The Business of Risk

COMMERCIAL GAMBLING IN MAINSTREAM AMERICA

Vicki Abt
James F. Smith
Eugene Martin Christiansen

UNIVERSITY PRESS OF KANSAS

Lyrics from "Easy Money," which appear in Chapter 6, used by permission.
Words and music by Billy Joel, © 1983 Joelsongs.

Published by the University Press of Kansas (Lawrence, Kansas 66045),
which was organized by the Kansas Board of Regents and is operated and
funded by Emporia State University, Fort Hays State University,
Kansas State University, Pittsburg State University,
the University of Kansas, and Wichita State University

Library of Congress Cataloging-in-Publication Data
Abt, Vicki, 1942–
The business of risk.
Bibliography: p
Includes index.
1. Gambling—United States.
2. Gambling—Social aspects—United States.
3. Gambling—Economic aspects—United States.
I. Smith, James F. (James Frederick), 1946– .
II. Christiansen, Eugene Martin, 1944– . III. Title.
HV6715.A46 1985 306′.482′0973 85-7491
ISBN 0-7006-0280-1
ISBN 0-7006-0281-X (pbk.)

Printed in the United States of America
10 9 8 7 6 5 4 3 2

Contents

List of Tables

Preface

This book is about the business of risk, or commercial gambling, and its entry into mainstream America in the late twentieth century. Readers stumbling over the phrase "commercial gambling" for the first time may wonder why the qualifier "commercial" is needed and whether gambling businesses are not for most people rather remote concerns. Many Americans still equate gambling with cards and dice and roulette wheels—far away in Las Vegas or Atlantic City. Adding to this sense of remoteness is the fact that the word's disapproving moral and religious overtones cloud distinctions. To the guardians of public morality gambling is Gambling and Wrong; so labeled it has been filed safely away, along with Drugs and Homosexuality, under the headings of "Vice" and "Deviance."

This simplistic view unfortunately overlooks everything that makes the business of risk an important development in contemporary American society. The neighborhood lottery agent and a Las Vegas craps table share a fundamental quality: they both offer games of unequal chance. There is a fundamental difference between gambling at games of equal chance and commercial gambling games that by definition ensure collective player losses. Kids tossing a coin for the last seat at a rock concert are gambling at a game of equal chance; their parents buying a lottery ticket at the corner newsstand are buying chance from a commercial business, in this case their State government.* The dif-

* We have used capitalization to distinguish clearly between states in general and the fifty States of the United States. The substantive meaning underlying this distinction is a function of the States' peculiar responsibility and role in the evolution of commercial gambling. Unlike nearly every other state—in which the national government normally includes commercial gambling within its legal

ference between these two games is that one of the kids is going to get to see the concert, while the lottery players collectively are going to lose a very substantial percentage (about 54 percent) of their investment to the state.

The operators of all commercial gambling games have a guaranteed advantage, an edge. Upon this edge and the attraction of risk an enormous institution has been raised. Today gambling is a major American leisure industry. *The Business of Risk* is a detailed examination of commercial gambling in the United States: from its colonial beginnings in private lotteries authorized by the Crown through the watershed elections of 1984, when voters brought gambling policies in this country full circle by approving every lottery initiative on the ballots and thus decisively affirmed their acceptance of the principle of funding government expenditures through State-operated lotteries. We have tried to give the controversial problems of illegal wagering and compulsive gambling their due importance in the larger context of activities a majority of Americans engage in legally and without harming themselves, their families, or their communities. We neither preach against gambling nor endorse it. Finally, we have not written a how-to-gamble book.

Instead we have used sociological insights and methodology to examine commercial gambling for the complex phenomenon that it is: a distinct set of games, each with its own structure and context, that interact with society and culture as well as with individual players' motivations to produce distinguishable gambling behaviors. Gambling games are not homogeneous, nor are they interchangeable products in the marketplace. *The Business of Risk* offers a model for evaluating the differential impact of each of the major commercial games on the individual and on society, or at the micro- and macro-levels of sociological analysis.

All studies, even the most determinedly objective, proceed from a particular point of view. Especially when the subject is as controversial and emotionally charged as cards and dice and horses, some bias on the part of the researcher is inevitable. The point of view—the bias—of *The Business of Risk* is the *public interest* in commercial gambling—not the casino operator's interest; not Internal Revenue's; not the financial interest of State treasuries; not the interests, hidden or disclosed, of

competence—commercial gambling has here remained a prerogative of the States. We use the term *State lottery* for lotteries operated by a State of the United States, in contrast to privately owned or operated lotteries authorized or franchised by governments of domestic or foreign jurisdiction. Such private lotteries are barred from interstate commerce and U.S. mails by federal law, and are generally illegal under State constitutions and statute law.

organized crime or free-lance criminal entrepreneurs; but the public interest, in the person of the ordinary citizen, who, walking down his neighborhood street or driving down the local freeway, encounters Big Gambling at a newsstand selling lottery tickets or a resort built on casino gaming.

What he should find, in our opinion, is something like the following: a recreational activity, perhaps newly legal, of ambiguous cultural status and imperfectly understood social and medical consequences, provided by honest operators at the lowest possible cost to both the consumer and society, and regulated under workable laws by knowledgeable and adequately paid regulators whose only interest in gambling is the public welfare.

What the ordinary citizen too often finds in fact is that the special interests in commercial gambling—operators, government, the media, and the Mob—have already and very effectively looked out for themselves, by creating a machine that processes conventional behavior into some outrageously excessive gambling revenues. The calculus of public policy requires numbers for its operation, and to this end *The Business of Risk* provides in an appendix estimates of gross wagering and gross revenues (or losses) for all of the major forms of commercial gambling in the United States. These statistics describe the financial dimensions of commercial gambling, which is the most easily quantifiable part of the equation. They are not a complete statement of the public interest in commercial gambling by any means. There are hundreds of thousands of jobs and billions of dollars of invested equity in the business of risk. This economic contribution of commercial gambling is also quantifiable and is summarized in Chapter 3.

But there is still more at stake. Commercial gambling by definition involves gamblers' losses. As we show, each game produces characteristic and widely varying levels of loss and in effect distributes these losses differentially among the general population. The magnitude and demographic distribution of gambling losses are not ordinarily factored into the policymaking process, for the reasons that these concepts are not usually understood by policymakers and are in any case much more difficult to quantify than gambling revenues. *The Business of Risk* supplies an objective basis for representing these important aspects of the public interest in commercial gambling in the formulation of gambling policy and law.

Yet another consideration is economic. Large-scale gambling operations concentrated into limited geographic areas strongly affect the nongambling economy. Some legalizations, of which Atlantic City casino gaming is the most prominent current example, are intended to change the nongambling economy in positive ways, to accomplish economic redevelopment. The extent to which this goal is realized does not, however, depend solely on the economic success or failure of casinos. There must also be strong, honest, competent, and disinterested government—meaning soundly conceived gambling law and effective regulation. This requirement has not been met in Atlantic City, with predictable results: the area's poor, who are not adequately represented at the institutional level of society where gambling policies are made and enforced, have not fairly shared in the tremendous economic growth casino gaming has stimulated. The Atlantic City experience also illustrates the political dimension of gambling legalizations: because State governments have the power to create new industries, and great individual and corporate wealth, by fiat, gambling initiatives and the new businesses they establish stress governments in unusual and powerful ways. In many cases government has failed under this stress and thereby failed to protect the public interest in commercial gambling.

Finally, gambling is being conventionalized. The self-limiting games that provided highly individualistic recreation for earlier generations have rapidly evolved into a commercial institution. Big Gambling—State lotteries, racetracks, OTB (off-track betting), casinos, bingo, and a marriage of convenience between mostly illegal bookmakers and the professional sports leagues—is transforming spontaneous and self-limiting play at gambling games into programmed behaviors indistinguishable from the mass consumption of television programs or designer jeans. The individual entrepreneuers—bookmakers and riverboat gamblers—who supplied preindustrial America with gambling services have been replaced by large-scale corporate and governmental operators, blessed by or identical with the State. This has added a very substantial cost to the price gamblers pay for their chosen leisure activity: in addition to the normal profits successful gambling businesses always earned, billions of dollars annually in gambling privilege taxes are extracted from gambling losses. The conventionalization of these traditional games is exacting a larger price as well: the social and cultural meaning of gambling is being altered beyond recognition. In the process the understandable social and psychological functions of a unique form of play are giving way to new institutional meanings that affect all of us, gamblers and nongamblers alike.

It is one of the tragedies of the American experience with gambling that its larger social functions have never been clearly appreciated. Earlier studies, both sociological and psychological, exaggerated the impact of gambling as play on most participants and underestimated or ignored altogether the impact of commercial gambling on society and the culture. *The Business of Risk* attempts to redirect attention to the social and cultural consequences of commercial gambling at a time when the relationship of gambling and society is undergoing wholesale transformation. Commercial gambling is in truth a risky business. It need not, however, be for American society a game of chance. Gambling can be analyzed through sociological methods and concepts, and it can be understood. If we are able to impart this understanding to the reader we will have succeeded in a difficult task.

We have received an enormous amount of help during our investigation of this most sensitive industry. Professor William R. Eadington of the economics department of the University of Nevada/Reno, the country's leading academic expert on gambling, has given freely of knowledge that extends beyond the Academy to the real world of gamblers and commercial games. Sam Kanchugar, director, news service bureau, the Jockey Club, gave generously of his time and unrivalled knowledge of racing in many long conversations. Dean Macomber, casino administrator at Bally's Park Place in Atlantic City, patiently explained the practical considerations that govern the conduct of casino games in practice as well as in theory. The staff of *Gaming Business Magazine* (now *Gaming & Wagering Business Magazine*)—Gary Selesner, former editor and now advertising manager at Trump Plaza; Michael P. Davis, associate editor; Paul Dworin, the current editor; and Irv Babson, publisher—helped run down countless pieces of information about an industry that lacks consolidated data and reporting. Thomas L. Aronson, executive secretary of the American Horse Council's racing committee, courteously shared both the Horse Council's store of information and his own unique understanding of the horse in American life. Dr. William R. Killingsworth and Will E. Cummings of Killingsworth Associates, who have quantified betting markets for everything from $2 bets to $10 million yearlings, have been generous with their data and knowledge. James E. Ritchie, the former executive director of the Commission on the Review of the National Policy Toward Gambling, and Stephen C. Fogleman of James E. Ritchie law offices, the country's leading practitioners of gambling law, provided clarifying insights into American gambling policies in the world of practical affairs. Jerome H. Skolnick, the author of *House of Cards,* a classic study of gaming legalization and control, and John Dennis Dombrink both added immeasurably to our understanding of the regulation of gaming. Michael D. Shagan of the New York City Off-Track Betting Corporation allowed us use of both his library of gambling materials and precise knowledge of OTB in the United States and other countries and has contributed greatly to our appreciation of the politics of commercial gambling. Stuart E.

Curtis, of the Tax and License Division of the Nevada Gaming Control Board, courteously and accurately answered many questions about Nevada casino operations.

Many people at Liberty Bell Park in Philadelphia have cooperated with us in our on-site observations of racetracks. We wish to thank especially Raymond A. Birbeck, president of Liberty Bell, and Michael F. Green, treasurer and director of Liberty Bell, for their cooperation. We also want to thank Nick Romano, veteran handicapper, for introducing us to drivers such as Sam Belote and Vito Truglio; to Bruce Saunders, owner/trainer of "Perky Fiddler," and his wife Ann-Lis; and to cashiers, other personnel, and various patrons who helped us understand the world of horse racing and handicapping.

Our understanding of casino gambling was enhanced by the insights of many individuals. Sam Landy, the "professor of chance," provided much background on the business of gambling in America, especially as it has evolved in Las Vegas. Bill Friedman, president of the Castaways Hotel and Casino in Las Vegas, shared his expertise in modern casino operation, and George Ayoub of the Sands Hotel in Las Vegas helped us understand the daily activities on the casino floor. Steve Hann and Ralph Delligatti in Atlantic City provided valuable information on the evolution of casino gaming in the East.

John Luckman and Howard Schwartz of the Gamblers' Book Club in Las Vegas helped us with much of our research into the history of gambling, as did the staff of the Special Collections at the University of Nevada, Las Vegas, library.

The manuscript was read at various stages by David Westby, associate professor of sociology at Pennsylvania State University, and he helped us formulate our conception of the crucial role played by the state in the growth of commercial gambling. The manuscript also benefited from the insights of Harold Abt and of Prof. Leon Chorbajian of the University of Lowell, editor of *The Arena Review.* Dr. Robert Bernoff and Dr. Sanford Nicol of the Pennsylvania State University, Ogontz Campus, patiently understood the demands that this study made on our time. Susan Pagano provided invaluable assistance in typing portions of the manuscript, and Robin Casten helped us with our library research.

Finally, we wish to acknowledge the example of Albert W. Merck, one of the four original members of the New Jersey Casino Control Commission, whose willingness to learn the intricacies of casino gaming and uncompromising commitment to exercise this knowledge to further the public interest in commercial gambling are a standard of public service and one of the inspirations for this book.

1

The Sound and the Fury

> Gambling is inevitable. No matter what is said or done by advocates or opponents of gambling in all its various forms, it is an activity that is practiced, or tacitly endorsed, by a substantial majority of Americans.
>
> —Commission on the Review of the National Policy Toward Gambling (1976)

Gambling is a universal cultural phenomenon: one of a relatively small number of activities that occur in nearly all societies and every period. People have been playing risky games for at least 4,000 years, and virtually every culture has evolved ways of letting its members stake something of value on an event of uncertain outcome. Gambling might be said to have had a determining role in the antecedents of American society: the Old Testament God created man with a natural propensity to bet, and the Biblical account of the genesis of Western civilization begins with Adam and Eve wagering a stake, their innocence, in the hope of adding knowledge to that stake. The theology is obscure: like gambling since, the social value and moral consequences of Adam and Eve's wager are matters of debate. To many, man's fall from grace and subsequent history are proof it was immoral, or a sucker bet, the first step down the road to ruin that is the antigambling reformers' contribution to cartography. To others, the wager was an act of self-actualization: with knowledge Adam and Eve acquired humanity, and from the human interdependence created by the loss of Paradise society began.

This metaphor illustrates the human experience with gambling: thousands of years later mainstream America is still playing the game, but both the stakes and the social significance of the activity have changed. A lot of modern gambling is no longer play. Fairly late in the history separating the Devil's Tree of Knowledge from the neighborhood lottery agent gambling was commercialized. Today it is a business: the business of risk. It is a big business, \$163 billion in gross wagering in

1983, with gross revenues (or losses) amounting to roughly 10 percent of that figure, or about $16.8 billion. And for the most part the business of risk is legal. Illegal wagering—mostly on the old American games of bookmaking and numbers—totaled some $28.9 billion, with gross revenues of about $5 billion, giving the Mob only about a 17 percent share of the market. This intelligence will be disturbing to much of the law enforcement establishment, which has made a practice of justifying part of its taxpayer-funded budgets with the spectre of fantastic Mafia earnings from illegal numbers and sports betting. The truth will also be disappointing to the media and to a lot of ordinary people who may never make a bet but enjoy reading lurid tales about violent men with guns catering to America's appetite for cards and dice and horses. Organized crime's participation in the business of risk is a fact, but *Godfather*-like stories obscure the historic changes now transforming gambling in America. The characteristics of gambling games and how they influence (and are influenced by) players and society in general are fundamentally more important than the legal status of the supplier. The real story is the expansion of commercial gambling in the last twenty years and the concentration of this business into increasingly powerful corporate and governmental operations. Because of these events American life may never be quite the same again.

Paradoxically, the knowledge for which Paradise was lost has notably scanted the game at which it was won. Fear and fascination—the knee-jerk reactions when the subject of gambling is raised—are poor substitutes for understanding. Gambling is not some mysterious monolith. There are subtle but significant distinctions among commercial gambling games. Similarly, gamblers are not all the same. Their motivations, their play, and the outcomes of their gambling vary according to the individual and the surrounding, or containing, culture.

This blind determination to keep gambling games and behaviors beyond the pale of "normal" life has made it impossible to see the true relationship of the business of risk to the state and to society. In large measure this is because the focus has been on the wrong things. Earlier studies tended to deal with gambling in monolithic terms and to consider all gamblers as if they were already—or had the potential to become—pathological gamblers. These two ideas inform most of the enormous popular and professional literature on the subject. Unfortunately, these concepts have served only to divert attention from more substantial issues and keep our knowledge of gambling behavior and the business of risk at rudimentary levels. A broader approach is required. This chapter reviews the public debate over gambling and brings the perspective of sociology to the study of gambling behavior and of the social forms in which this behavior occurs.

THE GAMBLING DEBATE

Gambling is an enduring controversy. Despite the fact that it is something most people do Americans have a great deal of difficulty in talking about it, or writing about it, dispassionately. Although the literature is enormous most of it consists of superficial romanticizing or moral preaching or hysterical antigambling tracts.[1] Histories of the subject acquire lurid titles with a remarkable consistency: *Fools of Fortune, Sucker's Progress, Play the Devil.*[2] Even serious discussions of the psychology of gambling usually fail to consider gambling's relationship to specific situations and the historical context that give meaning to the activity. Psychologists' concern with individual behavior causes most studies of the psychology of gambling to focus narrowly on individual actions and decisionmaking processes rather than the larger issues these behaviors raise.[3] Popular as well as professional writing about gambling generally reads like the result of a particularly long and difficult psychoanalysis: as if the collective American psyche, unable to deal rationally with the gambling proclivities of its id, has discharged the resulting psychological tensions in a marathon emotional writing jag. The product of this binge (which shows no sign of abating) is a fog of verbiage, a wordy miasma of misconceptions, stereotypes, loaded buzzwords, and simple misinformation through which the reality of gambling situations and gambling behavior has been almost wholly obscured. The rapid expansion of legal commercial gambling following the institution of a State lottery by New Hampshire in 1964 has intensified and further polarized the gambling debate, which is increasingly taking on the rigid characteristics of ideological polemic. As a preliminary to a more reasoned and less emotional perspective on gambling it may be useful to review the main points of this controversy.

On one side, legal commercial gambling is condemned by religious leaders who have historically equated all gambling with sin, and by secular critics, including psychiatrists professionally concerned with the treatment of "sick" or compulsive gamblers, moral reformers, and some elected officials, notably a succession of congressional and senatorial committees that in the last thirty years have established as doctrine the belief of many law enforcement professionals that illegal gambling bankrolls organized crime and is linked to various kinds of corruption.[4] Both secular and clerical critics tend to argue their views with an emotional fervor that recalls nineteenth-century revivalist preaching: they perceive a devil at large in the land, in the form of organized, concerted, and well-financed gambling industries, to which, in opposition, "there has developed in the United States and Europe a compulsive

[sic] gambling movement. It is a moral crusade similar in theory and practice to the moral crusade that was organized for the passage of the Volstead Act in 1919."[5] This call to arms—not, as one might suppose, from a cleric but from a professor of sociology—against the dangerous permissiveness of allowing people to gamble as they chose has been sounded regularly over the centuries, and not just by Americans; sermons on the evils of gambling are staples of the literature. Here is a seventeenth-century English writer:

> Gaming is an enchanting witchery, gotten betwixt idleness and avarice: an itching disease, that makes some scratch the head, whilst others, as if they were bitten by a Tarantula, are laughing themselves to death: or lastly, it is a paralytical distemper, which seizing the arm that man cannot chuse but shake his elbow . . . it renders a man incapable of prosecuting any serious action, and makes him always unsatisfied with his own condition . . . till he has lost sight of both sense and reason.[6]

Such statements reflect enduring attitudes in what might be called the moral economy of vice. Both drunks and the temperance movement need alcohol to function; for the rest of us a drink is optional, something we can take or leave alone. Betting serves a similar diversity of purpose: its abuse by a minority has provided steady employment for reformers ever since Adam and Eve.

On the other side of the gambling debate are those who believe that, in the words of the Federal Gambling Commission, "gambling is inevitable."[7] A variety of vested interests argue the positive values of commercial gambling and gambling behavior. These proponents include an increasing number of legitimate, publicly held corporations,[8] the significant fraction of American agribusiness engaged in horse breeding, and numerous State, county, and municipal governments that depend in part on gambling revenues. Even some professionals in the social sciences, attempting to be objective, go so far as to argue that gambling is no different from any other form of play or social game behavior. These social scientists apply value-free theories of decisionmaking and rational calculation developed by economists and psychologists to horse-race betting and casino gaming.[9]

Caught between these two opposing forces is the American public, along with the police and the courts. In an era of unprecedented violent crime we are reluctant to assign high priority to the enforcement of antigambling laws that at best proscribe activities which may be legal in neighboring jurisdictions and are in any case directed at victimless, and very popular, crimes. Sustained opposition to gambling itself has lacked broad public support,[10] and people often condone the lax enforcement of antigambling laws, an attitude reflected in a 1982 Gallup Poll showing that 80 percent of those surveyed favored at least some legal opportunities to gamble.

For all the vehemence with which it is being conducted, the public debate over gambling has remained for the most part remarkably uninformed. Both sides vastly oversimplify the complexities of gambling behavior and the operations of modern commercial gambling. Secular critics of gambling involved in the treatment of "junkie" gamblers are sometimes themselves reformed compulsive gamblers, and are in any case professionally exposed only to the most harmful effects of commercial gambling. The gambling industry and, perhaps more seriously, a growing number of State and local governments have large vested interests in further legalization. Neither operators nor their critics are disposed to an objective view of gambling. Both sides have failed to develop a perspective permitting a reasoned analysis of the interrelationships among gambling games, situations, structures, and participants. This failure would be of purely academic interest were it not for the fact that this debate is not confined to an ivory tower. In large measure, it has determined the country's gambling policies and laws.

The reception of English law into American judicial processes by separate acts of the original thirteen States between 1776 and 1784 had the practical effect of making gambling statutes enacted by Parliament prior to Independence the basis for American gambling law. This law was then applied to American circumstances in American courts by American judges who for the most part reflected basically Puritan views towards gambling. Overwhelmingly, their opinions articulated an antigambling rationale, and so an antigambling bias was introduced into the American legal system.[11] Gambling has generally remained a matter of State jurisdiction, and in spite of sporadic relaxations antigambling law and enforcement grew progressively more rigorous, until by 1900 gambling prohibitions were firmly embedded in State constitutions and statute law.

This complex legal edifice contained a serious structural defect: the American propensity to gamble. Puritan and clerical prejudice had succeeded in making gambling illegal but failed to alter American gambling behavior. From colonial times the statutory treatment of gambling had been marked by ambivalence: legal proscriptions alternated with gambling authorizations, usually for specific games and purposes. Economically weakened by the mercantilistic policies of England and lacking adequate systems of banking and taxation the colonies turned to lotteries as a method of public and private finance.[12] Public works of all kinds—highways, bridges, dams, fortifications, sewers and so forth—as well as schools, colleges, hospitals, and even churches were all funded by channeling the American demand for opportunities to bet through lotteries. This method of public finance was continued by the States following 1776 in the form of State-franchised private lottery companies, and their success in generating revenues is convincing evidence that gambling, at least at lotteries, enjoyed a considerable measure of social approval regardless of its legal status. As the nineteenth century progressed horse-race betting in the East and casino gaming at eastern spas and along the frontier became firmly established even while gambling proscriptions were being tightened, and, with the turn of the century, Americans' irrepressible propensity to gamble began to erode the States' gambling prohibitions. In 1931 Nevada legalized casino gaming along with most other forms of gambling,[13] and during the next decade pari-mutuel racing was legalized along the eastern seaboard and in parts of the Middle West. For a generation following World War II legal commercial gambling was confined to racetracks and Nevada casinos, but in 1964, with the start of the first State lottery in New Hampshire, a second wave of legalizations began that shows no sign of abating.[14] In the next twenty years twenty-two jurisdictions authorized lotteries; New York and Connecticut authorized government-operated off-track betting (OTB); pari-mutuel *jai-alai* spread from Florida to Connecticut, Rhode Island, and Nevada; and New Jersey legalized casino gaming in Atlantic City.

Today American commercial gambling is an industry of enormous dimensions. Thirty-six States allow some form of pari-mutuel betting; twenty-one States and the District of Columbia have authorized State-operated lotteries, of which eighteen are currently operating and four are in various stages of implementation; eight States allow card rooms; two States allow casino gaming; and one State (Nevada) allows bookmaking on team sports such as National Football League (NFL) games. Approximately 80 percent of the population has ready access to some form of legal commercial gambling. In 1983 Americans lost some $11.8 billion to legal gambling businesses. Another $5 billion was lost to illegal operations, principally numbers games and bookmakers, for a total expenditure of $16.8 billion.[15]

The issue of whether to allow gambling is moot. It is allowed. The debate should therefore be how to devise meaningful policies and effective laws and regulation for commercial gambling. Meaningful policies and effective laws and regulation cannot be created from the assumption that gambling is a sin and inherently evil. Yet most studies of gambling continue to be marred by an antigambling bias. In large measure this bias derives from an obsessive focus on "problem," or compulsive, gambling. It is important, therefore, to evaluate compulsive gambling and its relation to the availability of legal opportunities to gamble.

PATHOLOGICAL GAMBLING

Nearly all observers who see gambling as evil and gamblers as actual or potential social problems grossly overestimate the importance of gambling for most people. While gambling is indeed a growing phenomenon in the United States, there is no reason to assume that it is a preoccupation for every American or even for every gambler. Gambling is the central fact only in the lives of problem or compulsive gamblers. Indeed, involvement with gambling to the exclusion of other things, the *compulsion* to play, are among the usual criteria for determining that an individual has a gambling problem.[16] For everyone else gambling is just one of many interests. An idea of the relative importance of gambling in American lives can be formed from calculating per capita losses: the $16.8 billion lost in 1983 works out to about $101 for every adult American. The survey of American gambling behavior conducted for the Federal Gambling Commission in 1975 estimated average per capita annual wagering at $150 for all adults and $387 for adults who bet, and average annual losses of about $30 per person over 18.[17] Even allowing for the possible understatement of losses inherent in any survey results there has been a massive increase in gambling expenditures since 1974.

A problem with gambling, or alcohol or narcotics or video games, can certainly have unpleasant or even tragic consequences. But many Americans gamble, drink, play Pac-Man, and indulge in other potentially addictive activities without becoming obsessed with them. Most Americans, including compulsive gamblers, are going to gamble regardless of the presence or absence of legal opportunities to do so. The failure of gambling prohibitions, enacted and enforced at every level of government over a period of two hundred years, to "reform" or even markedly to alter the American propensity to gamble is ample testimony to this fundamental fact. In focusing their attention on compulsive gamblers and their ire on the suppliers of gambling services, the critics of legal gambling ignore the overriding cause of our present dilemma: the demand for opportunities to gamble is deeply rooted in American society.

The extent of compulsive gambling behavior is critical to the rational discussion of gambling. How frequently does this behavior occur in the unstimulated population? Does the mere availability of legal but unpromoted commercial gambling significantly increase the incidence of compulsive gambling? Does the unrestricted advertisement of gambling by private or government operators create compulsive gambling that otherwise would not exist or stimulate latent compulsive gambling?

The answers to these questions have important public policy and legislative implications. There have been numerous estimates of the incidence of compulsive gambling.[18] The most serious attempt to date to answer this question is the 1975 survey of American gambling behavior conducted by the Survey Research Center (SRC), whose findings regarding compulsive gambling have, by virtue of their comprehensive nature, a claim to be authoritative.[19] Relying on this survey, the Federal Gambling Commission concluded that 0.77 percent of the national population (or about 1.1 million persons over 18) were "probable" compulsive gamblers and another 2.33 percent were "potential" compulsive gamblers. The former statistic was much higher for Nevada residents, who are more exposed to legal commercial gambling: 2.62 percent "probable" compulsive gamblers and 2.35 percent—virtually the same as the percentage nationally—"potential" compulsive gamblers.[20] This finding led the commission to conclude that when widely available, legal commercial gambling leads to significant increases in compulsive gambling behavior:

> Not only is the incidence of compulsive gambling higher in Nevada than in the national sample, but the ratio of probables to potentials is as well. This is consistent with the hypothesis that widespread availability of gambling in a legal form leads a portion of those classified as potential compulsive gamblers to actualize their potential compulsion. This effect is more pronounced for women than for men and is also consistent with the observation that women are more easily accepted into legal gambling environments than into illegal operations, where the player frequently has to establish a credit rating; this may be a difficult matter for women who are dependent on their husbands financially.[21]

The commission concluded that in 1974 approximately 1.1 million Americans were compulsive gamblers. The numerous subsequent legalizations and apparent growth of illegal sports betting since 1974, when taken together with the commission's hypothesis that availability of legal gambling leads to increased compulsive gambling behavior, suggest that the number of Americans who gamble compulsively is higher today. Compulsive gamblers constitute a social problem of major proportions. The certainty that further legalization will occur means that the already large number of compulsive gamblers will grow. What is to be done about this?

Many religious and secular critics of decriminalization have a simple solution: return to prohibition. Make all gambling once again illegal, these critics say, rigorously enforce antigambling laws, and compulsive gambling will cease to be a problem. This has a certain plausibility. It seems reasonable, for example, that without legal opportunities to gamble susceptible individuals will not develop into compulsive gamblers. The realities of gambling and gambling behavior are, however, more complex than antigambling reformers are willing to admit, and the dilemma created by the presence of significant numbers of potential compulsive gamblers in the general population unfortunately resists such simple solutions.

Compulsive gambling presents policymakers with a complex set of choices. In deciding whether to allow a given form of commercial gambling, legislators and citizens must weigh the potential benefits—tax revenues, economic contributions, the provision of legal, honest, effectively regulated outlets for an already existing demand for gambling opportunities—against the social ills that may result from legalization. They should also consider the needs and preferences of the vast majority who are not potential compulsive gamblers.

A general principle of social policy is at stake here. If a society prohibits activities or substances because they are abused by a minority it often creates situations in which the majority suffers, either by being deprived of legal access to something it enjoys or because the resulting market for illegal suppliers leads to the rise of an organized criminal underworld. Legal proscriptions of selected behaviors have historically created as many problems as they have solved. Prohibition is the classic American example. The massive illegal bookmaking on team sports that pervades American life is another case in point: the United States is one of the few Western industrialized countries that does not allow sports betting and the only one to tax legal winnings as income,[22] policies that have combined to create perhaps the world's largest market for illegal bookmaking. Like the organized crime that supplied Americans with bootleg whiskey in the 1920s, our present illegal gambling problem is a self-inflicted wound.

Such "reform" involves a fundamental consideration of social policy: in whose interest are such policies to be made? If the solution to abuse by a minority—of activities or substances or even freedoms—is prohibition for everyone *anything* can become "wrong," and society is faced with a kind of tyranny. It is a basic tenet of democracy that in a free society people live the way they want to live, not the way some reformers, however well-intentioned, think they should. If large-scale gambling raises a number of intractible social issues—and it certainly does—turning gambling into a buzzword like communism or homosexuality only makes it more and not less difficult to resolve these issues. Devil-theories of gambling may have their place in church, but they are disastrous public policy.

To view gambling as inherently evil is a kind of scapegoating. Complex social problems generally have complex causes: blaming only one and overlooking all the others is unlikely to improve matters. It is easy and often emotionally satisfying for social reformers to argue that if society can only rid itself of a particular harmful activity all will be well. The fallacy in such arguments is that nothing—be it gambling, alcohol, or nuclear energy—is always in all circumstances bad. Value in this sense is a complex function of control, situation, regulation, and use. Like fire, gambling can lead to tragedy if it gets out of control, but like fire it can serve useful purposes. It is not inherently evil because of its potential negative effects.

A multitude of devils plague modern life. Gambling is one, perhaps, to some people but not to the majority and is by no means the source of all evil. In the context of a basically healthy society the question of whether to allow commercial gambling should not, as many clinical researchers and social critics argue, be decided solely in terms of the potential risk of increased compulsive gambling. Compulsive gambling is only one of the factors that should weigh in the decision to legalize. Without in any way minimizing the problem of compulsive gambling for affected individuals, it does not seem to us to constitute an unacceptable social risk of legalizing activities most Americans clearly approve of and enjoy without incurring unaffordable losses.

This more balanced evaluation of the medical implications of legalization for society as a whole derives from extensive study of gamblers in actual gambling situations, as opposed to clinical observations of advanced stages of compulsive gambling in isolation from the real-world gambling scene. Explanations of gambling behavior based on a pathological model invariably focus on the gambler to the exclusion of the gambling event. Such studies almost always emphasize the end result of long-term heavy betting, which usually involves serious economic and social loss. Moreover, many clinical researchers misunderstand the nature of gambling. The unfairness of all commercial games, which by definition have an advantage or edge that ensures revenues for the operator and losses for players, is used as the basis for a narrowly economic argument against the rationality of gambling: since gamblers voluntarily engage in activities that must *a priori* result in financial loss they are irrational and, if regular gamblers, "sick" because they are preoccupied with activities that almost inevitably lead to ruin.

This argument has several defects. First, there is much evidence to suggest that gamblers behave rationally even in narrow economic terms. Observations in a wide variety of times and places have shown that gamblers are realistically aware of their chances of winning and conduct their wagering with deliberation and disciplined concentration.[23] Casino patrons tend to take the best odds,[24] and horseplayers tend to bet favorites[25] and make rational use of information concerning the prospects of each horse or betting interest.[26] In the short term most gamblers are economically rational; each gamble is evaluated according to odds, expected return, alternative betting opportunities, and a number of other structural characteristics.[27] It is only over extended series of gambles that the built-in edge of commercial games grinds away the players' bankrolls. A gambler who believes he will lose any particular gamble, and that his loss would outweigh any possible reward in terms of recreation or status, might, arguably, be judged irrational in this narrow economic sense. But no gambler loses every bet: there are inevitable streaks of good and bad fortune. It is in fact this unpredictable alternation of loss and gain that is one of the satisfactions of gambling; loss, in other words, far from being evidence of irrationality, is intrinsic to the utility of gambling activities. To say that every gambling situation demands irrational behavior is roughly equivalent to saying that every cocktail party leads to drunkenness or, worse, to alcoholism.

A second and more serious fallacy with the pathological model becomes apparent when it is used to explain gambling motivations and the dynamics of play. The inadequacy of the argument from narrow economic rationality derives from its assumption that the only measure of the utilities of gambling consumption is monetary—that gambling can be valued solely in terms of gain or loss. This assumption is clearly at odds with reality. Few racetrack and casino gamblers we questioned mentioned the possibility of monetary gain as their primary reason for gambling.[28] Most said they gambled because they liked the excitement, the escape from everyday routine, or the company of gambling cronies.[29] Gamblers who seek these satisfactions exercise rational choice in deciding to spend (or lose) money at gambling. Reductive economic theories of behavioral motivation were too simplistic when they were proposed by Karl Marx as explanations of social conflict in history and such an approach is equally misleading as an explanation of gambling behavior. The confusion arises from the fact that in gambling money is used as the stake and payoff. Money is the agreed-upon measure of worth in our society, and as such it is the obvious and appropriate medium for gambling. It is not, for most gamblers, the end. Money heightens player involvement and provides an easy measure of outcomes, but gain or loss is not always or even usually the primary motivation. Players gamble *with* but not always *for* money.

Nor is it necessarily true that compulsive gamblers gamble in order to lose. There is a psychological fallacy underlying this common assertion. It is all too emotionally satisfying to adopt a "just desserts" model of causality—to make causal links between motivations, intentions, and results. Compulsive gambling is pathetically a bad result, and it is very tempting to conclude that this behavior is prompted by self-destructive intent. Evil intentions, however, are not necessary to produce evil consequences, just as well-intentioned activity—like the "reform" embodied in the Volstead Act—does not always lead to social improvements. Much of sociology deals with the latent and unintended consequences of individual social actions. Many areas of modern life provide examples of persons reaping more or less than they sowed, and "just desserts" is often more a product of wishful thinking than a reflection of reality. For good or ill, this appears to be especially true of gambling. We do not agree that all compulsive gamblers "deserve" their destructive losses because by incurring them they are satisfying the demands of psychological traits.

So far we have been using the terms *compulsive* and *pathological* without defining them. As noted, researchers using the pathological model commonly assume elements of compulsion and self-destruction in gambling, because they know that in the long run gamblers will lose. Our own research makes us question both of these traditional notions. Perhaps because so much of the study of gambling has depended on observations of members of Gamblers Anonymous (G.A.), gambling is portrayed as out-of-control, painful, compulsive behavior. As with its counterpart, Alcoholics Anonymous (A.A.), membership in G.A. is voluntary. When the pain or economic consequences of compulsive gambling reach a crisis point the gambler joins G.A. in order to stop. Consequently, to use G.A. members as representative of the gambling population is a little like sampling traffic court to find representative drivers, or Alcoholics Anonymous to find typical drinkers.

It is clear to us from our research that even among the ranks of "problem" gamblers there are persons who because of their financial or emotional resources never reach a crisis point, who never experience the pain of gambling-induced self-doubt or self-loathing, and who do not wish to stop gambling. Indeed, most gamblers do stop intermittently, whenever they can no longer afford to stay in action. We can still label these heavy bettors "problem" gamblers, either because they assign gambling an inordinately high priority in their lives or because they have reached very high levels of wagering. Many of these heavy bettors are however more usefully characterized as *obsessive* rather than compulsive gamblers.

Obsessive behavior may be defined as any behavior that takes over an individual's life and becomes central, all-engrossing, and perhaps all-consuming within definable boundaries of control. There are religious obsessions, sexual obsessions, and work obsessions—in short, any imbalance from the Aristotelian dictum of moderation in all things. All obsessions can be difficult to live with, and to their families obsessive gamblers, like workaholics or alcoholics, can be disruptive and perhaps destructive. But unless the gambler himself makes his family a higher priority than his playing—and by definition the obsessive gambler does not—he will not feel the pain his absence from the home causes and so will have no motivation to stop gambling until his financial resources are exhausted.

What differentiates the obsessive gambler from the compulsive gambler is not the effect his behavior has on those around him but how he handles his betting and its effect on his life and self-image. On the one hand, because of the one-dimensional focus of his life the obsessive gambler dare not give up gambling; on the other, his gambling is controlled: he will stop playing before reaching the limit of his resources. These individuals do not bet the mortgage payment or the assets of their businesses or write bad checks; if they did they could not return to the gambling scene and get back into action. Instead of losing everything, they go back to their jobs and families, save up some money, and reward themselves with more gambling at the next opportunity. They are controlled gamblers, even though they invest virtually all their leisure time and disposable income in gambling. Unlike compulsive gamblers, whose gambling may cross the boundaries of socially acceptable behavior, obsessive gamblers are unusual principally in the object of their obsession: sports fanatics, joggers, dedicated athletes, performers, and workaholics who give themselves wholly to their jobs or professions—all of whom are usually considered to be "normal"—are fundamentally similar personalities. The dimensions of the problem of compulsive gambling have been overstated by the inclusion in psychologically oriented studies of these obsessive, heavy, but controlled gamblers. The differentiation between obsessive and compulsive gamblers is a necessary prerequisite to an accurate evaluation of this problem and of the social risk of legal commercial gambling.

As the foregoing discussion demonstrates, simple solutions to the problems raised by legal commercial gambling are likely to prove ineffective in practice, for the reason that these solutions focus on the individual to the exclusion of the larger social context. Compulsive gamblers, perhaps because of the pathos of their predicament, have been especially cursed by the purveyors of simplistic nostrums. It is all too easy, in trying to help these unfortunate people to work off the resulting emotional involvement on some convenient villain—usually the nearest gambling business.

By failing to take into account the gambling propensities of the noncompulsive majority that gave rise to commercial gambling in the first place "reform" channeled in this direction will continue to fail to resolve our present dilemma. Even if there were no compulsive or obsessive gamblers commercial gambling would remain an enterprise with far-reaching consequences for American society. Gambling, on the scale it is presently being conducted in the United States, raises fundamental social issues. It poses serious questions for our democratic capitalist system, and it is modifying the socio-cultural values of Americans in ways only dimly understood. Only a few years ago, in a landmark study of the regulation of gaming in Nevada, Jerome Skolnick termed casinos a "pariah industry,"[30] a half-outlawed, half-legal multi-billion dollar business, alternately and inconsistently reviled and embraced by mainstream America, that because of its ambiguous legal, cultural, and sociological status has created unique and heretofore insoluble problems for society. Commercial gambling has continued to expand since Skolnick's study, but little progress towards resolving the dilemma he so thoroughly elucidated has been made. Gambling, though indulged in by many Americans, is still considered socially deviant behavior; but commercial gambling should no longer be considered a pariah.

This comfortable hypocrisy, that gambling is deviant and pathological, is the root cause of our inability to deal rationally with gambling behavior and the commercial gambling industry. The point cannot be made too strongly: legal commercial gambling raises profound issues for our society and capitalist system precisely because it is so perfectly integrated into mainstream American life. If gambling were truly deviant, if racetracks and lotteries and casinos did not satisfy a widely and deeply rooted demand, the problems created by gambling would be trivial, and confined to the small segment of the population liable to become compulsive gamblers. Instead we find:

that in just five years of some of the most explosive growth in the history of American business, Atlantic City casinos were (in 1983) generating gross revenues (or player losses) approaching $5 million a day, with single-day individual casino wins exceeding $1 million an increasingly routine experience;

the rapid expansion of State lotteries and their transformation from "benign" weekly and monthly drawings to an aggressive form of gambling offering daily drawings, instant ("paper slot machine") games, player-active numbers games, and in 1984, on an experimental basis, player-active lottery video games that potentially can put the combined attractions of Pac-Man and "one-armed bandits" in the more than 100,000 outlets selling lottery tickets to some 56 percent of the U.S. population;

the imminent expansion of off-track betting to Illinois, and then to other major pari-mutuel racing States;[31]

the utilization of advanced communications technology to bring live televised horse racing ("simulcasting") into neighborhood OTB shops and to homes via closed-circuit television in conjunction with racetrack-operated telephone deposit-account betting;

the continuing rapid growth of bookmaking on team sports into an illegal commercial gambling business of massive proportions.[32]

The list could easily be extended. A historic confluence of forces—government's need for new, "painless" sources of revenue, private industry's ingenuity in supplying ever more attractive opportunities to gamble, changing public mores and attitudes, and above all the gambling propensities of mainstream America—has combined to make legal commercial gambling, with gross wagering estimated at nearly $135 billion in 1983,[33] one of the largest leisure industries in the United States.

Gambling is not, as we like to believe, some sort of "fringe" activity that isn't really competitive with the mainstream economy. Gambling competes too well. Some years ago, in the early morning hours at one of the restaurants in Caesars Palace in Las Vegas an old, successful, and respected gambler was musing on the business in which he'd spent his life. "Give me a dozen of these," the gambler said, indicating with a jeweled index finger the casino floor, "and permission to put them anywhere I choose, and with them I can destroy the economy of any city in the world." We have come to believe he had a point. To paraphrase another, fictional gambler, American commercial gambling today is bigger than U.S. Steel.[34]

The time is long past when taking refuge in the myth of gambling as deviance and relegating commercial gambling to the status of a pariah industry can pass for meaningful responses to the phenomenon of gambling. The difficulties that have been created by these shopworn attitudes should by now be apparent. Compulsive gamblers receive an excess of attention and far too little real help from authorities reluctant to assume responsibility for the problem. Consistent gambling policies are made impossible by contradictory gambling laws and public apathy. The federal tax treatment of legal winnings is an incentive to massive illegal gambling, while the task of supplying an enormous public demand for sports betting is left to the underworld. In all, regulation of the entire industry, legal and illicit, may accurately be characterized as too little and too late. If society is to avoid a disaster gambling must first be seen clearly, without bias or prejudice, for what it is: conventional behavior practiced by most Americans. Next must come a perspective that differentiates among gambling games within the general context of leisure and play. Finally gambling games and behaviors must be located within historical processes that are transforming many areas of American life.

THE SOCIOLOGICAL PERSPECTIVE

No single perspective is adequate for an understanding of something as complex as gambling. In rejecting the psychological approach to an explanation of mainstream American gambling behavior we are not discounting the real contributions of psychology to the study of compulsive gambling, individual gambling careers, and individual risky decisionmaking. In all these areas psychologists have added to our knowledge. Gambling, however, is more than a series of individual risky decisions. It is an activity with specific structures and contexts that exist regardless of individual motivations. The psychological approach, with its focus on the individual, overemphasizes stability and consistency of personality as well as personal motives and judgments in explaining gambling behavior. At the same time it underestimates the significance of the games themselves, the other actors, and the gambling situation as an enclosed system offering many alternative behavior options. As we have noted, where compulsive gambling is concerned this emphasis produces useful results. Like other compulsions, uncontrollable gambling is a manifestation of individual psychological traits for which gambling situations are the occasion but not the cause. But, while it is certainly true that each gambler has his or her own psychological goals, perceptions, and interpretations of the gambling scene, the "worlds of reality" gamblers inhabit are largely situational—and not the autonomous creations of individual psyches. From buying lottery tickets to shooting craps the structure of their experience relies heavily on socially constructed systems of meaning: on norms and ideologies that define games, playing strategies, and what constitutes winning and losing. No analysis of individual gamblers, however complete or profound, can reveal these

meanings. Gambling cannot profitably be studied in isolation from its social context.

What is needed is an overview, a perspective that takes in not only gamblers individually but the games themselves, within specific cultural contexts that are the product of particular historical processes. Sociology provides this perspective. Along with the steady accretion of clinical studies, a sociology of gambling has developed. This literature has sought to apply the sociology of leisure to the study of gambling as games and play.

In his landmark theory of games,[35] Roger Caillois, building on the seminal work of Johan Huizinga,[36] classifies lotteries, casinos, and pari-mutuel betting as (primarily) games of chance *(aléa)* located on the margins of the social order.[37] Gambling, however, is not asocial: play at games of chance[38] "presuppose[s] not solitude but company" and is fundamentally a social activity. Through this social aspect of play, games, including gambling games of chance, are involved in relationships that cross over all four of the categories into which Caillois analyzes play: chance *(aléa),* competition *(agon),* mimicry, and vertigo *(ilinx).* Horse racing, for example, is "typical *agon* for the jockeys [and] at the same time a spectacle which . . . stimulates *mimicry* and is also a pretext for betting, through which the competition [of the horses and jockeys] is a basis [or object] of *aléa.*"[39] These relationships may have a psychological dimension: "In games of chance . . . a special kind of vertigo seizes both lucky and unlucky players. They are no longer aware of fatigue and are scarcely conscious of what is going on around them. They are entranced by the question of where the ball will stop or what card will turn up. They lose all objectivity and sometimes gamble more than they have."[40] The social activity of roulette—and not a psychological trait—produces vertigo that robs the player of his objectivity and may thereby stimulate excessive loss regardless of his motivation for playing roulette (which may, of course, include a conscious or unconscious desire to experience vertigo). This explanation of excessive—not compulsive—gambling requires, as we have said, a context and structure beyond the individual player's personality. It is, most certainly, not the same thing as individual decisionmaking. Gambling cannot exist without a social system in which to gamble; paradoxically, Caillois suggests that a society such as ours where "the entire social structure rests upon [*agon,* or competition]" may not be able to exist without the socialized chance of gambling: "*agon* and *aléa* no doubt represent the contradictory and complementary principles of a new social order. Moreover, they must fulfill parallel functions which are recognizably indispensible. . . ."[41] The kind of play that is gambling provides an escape from the discipline of work and from the boredom and routine it engenders. For Caillois and Huizinga, by reintroducing chance in the (socially constructed) forms of racetrack and lottery and casino games into societies ruled by competition, gambling frees us, if only temporarily, from the tyranny of rational order.

Erving Goffman extends the sociology of gambling to the prosaic world of "everyday" situations.[42] He argues that orderly social life at the most pragmatic levels is made possible by unspoken rules of social interaction, or rituals, that serve to sustain the action of society. Gambling games offer a particular kind of action: consequential, avoidable chance. All games, including gambling games, have as their rationale the game itself; observing players in action we do not have to know anything about their individual personalities to understand their moves and strategies. The gambler, in other words, does not autonomously generate gambling behavior from his own psyche. The games he plays are cultural in origin, social constructions of risk. A society, Goffman is saying, gets the games—and the gambling—it deserves. Our competitive and materialistic culture, where money is central to real and symbolic values, is as responsible for the game of *Monopoly* as is Parker Brothers. In *Monopoly* collecting money, buying symbolic properties, and building token houses are acceptable behavior toward the prescribed end of bankrupting other players. Outside the game these houses and deeds are valueless: the winner of a State lottery, for example, would be outraged if his payoff were in *Monopoly* money. The excitement of and motivation for *Monopoly* reside in the game, but its rules and roles, and its meaning, are conventional and derive not from the players but from their culture.

So with gambling. Goffman is less sure of the liberating qualities of gambling than Huizinga and Caillois: individuals, he argues, whatever their motives for engaging in this kind of action, are not free even in the gambling situation to create their own worlds of meaning. Like *Monopoly,* gambling is conventional: as with other social activities all gambling situations contain rules and roles; the meaning of betting, as distinct from the monetary value of a bet, can be arrived at only through subjective utilities that are by no means necessarily economic. A nickel pot is worth a nickel, but the value of gambling for a nickel pot to any particular individual is objectively incalculable. In Goffman's perspective the social valuation of gambling is likewise a subjective calculation. Gambling is not a pathology, but a specific form of social behavior that occurs only within a given system of internally consistent, culturally determined, and socially agreed-upon meanings. Action and its social context are inseparable.

One of Goffman's contributions to the sociology of gambling is the brief but cogent description of gambling games in the opening pages of "Where the Action Is," which provides a solid underpinning for his examination of interactive gambling behavior. As we have noted, the failure to look carefully at the games gamblers play is one of the principal shortcomings of the psychological literature. The structural analysis of games that is the subject of the next chapter, while primarily an exercise in structural functionalism, derives its significance from one of the most basic theoretical approaches within the sociological perspective: symbolic interactionism.[43] The ideas of George Herbert Mead, presented in *Mind, Self and Society,*[44] center on the importance of games for the development of society and the socialization of the child. It is through games that the child learns to play roles in society and, in the process, develops a sense of self and internalizes cultural meanings. These ideas underly much of the work, by Howard Becker, David Matza,[45] and others, on "deviance"—including gambling—as conventional behavior. In these studies the complex question of how a person comes to define himself as a gambler, or any other "deviant," is addressed within the framework of symbolic interaction.

Becker's classic study of deviant careers, "Becoming a Marijuana User," offers a sociological explanation for social pathology: we can learn deviance just as, and just as easily as, we can learn "acceptable" behavior.[46] Rather than assuming users are motivated by happenstance or some personality disturbance, Becker argues that marijuana use is the result of several interrelated conditions: an available, secure supply, an appropriate time and place, and the example of other users. These conditions are met through a complex social interaction between the novice and more experienced marijuana smokers. Following his initiation the novice develops routines of secrecy, redefines his earlier (and of course culturally, and not psychologically, derived) notions regarding the morality of smoking marijuana, and associates regularly with other marijuana smokers. Becker concludes: "Instead of the deviant motives leading to the deviant behavior, it is the other way around; the deviant behavior in time produces the deviant motivations." The parallel with Goffman's findings is exact: The sensations produced by marijuana, like the satisfactions of *Monopoly* or the excitement of gambling, which are internal and intrinsic to the game or drug, not to the personality of the individual, become the motivation for the "deviance" of gambling or smoking marijuana. These sensations and satisfactions are sought and experienced through interactive social behaviors that only occur in the social contexts of gambling or marijuana-smoking situations; and over time elaborate interactive rituals develop in the gambling or drug subculture that transform individual actions into definite patterns of everyday social behavior.

A similar approach underlies Henry Lesieur's *The Chase,* a study of pathological gamblers seeking to repeat a big win they, or their gambling acquaintances, once experienced.[47] Jay Livingston and Igor Kusyszyn adopt a similar view in their description of the stages through which problem gamblers progress in learning the role of sick players.[48] The compulsive gambler may not have personality problems at the outset of his eventual downfall, but over time, through differential association and immersion in gambling situations and the resulting congruence of the gambler-role and his identity, he becomes a different individual and his behavior becomes pathological. In this view a "gambling personality" is not so much a cause of gambling as it is one of gambling's effects on the individual. Here, as in Goffman's analysis, the importance of socially and culturally constructed roles in determining gambling behavior emerges. On entering gambling situations individuals assume one of many possible gambler-roles, one of which is the role of compulsive gambler.

We can at this point summarize the insights into gambling and gambling behavior provided by symbolic interactionism. These are: (1) the importance of games; (2) the conventional nature of most behavior, even behavior usually considered deviant; and (3) an understanding of the process of socialization into deviant careers. Symbolic interaction is essentially biography rather than history. Its primary focus is on the individual within social situations. In order to arrive at a complete understanding of the social functions of gambling games, however, a second sociological approach is needed. This second approach is structural functionalism.

One of the functions of society is to provide mechanisms that enable people to deal with and control potentially dangerous situations. Many social rituals perform this function: for example, a funeral helps mourners adjust to the loss of a loved one. For the great majority of Americans who gamble without becoming compulsive, gambling, like other forms of play, performs analogous social functions. For most people gambling is a healthy recreation. It provides escape from both the uncertainty and the boring routine of modern life by reinforcing, in familiar and highly ritualized surroundings, conventions and roles that let gamblers feel, at least for the duration of the game, that they are the masters of their fates. Some of the more structured gambling situations, such as horse-race betting, allow gamblers to confront the probabilistic, chancey nature of existence within the comforting bounds of ritual order. Other games, of which craps is an example, give players the subjective (and in this case illusory) feeling of influence (by throwing the dice) over the outcome of the gambling event. State lotteries have the perhaps more dubious function of offering the hope, against astronomical odds, of striking it rich to people who in a capitalistic system have few realistic prospects of realizing the American dream. Games may vary in the satisfactions they offer, but all gambling, and many other games and sports as well, have in common the major social function of the disenchantment of chance by subjecting it to the rules of play. In the most ordered and technically proficient culture there remains an unpredictable and uncontrollable challenge to personal survival arising from the random nature of events. Gambling, with its predictable uncertainties, tames chance and turns it—for most people—to useful social purpose.[49]

In contrast to symbolic interaction, structural functionalism does not focus attention on the biography of the individual or on the process by which he internalizes external social facts or rules. The structural functionalist assumes that order is "out there," created by society independently of the individuals living within it. Order is a social fact that functions to maintain the integrity of the system. Structural functionalism attempts to explain social forms and rituals not in terms of the psychological motives of individual participants, but rather in terms of the often latent functions these activities have for the survival of society itself. In this view society is a thing *sui generis,* and as such has its own survival mechanisms, or cultural subsystems, that perform different and specialized functions to get the job of society done. Each of these systems of action, or social institutions, can be conceptualized separately within its own boundaries, and yet each is interconnected with other systems, in much the same way as one's cardiovascular system is separate from but related to one's muscular system.[50]

Most studies in the sociology of gambling have, at least implicitly, some underlying basis in structural functionalism. Gamblers and gambling are seen as fulfilling certain functions for society. Several structural functionalist studies also look at the various ways a gambling structure maintains itself. For example, Irving Kenneth Zola's "Gambling in a Lower Class Setting" shows how the role of a good gambler among fellow gamblers functions as a chance for individuals to practice a productive presentation of self: being a good winner or loser has positive functional value for the gambler and also helps to maintain the game.[51] Goffman similarly speaks of structural mechanisms that "cool out" the loser and keep him from disrupting the game.[52] Robert D. Herman, in his study of the racetrack, looks at the function of various structural aspects of gambling in the context of the gambling situation. Money, for example, functions to "verify the decisionmaking process" of betting a horse; it also "verifies the involvement of the bettor in the action."[53] All of these studies speak to those aspects of the gambling situation that facilitate the involvement and participation of gamblers. While maintaining the action, Herman suggests that these mechanisms of involvement—tote boards, for example, which "give prominence to the total amounts of money wagered and information concerning the odds"—also emphasize the importance of "weighing alternatives, making decisions, and signaling these decisions by attaching money to them." Further, through these system-maintaining devices players emulate traditional entrepreneurial roles—in this case the role of the investor watching the stock market ticker-tape—which are of course basic mainstream American cultural values: "Gambling, by this view, is less dysfunctional than it appears to be to those who judge it solely by standards linked to the production of goods."[54]

We argue that commercial gambling caricatures the nineteenth-century ideology of enterprise—sober individual risk-taking, thrift, effort, and self-denial—that legitimated investment capitalism in a democracy.[55] These values constituted what Max Weber called "the Protestant ethic,"[56] which is caricatured insofar as the gambler invests in the present—in a chance for immediate, materialistic rewards and payoffs in an atmosphere of self-indulgence. Gambling thus exemplifies a reversal of American values:[57] the ethic of saving, of self-denial and capital accumulation, has been replaced by an ideology of hedonistic consumerism, which Christopher Lasch has perceptively termed the culture of narcissism.[58] Today Americans eagerly consume disposable time and wealth. The accumulation of capital is no longer as important to most people as the search for ways to use money in pursuit of pleasure and status. This emphasis on consumption is quite functional in a modern capitalistic society. By embracing gambling and so enthusiastically caricaturing the work ethic of our parents, mainstream Americans truly mirror a historic cultural change.

The structural characteristics of gambling fit the times extremely well. Caillois observes that the lottery of heredity has always been resented by egalitarian societies;[59] for this injustice of biology, the unflinchingly democratic odds of casino games, which are the same for everyone whether the wager is large or small, is a measure of social compensation. From roulette to slot machines, these games of pure chance are equally accessible to anyone with the money for a minimum bet.[60] In contrast the odds at pari-mutuel horse racing are neither egalitarian nor stable,[61] but in their teasing fluctuations at once facilitate and stimulate and emphasize the consumer's decisionmaking process. As well as Zola's lower-class betting milieu, racetracks and casinos are prototypical arenas for the displays of money that in this country confer power and prestige.

The peculiar "fit" between gambling and capitalism was first suggested by Edward Devereux in an early functional analysis of gambling as a kind of safety valve for the unfulfilled hopes of the lower classes.[62] In Devereux's view modern capitalistic society contains a basic contradiction, between the ideal of equality of opportunity and the actual inequality of capitalistic economic institutions, that gambling, through its ability to provide an outlet for the frustrated hopes of less fortunate classes, has helped to obscure: "Upon gambling can be heaped the onus of responsibility for our collective guilts. Gambling must be tolerated, even allowed to flourish, in practice, since its elimination would leave the contradictions of capitalism untouched and over-exposed. The pretense that we aim to eliminate it must, however, be maintained."[63] We find a number of pleasing ironies, and more than a measure of truth, in Devereux's image of a capitalistic system founded by antigambling Puritans held hostage to a roulette wheel.

One of the more recent and comprehensive studies of the sociology of gambling, by D. M. Downes et al., attempts to combine Caillois's sociology of games and play and Devereux's structural functionalist hypothesis with an effort to ascertain empirically the sociological functions of gambling considered as a game.[64] This attempt inadvertently points up several limitations common to all such studies. The literature to date on the sociology of gambling has failed to differentiate in any very thorough and rigorous way among the highly diverse structures of the games used in commercial gambling.[65] Devereux's thesis of the safety valve function of gambling may help explain the rapid institutionalization of State lotteries, but it is certainly less helpful in explaining the appeal of casino games like blackjack or baccarat, whose players come from the middle and upper strata of American society. A more general defect of these studies is that sociologists, while recognizing that gambling has social functions, have in their desire to generate quantifiable data (Downes) or make *in situ* observations (Herman and Zola) often fallen into precisely the methodological (if not conceptual) error they try to avoid: the trap of psychological reductionism.

One of the earliest sociologists, Emile Durkheim, pointed out in his classic study *Suicide*[66] that one cannot arrive at an understanding of social functions by studying individual intentions and actions. Durkheim concluded that the difference in suicide rates among countries could only be explained by variations in the mechanisms of social cohesion in different societies, not by the personalities of individuals living in these societies. In other words, suicide cannot be attributed to personality problems. Similarly, society is not reducible to the sum of its parts. The latent functions of social phenomena cannot be elucidated by questioning individuals about their motives or intentions or through personality studies. Psychology, in short, is an avenue of research into the individual personality; but it does not lead very far toward an understanding of social constructs and behaviors, such as gambling and gambling games, or of society.

A third defect in the literature is that it is ahistorical and, in a peculiar sense, acultural as well. Neither symbolic interactionists nor structural functionalists have taken sufficient account of the larger historical processes that are affecting games and gamblers, society, and the social meaning of gambling.

There is a third approach within sociology, one that has not previously been applied to the sociological study of gambling.[67] This approach is conflict theory. Like gambling, conflict theory is not a homogeneous entity. Conflict theory recognizes that there may be important differences in the bases for social conflict, in how social conflicts are resolved, and in whose interest they are resolved. But conflict theory has the important advantage of being oriented toward a historical view of social phenomena. This approach seeks to explain social behavior as motivated by the quest for power among competing individuals or interest groups.[68] Conflict theory does not assume social consensus or functionally interrelated natural subsystems cooperating to maintain society. Instead, conflict theory assumes there is no single macro-entity or process called society. Rather, society is whatever the individual or group in power defines it to be. This approach would define the contemporary gambling scene as a result of a history of competing interests—one that would spread gambling opportunities, and one that would prohibit or severely constrain such opportunities.

Conflict theory explains relationships among a series of events dynamically related through history more effectively than does the structural approach, which posits a static, self-maintaining, perfect-state model of society in which norms exist virtually unchallenged. According to conflict theory, actors within any situation represent interests, and their actions are strategies. Conflict theory speaks of bargaining, staking new claims, and shifting alliances depending upon changing situations. No one has permanent, nonmaterialistic, nonspecific loyalties in a world defined by conflict theory. This conception clearly opposes a world of *a priori* values or unchanging social functions.

Conflict theory specifies conflict as the mechanism of historical change. Marx generally argued that the history of legal, political, and cultural "superstructures" is ultimately the product and reflection of underlying shifts in economic relationships. Values and norms are ideologies that serve to legitimate and maintain the position of those currently in control of the social structure. Weber, though also a conflict theorist, believed Marx was mistaken in making economic forces the sole determinants of history and the structure of society. For Weber ideas were not simply reflections of underlying interests. He was aware of the role ideas play in strengthening and guaranteeing the position of interests within a given social order. In Weber's view, people also have non-material interests and beliefs about the world. These beliefs are not simply rationalizations of economic interests but exist in their own right. Both variations of conflict theory agree, however, that for a group to maintain power—regardless of its particular interest—it must eventually justify its position through cultural mechanisms of legitimacy and authority.[69] As we will show in Chapter 6, this relates directly to the history of commercial gambling in America.

Conflict theory explains a number of seeming contradictions within the gambling scene. For instance, a clergyman with a personal moral bias against gambling might allow his congregation to sponsor a weekly bingo game or raffle if he sees these activities as revenue producers for his parish.[70] Similarly, a State or locality that prohibits gambling in accordance with the expressed moral reservations of its citizens may be persuaded to legalize lotteries or racetracks or casinos in an attempt to raise revenues without direct taxation and justify the action with the arguments that gambling revenues are "painless" taxes, or will go to the arts or the elderly or the poor, or for some other especially deserving purpose.

Conflict theory may be applied to very specific gambling situations, including the actual playing of games. As Caillois notes, gambling contains elements of competition. Conflict theory can explain gambling as an attempt by players to beat each other (in pari-mutuel betting) or the house (at casino games) by adopting strategies to maximize their self-interests, whether that is winning money, having a good time, or just experiencing the excitement of action. Applications of conflict theory at this level need not be restricted to gambling behavior. When individuals responsible for regulating commercial gambling leave modestly salaried government posts for more highly paid positions in the gambling industry they follow a time-honored precedent established by the government regulators of virtually every major industry in the United States: like gamblers, or casinos and racetracks, these people use gambling to maximize their self-interest.[71] Individual movements from one gambling interest to another are in fact common at every level, even among gamblers themselves. Bookmakers are frequently recruited from the ranks of serious bettors.[72] Ken Uston, a card-counter whose profession cast him and casinos in adversarial roles, capitalized on his experience by writing books on blackjack and eventually running blackjack seminars under the auspices of a casino.[73] Both Uston and the bettor-turned-bookmaker use gambling as a means to a rational end; the variations on similar shifts between roles and interests created by gambling are numerous.

Finally in this review of methodological approaches to the study of the sociology of gambling there is the importance of history. As one major form of commercial gambling after another enters mainstream America they do so as the result of historical processes that are unique and could not be predicted by any sociological or economic model. Conflict theory can explain how State lotteries have grown in just twenty years from an acknowledged failure to the second largest commercial gambling game in the United States. But it could not have predicted this surprising turn of events. Moreover, the anticipated introduction of a new technological contrivance, electronic video gaming devices, into State lottery operations while an enormously popular indigenous gambling activity like sports betting remains proscribed is explainable only in specific historical terms. As these examples show, commercial gambling is more than the sum of the motivations of individual gamblers. It is that sum and the product of diverse and complex historical factors as well. Gambling is not a single activity but a set of diverse activities that are related to the unique complex of structures and contexts that are particular to each game.

Thus, it is clear that a broader focus and a reframing of the issues are necessary to understand the business of risk. The nature of gambling has changed as it has evolved from sub rosa activities, run by individual entrepreneurs or springing up spontaneously among a group of players, to legitimate businesses run by public corporations and even governments. Society can no longer afford to focus almost exclusively on individuals and the problems some of them have with gambling. It can no longer take refuge in a moral crusade to prohibit behavior most Americans enjoy. And the relationship between Big Gambling and American society can no longer go unexamined. By analyzing the real differences among gambling games, by focusing on the major forms of legal commercial gambling, by taking a detailed look at the many types of gamblers, and by looking at the relationship of commercial gambling to our society and our culture, we offer an alternative view of issues that have been clouded by much sound and fury and suggest some more practical ways to deal with commercial gambling in mainstream America.

NOTES

1. Examples of superficial romanticizing include Lucius Beebe, *The Big Spenders* (New York: Doubleday, 1966); Alexander Gardiner, *Canfield: The True Story of the Greatest Gambler* (Garden City, N.Y.: Doubleday, Doran, 1930); Will Irwin, *Confessions of a Con Man* (New York: B. W. Huebsch, 1909); Robert Irving Warshaw, *Bet-A-Million Gates: The Story of a Plunger* (New York: Greenberg, 1932). A recent representative hysterical antigambling tract is Tomás Martinez, *The Gambling Scene: Why People Gamble* (Springfield, Ill.: Charles C. Thomas, 1983). Moral preaching includes John Morris, *An Exposure of the Arts and Miseries of Gambling* (Cincinnati, Ohio, 1843); W. T. Stead, *Satan's Invisible World Displayed* (New York: World Publishing, 1972). For a sober, thorough, and excellent overview of American moral views of gambling see Raymond C. Bell, "Moral Views on Gambling Promulgated by Major American Religious Bodies," in *Gambling in America: Final Report of the Commission on the Review of the National Policy Toward Gambling* (Washington, D.C.: GPO, 1976), Appendix 1, pp. 161–239.

2. John Philip Quinn, *Fools of Fortune* (Chicago: G. Howe, 1890); Herbert Asbury, *Sucker's Progress: An Informal History of Gambling in America from the Colonies to Canfield* (New York: Dodd, Mead, 1938); Henry Chafetz, *Play the Devil: A History of Gambling in the United States from 1492 to 1955* (New York: Clarkson N. Potter, 1960).

3. The basic text on the psychology of gambling is Edmund Bergler, M.D., *The Psychology of Gambling* (New York: Hill and Wang, 1957). Representative examples of the literature include William E. Aubrey, "Altering the Gambler's Maladaptive Life Goals," *International Journal of the Addictions* 10 (1975):29–33; Robert M. Lindner, "The Psychodynamics of Gambling," *Annals of the American Academy of Political and Social Science* 269 (May 1950):93–107; Robert Ladouceur and Marie Mayrand, "Evaluation of the 'Illusion of Control,'" in *The Gambling Papers: Proceedings of the Fifth National Conference on Gambling and Risk Taking,* vol. 4, *Studies in Gambling Behavior,* ed. William R. Eadington (Reno: University of Nevada, 1982), pp. 61–78; Jay Livingston, "Compulsive Gambling: A Culture of Losers," *Psychology Today* 7 (March 1974):51–55; Henry Lesieur, *The Chase: Career of the Compulsive Gambler* (Garden City, N.Y.: Anchor Press, 1977); Igor Kusyszyn, "Compulsive Gambling: The Problem of Definition," *International Journal of the Addictions* 13 (1978):1095–1101.

4. Bell, "Moral Views on Gambling," is the best summary of American religious views concerning gambling. Protestant Christians have been the severest critics: Lycurgus M. Starkey, Jr., is representative: *The Christian Church and Gambling* (Washington, D.C.: General Board of Christian Social Concerns of the Methodist Church, n.d.); "Christians and the Gambling Mania," in *Gambling,* ed. Robert Herman (New York: Harper and Row, 1967); and *Money, Mania, and Morals: The Churches and Gambling* (New York: Abingdon Press, 1964). Moral reformers have often viewed gambling, legal or not, as an evil most effectively prevented by social institutions rather than law and enforcement measures: "Whether [antigambling] efforts will prevail over the vested gambling interests depends . . . upon the moral tone of our present and future citizenry. . . . Important in this molding process are the church, the home, the school, motion pictures, books, magazines, and newspapers. Courts and police are prosecuting rather than preventive agencies." Paul S. Deland (managing editor of the *Christian Science Monitor),* "The Facilitation of Gambling," *Annals of the American Academy of Political and Social Science* 269 (May 1950):21–29. The development of the doctrine of organized crime's control of, and financial dependence on, illegal gambling is examined in Peter Reuter and Jonathan B. Rubinstein, "Fact, Fancy, and Organized Crime,"

Public Interest 53 (Fall 1978):45–67. The relationship of antigambling law enforcement and police corruption is examined in Jonathan Rubinstein, "Gambling Enforcement and Police Corruption," in *Gambling in America,* Appendix 1, pp. 600–632. Robert F. Kennedy, "The Baleful Influence of Gambling," in *Gambling,* ed. Herman, pp. 169–77, is a succinct statement of this doctrine. The Kefauver committee's *Report on Organized Crime: Report of the Special Senate Committee to Investigate Organized Crime in Interstate Commerce* (New York: Didier, 1951) and the McClellon committee's *Gambling and Organized Crime: Report of the Committee on Government Operations by its Permanent Subcommittee on Investigations,* 3 vols. (Washington, D.C.: GPO, 1962) are the most important statements of this doctrine by Congress. See also the discussion of illegal gambling in the Appendix.

5. Martinez, *The Gambling Scene,* p. 152.

6. Charles Cotton, *Games and Gamesters of the Restoration: The Compleat Gamster* (1674; London: Kennikat Press, 1930). Compare Ernest E. Blanche, chief statistician for the United States Army general staff's logistics division: "The mathematical odds or probabilities in all gambling games are so determined that only the operator . . . can win during the continued conduct of the games. . . . The following summaries of the more popular ways of losing money may make each suggested game a loathsome, sickening purgative." "Gambling Odds are Gimmicked!," *Annals of the American Academy of Political and Social Science* 269 (May 1950):77–80.

7. *Gambling in America,* p. 1. The commission was created by Congress in the Organized Crime Control Act of 1970 (P.L. 91–452) for the purpose of conducting "a comprehensive legal and factual study of gambling in the United States and existing Federal, State, and local policy and practices with respect to legal prohibition and taxation of gambling activities and to formulate and propose such changes in those policies and practices as the Commission may deem appropriate." The commission's membership comprised four senators, four representatives, and nine other persons, including the chairman, Charles H. Morin, and executive director, James E. Ritchie. The commission handed up its final report in 1976.

8. A number of racetracks and vendors of pari-mutuel betting systems have been publicly traded for years. Prominent examples include Santa Anita Companies (NYSE, the operator of a major Southern California racetrack), Churchill Downs (OTC, the operator of the Kentucky racetrack holding the Kentucky Derby), General Instrument Corporation (NYSE, a vendor through its subsidiary American Totalizator of pari-mutuel betting systems), and many other companies. Since the enactment by the State of Nevada of corporate gaming acts in 1967 and 1969 publicly traded corporations have come to dominate casino gaming. Hilton Hotels (NYSE), Holiday Inns (NYSE), Caesars World (NYSE), Showboat (AMEX), Ramada Inns (NYSE), and MGM Grand Hotels (NYSE) are examples. State lottery games are supplied by private sector vendors that are for the most part publicly traded: Bally Manufacturing (NYSE, through its subsidiary Scientific Games), GTECH (OTC), Syntech International (OTC), and other companies.

9. Rational decisionmaking analyses include William J. Corney and William Theodore Cummings, "Information Processing Biases and Gambling Behavior," in *The Gambling Papers,* ed. Eadington, pp. 120–30; William R. Eadington, *The Economics of Gambling Behavior: A Qualitative Study of Nevada's Gambling Industry,* Bureau of Business and Economic Research Report no. 11 (Reno: University of Nevada, 1973); Terry J. Knapp, "A Functional Analysis of Gambling Behavior," in *Gambling and Society,* ed. Eadington, pp. 276–94; R. N. Rosett, "Gambling and Rationality," *Journal of Political Economy* 73 (December 1965):595–607; N. Kogan and M. A. Wallach, "Risk Taking as a Function of the Situation, the Person and the Group," in *New*

Directions in Psychology III, eds. George Mandler, Paul Mussen, Nathan Kogan and Michael A. Wellach (New York: Holt, Rinehart and Winson, 1967).

10. See Thomas W. Mangione et al., "Citizen Views of Gambling Enforcement," in *Gambling in America,* Appendix 1, pp. 240–300; Frederick Pratter and Floyd J. Fowler, Jr., "Police Perceptions About Gambling Enforcement," ibid., pp. 461–93; James M. Kretz and Carol H. Duncan, "Police Attitudes Toward Gambling Enforcement," ibid., pp. 565–73; Carol H. Duncan, "State and Local Gambling Enforcement: Arrest, Disposition, and Sentencing Statistics," ibid., pp. 679–744; and Peter Reuter, "Enforceability of Gambling Laws," ibid., pp. 551–64; Kathleen M. Joyce, "Public Opinion and the Politics of Gambling," *Journal of Social Issues* 35 (Summer 1979):144–65; Judge John M. Murtagh, "Gambling and Police Corruption," *Atlantic Monthly* 206 (November 1960):49–53.

11. Cornell Law School, G. Robert Blakey, supervisor, *The Development of the Law of Gambling: 1776–1976,* prepared for National Institute of Law Enforcement and Criminal Justice, Law Enforcement Assistance Administration, United States Department of Justice (Washington, D.C.: GPO, 1977), pp. 39ff., 59–61. This massive review of American gambling law is supplemented by G. Robert Blakey and Harold A. Kurland, "The Development of the Federal Law of Gambling," *Cornell Law Review* 63 (August 1978):923–1021. There is an excellent summary of federal gambling law and regulation in *Gambling in America,* pp. 11–33, with extensive, detailed, and accurate notes.

12. The best history of American lotteries is John Samuel Ezell, *Fortune's Merry Wheel: The Lottery in America* (Cambridge, Mass.: Harvard University Press, 1960). For lotteries in England see C. L'Estrange Ewen, *Lotteries and Sweepstakes: An Historical, Legal, and Ethical Survey of Their Introduction, Suppression, and Re-establishment in the British Isles* (London: Heath Cranton, 1932; New York: Benjamin Blom, 1972). Ewen provides extensive selections from original source materials and is the best history of English and colonial lotteries. John Ashton, *A History of English Lotteries* (1893; reprint, Detroit, Mich.: Singing Tree Press, 1969), provides source materials of an anecdotal nature. Chafetz, *Play the Devil,* pp. 20–28, provides useful anecdotal material. See also Asbury, *Sucker's Progress;* Eric J. Bender, *Tickets to Fortune: The Story of Sweepstakes, Lotteries, and Contests* (New York: Modern Age Books, 1938); Harry Bischoff Weiss and Grace M. Weiss, *The Early Lotteries of New Jersey* (Trenton, N.J.: Past Times Press, 1966); Francis Emmett Williams, *Lotteries, Laws, and Morals* (New York: Vantage Press, 1958); George Sullivan, *By Chance a Winner: The History of Lotteries* (New York: Dodd, Mead, 1972).

13. Lotteries, except keno, and pari-mutuel betting remained prohibited.

14. The evolution of legal commercial gambling has been on a State-by-State basis and can best be followed in *The Development of the Law of Gambling.* Aspects of this evolution are summarized in Fact Research, Inc., "Gambling in Perspective," in *Gambling in America,* Appendix 1, pp. 1–101. Chafetz, *Play the Devil,* is a good general history of American gambling. See as well Mark H. Haller, "The Changing Structure of American Gambling in the Twentieth Century," *Journal of Social Issues* 35 (Summer 1979):87–114.

15. See the Appendix for a summary accounting of legal commercial gambling losses and a discussion of various estimates of illegal gambling.

16. There is an enormous literature on the definition of compulsive or pathological gambling. A recent, brief summary of this literature is Nancy Ashton, "Gamblers: Disturbed or Healthy?," in *Gambling Today,* ed. David Lester (Springfield, Ill.: Charles C. Thomas, 1979), pp. 53–70. See as well Chapter 4.

17. Maureen Kallick, Daniel Suits, Ted Dielman, and Judith Hybels, Survey Research Center, Institute for Social Research, University of Michigan, "Survey of

American Gambling Attitudes and Behavior,'' in *Gambling in America,* Appendix 2, pp. 93–95. The estimates of gambling expenditures given in this survey are discussed in the Appendix.

18. The most widely quoted estimates range from 2 percent to about 6 percent of the U.S. population. For the 2 percent figure, see Robert L. Custer, ''Description of Compulsive Gambling'' (paper prepared for the American Psychiatric Association Task Force on Nomenclature for inclusion in its Diagnostic Statistical Manual III, 1976); and for the 6 percent figure, see *Gamblers Anonymous* (Los Angeles: G. A. Publishing, n.d.).

19. Kallick, ''Survey of American Gambling,'' in *Gambling in America,* Appendix 1, pp. 417–54.

20. *Gambling in America,* pp. 73–74.

21. Ibid., p. 74.

22. For the federal tax treatment of winnings see John L. Kellogg, ''The Federal Tax Treatment of Winnings, Losses, and Expenses of the Sports and Casino Bettor,'' in *The Gambling Papers,* ed. Eadington, 5:1–25; and *Gambling in America,* pp. 14–18. Citing the stimulus to illegal gambling and interference with State gambling policies created by the inclusion of legal winnings in taxable income as reasons, the commission recommended ''that winnings derived from legal gambling entities be excluded from gross income, with the affirmative burden being placed upon the taxpayer to declare the income and prove the legality of the source'' (p. 15). Successive administrations have declined the commission's recommendation, even to the limited extent of repealing withholding from legal payouts. In 1982, Assistant Secretary of the Treasury for Tax Policy John E. Chapoton testified against bills to repeal or limit withholding on the grounds that the argument ''that the imposition of withholding . . . creates an incentive for patrons to wager with illegal bookmakers . . . proves too much. . . . One must ask . . . why . . . bettors prefer to place their bets with illegal bookmakers. One natural conclusion is that some, if not a substantial portion, of these bettors must be attempting to avoid the reporting and withholding requirements of current law. . . . Reduced to its essential points, this argument asks us to condone implicitly a failure to report income by making it easier to win at legalized establishments and not report winnings. . . . Treasury simply cannot stand by and acquiesce in a change which will encourage, rather than discourage, the failure to report income accurately.'' In other words, Treasury recognizes the inclusion of legal winnings in taxable income is an incentive to illegal gambling, further recognizes that withholding from legal payouts is a further stimulus to illegal gambling, and wants to continue both policies. John E. Chapoton, statement, House Committee on Ways and Means, 97th Cong., 2d sess., *Hearings before the Subcommittee on Select Revenue Measures,* March 16, 1982. Chapoton's solution to the problem of the diversion of legal wagering to illegal operators caused by withholding requirements is ''increased enforcement of the withholding laws'' (Chapoton, letter to Sen. Paul Laxalt, May 21, 1982).

23. See, for example, Erving Goffman, ''Where the Action Is,'' in *Interaction Ritual: Essays on Face-to-Face Behavior* (New York: Pantheon Books, 1967, 1982); Robert D. Herman, ''Gambling as Work: A Sociological Study of the Racetrack,'' in *Gambling,* ed. Herman; Otto Newman, *Gambling: Hazard and Reward* (London: Athlone Press, University of London, 1977); Irving Kenneth Zola, ''Observations on Gambling in a Lower Class Setting,'' in *Gambling,* ed. Herman, pp. 19–31.

24. The fact that craps, which offers bets with house advantages ranging from 1.402 percent to 16.667 percent of handle has in practice an effective average edge of 2 percent to 3 percent is convincing evidence that most players choose the most favorable odds. See the Appendix for a fuller discussion.

25. In horse racing, favorites are established by the subjective opinions of published handicappers (the "morning line") and subsequently by the process of pari-mutuel betting, which establishes the *odds paid,* or return on investment, for each betting interest. In 1981, for example, favorites won 32 percent of U.S. thoroughbred races. *The American Racing Manual* (Hightstown, N.J.: Daily Racing Form, 1982), p. 234.

26. That this is the case is most persuasively demonstrated by the weak efficiency of pari-mutuel betting markets. See the discussion of pari-mutuel betting in Chapter 3.

27. These structural characteristics are discussed in Chapter 2. Economic rationality in risky decisionmaking is analyzed by Theodore Tsukahara, Jr., and Harold J. Brumm, Jr., "Economic Rationality, Psychology and Decision-Making under Uncertainty," in *Gambling and Society,* ed. Eadington, pp. 92–107.

28. Since the opening of Resorts International in Atlantic City in 1978, we have been conducting an on-site study of gambling at racetracks in New Jersey, New York, and Pennsylvania and casinos in Atlantic City and Nevada. In the course of this study we have interviewed persons at all levels of commercial gambling, including most especially racetrack and casino executives and employees. We have also been conducting extensive interviews with gamblers at these establishments, and designed a detailed questionnaire that has been administered to more than one hundred casino patrons and horseplayers. These interviews have employed forced-choice and open-ended questions that, among other things, elicit information about the kinds of games preferred, the kind and location of gambling establishments patronized, the reasons for this patronage, perceptions of success or failure at gambling, levels of wagering, and reactions of friends and relations to gambling. We also explored gamblers' careers or histories, including questions relating to initial introductions to gambling. Data collection and analysis are on-going, but preliminary findings have been presented in several papers. Final study results will include a comparison of respondents to a control group of nongamblers from a randomly distributed questionnaire. We are especially interested in comparisons of socioeconomic status, leisure interests, marital and occupational stability, social networks, and attitudes about "luck," "fate," and the gamblers and nongamblers themselves. Data to date do not support the accepted psychological stereotypes of compulsive gamblers, nor do gamblers appear to differ significantly from the control group. Unlike Ted E. Dielman, "Gambling: A Social Problem?," *Journal of Social Issues* 35 (1979):36-42, we have found no indications of social or personal disorganization among racetrack and casino gamblers, who on the contrary are quite *conventional.* It was this finding that prompted us to rethink the issue of gambling as deviance/pathology and/or related to general social disorganization.

29. Compare the findings of the University of Michigan's Survey Research Center survey: 86 percent of trackgoers and 78 percent of casino patrons gave "to have a good time" as their reason for gambling, with "to make money" the reason of 33 percent and 36 percent of these respective groups. "Excitement" (the primary reason given by 51 percent of trackgoers and 46 percent of casino patrons) and "challenge" (40 percent and 41 percent, respectively) were also more common motivations than making money. Kallick, "Survey of American Gambling," in *Gambling in America,* Appendix 2, pp. 45-48.

30. Jerome H. Skolnick, *House of Cards: Legalization and Control of Casino Gambling* (Boston: Little, Brown, 1978). This classic study is usefully supplemented by John Dennis Dombrink, "Outlaw Businessmen: Organized Crime and the Legalization of Casino Gambling" (Ph.D. diss., University of California, Berkeley, 1981), with much valuable material on Atlantic City.

31. Off-track betting has been an issue in California since the early 1970s. Prior to 1983 the various interests that comprise the State's racing industry were unable to agree

on a format for OTB; during the summer of that year, however, an industry accord was reached on an off-track betting proposal embodied in Assembly Bill 1517, which despite considerable support failed to pass the legislature due to opposition from the State's attorney general and governor, who threatened to veto the bill. The legislation's prospects for enactment in 1984 are unclear at the time of writing; there is, however, widespread expectation that off-track betting is an inevitable development in the majority of racing States. As of 1984, Illinois is the State most likely to legalize off-track betting.

32. For a discussion of illegal sports betting and other forms of illegal gambling, see the Appendix.

33. For the derivation of this estimate see the Appendix.

34. Mario Puzo, *The Godfather* (New York: Putnam, 1969).

35. Roger Caillois, *Man, Play, and Games,* trans. from *Les jeux et les hommes* (Paris: Gallimard, 1958) by Meyer Barash (New York: Schocken Books, 1979).

36. Johan Huizinga, *Homo Ludens: A Study of the Play-Element in Culture* (Boston: Beacon Press, 1955).

37. Caillois, *Man, Play, and Games,* pp. 41, 54.

38. And, in fact, all four of Caillois's categories of play: *aléa,* competition *(agon),* mimicry, and vertigo *(ilinx).* Ibid., p. 40.

39. Ibid., p. 72.

40. Ibid., p. 73.

41. Ibid., p. 157.

42. Goffman, "Where the Action Is," pp. 149–270.

43. For a general discussion of symbolic interactionism see Jerome Manis and Bernard Meltzer, eds., *Symbolic Interaction: A Reader in Social Psychology* (Boston: Allyn & Bacon, 1972); Anselm Straus, *George Herbert Mead on Social Psychology* (Chicago: University of Chicago Press, 1964); Don Martindale, *The Nature and Types of Sociological Theory* (Boston: Houghton Mifflin, 1960); Ruth Wallace and Alison Wolf, *Contemporary Sociological Theory* (New York: Prentice Hall, 1980).

44. George Herbert Mead, *Mind, Self and Society* (Chicago: University of Chicago Press, 1934).

45. Howard Becker, *Outsiders: Studies in the Sociology of Deviance* (New York: Free Press, 1963); David Matza, *Delinquency and Drift* (New York: Wiley, 1964).

46. Becker, "Becoming a Marijuana User," *American Journal of Sociology* 59 (November 1953):235–42.

47. Lesieur, *The Chase.*

48. Livingston, "Compulsive Gambling: A Culture of Losers," pp. 51–55; Kusyszyn, "Compulsive Gambling," pp. 1095–101.

49. This theme is developed by Mary Douglas and Aaron Wildavsky, *Culture and Risk* (New York: Random House, 1982).

50. For a discussion of Durkheim and modern sociological structural functionalism see Robert K. Merton, *Social Theory and Social Structure* (Glencoe, Ill.: Free Press, 1957); Talcott Parsons and Edward Shils, eds., *Toward a General Theory of Action* (New York: Harper, 1951); George Simpson, *Emile Durkheim* (New York: Thomas Y. Crowell, 1963); Wallace and Wolf, *Contemporary Sociological Theory.*

51. Zola, "Observations on Gambling in a Lower-Class Setting," pp. 353–61.

52. Goffman, "Where the Action Is."

53. Herman, "Gambling as Work," p. 101.

54. Ibid., p. 107.

55. Vicki Abt and James Smith, "Playing the Game in Mainstream America," in *World of Play,* ed. Frank E. Manning (West Point, N.Y.: Leisure Press, 1983).

56. Max Weber, *The Protestant Ethic and the Spirit of Capitalism* (New York: Charles Scribner, 1930).

57. Not coincidentally, at a time when real investment opportunities are largely foreclosed within the economic system, at least for the lower classes. For many of the multi-million dollar lottery prizewinners whose rags-to-riches biographies are regularly reported in the press investments in the local State lottery may indeed be the most likely chance of exchanging their rags for a piece of the American dream.

58. Christopher Lasch, *The Culture of Narcissism: American Life in an Age of Diminishing Expectations* (New York: Warner Books, 1979).

59. Caillois, *Man, Play, and Games,* p. 158.

60. Games of mixed chance and skill (e.g., poker, baccarat, and blackjack) are not as democratic: skill, which is a function of biology to the extent that intelligence and stamina are factors in its development and exercise, partially determines the odds at which these games are played. See Chapters 2 and 3.

61. Here also skill is a factor, in that considerable expertise is required to use the information reflected in the constantly shifting pari-mutuel odds to best advantage. See Chapters 2 and 3.

62. Edward C. Devereux, Jr., "Gambling and the Social Structure: A Sociological Study of Lotteries and Horseracing in Contemporary America" (Ph.D. diss., Harvard University, 1949).

63. Devereux, quoted in D. M. Downes, B. P. Davies, M. E. David, and P. Stone, *Gambling, Work and Leisure: A Study across Three Areas* (London: Routledge & Kegan Paul, 1976), p. 79.

64. Ibid.

65. Goffman, as has been noted, is an exception, but the essay form of "Where the Action Is" did not lend itself to an exhaustive treatment.

66. Emile Durkheim, *Suicide* (1897; Glencoe, Ill.: Free Press, 1964).

67. A notable exception is Skolnick's *House of Cards.*

68. For a good overview of sociological conflict theories see Reinhard Bendix and Seymour M. Lipset, eds., *Class, Status and Power* (Glencoe, Ill.: Free Press, 1953); Percy S. Cohen, *Modern Social Theory* (New York: Basic Books, 1968); Irving Louis Horowitz, ed., *The New Sociology: Essays in Social Science and Social Theory in Honor of C. Wright Mills* (New York: Oxford University Press, 1964); Graham C. Kinloch, *Ideology and Contemporary Sociological Theory* (New York: Prentice Hall, 1981); Wallace and Wolf, *Contemporary Sociological Theory.*

69. A detailed comparison of various conflict theories can be found in H. H. Gerth and C. Wright Mills, trans. and eds., *From Max Weber: Essays in Sociology* (New York: Oxford University Press, 1958); Reinhard Bendix, *Max Weber: An Intellectual Portrait* (New York: Anchor Books, 1962); Julien Freund, *The Sociology of Max Weber* (New York: Vintage Books, 1969); T. B. Bottomore, "Marxist Sociology," in *International Encyclopedia of the Social Sciences,* ed. David L. Sills (New York: Free Press, 1968), 10:46–53; Robert Friedman, *Marxist Social Thought* (New York: Harcourt, Brace and World, 1968); Claus Offe, "Political Authority and Class Structures: An Analysis of Late Capitalist Societies," *International Journal of Sociology* 2 (Spring 1972):73–108; and Robert Alford, "Paradigms of Relations Between State and Society," in *Stress and Contradiction in Modern Capitalism,* ed. L. Lindberg (Lexington, Mass.: Heath, 1977), pp. 145–59.

70. Many clergymen do see gambling as an acceptable revenue producer, at least for religious institutions. Charitable gambling is allowed in nearly every State, and, if charitable bingo is included, generates several hundred million dollars in revenues

annually. See the Appendix for a more detailed estimate of charitable gambling handle and revenues.

71. This is not to beg the important and difficult questions of public policy that are raised by the movement of regulators and other persons who by virtue of public office are in positions to influence gambling policies or businesses, from government to the gambling industry. Conflict of interest *while the individual still exercises regulatory power* is an ever-present and serious problem. Government's ability to compete with the gambling industry for talented personnel is also questionable in many States; it is clearly in the public interest to have regulators of the highest caliber, but when middle-level gambling industry executives are more highly paid than the highest elected officials, as is very often the case, it may be impossible to attract qualified persons to regulatory agencies or keep them from moving into the industry. These issues are dealt with in more detail in Chapters 5 and 7; the interested reader is referred to Skolnick's *House of Cards* for a perceptive and extensive analysis of the problem.

72. The best account of bookmaking careers is Peter Reuter, *Disorganized Crime: The Economics of the Visible Hand* (Cambridge, Mass.: MIT Press, 1983), pp. 26–29.

73. See for example Ken Uston, *Million Dollar Blackjack* (Hollywood, Calif.: Scientific Research Services, 1981). This is the most recent of three books Uston has written on blackjack. The Treasury Casino in Las Vegas sponsored Ken Uston's blackjack seminars, at which counters were allowed to play under certain time and betting limitations.

2

The Games: A Structural Analysis of Commercial Gambling

Un coup de dés n'abolira jamais le hasard.

—Mallarmé, "Poesies"

I believe in the best moves.

—Bobby Fischer

The words *game, gamble, gambler,* and *gambling* derive from the Old English *gamen* (game) and *gam(e)nian* (to sport or to play or to game). The primary meanings of *gamen* and *gam(e)nian* were amusement, delight, fun, mirth, and sport, suggesting a generally positive cultural valuation of these activities. Not until the early sixteenth century do the words *to game* and *gaming* appear with the sense of playing at games of chance for prizes, stakes, or wagers. So used, these words immediately acquired normative meaning: of the thirteen sixteenth-century examples cited by the *Oxford English Dictionary* of *game, to game, gaming, gaming-table,* or *gamester* in the sense of gambling, seven, including the earliest,[1] concern losses or other evil consequences of gaming for monetary stakes; the other six examples have neutral connotations, and none reflect a positive view of the activity. *To gamble, gambler,* and *gambling* appear later, as eighteenth-century slang words of moral reproach.[2] This etymology is not encouraging; gambling entered the language under a cloud.

Not all games are gambling, but all gambling is fundamentally a game. This is an important distinction: conventional gambling behaviors (but not obsessive or compulsive gambling) are play. This word also comes from Old English: *plega* (play) and *plegan* (to play). According to Huizinga,[3] these words and their Old Saxon *(plegan),* Old Frisian *(plega),* and Old High German *(pflegan)* counterparts share among their primary meanings the elements of challenge, danger, risk, and chance, all within a single field Huizinga termed the *play-sphere,* where some moral or material thing is at stake. Huizinga found an underlying semantic relationship between *play* and *contest,* extending from metaphor in Anglo-Saxon poetry and "trifling games" to "bloody and mortal strife," all "comprised, together with play proper, in the single fundamental idea of a struggle with fate limited by certain rules."[4] The linguistic development of play in English is marked by a division between purposeful activity of a recreative or divertive nature and idleness; in the latter usage, play acquires the sense of "to cease work" as distinct from exercise or busy occupation. Idle play was no less serious than armed battles: in the *OED*'s earliest reference to play in the sense of gambling, a dice player demands of St. Bernard "yf he wolde playe his hors ageynst his sowle."[5]

Life here or hereafter is not generally a stake in contemporary American games, but play remains an essential part of living. For children play is the principal activity. Childhood games are commonly "make-believe" versions of adult occupations; in playing these games children are socialized into the grownup roles that with the passage of years often become realities. In his influential study of the sociology of games, Roger Caillois concluded that the spontaneous improvisation and joy of early successes at play create a need for gratuitous difficulty—for ever-more ingenious games deriving more and more closely from the "real" world and reflecting more and more exactly the moral and intellectual values of the culture. In Caillois's view, playing games is civilizing: through play children learn.[6]

Gradually this learning process is institutionalized as school and made involuntary, and thereby ceases to be play. With adulthood come work, a career, and personal responsibilities that, although voluntarily accepted, transform the play of childhood into the involuntary obligations of "real" life. Society divides time into two spheres: work and leisure. In the sphere of work involuntary activities govern; but in leisure time people are free. This remains the domain of games and play.

Games are the social structures of leisure time. True games cannot be productive of economic ends; in this they are distinguished from work. Athletics, for example, is play for most people, but for professional football players, football is work and not play. Pro football is still recognizably the game played at school, transformed into institutionalized leisure and turned to commercial purposes: it is a livelihood for the players, and a very substantial business for the members of the National Football League. Role and social function, in other words, are defining characteristics of games and play. Like psychologists who study gambling behaviors in clinical surroundings, game theorists and economists seek to explain games and play through computer models that bear little relation to the actual environments where these activities occur. Both disciplines have made important contributions to an understanding of play. But no human behavior is fully intelligible considered apart from its social surroundings. To completely understand games and play, including gambling, these behaviors must be examined in their social contexts.

In its various forms, gambling is one of the most popular adult games. Conventional gambling is part of the domain of leisure and conforms to Huizinga's definition of play:

> Play is superfluous. The need for it is only urgent to the extent that the enjoyment of it makes it a need. Play can be deferred or suspended at any time. It is never imposed by physical [or, we might add, psychological] necessity or moral duty. It is never a task. It is done at leisure, during "free time." . . . Play is distinct from "ordinary" life both as to locality and duration. . . . It is "played out" within certain limits of time and place. It contains its own course and meaning.[7]

Contrary to what Caillois and others have claimed,[8] Huizinga did not exclude wagering at games of chance from his definition of play.[9] The distinguishing element is the purpose of the activity. Gambling for pleasure is play, even though money is at stake. Conversely, the gambling of professionals falls outside Huizinga's definition. Like professional football players, professional poker players, blackjack card-counters, and professional handicappers exercise their skill not for pleasure but to realize financial gains. Uniquely among gambling behaviors, the activities of these specialized gamblers produce long-term financial gains and therefore constitute work. Similarly, obsessive and compulsive gambling fail to meet an important criterion of play. Both are the product of emotional and psychological necessity, and consequently lack the essential qualities of voluntary and spontaneous behavior.

It is one of the central arguments of this book that professional, obsessive, and compulsive gambling are nonconventional behaviors and are very different from conventional gambling in their individual effects and social implications. The exact nature of these differences, and their consequences for both individual gamblers and society as a whole, are explored in Chapter 4. The fact and the importance of these behavioral differences are, however, fundamental to the discussion of gambling games that follows. As sociological concepts, *conventional* and *nonconventional,* regardless of the behavior to which they are applied, are culturally determined qualities, not functions of individual psychological traits. These terms are norms of behavior, not behaviors themselves. Their application to gambling yields significant advances over previous studies. Psychology is able to make only limited and very gross distinctions among the great variety of gambling games and behaviors. Moralists and religious critics make no distinctions at all: in their view all gambling is equally and intrinsically evil.

By placing the moral and psychological understanding of gambling into the wider context of the sociology of games and play and subjecting these phenomena to sociological analysis, some centuries-old misconceptions about activities that are inextricable parts of the culture are cleared away. Nothing has so impeded a rational understanding of gambling as the confusion of normative values with social function. In studying behaviors labeled "deviant" by prevailing cultural norms the question of perspective is all-important. Gambling and the cultural status of gambling are different things. In separating the two it is essential to keep in mind another crucial element of Huizinga's definition of play: "Play lies outside the antithesis of wisdom and folly, and equally outside those of truth and falsehood, good and evil. Although it is a non-material activity it has no moral function. The valuations of virtue and vice do not apply here."[10]

Huizinga's comment points up a basic error of social reformers. They have trouble with play precisely because it is an end in and of itself. Social reformers evaluate all activities, including play and games, as to their external productive effects. Play must uplift, or be profitable, or be somehow useful either to the state or to the community or to the individual. It can't just be pleasurable for pleasure's sake. This is, in effect, a secularization of the Protestant ethic: all social activities have to have a teleological purpose. Gambling can't be valuable in and of itself—because it is exciting or fun or an escape or whatever. It must be useful; it must generate revenues for education, or combat illegal gambling, or redevelop a depressed area. No gambling legalization was ever justified for the purpose of having fun.

American society has forced games and play into a Procrustean bed: the Protestant ethic of utilitarianism, thus perverting their real meaning. In order to make play fit, it has been commercialized: to make play useful, Americans do it for profit. Christopher Lasch, in his critique of American culture, sums up the American perversion of play: "The very uselessness of games makes them offensive to social reformers, improvers of public morals, or functionalist critics of society . . . yet the 'futility of play,' and nothing else, explains its appeal—its artificiality, the arbitrary obstacles it sets up for no other purpose than to challenge the players to surmount them, the absence of any utilitarian or uplifting object. Games quickly lose their charm when forced into the service of education, character development, or social improvement."[11]

The meaning of games—including gambling games—and play is not utilitarian but intrinsic. They are valuable because they are fun. Gamblers intuitively know this. That is what is meant by the "love of action." It is the use of money in gambling that has so confused everyone. Because the medium is money, which is won or lost, people have assumed the medium is the meaning. It is not. Gambling is not meaningful solely because it leaves gamblers richer or poorer; the games—the action, the excitement, the escape—are in and of themselves meaningful. Precisely because money is neutral, and only acquires meaning by virtue of how it is made or spent, Americans reduce the value of all activities to their monetary worth. It is not whether they win or lose, even in gambling games, that should matter to players, but the experience of playing the game. By commercializing gambling, and especially forms of gambling that make unaffordable losses possible and in fact probable if one plays long enough, we have perverted it. The longer one plays the more one ought to enjoy it—not the more one should lose. A. Alvarez recounts the anecdote of the expert poker player who because of his skill consistently wins and then goes out onto the casino floor and loses it all on craps—where his skill is of no avail—just for the action.[12] The point is not that he wants to lose, but that the money involved is irrelevant.

THE STRUCTURAL CHARACTERISTICS OF COMMERCIAL GAMBLING

In Chapter 1, structural functionalism was discussed in the context of commercial gambling. In this and the following chapter we apply structural functionalism to the analysis of gambling games. Each form of commercial gambling will be seen to have unique characteristics, and we will show that these characteristics have profound implications for the formal control of gambling. Moral and religious reformers consider all forms of gambling to be essentially similar and argue that blanket prohibitions would eliminate both pathological gambling behavior and the adverse effects of noncompulsive gambling, including illegal betting and the revenues it generates for organized crime. Unfortunately for the generally well-meaning proponents of simple solutions to these intractable problems, the structures of the major illegal games, bookmaking and numbers, place these activities effectively beyond the reach of legal proscriptions. Bookmaking on NFL football, for example, provided there is substantial public demand for it, cannot be eliminated—or even markedly reduced—through any constitutional combination of statutory prohibition and law enforcement. The failure of legislators (for whatever reasons) to recognize this fact has resulted in wholly unenforceable antibookmaking laws[13] and the misallocation of scarce police and judicial resources. At the same time, government neglects or ignores entirely important aspects of commercial gambling that are amenable to formal control and regulation.

Gambling may be defined in terms of the characteristics that distinguish one game from another and collectively constitute the activities in which gamblers engage. The identification of characteristics common to all gambling activities is, to some extent, subjective. D. B. Cornish,[14] following David Weinstein and Lillian Deitch[15] and the 1951 British Royal Commission on Betting, Lotteries, and Gaming,[16] proposes ten such characteristics: *frequency of opportunities to gamble; payout interval; range of odds; range of stakes; degree of player participation; opportunity for the exercise of skill; probability of winning a particular bet; payout ratio; association of the gambling activity with other attractions;* and *whether the gambling is on a cash or a credit basis.* To these we have added three structural chracteristics that are of special importance in the analysis of American commercial gambling: *price; the intrinsic interest (or play value) of the game or activity;* and *the extent of knowledge needed to enter into the game,* which in some cases constitutes a barrier to participation. Because the meaning of several of these terms differs from common English usage a brief definition of each may be helpful. (Additional definitions appear in the Glossary.)

Frequency of opportunities to gamble is a function of the rate at which gambling events occur and may range from an annual sweepstakes, at one extreme, to the continuous action of slot machine play, at the other. This constitutes the action of gambling and largely determines the handle generated from each gambling game. (The relationship of frequency of gambles to handle, and its importance to gamblers and gambling operations, is discussed in greater detail in the Appendix.)

Payout interval is closely related to the frequency of opportunities to gamble. At most casino games, for example, payouts are immediate. In other forms of gambling, such as bookmaking or lotteries, hours or days may elapse between the gambling event and payouts to winners.

Frequency of opportunities to gamble and payout interval are the principal factors governing the rate of gambling activities. In general, more frequent opportunities to gamble and shorter payout intervals allow gamblers to gamble at faster rates and thereby to develop patterns of repetitive gambling.

The word *odds* means, variously, chance; both the *a priori* and the subjective probabilities of any given outcome of uncertain events, including events used for gambling, such as horse races or the turn of a roulette wheel; and the return (or *odds paid*) on successful gambles in relation to the amount staked. State lottery Lotto games, for example, may have *fixed odds* of winning but *pari-mutuelly calculated odds paid,* meaning that the probability of winning is determined by the operator while the value of a winning Lotto ticket is a function of the number of winning selections in relation to the total amount bet on the Lotto game. It plays like roulette but pays like a horse race. Fixed odds or probabilities of winning are precisely knowable prior to the gambling event, in this case the drawing of winning Lotto numbers. Pari-mutuel odds paid are known only after the gambling event has gone to a decision and the number of winners is determined.[17]

The relationship of odds of winning to odds paid is illustrated by a Lotto game concluded by the New York State Lottery on September 26, 1983. The game required players to select six numbers, with a minimum bet of $1 for two six-number selections (or games), prior to a public drawing of the winning six-number combination. The fixed odds of winning the regular first prize in this game were as follows: "Six winning numbers in one game panel. Odds—1 : 3,838,380. Odds on a $1 bet (two panels)—1 : 1,919,190."[18] The allocation of prize monies, or odds paid, were not, however, related to these odds of winning: "Prize amounts . . . will be paid on a parimutuel basis. Each week 40 percent of that week's sales revenue (less 2% Prize Fund Reserve) is allocated as the winning pool for the payment of the following prizes: First Prize: Regular First Prize—50% of the winning pool plus any first prize money carried forward from previous weeks."[19] Because of the enormously high odds against selecting the winning six-number combination, Lotto game drawings sometimes fail to produce any first prize winners. In this case, in New York and several other lottery States, all or a portion of the first prize pool is carried over to succeeding weeks until someone wins. Lotto games can create very large prizes, the record to date (September 1984) being $40 million won by a printer in an Illinois Lottery Lotto drawing.[20] The New York State Lottery Lotto drawing on September 26, 1983, however, produced no less than forty-six winners, each of whom had selected the winning combination of 2, 6, 15, 20, 26, and 30. The result was a prize of $49,952.80 for each winner—a substantial amount of money, but much less than the $6 million prize advertised prior to the drawing on the assumption fewer people would win.[21]

Stakes are the amounts wagered. The range of stakes varies considerably among the different forms of commercial gambling. Lotteries commonly allow stakes of from $1 (or less) to $5, while in pari-mutuel betting the range of stakes is normally $2 to $100 for a single ticket. Casino games with minimum stakes of $1,000 or more, while not common, are occasionally found.

Together with frequency of opportunities to gamble, odds and stakes govern the rate of change in a gambler's net worth. High-odds, variable-stakes gambling facilitates sudden changes in net worth, while in low-odds, small-stakes gambling changes in net worth are both more gradual and more predictable. Betting modest sums on favorites to show on high-quality (and therefore of consistent form) horse racing, for example, will usually result in relatively slow and modest fluctuations in the bettor's net worth, and is an often-recommended strategy for novices who do not want to expose themselves to large losses. At casino table games, on the other hand, where both odds and stakes are variable over a considerable range and action is continuous, great changes in net worth may occur in very short periods of play. As one racetrack owner of our acquaintance remarked upon the conclusion of his first, brief, and disastrous experience with casino gaming, "Things happen fast out there."

The *price* of gambling is the percentage of the gross amount wagered (or *handle*) retained by the operator of a commercial gambling business. This price (which is called *retention* in pari-mutuel accounting and *win* in casino gaming accounting) is equivalent to the losses incurred by gamblers collectively over the long term.[22] The price of commercial gambling is highly variable, ranging from less than 2 percent for some bets at casino table games to more than 50 percent in most State lotteries. Over the long term and provided he or she exercises adequate skill (where relevant), the price an individual pays for gambling will approximate the price of that form of gambling for all gamblers collectively. The outcome of a short series of gambles may, however, bear little relationship to the real price of gambling. For a gambler who makes one bet, loses, and stops, the price of gambling is 100 percent. Conversely, a gambler who makes one bet, wins, and quits, pays no price for gambling and instead realizes an absolute financial gain. Notwithstanding these short-term fluctuations, the price of gambling is, for gamblers collectively over the long term, calculable for all commercial gambling activities.[23]

Odds and price are frequently confused by gamblers and even by the operators of commercial gambling businesses. Odds and price are related in that commercial gambling at fixed odds, such as casino gaming, must ensure a sufficient return to the operator to cover expenses, tax liabilities, and profit. Odds paid and price may, however, be only indirectly related, as in pari-mutuel betting.

Player participation and *the exercise of skill* are related but distinct characteristics of gambling activities. Pulling the handle of a slot machine is participation but does not involve skill; counting cards at blackjack combines both characteristics into a single activity. Player participation and the exercise of skill correlate positively with increasing levels of involvement in gambling.

The probability of winning a particular bet and *payout ratio* are normally inversely related variables that together provide a continuum of risk/reward values that are crucial elements of individual choice among the various forms of gambling. Gambling activities that offer only a segment of this continuum—for example, monthly lotteries, where the single gamble offered is of very low probability of winning and very high reward, or ratio of payout to investment—interest a relatively small number of gamblers. Conversely, gambling activities that cover the entire continuum, such as casino gaming, meet a broader range of individual interests and consequently enjoy much wider popular appeal.

The pre-eminent example of the *association of gambling with other activities* is bookmaking on professional football, which, though illegal on a commercial basis outside of Nevada, is (with gaming) one of the two largest gambling games in America. Pari-mutuel sports, especially horse racing, are similar examples of the association of gambling with other attractions. Nevada casinos, particularly those situated along the "Strip," are located within resort complexes that offer a variety of nongambling entertainment and recreation (including golf, tennis, swimming, and other participant sports), dining facilities of every description, and "name" performing talent, in carefully designed fantasy surroundings that of themselves constitute a considerable attraction and fully deserve the sobriquet "adult Disneyland." These attractions—horse racing, football, resort environments, and so forth—can all be pursued for their own sake, apart and distinct from gambling. The intrinsic value of these attractions adds a nongambling dimension to the significance of commercial gambling within the larger context of American leisure. Gambling, in other words, is not just a series of risky financial transactions. It is directly and intimately related to the most popular American spectator sports and to the vacation/resort industry as well.

Credit is generally assumed to increase the risk of unaffordable losses. The merits of this assumption are evaluated below, in the context of casino gaming.

Intrinsic play value and *the extent of knowledge required for a particular gambling activity* are related characteristics that, like player participation and the exercise of skill, correlate positively with increasing levels of involvement in gambling. Both vary over wide ranges among commercial games. Passive forms of gambling, of which lottery drawings are the best example, have little or no intrinsic play value. Active forms of gambling, which include pari-mutuel betting as well as virtually all casino games, are generally intrinsically interesting to play. This interest may be physical (pulling slot-machine handles, throwing dice, manipulating video gaming devices), emotional (watching slot reels revolve to their stop or horses run to the finish line), or intellectual (handicapping races, counting cards at blackjack). In all cases the intrinsic interest is a reinforcement to gambling activities that is distinct from the risk of loss and the possibility of gain. The special knowledge required for particular forms of gambling is a close functional analogy. Pari-mutuel racing is the best example: there is a high minimum level of knowledge needed to bet horses, and a very great deal more knowledge that horseplayers may acquire if they choose. To the uninitiated this entry-level knowledge requirement is a barrier to participation, but to bettors who have made the necessary investment of time and mental application the possession of this special knowledge is reinforcing: knowing how to read the *Racing Form* is useful only at racetracks and OTB offices.

THE CONTEXT OF GAMBLING

As games, or formal structures, the various forms of commercial gambling may be analyzed in terms of four contextual variables: (1) place; (2) situation (or environment); (3) ownership and operation (whether private for profit or nonprofit purposes or government); and (4) purpose.

Place

The geographic location of commercial gambling operations is an obviously important but often-overlooked variable. Racetracks and off-track betting offices, for example, may offer identical opportunities to gamble and yet, because of their different geographic locations, interact in very dissimilar ways with society at both the micro- and macro-levels. The geography of sales outlets profoundly influences both the extent and the demographics of public participation in a given form of gambling. Prior to the 1970s both gaming and pari-mutuel horse racing were geographically restricted, gaming to the isolated State of Nevada and (legal) horse-race betting to racetrack grounds. Regular participation in either form of gambling was effectively restricted to persons with substantial amounts of leisure time and disposable income, a day at the races or a trip to Las Vegas being both time-consuming and expensive.

The extension of gaming to Atlantic City and the legalization of off-track betting by New York and Connecticut since 1970 has lowered or removed entirely the geographic barriers to participation in these games for tens of millions of Americans. Wider geographic availability has in turn lowered both the time and money costs of gaming and pari-mutuel racing, with the result that both forms of gambling are now accessible to virtually every resident of these and neighboring States. This geographic change is reflected in the demographics of off-track betting and East Coast gaming: both industries are successfully marketing gambling opportunities to segments of the population that were effectively beyond the reach of racetracks and Las Vegas casinos.

Not all forms of commercial gambling are constrained by geography. Illegal bookmaking, which takes advantage of the geographic and legal restrictions on team sports and horse-race betting, is for the most part conducted over telephones that may be located anywhere, and are in any case frequently changed to avoid disruption of service by police. Bookmaking is in fact the first major form of commercial gambling to be transformed by the twentieth-century revolution in communications technology. The face-to-face transactions between bookmaker and bettor that were so prominent a feature of the nineteenth-century American gambling scene have, outside Nevada, almost wholly disappeared. Many regular sports bettors never see the person who books their bets, their personal contact with the betting operation being limited to periodic settlements with the book's collection agents, or "runners."[24]

The stimulus to the technological transformation of bookmaking was police enforcement of antibookmaking laws: telephones, once they had become ubiquitous, were the safest way to conduct this business. Paradoxically, the legalizations that in the 1960s began to selectively erode the American gambling prohibition have set in motion economic changes that are driving the pari-mutuel industries in a similar direction. Today the modern communications technology of closed-circuit television is being married to various forms of legal off-track betting to make live horse racing and betting available either in betting shop or teletheater environments ("simulcasting") or subscribers' homes. The vendors of on-line lottery terminals and video versions of casino games are actively exploring analogous applications of communications technology to their devices. Lawmakers permitting, the wider dispersal of both lottery and gaming activities through electronic means is a probable future development in American commercial gambling.[25]

SITUATION

The situational, or environmental, aspect of commercial gambling is a second important contextual variable. Nevada and Atlantic City casinos are designed as timeless, hermetic environments of near-monastic abstraction and isolation from the real world. Reality is excluded—there are no clocks and generally no windows in casinos—and replaced by a concrete, tangible fantasy where every stimulus conduces to gambling. In contrast, State lottery tickets are purchased (and in the case of "instant" lottery games are often played) in the most prosaic neighborhood environments: newsstands, bars, small grocery stores, and so forth. Unlike casinos, State lotteries are perfectly integrated into the real world.

Ownership and Operation

The ownership and operation of American commercial gambling covers the spectrum from state capitalism to private enterprise. Curiously enough, in terms of micro-level social interactions this contextual variable is relatively unimportant: commercial gambling operators, whether civil servants or private businessmen, tend to interact with their clientele in similar ways. At the macro-level of interaction, however, the ownership and operation of commercial gambling have profound implications. As will be discussed in detail, there is an enormous cultural difference between a privately operated casino and a State-operated lottery. Betting against the house is consistent with prevailing cultural norms; betting against the state is not. Public ownership and operation of commercial gambling is a relatively recent development, dating only from the 1960s. Its implications are not yet fully understood, partly because this development has been regarded from psychological and legal perspectives that do not encompass social and cultural change. From the perspective of sociology, however, the ownership and operation of commercial gambling raises new and important questions concerning the meaning of gambling in American society.

Purpose

In American jurisdictions legal commercial gambling has, almost invariably, a statutory purpose or purposes. There is no free entry to American gambling markets; the suppliers of legal commercial gambling opportunities are highly regulated franchisees who, in return for permission to operate a gambling business, are required to raise government revenue, contribute to economic development or redevelopment, compete with illegal gambling, and so forth. To the extent that these statutory purposes govern commercial gambling operations they are important determinants of both micro- and macro-level interactions between commercial gambling and society.

There is a second reason for examining the statutory purposes of legalizations. This statutory language is the public justification, or rationale, of lawmakers for legalizing activities that in normative terms are still vice. This rationale must be sufficiently persuasive, with both the public and the news media, to absolve the makers of laws that enable gambling of the normal penalty for violating a cultural norm: that is, failure at the next election. Legislators voting to legalize other popular vices constituting "victimless crimes," such as the recreational use of marijuana, would not survive their next election, and consequently these vices remain crimes despite the fact that smoking marijuana is a widespread behavior.[26] In some sense, then, the statutory purposes of legalizations reflect society's purposes in allowing an activity, gambling, that by prevailing norms is wrong. And if this is true, the actual consequences of legal gambling can be compared with the statutory purposes of enabling legislation to provide a measure of how well a given form of commercial gambling is fulfilling its social function. Further, these purposes can themselves be tested, both for internal logical consistency and against social realities, as a means of evaluating how effective our gambling policies are. We will return to these questions in Chapter 7.

THE STRUCTURAL ANALYSIS OF GAMES AND GAMBLING POLICY

At the micro-level of sociological analysis the gambles (that is, the particular risky choices offered by commercial games), structural characteristics, and contextual variables of each commercial game are significant determinants of gambling behaviors. At the macro-level these structural features largely determine the relative appeal of the various games or the substitutability of one gambling opportunity for another. The substitution quotient of gambling games is a measure of their ability to compete for the same market. In addition to their obvious significance for the managers of lotteries, racetracks, and casinos, substitution quotients have important implications for efforts to eliminate illegal gambling by providing competitive legal alternatives. Finally, structural characteristics govern the extent and intensity of public participation in commercial gambling. Each game stimulates a characteristic mix of gambling behaviors, a fact that should be a fundamental consideration in formulating gambling policy.

The major contemporary American commercial gambling games are: State-operated lotteries, including State-operated numbers games; illegal numbers games; legal privately owned and operated casinos; the largely private pari-mutuel horse- and greyhound-racing industries;

government-operated pari-mutuel off-track betting; privately owned and operated pari-mutuel *jai-alai;* legal bookmaking (in Nevada); illegal bookmaking; bingo; and poker and related card games. The aggregate amount gambled on these games constitutes the annual gross wager of the United States, which was approximately $163 billion in 1983. Gross revenues to operators from this wagering, or expenditures (losses) of gamblers, were approximately $16.8 billion.[27]

All of these games are commercially important, in that each is played by millions of Americans and generates very substantial operator revenues. Bingo is a big business that in 1983 was legal in forty-five States and the District of Columbia[28] for charitable and limited commercial purposes.[29] A 1981 Supreme Court decision upholding an appellate court ruling in a Florida case that effectively barred State and local law enforcement agencies from regulating bingo games on the Seminole Indian reservation has resulted in an explosive growth in bingo operations on reservations throughout the United States, despite the opposition of the Justice Department and State officials who argue that Indian bingo games compete unfairly with church and charity gambling.[30] Although reliable current estimates of the amounts wagered on bingo nationally are not available, the Survey Research Center estimated the 1974 bingo handle (gross wagering) at $1.7 billion and operator revenues (player losses) at $551 million;[31] today both statistics are certainly larger. We estimate that approximately $3 billion was wagered legally on bingo in 1982.[32] In addition to bingo, many States allow charitable (''Las Vegas night'') gaming. Unfortunately, reliable estimates of the volume of charitable gaming apart from bingo are lacking. In New York (which has both a State lottery and on- and off-track pari-mutuel betting) 1,378 charitable, religious or nonprofit organizations won $4,641,241 from ''Las Vegas night'' games in 1982.[33] North Dakota, a sparsely populated State, provides a contrast. Prior to 1981, the only legal gambling was noncommercial bingo, raffles, and lottery-like games. The legalization (in July 1981) of charitable and nonprofit $2 blackjack resulted in gross winnings (that is, player losses) of $3.5 million in the first three months.[34] Commercial card rooms, usually for poker, are legal in eight States. The most significant operations are located in California, where more than 325 card rooms in eighty cities provide some 2,200 legal poker seats that are rented by players (who gamble among themselves, the house having no stake in the games) for $2 to $20 per hour, depending on the size of the game.[35]

The highly decentralized organization of bingo, card rooms, and charitable gaming and the absence of reliable financial reporting on these activities place a meaningful structural analysis of these games beyond the scope of this book.[36] Illegal bookmaking, which is second only to casino gaming in terms of gross wagering, presents similar problems in the collection and evaluation of data: illegal operators obviously do not publish annual reports or file 10K forms with the Securities and Exchange Commission.[37] Three major forms of legal gambling—casinos, pari-mutuel betting, and State lotteries—account for the overwhelming portion of the remaining gross wager of the United States. In the next chapter we examine these dominant forms in terms of their structural and contextual differences.

NOTES

1. "An olde man can play, and keepe his gratuitie, Of death the remembrance his gamning ought to be." Alexander Barclay (1475?–1552), *The Mirror of Good Manners* (1510). *The Compact Edition of the Oxford English Dictionary* (Oxford: University Press, 1971), vbl. sb., "gaming," pp. 1, 111. The *OED* does cite an earlier (1340) reference to "gemenes of des," ibid., s.v., "game," pp. 1, 111.

2. Apparently these words are dialectical survivals of *gam(e)nian;* the verb itself is not found until 1775–1786. Ibid.

3. Huizinga, *Homo Ludens,* pp. 37–42.

4. Ibid., pp. 40–41.

5. Caxton, tr., *Cato,* Bk. iv b (1483); *OED,* s.v., "play," pp. 2, 204.

6. Caillois, *Man, Play, and Games.*

7. Huizinga, *Homo Ludens,* pp. 8–9.

8. Caillois, *Man, Play, and Games,* p. 5.

9. Huizinga, *Homo Ludens,* pp. 52–53: *Playing* or *gambling* at roulette is distinguished, if narrowly, from the "business" of stock exchange "machinations," and the origins of the business of life insurance are traced to wagering "on future eventualities of a non-economic nature."

10. Ibid., p. 6.

11. Lasch, *The Culture of Narcissism,* p. 182.

12. A. Alvarez, "A Reporter at Large: Poker World Series," *New Yorker,* March 7, 14, 1983.

13. The issues of gambling legalizations and criminalizations are related through the substitutability of gambling games. Legal State lottery numbers, for example, are an imperfect substitute for illegal numbers in that payouts are usually lower and runners are not employed as sales agents. At the same time, legalization of numbers both increases the market for this form of gambling and makes enforcement of antinumbers game laws an exceedingly difficult proposition. There is a considerable literature on the enforceability of antigambling laws. See Virgil W. Peterson, "Obstacles to Enforcement of Gambling Laws," *Annals of the American Academy of Political and Social Science* 269 (May 1950):9–20; Peter Reuter, "Enforceability of Gambling Laws," in *Gambling in America,* Appendix 1, pp. 551–64; and Thomas W. Mangione and Floyd J. Fowler, Jr., "Enforcing the Gambling Laws," *Journal of Social Issues* 35 (1979):115–28. Peterson and Reuter conclude that antigambling laws are poorly enforced and massively violated in

most of the United States. Mangione and Fowler decide that laws against commercial gambling, particularly numbers and street-level bookmaking, are enforceable, given adequate community support, the use of police with gambling expertise, effective prosecution, meaningful statutory penalties, and the willingness of courts to impose these penalties. The findings of the Knapp commission, which investigated antigambling law enforcement-related police corruption in New York in the early 1970s, suggest that the conditions recommended by Mangione and Fowler are unlikely to obtain in the real world. Enforcement efforts did not reduce illegal commercial gambling but did result in systematic corruption of the New York Police Department. Following the Knapp investigation the discretion of uniformed patrolmen as regards illegal gambling was severely limited and infractions of antigambling laws were routinely referred to specialized vice units, the number of men assigned to antigambling enforcement was reduced, the number of arrests under antigambling laws dramatically declined, and the enforcement of antigambling laws generally became a low-priority activity. Knapp Commission, *Report of Commission to Investigate Allegations of Police Corruption and the City's Anti-Corruption Procedures* (New York: George Braziller, 1973), and Alan Kornblum, *The Moral Hazards* (Lexington, Mass.: D. C. Heath, 1976).

14. D. B. Cornish, *Gambling: A Review of the Literature and Its Implications for Policy and Research,* Home Office Research Study no. 42 (London: Home Office Research Unit, 1978), pp. 138–41, 166–72.

15. David Weinstein and Lillian Deitch, *The Impact of Legalized Gambling: The Socioeconomic Consequences of Lotteries and Off-Track Betting* (New York: Praeger, 1974), pp. 150–53.

16. Royal Commission on Betting, Lotteries, and Gaming 1949–1951, Henry Urmston Willink, chairman, *Report* (1951; reprint, London: Her Majesty's Stationery Office, 1956), pp. 58–60.

17. Racetracks and *jai-alai* frontons provide *tote boards* that display approximate pari-mutuel odds paid for simple pools, including *win, place, and show* pools. Pools involving more than three betting interests, such as triples (the selection of the first three betting interests in order of finish), exceed the display capacities of tote boards, requiring investors in triple pools to "bet blind"—to invest with no certain knowledge of the value of winning selections.

18. New York State Lottery, "Rules and Regulations," Rev. 2/10/83.

19. Ibid.

20. E. R. Shipp, "$40 Million Lottery Award is Won by Chicago Printer," *New York Times,* September 4, 1984.

21. Robert Carroll, "Lotto Winners Take It & Lump It," *New York Daily News,* September 27, 1983.

22. The *price of gambling,* which is the *expected value* (EV) of a game to its operator, must be distinguished from the expected value of a particular gamble. The expected value from choosing some alternative is a concept of economics that may be applied to gambling decisions, and other risky decisions, with a degree of mathematical precision that may in (subjective) reality be spurious. See Peter H. Aranson and Roger LeRoy Miller, "Economic Aspects of Public Gaming," *Connecticut Law Review* 12 (Summer 1980):822–53. Goffman, "Where the Action Is," pp. 149ff., employs the related concept of *expected utility* to arrive at a measure of the economic meaning of betting.

23. Gambling may obviously entail other expenses, such as racetrack admissions, travel costs, and so forth, that are not functions of the gambling activities themselves. While these nongambling but gambling-related expenses are significant considerations, only the *cost of gambling itself* is meant by *price* as used here.

24. For an authoritative description of illegal bookmaking operations see Peter Reuter and Jonathan Rubinstein, *Illegal Gambling in New York: A Case Study in the Operation, Structure, and Regulation of an Illegal Market* (Washington, D.C.: GPO, 1982), pp. 49-59.

25. Andrew Pollack, ''Electronics Invades Gambling,'' *New York Times*, January 21, 1984.

26. For a comparison of gambling and marijuana use as vices and as examples of criminalization see John Dennis Dombrink, ''Outlaw Businessmen,'' pp. 14–16, 255–56.

27. Summary data for each of these forms of gambling, including the jurisdictions where each is allowed (1983), the gross amount wagered (handle), and gross revenues (gamblers' losses), are given in the Appendix.

28. *Gaming Business Magazine*, July 1983, p. 16.

29. Most jurisdictions restrict bingo licenses to charitable, religious, or nonprofit organizations. In New York, for example, 3,195 such organizations were licensed to conduct some 144,000 bingo programs in 1982. A total of $225,461,239 was gambled on these bingo cards, producing $62,352,249 in operator profits (player losses). New York State Racing and Wagering Board, *Annual Report* (1982), p. 9. A few States allow noncharitable organizations, such as county governments, labor unions, veterans, and political groups, to conduct bingo. *Gambling in America*, pp. 161–62.

30. *New York Times*, ''Bingo Boom Brings Tribes Profit and Conflict,'' March 29, 1983. Indian bingo has attracted some prospective operators of dubious reputation; see *Wall Street Journal*, ''Indian Bingo Inc. Has Big List of Reasons Stock Is Risky, as It Plans Initial Offering,'' July 1, 1983.

31. Kallick, ''Survey of American Gambling,'' in *Gambling in America*, Appendix 2, pp. 94-96, 105.

32. Derived from reported legal bingo wagering in several States, extrapolated, as per capita wagering, to the remaining States that allowed bingo in 1982. See the Appendix. The most extensive recently published bingo (and charitable gambling generally) handle estimate is contained in ''Bingo and Break Opens [pull tabs] Becoming Big Business,'' *Public Gaming Magazine*, November 1983, pp. 39–48. This analysis is likewise derived from reported State bingo wagering totals, and puts the 1982 legal bingo handle at $3.8 billion.

33. New York State Racing and Wagering Board, *Annual Report* (1982), p. 9.

34. *Wall Street Journal*, ''In North Dakota, a Blackjack Game is an Act of Charity,'' January 14, 1982.

35. *Gaming Business Magazine*, July 1983, p. 16; January 1981, p. 38; March 1983, pp. 7-10.

36. A study of charitable and nonprofit bingo and gaming is a special desideratum in that these activities put gambling that is commercial in all but name into the hands of those—churches, charities, and so forth—least able to control it.

37. The prinicipal source of information regarding illegal bookmaking is arrest records and reports of criminal investigations filed by police or other law enforcement agencies. See Peter Reuter, *Disorganized Crime*, p. 233. This is a landmark contribution to this subject that should be consulted by anyone with an interest in illegal gambling. See as well Peter Reuter and Jonathan Rubinstein, *Illegal Gambling in New York;* Reuter and Rubinstein, ''Fact, Fancy and Organized Crime,'' pp. 45–67; Mark Haller, ''Bootleggers and American Gambling 1920–1950,'' in *Gambling in America*, Appendix 1, pp. 102–43; and David Johnson, ''A Sinful Business: Origins of Gambling Syndicates in the United States, 1840–1887,'' in *Police and Society*, ed. David Bayley (Beverly Hills, Calif.: Sage Press, 1977).

3

The Major Forms of Commercial Gambling: State Lotteries, Casinos, and Pari-mutuel Betting

> Strangers at the same table find that a slight camaraderie is generated by a joint and mutually visible exposure to fate.
>
> —Erving Goffman, "Where the Action Is"

A snapshot of contemporary commercial gambling would discover a varied and somewhat deceptive landscape. The most prominent features, conspicuous in their gaudy isolation from workaday America, are two hundred-odd casinos concentrated in resort towns at either end of the continent, appearing by night as handfuls of variegated neon flung down upon the Nevada desert and along the Jersey shore. Scattered across the country (except in the most firmly Protestant States of the old Confederacy) are some 230 pari-mutuel horse and greyhound racetracks that preserve a sport of preindustrial times in surroundings ranging from park-like grounds to modern, antiseptic betting plants. On the outskirts of New Haven, Connecticut, a 2,200-seat, 24′ × 32′-screen teletheater many horsemen fear as a harbinger of the future offers the world's first horse racing without live horses,[1] while in Florida and New England frontons for the old Basque game of *jai-alai* compete with native recreations for leisure dollars. These games register clearly in the photograph, their buildings and real estate a concrete presence in hundreds of communities. Other forms of commercial gambling are less distinct. New York and Connecticut provide their citizens with neighborhood off-track betting services through offices that blend into the retail shops of main streets and shopping centers. OTB and a growing number of racetracks also accept telephone bets, which, like the transactions of brokers and bookies, are of a private nature and do not appear in the snapshot at all. And at the opposite extreme from the separation of gambling and society represented by the hotel/casinos of Las Vegas are more than 100,000 nearly invisible State lottery sales outlets: the newsstands, delicatessens, supermarkets, bodegas, drugstores, restaurants, and bars through which this form of commercial gambling has been perfectly integrated into ordinary, everyday American life.

It is a remarkable view. Sixty-six million Americans—40 percent of the adult population—gambled at legal commercial games in 1982.[2] Their aggregate wagering against casinos and in State lotteries or among themselves at racetracks and frontons exceeded $125 billion.[3] Their aggregate losses at these games were $10.5 billion.[4] Very loosely, all of this activity is gambling, and to many people there is no difference between a dollar won at blackjack or lost on an ill-chosen horse. To say all bets are equally immoral is a defensible position, for a moralist, but the social implications of different kinds of betting vary over an enormous range, and hence the social valuation of commercial gambling is a rather more complex question. In order to understand the meaning of this snapshot it is necessary to begin to make distinctions among the various commercial games. Craps and million-dollar Lotto drawings are both games of chance, but they create different degrees of risk and wildly dissimilar kinds of "action." Racetracks and OTB offices may offer identical wagers, but they are not identical in their relationship to society.

The conviction that the world can be made a better place by regulating behavior runs deep in America—deeply and strongly enough to have produced the Volstead Act.[5] Conscious or not, this conviction continues to animate most of the individuals and organizations—academics, editorial boards, psychiatrists, politicians, and bureaucrats—who would guard the public interest where gambling is concerned. No one else, and certainly not gambling interests, is likely to assume this burden. It is thus a doubly unfortunate paradox that the reformer's perspective is a coarse one. Whatever their moral and ethical similarities, the major forms of commercial gambling are not alike in their practical consequences for mainstream America. Each of these games—lotteries, casinos, and pari-mutuel betting—is more or less profitable, more or less expensive, more or less fun, and more or less dangerous, depending on one's point of view, to individuals and society. Fortunately we do not have to guess about these qualities. It is possible to say, with a great deal of precision, that the cost of lottery tickets is higher than a $2 bet on a horse. The rates at which racetracks and casinos extract money from the general public are not the same, and are, at least in relative terms, both knowable and predictable. The answers to these questions, and to many other difficult issues the expansion of legal gambling has raised, may be found by analyzing the major commercial games through the structural characteristics and contextual variables discussed in the preceding chapter and comparing the results. We begin with State lotteries.

STATE LOTTERIES

A lottery may be defined as a game in which chances to share in a distribution of prizes are determined by lot, or drawing. For a lottery to constitute gambling three elements must be present: *chance, consideration,* and *prize.* If, for example, the tickets in a drawing are free a lottery is not gambling, even if prizes of substantial value are awarded. Generally, for lotteries to come under gambling laws lots or chances must be purchased or otherwise received in return for a consideration. Supermarket drawings, in which prizes are distributed to customers by drawing coupons given away as promotions, are not usually considered to constitute gambling for this reason. The element of chance in lotteries is less easily defined. Three specific rules are relevant in American gambling law:

(1) Under the ‘‘English’’ or ‘‘pure chance’’ rule the determination of winners is by pure chance; if any element of skill contributes to the determination of winners there is no lottery.

(2) Under the ‘‘dominant factor’’ rule skill may contribute to the determination of winners but chance is, in a quantitative or causative sense, the dominant factor. Thus, even if the determination of winners should involve numerous acts of skill (as the selection of a series of winning football teams or the winning horses in a series of horse races by systematically applying criteria to sports or race information) there is still a lottery if the quantitatively dominant factor in determining winners is chance.

(3) The ‘‘integral factor’’ rule essentially weakens the ‘‘dominant factor’’ rule so that regardless of the relative proportions of chance and skill there is a lottery if chance is an integral part of the determination of winners. In the example cited above, a lottery based on the outcome of a series of horse races would be a lottery as long as chance is in a qualitative sense integral, and therefore dominant over skill, in determining winners.

State lotteries generally conform to the ‘‘pure chance’’ rule: that is, player skill is not a factor in the determination of winners. Player participation, which is sometimes confused with skill by players themselves, is a characteristic of illegal and State lottery numbers games in that players may select any three-digit (or, in some games, two-digit or four-digit) number to bet on, but this choice has no statistical effect on the chance of wining.[6]

STRUCTURAL CHARACTERISTICS OF STATE LOTTERIES

Unlike casinos and horse racing State lotteries are a recent development in American commercial gambling. Whereas the older casino and pari-mutuel betting activities have remained essentially unchanged for generations, State lotteries are dynamic and still evolving. The "snapshot" description of structural characteristics appropriate to gaming and pari-mutuel betting would be misleading if applied to lottery games, which are not yet frozen in time. We will therefore analyze the structure of lottery gambling in the context of the history of State lotteries.

In 1963 the New Hampshire legislature, which was constitutionally prohibited from levying a progressive income tax and consequently relied heavily on alternative revenue sources, including "sin taxes" on the purchase of alcohol and tobacco, authorized a State-operated sweepstakes based on the outcome of horse races for the benefit of public education. Following a successful referendum in the 1966 general election the New York legislature instituted a monthly lottery, also in aid of education. To date (1984) twenty-one States[7] and the District of Columbia have followed suit.

Initially State lotteries were extremely "benign" forms of gambling. In New Hampshire the first lottery consisted of two biannual sweepstakes, with tickets priced at $3. The New York lottery was originally limited to not more than twelve drawings a year; tickets were priced from $1 to $2, had to contain the name and address of the purchaser, and could be sold only by banks, telegraph companies, hotels, and municipalities.[8]

An analysis of the structural characteristics of these two lotteries reveals them to have been almost perfectly calculated to limit the public's participation. The long intervals between opportunities to play dictated very slow rates of gambling, with the likelihood that many persons would lose interest in the games altogether once their novelty had worn off. The very high odds and very low probability of winning a prize[9] produced few winners and a very unequal distribution of winnings, again contributing to declining player interest. Neither lottery offered opportunities for player participation or the exercise of skill, and while the games were very easy to learn they had little or no intrinsic play value. Both lotteries quickly proved unpopular. The first annual New Hampshire Sweepstakes (held in 1964) sold only $5.7 million worth of tickets, far short of the $10 million that had been predicted. Sales declined each year thereafter, falling to $2.5 million with the start of the New York Lottery in 1967, and revenues fell far short of expectations. The New York Lottery produced similarly disappointing results, with sales in the monthly drawings declining steadily and total sales, including a series of special drawings, of only $70 million in 1971. Annual per capita sales in 1970 were about the same for both lotteries: $2.67 for New Hampshire and $2.60 for New York.[10] As a source of government funds State lotteries appeared to be stillborn.

The States' lottery initiative might have ended at this point had not one of what we have defined as the contextual variables of commercial gambling forced alterations in the games that stimulated sales—that is, more gambling. This variable was the lotteries' purpose. The New Hampshire and New York lotteries were revenue measures.[11] As such, they are the purest example of what Jerome Skolnick has called the "economic imperative" in the evolution of commercial gambling—the tendency for the revenue and economic purposes of gambling legalizations to dominate all other considerations.[12] In obedience to the revenue imperative there began a still-continuing series of State-initiated changes in the structural characteristics of lottery games that have made these lotteries competitive in nearly all segments of the market, and currently perhaps the most aggressive form of commercial gambling in America.

The first step in this transformation was taken by New Jersey. On December 16, 1970, the New Jersey State Lottery placed on sale 50¢ tickets in a weekly lottery based on a six-digit number,[13] at one stroke lowering the lottery stake and increasing the frequency of gambles. Success was immediate. Sales totaled $73 million in the first half-year and $124 million in the following twelve months, for an average annual per capita sale of $17.[14] New York responded by lowering its ticket price to 50¢ and eliminating the requirement that the purchaser's name and address appear, and by allowing any convenient retail business to become a lottery outlet.[15]

Weekly drawings quickly became a standard feature of State lottery menus. The New Jersey Lottery continued to modify the structural characteristics of its games to increase the range and intensity of public participation. Payout ratio was the next parameter to change. On March 17, 1971, Edward Henry, of Morristown, New Jersey, became the first person to win $1 million in a State lottery.[16] This award initiated an evolution of lottery prize structures culminating in multi-million dollar Lotto games that in the 1980s have stimulated unprecedented ticket sales and made State lotteries tremendously appealing to persons willing to gamble against astronomical odds in the hope of winning a fortune.

In November 1972 the New Jersey Lottery further increased the frequency of lottery gambles by introducing the first daily drawing.[17] The next step in the transformation of State lotteries from long-interval games into high-frequency, repetitive stimulus-response gambling was taken by the Massachusetts State Lottery, which on May 28, 1974, sold the first instant game lottery tickets. Like daily drawings and million-dollar prizes, instant games were quickly adopted by other State lotteries.

Instant games also added an element of player participation to lottery gambling. These games (''paper slot machines'') are played by scratching a chemically treated window on the ticket to reveal a number or symbol indicating whether the player has won or lost. The purchaser was no longer a passive consumer: like the slot-machine player, who pulls the handle of one-armed bandits for the suspense of watching the reels revolve, instant-game players interact physically with lotteries through the medium of tickets that ingeniously combine color and suspense with the challenges of game-playing and puzzle-solving on small cardboard squares.

These tickets are a neglected[18] but extremely important characteristic of State lottery gambling. Unlike pari-mutuel tickets, which are simple receipts and quite incidental to horse racing or *jai-alai,* lottery tickets are the medium through which lottery games are played. These games are commonly associated with other activities through the use of themes, which are the basis for ticket graphics and for much of the lotteries' print and electronic advertising, as well as the televised drawings that are regularly scheduled in many lottery States. The appeals of most of the State lottery game themes in general use over the last few years are, with one exception, to normative cultural values; the marketing of lottery tickets often resembles the United States Treasury's promotions of Series E Savings Bonds more closely than racetrack or casino advertising. The most popular game themes include the following:

Sports: Sports of all kinds are used for lottery game themes. An example is ''Touchdown,'' a football theme game started by the New Jersey Lottery in December 1976 that ended with a ''Super Bowl '77 Drawing'' for a top prize of $1 million. Baseball—the ''national pastime''—and horse racing are also frequent game theme choices. The association of these sports with illegal (football and baseball) and legal (horse racing) gambling is sometimes but not usually overtly acknowledged.

Wealth and winning: The excitement of winning and the chance of winning great wealth are traditional lottery themes. Both are frequently used by State lotteries. For example, in 1978 the Massachusetts State Lottery's games included, in addition to the instant ''Baseball Game'' and "Football Game," a weekly "Big Money" game with a $1 million prize drawn on a weekly "Big Money" television show. The enormous Lotto game prizes of the last two years have given new importance to the theme of winning great wealth in many State lotteries.

Luck: Luck is another traditional lottery theme. The New Jersey State Lottery, for example, incorporates a four leaf clover in its logo and used "Lucky Horoscope," which employed the twelve signs of the zodiac, as the theme of an instant game started in 1978. Luck is the basic theme choice for State lottery numbers games, which generally ask players to play "your hunch" or "your lucky number" as an impulse gamble. The New York State Lottery's 1983 numbers advertising is representative.

Patriotism: Appeals to patriotism are frequent. The bicentennial of the United States was used for numerous game themes. For example, the New Jersey State Lottery held a "1776" instant game, with a prize of $1,776 a week for the life of the winner. The Illinois State Lottery had an instant "President's Game" as a "bicentennial tribute to our nation's presidents."[19] A variation is the association of lottery games with particular State symbols or identities, of which the Vermont Lottery's 1978 weekly "Green Mountain Game," which exhorted players to "Take a Chance on Vermont," and the Pennsylvania State Lottery's use of the "Keystone State" seal on its tickets—like a State "good house-keeping seal of approval"—are examples.[20] Seasonal themes are also used: in 1983 the Pennsylvania State Lottery included Santa in its Christmas season advertising, associating the lottery with the holiday spirit in one of the oldest American political ploys: the state as Santa Claus.

Casinos and Other Forms of Gambling: Dice, roulette wheels, slot machines, poker and other card games, and so forth are used as themes by many lotteries. Examples are "Jersey Casino," an instant game introduced by the New Jersey State Lottery in 1978, and "Wild Deuces," a 1978 instant game of the Michigan State Lottery. The use of casino games as themes is the major exception to the State lotteries' appeals to normative values in their promotion of lottery gambling.

The degree of player participation in State lotteries was further increased when the New Jersey State Lottery introduced the nation's first legal numbers game, "Pick-it," on May 22, 1975.[21] "Pick-it" allowed players to choose their own three-digit number in a daily drawing. Like previous innovations, legal numbers was a success, replacing the daily game in 1976 and accounting for 50.2 percent of the New Jersey Lottery's gross sales in 1977[22] and two-thirds in 1979. Legal numbers was rapidly adopted by other State lotteries, with fifteen States operating numbers games in 1983.

The evolution of State lotteries from passive annual and monthly games into high-frequency, player-active gambling is still continuing. The next stage is widely expected to be the "player activated lottery machine," or "PALM"—electronic video gaming devices combining the features of nongambling video games such as Pac-Man and the video poker and blackjack that is an increasingly important feature of Nevada and Atlantic City casinos. The introduction of these video devices into State lotteries has been delayed by questions of legality under lottery laws. In August 1981 shortly after the State's lottery director announced plans to install video poker and blackjack games in hotels, bars, and stores on a trial basis,[23] New York's attorney general said the games were of "questionable legality" and would possibly violate the State constitution.[24] A year later the attorney general of New Jersey ruled that player-operated video bingo (a video game in which an astronaut looks for buried treasure) and a five-digit video matching game fell within statutory and judicial definitions of slot machines, and, further, that "there is no constitutional or statutory bar to the incorporation of a consumer-operated video games terminal into . . . the New Jersey State lottery."[25] The award of a contract for three hundred of these games became embroiled in allegations of conflict of interest between the vendor, Syntech International of Dallas, Texas, and the chairman of the New Jersey State Lottery Commission, and on March 1, 1983, Gov. Thomas Kean signed into a law a bill prohibiting the use of video gaming devices by the lottery, saying, "It is critical that public perceptions of the operations of the lottery remain completely above reproach."[26] In September 1982 the attorney general of Vermont, after reviewing the conflicting opinions of the attorneys general of New York and New Jersey, ruled that video gaming devices resembling "video games of skill, like Space Invaders or Pac-Man" but "the outcome of [which] would depend purely on chance" were "within the meaning of Vermont law . . . not a lottery, and so beyond the authority of the Lottery Commission to operate."[27]

Washington State became the first jurisdiction to specifically authorize video lottery devices when on July 16, 1983, Gov. John Spellman signed a bill establishing a Washington State Lottery.[28] The first legal use of video lottery devices was in August 1983, when the Lions Club of Ft. Calhoun, Nebraska, installed four such machines in taverns under the State's charitable lottery laws. The video devices have proven extremely popular, and a number of Nebraska municipalities expressed interest in operating video lotteries.[29] Nebraska's video lottery terminals, or VLTs, survived a court test when Douglas County District Court Judge Theodore Carlson ruled on January 16, 1984, that the terminals could legally be used in lotteries. In March 1984, however, the Nebraska legislature approved a bill banning all video and mechanical lotteries after January 1, 1985;[30] absent further legislative action, therefore, the Nebraska video lottery experiment will end on that date. On August 1, 1984, the Illinois Lottery began a six-month test of three hundred VLTs provided by Scientific Games, a subsidiary of Bally Manufacturing, that is widely expected to determine the immediate prospects for video lottery gambling. The video machines, which are installed in taverns, have aroused considerable opposition from Chicago suburban governments, and the State legislature is expected to create a commission to study their legality.[31] The legal impediments to the implementation of video lottery machines are formidable but if the wholesale legalizations of the last twenty years are a guide to the future these impediments—provided VLTs prove popular—will eventually be overcome.

State Lotteries Today

State lottery gambling today bears little or no resemblance to the original New Hampshire and New York lotteries. The monthly and weekly drawings that were initially the lotteries' principal games are disappearing from lottery menus. The New York State Lottery, which has overcome its early difficulties to become one of the nation's largest, is representative of current trends in lottery "product lines." For 1982 only instant, Lotto, and numbers games were offered. Table 1 shows the fiscal 1983 sales and revenues for the New York State Lottery.

TABLE 1
NEW YORK STATE LOTTERY: FISCAL 1983 SALES AND REVENUES

Game	*Sales*	*Revenues*
Instant Games	$ 87,124,000	$ 52,274,000
Lotto	279,259,000	167,556,000
Numbers/Win 4	278,584,000	139,291,000
TOTAL	644,967,000	359,121,000[a]

Source: New York State Lottery, *Annual Report* for the year ending March 31, 1983.

[a] Revenues of $262.4 million, or 40.7% of sales, are earnings for the State; $286 million, or 44.3% of sales were allocated to prizes; the balance, $97 million, or 15%, are used for expenses or to satisfy other lottery obligations.

Like casinos, which offer games and gambling opportunities to suit every taste, modern lottery menus appeal to a broad spectrum of the population. Instant games provide rapid frequency of play. On-line computer systems, first used in 1975 to process New Jersey's legal numbers game, have dramatically shortened payout intervals, enabling winners to reinvest their winnings in more lottery tickets. Lottery games and prize structures now offer a wide range of odds and payout ratios, from $1 to more than $1 million for a single $1 to $5 ticket. Recent instances of enormous prizes—the record to date being $40 million[32]—in Lotto games have made State lotteries the greatest purveyors of hope, albeit at astronomical odds, in American commercial gambling. Advertisements relate lottery gambling to ordinary life by emphasizing the homes, cars, clothes, and other material things lottery winnings can buy, and televised drawings featuring film and television celebrities add the glamorous fantasy that was once exclusive to casino gaming.

The transformation of lottery gambling has not been total. For the most part lottery games remain easy to learn. Moreover, as games—with the prospective exception of video lottery games—lotteries are still limited in play value in comparison with casinos and horse racing. Of all lottery structural characteristics this has been perhaps the most resistent to change. This relatively low intrinsic play value has forced lottery operators to adopt a "product line" strategy unique in American commercial gambling. Unlike roulette or blackjack or the Kentucky Derby, of which the public never seems to tire, State lottery games have finite and often quite short lifetimes. Novelty is an essential element in their appeal, and new games appear on a regular basis, to be succeeded in turn by still newer games in a continuous series. In this way State lotteries substitute for intrinsic play value the "newness" that is one of their distinguishing characteristics.

The Context of Lottery Gambling

Place: State lotteries have a larger number of sales outlets than any other form of legal commercial gambling. Reliable totals of the number of newsstands, supermarkets, candy and tobacco sellers, gas stations, bars, restaurants, hotels, and other retail establishments that act as State lottery ticket agents are not available, but from a review of recent annual reports the total must exceed 100,000 in the eighteen currently operating lotteries. These sales outlets are moreover widely dispersed geographically; only Nevada slot machines, perhaps, are comparable in this respect. The practical effect of this contextual characteristic is to make lottery games by far the most accessible form of legal commercial gambling. Generally speaking, the lottery States no longer make any attempt to restrict adult access to these games: the networks of sales outlets typically expand until tickets are readily available to everyone in the jurisdiction. In 1983 approximately 42 percent of the U.S. population resided in jurisdictions with lotteries. When the lotteries authorized in 1984 by the voters of California, Missouri, Oregon, and West Virginia are started this figure will rise to approximately 56 percent.

Situation: The accessibility of lottery gambling is reinforced by its almost perfect integration into everyday life. The bulk of lottery sales are through stores, newsstands, delicatessens, and other retail businesses. To a greater extent than any other form of legal commercial gambling State lotteries are a neighborhood activity. Buying a lottery ticket—and playing an instant game—is part of ordinary life. State lottery games are woven into the fabric of their communities, and this, together with the wide geographic dispersion of sales outlets, is conducive to habitual lottery play. Like illegal numbers, many State lottery tickets are purchased as a daily routine: at the same time of every day, like, and perhaps with, the morning newspaper or the evening's groceries.

Ownership and Operation: All State lottery operations are agencies of State government.[33] State ownership and operation of lotteries is a legacy of the nineteenth-century scandals involving State-franchised private lotteries: the laws prohibiting them remained in force, and formed the statutory background for modern lottery initiatives. No legislature has been eager to invite repetition of the preceding century's experience with private lottery companies.

As examples of virtual state capitalism the State lotteries are almost unique in American commercial gambling.[34] From the inception of the New Hampshire Sweepstakes in 1963 State ownership and operation of lotteries has raised questions about the propriety and social implications of government-run commercial gambling. The issue is not, as critics of lotteries often claim, the wisdom of government dependency on gambling revenues. All American legal commercial gambling, with the exceptions of charitable bingo and "Las Vegas night" gaming, has been authorized in whole or in part to raise government revenue as a supplement or an alternative to involuntary taxation. Nor is the propriety of putting the State at financial risk, as may theoretically be the case in numbers gambling at fixed odds, a real issue. Over time the operator of the games offered by modern lotteries will certainly win.[35] The real issue is that the lotteries are State agencies exercising the States' powers and authority as entrepreneurs with a direct interest in the promotion of gambling. The implications of this government presence in gambling are succinctly stated by tax analyst Frederick D. Stocker: "The real significance of the lottery and other forms of publicly sponsored gambling . . . lies not in the revenue but in the change it signifies in our national conception of the nature and functions of government. . . . It may be that the fiscal crisis of the states, in leading legislatures to cast about desperately to find forms of sin in which a state monopoly can be established, will bring about a fundamental alteration in our traditional views of the relation of government to the private economy.''[36]

The States' entrepreneurial role in the lottery industry has had important consequences for the interaction of this form of gambling with both individuals and society as a whole. First, the revenue imperative has governed the evolution of lotteries to the nearly complete exclusion of other considerations, changing them from passive games with narrow popular appeal to a highly aggressive form of gambling. Secondly, largely because of the revenue imperative State lotteries extract a higher percentage (an average 54 percent) of the handle, or gross sales, than does any other commercial gambling game.[37] From the consumer's point of view this makes lottery tickets the most costly of all commercial gambles.

The high price of lottery gambling may appear to be inconsistent with the widespread and rapidly growing popularity of lottery games. In fact, State lotteries are the least price-sensitive form of gambling. There are three reasons for this. First, people who buy lottery tickets are, as a group, much less sophisticated gamblers than the clientele of racetracks or casino table games. Thus, although many States require their lotteries to print both the odds or probabilities of winning and the odds paid for individual lottery gambles this information is to many players like the lists of additives and ingredients on cereal boxes or the proverbial fine print in contracts: hard to read and therefore easy to ignore. As a result many lottery players have only a vague idea of the price of lottery gambling. Secondly, even if they are aware of this high price, less expensive forms of gambling (with the important exception of illegal numbers) may not be readily available. Horse racing, while both cheaper and legal in thirty-six States, requires sophisticated skills that most lottery players do not possess. Slot machines, which are also cheaper and even easier to play than lotteries, are legally available only in Nevada and Atlantic City.

Finally, and most importantly, neither horse racing nor gaming are good substitutes for lotteries with respect to payout ratios. The purchaser of a lottery ticket is buying a dream: the chance to win a million dollars, and even millions of dollars, by risking a trivial stake, perhaps only 50¢ or a dollar. Empirically, neither the odds against realizing this dream nor its comparatively high price appear to be relevant in calculating the marginal utility of lottery expenditures. There is a cultural as well as a political economy of commercial gambling.[38] The value society places on wealth, and the social and economic realities of its distribution, are important factors in the reception of lotteries in mainstream America.

Like the social costs of commercial gambling, dreams are difficult to quantify, but they are nevertheless part of the equation. The satisfaction of some deeply rooted American cultural needs is an underlying motivation for the prosaic, conventional act of buying a lottery ticket.

A third criticism of State lotteries is that their high takeout combines with the predominantly lower-income demographics of many major lottery markets to make lotteries a highly regressive form of taxation. The Survey Research Center found that people with incomes under $10,000 earned 11.49 percent of total household income but contributed 24.68 percent of State lottery losses and, in comparing different forms of commercial gambling with sales and excise taxes, concluded that lotteries were ''considerably more regressive than the sales tax.'' Of all commercial gambling games the SRC found only numbers, historically played by the inner-city poor, and sports cards, a game for small unsophisticated sports bettors that is an even worse gamble in terms of odds and price than State lottery games, to be more regressive than lotteries.[39] A number of other professional studies have arrived at similar conclusions. Michael Spiro, an economist, determined from a sample of Pennsylvania Lottery winners that, if losses are considered a voluntary tax, in the early 1970s this lottery was ''highly regressive for the *subset of the population who won in the lottery*'' and probably regressive for most income ranges of Pennsylvania's general population.[40] Consultants Roger E. Brinner and Charles T. Clotfelter, after reviewing Spiro's data together with telephone surveys of Connecticut and Massachusetts residents and performing their own analysis of 108 Massachusetts Lottery winners between 1972 and 1974 similarly conclude that State lotteries are ''a particularly inequitable revenue base'' inasmuch as ''the revenue collected [from lotteries] constitutes a regressive tax [that] is all the more objectionable in light of the fact that many states appear to have adopted lotteries rather than implementing or expanding progressive income taxes.'' These negative tax considerations are offset, in Brinner and Clotfelter's view, by their social value: lotteries simultaneously impose a tax (the inevitable losses players incur at this high takeout commercial gambling game) and create a good (lottery gambles, which have the recreational and other consumption values discussed at length in Chapter 4). In other words, lotteries are a regressive tax that produce a social gain.[41]

Whether there has been any marked change in the tax incidence of the eastern and middle western State lotteries since the 1970s is problematical. An analysis of the first 14,020 winners in the new (November 1982) Washington State Lottery shows that 18.3 percent of claimants were from households with annual incomes of $10,000 or less.

This statistic may very roughly be compared to the 24.8 percent of losses contributed by persons with annual incomes of $10,000 or less reported by the Survey Research Center, suggesting that the Washington State Lottery may be somewhat less regressive.[42] Lottery game menus almost certainly appeal to a wider range of the general population than they did in the early 1970s. It is therefore possible that participation in lottery games is more reflective of the demographics of individual lottery markets than was the case a decade ago. If so, the legalization of a lottery in a State with relatively up-scale demographics might result in less regressive lottery revenues. The question is complex: participation rates in different forms of gambling are affected by many variables, including the availability of various commercial gambling games. Enough changes have occurred in State lotteries since the studies reviewed here, however, to warrant a second look at the issue of lottery regressivity.

A fourth issue raised by the States' ownership and operation of lotteries concerns regulation. By electing to own and operate lotteries the States have abrogated the private operator/State government regulator relationship that elsewhere serves as the basic control mechanism for legal commercial gambling. While the lottery States have devised a variety of more or less *pro forma* regulatory arrangements for their lotteries, they are essentially regulating themselves. One aspect of this merged entrepreneurial and regulatory role is particularly disturbing. State lottery agencies are by and large administrative in function; the lottery games themselves are provided by vendors from the private sector. Several of these vendors make, or are owned by companies that also make, slot machines and video games. Lottery administrators, who have statutory responsibilities to generate revenue from lottery sales, are naturally interested in any games or devices, including video gaming devices, that promise to increase sales. The result is that lottery administrators, who are State employees but in their capacity as lottery operators are just as subject to the revenue imperative as any privately owned racetrack or casino chief executive, become *de facto* lobbyists for the vendors of lottery games and gaming devices. This has produced some awkward situations in New York and New Jersey regarding proposals from State lottery administrations to introduce lottery video games manufactured by vendors from the private sector, with, in New Jersey, allegations of possible conflict of interest leading to the indictment of the chairman of the State Lottery Commission.[43] Because video lotteries appear to require legislative approval,[44] and because to vendors the prospective value of contracts to install video lotteries is great, the potential for similarly awkward situations exists in other lottery jurisdictions. This recent and as yet unfinished history makes it clear that because the normal private operator/government regulator relationship that is the basis for regulating other forms of commercial gambling does not function for State lotteries an essential control over the introduction of new forms of gambling in the guise of ''lottery'' games is missing.

Purpose: As we have noted, State lotteries have been authorized primarily for the purpose of raising revenue.[45] Other common justifications for legalizing gambling—to provide competitive legal alternatives to illegal gambling and to finance the economic development of depressed areas—were not usually among the original purposes of State lotteries. As revenue measures State lotteries have been successful: in 1983 an estimated $2.2 billion in government funds was generated from this ''voluntary taxation.''

When in the mid 1970s States began adding legal numbers games to their lotteries they typically justified their actions by adding to lottery laws the further purpose of providing a competitive legal alternative to illegal numbers games. Numbers, or policy, is a long-established American lottery game that is traceable to sixteenth-century Italian and eighteenth-century London lotteries. On both sides of the Atlantic during the eighteenth and nineteenth centuries lottery tickets were expensive, and many persons, unable to afford the price of a whole ticket, either purchased a piece of one or bought an ''insurance policy,'' for a penny or two, on what they expected to be the winning number. These ''policies'' were sold by retailers who received a commission on these ''numbers'' sales from the private lottery companies. In the early decades of the twentieth century numbers became a popular game in Harlem and other ghettos of the black or poor, and was eventually organized by bootleggers, who were able to capitalize numbers banks and provide managerial and organizational skills, or muscle, depending on one's point of view. Illegal numbers remains the gambling game of choice in many eastern and midwestern inner cities.[46]

In practice the original revenue purpose of State lotteries and the justification that legal numbers games could reduce illegal gambling have proven contradictory. In order to raise the maximum revenue State lottery numbers generally offer lower payouts than illegal numbers. Moreover, legal numbers games do not usually employ runners or extend credit and tend to be most heavily marketed in neighborhoods where illegal numbers are not well established. The result of this combination of factors has been twofold: the total market for numbers has been expanded as new players are drawn to the legal game, and a new market equilibrium evolves, with parallel legal and illegal numbers operations supplying demographically distinct segments of this expanded market.

State lottery numbers games are not good substitutes for illegal numbers.[47] The structural characteristics and purpose of State lotteries preclude effective competition with their illegal counterparts. The stated justification for legalizing numbers—to reduce illegal gambling through the provision of a competitive legal alternative—is, practically speaking, window-dressing for the addition of a popular, player-active game to lottery menus. The *function,* as opposed to the stated *justification,* of legal numbers is to generate government funds from a new market. Perhaps more clearly than any other form of commercial gambling, State lottery numbers games illustrate the tendency of the economic imperative to outweigh other social considerations in the evolution of gambling policy.

The public policy questions raised by State lotteries have become more pressing as a result of the 1984 elections. Voters approved lottery initiatives in four States—California, Oregon, Missouri, and West Virginia—by a nearly two-to-one margin[48] and rejected none. Other forms of gambling did not fare as well: the single pari-mutuel racing legalization (Missouri) on the ballots was approved but two casino measures (in Colorado and Arkansas) were defeated, and in Oregon the voters amended that State's constitution to specifically prohibit casinos while overwhelmingly approving a State lottery. It now appears that State lotteries will dominate U.S. commercial gambling for the remainder of the century. This development—which would have seemed the most improbable fantasy only ten years ago—has profound implications, not only for other gambling businesses but for American leisure and society as a whole. We examine these implications more closely in Chapter 7.

CASINO GAMING

Commercial casino gaming is legal in two jurisdictions, Nevada and, following the approval of a referendum in 1976, Atlantic City, New Jersey.

Casino Games

To a far greater extent than any other form of commercial gambling casinos offer a variety of games. Where pari-mutuel horse racing generally allows a dozen or so different wagers (win, place, exacta, daily double, and so forth) on a single event (the horse race) and State lotteries provide even fewer wagers in, at most, half a dozen games, American casinos contain gambling activities of every description: from the native card games of poker and blackjack to the Chinese domino game of *pai gow,*[49] the quintessentially American craps and the European roulette and baccarat, the Chinese lottery game of keno, bingo, pari-mutuel *jai-*

alai, bookmaking, and of course slot machines.[50] The great variety of gambling activities somewhat complicates the structural analysis of casino gaming in that elements of chance and skill vary from game to game. A brief discussion of these differences follows.

Games of Pure Chance: Roulette, craps, big six wheels, and slot machines are games of pure chance. Such games offer risk but no uncertainty: at the odds paid by casinos the player cannot win at games of pure chance over the long term; at best he or she can slow the rate of loss by choosing those bets that produce the smallest advantage for the house, such as the ''Don't Pass'' line at craps. Casino games of pure chance utilize a randomizing device, such as a roulette wheel or dice (a slot machine is a player-operated randomizing device), to produce events, or series of events, of individually random outcome but mathematically calculable probability and, hence, of known frequency. Provided the randomizing device is fair enough to subject each event (roll of the dice, turn of the roulette wheel) to the law of independent trials[51] the true likelihood of the outcomes of these events is immutable, and may *a priori* be calculated for any of these games.

Statistical, or *a priori* or *true, probability* is a mathematical expression of the likelihood that one of a number of possible but uncertain outcomes of an event, or series of events, will occur. Operators of games of pure chance calculate the likelihood of all possible outcomes of trials of the randomizing devices used for gambling, and relate the statistical probabilities these calculations yield to the terms, or odds, of the games they offer. These odds are fixed, and vary sufficiently from statistical probability or ''true odds'' to guarantee the operator a positive return, or house edge or advantage, from all possible series of independent trials of the house's randomizing devices. The player who plays these games at the operator's odds has, for all possible series of plays and bets, a negative expectation of gain: in other words, if he plays long enough he must, *a priori,* expect to lose. A game of pure chance can only be ''beaten'' by the player's taking advantage of a temporarily favorable short-term series of bets and ending the series while he or she is ahead.

Games of Pure Skill: Tic-tac-toe, checkers, and chess are games of pure skill. Chance is not a factor in determining the outcome of these games. Checkers and chess are games of perfect information; in other words, there is always a best move, and for each game there are best series of moves. Checkers has been completely analyzed and the results of the analysis written in computer programs which never lose. The analysis of chess involves very large numbers and is not yet complete; this analysis is however a finite problem, and, given enough calculation, will eventually result in the perfect game of chess. Games of pure skill are not used for commercial gambling: were a casino to offer chess, for example, Bobby Fischer, and not the house, would win.

Games and Mixed Chance and Skill: Blackjack and baccarat, as well as poker, bridge, backgammon, and a variety of other games often played for money or stakes of some kind, are games of mixed chance and skill. In varying proportion both chance and skill are factors in determining the outcome of these games. The most important commercial gambling game of mixed chance and skill is blackjack, which, from the casino's point of view, suffers from the defect that (unlike each turn of a roulette wheel) each card of a series dealt from one or several decks is not subject to the law of independent trials: in other words, the *a priori* probability that the next card dealt will be a particular card (say, a ten or face card) is a function of the preceding cards in the series. With this information available (from counting the cards) a series of bets with a positive expectation of gain may be devised. Chance, however, in the form of short-term anomalies in the succession of cards in a series, is still present, and even a betting strategy with a positive expectation of gain may also involve a sufficiently high element of ruin that the player loses his investment. The determination of optimum player strategy in baccarat is a complicated mathematical problem; it appears, however, that even assuming optimum strategy the element of skill is not sufficient to produce a positive expectation of gain for players of baccarat in American casinos.

Structural Characteristics of Casino Gaming

If the gambling offered by the first State lotteries elicited limited ticket sales from a comparatively narrow segment of the population modern casino gaming represents the opposite extreme: action, in a variety of forms and essentially without limit, for everyone. Analysis of the characteristics of gaming suggests that modern casinos appeal to a broader range of Americans and stimulate higher per capita play—and extract higher per capita losses—than any other form of commercial gambling. For this reason the structural characteristics of gaming are unusually important.

Entry-level Knowledge: There is no significant entry-level knowledge barrier to casino gaming. Anyone can pull the handle of a slot machine. Big six wheels are very simple to play, and keno only slightly more complicated. Roulette, craps, and blackjack, in roughly this ascending order, offer more complexity, but (with the growing exception of craps, a World War II–generation game whose popularity among younger people has been eclipsed by blackjack) are familiar to most Americans. Only baccarat is relatively unknown: many casinos place their baccarat tables apart from the casino floor and staff these games with formally dressed dealers and attractive female shills to create an aura of "foreign" exclusivity calculated to attract very "high rollers." Baccarat will usually have the highest table minimums in the casino, and, while in reality a simple enough game to play, it is presented as a ritual activity for initiates.

Intrinsic Interest: Casino games (big six wheels are an exception) have considerable play value. Slot-machine and table-game activity is typically prolonged for hours, and the catalogue of casino games is relatively stable over time: unlike State lotteries, which are compelled to introduce new games on a regular basis to maintain player interest, casinos are conservative as regards their "product line." The only recent significant change in table gaming has been a tremendous rise in the popularity of blackjack since the 1960s, a phenomenon commonly attributed to the publicizing of card-counting strategies. In contrast to the essential conservatism of table gaming, casino slot operations, after remaining relatively unchanged for decades, have in the last five years become increasingly dynamic: dollar slots, single and linked progressive jackpot machines, carrousels, and a variety of electronic video slot machines and gaming devices have been successively introduced, with the result that slot-machine gaming, particularly in Atlantic City, is undergoing rapid evolution.

Player Participation and the Opportunity to Exercise Skill: Most casino games require some degree of player participation. Craps and slot machines are in fact classic examples of player-active gambling. It is important, in considering the functions of participation and skill in gaming activity, to distinguish between the objective element of skill present in a particular game and the player's subjective perception of such skill.

For example, it is objectively true that the exercise of skill can influence the outcome of a session at blackjack. At craps or slot machines, however, all possible strategies have negative expectations of gain over extended periods of play. Player participation in these games—shooting dice or pulling the handle of a slot machine—may contribute, consciously or subconsciously, to the subjective but erroneous perception that participation can affect the game's outcome—in other words, to the illusion of control over the gambling event. In the case of slot play a subjective perception of control is wholly illusory. (The "play" of a slot thief, or "mechanic," is of course an exception.) At craps the player can, objectively, control to some extent his rate of loss by choosing from among the game's variety of odds, but as with slot machines (again, excluding dishonest play) any perceived control over the behavior of the

dice themselves is an illusion. Illusory or not, however, subjective perceptions of control can powerfully influence behavior. In casino gaming and gambling generally degrees of player participation and opportunities to exercise skill are strongly correlated with increasing levels of investment in the game.

Frequency of Opportunities to Gamble, Payout Intervals, Bet Size, and Payout Ratios: Casinos offer a wide range of frequency of opportunities to gamble, from the leisurely pace of keno to the continuous action of slot machines, craps, and blackjack. Payout intervals in these latter games are short, payouts being almost immediate. High frequency of gambles and immediate payouts facilitate the rapid cycling, or churning, of money. Like pari-mutuel betting, where "churn" is an important component of the handle, or gross wagering, casino gaming, especially table games, depends upon this rapid cycling of money to produce large dollar wins (player losses). As we will see, the casino's "edge" or advantage over the player is quite small, 2 percent or less for some table game bets. This small edge, however, operates each time a hand of blackjack is dealt or a craps bet is decided—more than fifty times an hour in efficiently dealt games, compared with nine times an evening in the course of the usual nine-race program at horse-racing tracks. (At racetracks there is a much higher edge—typically 18 percent or so in 1983.) This rapid repetition of small house edges "grinds" the player's bankroll away at predictable rates. Casinos use these rates to monitor the gambling of players they "comp," or offer complimentary room, board, airfare, and other services. As long as the player gambles long enough at high enough stakes he or she will be invited back, at the casino's expense, especially if he or she wins: over the long term the house edge will ensure player losses sufficiently large to cover the cost of "comps" and produce a profit for the casino.[52] The continuous nature of gaming has a second consequence. Unlike racetrack betting or weekly lotteries, players have no time to reflect on their financial position between gambles. Casinos reinforce this uncertainty with carefully calculated distractions—free drinks, flashing mirrored lights, provocatively dressed women, and in areas of the casino floor devoted to slot machines the jangle of coins and bells announcing jackpots. The result is that it is easier to lose track of one's wins or losses inside a casino than at any other commercial gambling game.

Ranges of Odds and Stakes: Casinos offer wide ranges of odds and stakes, from small-stake/low-odds nickel slot machines to craps and blackjack, where highly variable odds and stakes are available on each hand dealt. The practical effect of variable odds and stakes is to introduce into gambling activities the element of variable rates of change in net worth. At nickel slots, for example, the single small (5¢) stake and the machine's fixed odds dictate a constant, relatively slow rate of change in the player's net worth: his bankroll will, if he plays long enough, be ground away to zero over a calculable period of time. In contrast, craps players may have a number of bets of different sizes at different odds riding on a single role of the dice. Some of these bets may go to a decision on a single roll while others may take several to be decided; moreover, craps players can vary both the size of their bets and their odds over a considerable range from roll to roll. The variable nature of odds and stakes at craps, and at other table games, gives the careful player the ability to regulate his gambling through money management. At the same time, by allowing careless or compulsive players to multiply the rate of change in their net worth, games of variable odds and stakes create opportunities for large wins or large losses not present in games where stakes and odds are fixed, or are variable only within narrow ranges.

There are clear policy implications here: high frequency commercial gambling at variable odds and stakes, of which casino table games are the extreme example, is far more likely to extract unaffordable losses from undisciplined gamblers than slow games with narrow ranges of odds and stakes, such as weekly or monthly lotteries. Further, assuming highly extractive games are allowed the rate at which the continuously recycling money is extracted from players is heavily influenced by the ratio of minimum to maximum stakes. These table limits are the "headroom" within which players are able to manage their money. High minimum and low maximum stakes constrict this headroom and thereby increase the rate at which players lose. For example, a $2 minimum and $500 maximum allows players to double their bets (and so recover their losses if they win before reaching the table maximum) eight times; a $500 minimum and $5,000 maximum takes a larger percentage of player bankrolls for each bet and allows the doubling of losses only three times before the table limit is reached. The competitive environment of Nevada gaming ensures relatively high minimum-to-maximum bet ratios. In Atlantic City in 1978, however, when Resorts International had a monopoly on gaming and queues outside the casino's doors were a frequent sight, the casino had an obvious incentive to set high minimum/low maximum table limits: such limits would "tap out" players rapidly and thereby increase the turnover of seats at the gaming tables. This became the most hotly debated of all policy issues prior to the opening of the Resorts casino in May 1978, with Resorts proposing $5 minimums, Albert Merck, a member of the Casino Control Commission, $2 minimums, and the Commission staff $1 minimums with maximums at the casino's discretion. The casino won. Resorts opened under a

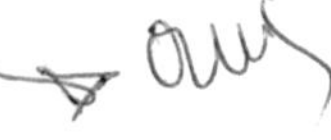

compromise rule allowing 90 percent of the tables a $5 minimum. Due in no small measure to this commission action Resorts won $134 million in its first 220 days of (monopoly) operation—more than twice its $50 million capital investment.[53]

Price: The price of casino gaming is frequently a matter of some confusion. First, unlike State lotteries and pari-mutuel betting, there is no statutory takeout or retention from table games.[54] Secondly, casinos do not report handle for table games,[55] and players are unlikely to have any very precise idea of their gross wagering due to the high frequency of gambles and variable stakes that are characteristics of casino gaming.

The absence of accurate handle figures for table games makes it impossible to calculate the price of gaming by the method used for State lotteries and pari-mutuel betting. Casino revenue accounting substitutes for the handle (or sales) and takeout (or retention) that are used by racetracks and State lotteries the concepts of *drop, win,* and *hold.* A brief discussion of these concepts is helpful in understanding the price of casino gaming.

A player who exchanges $100 for the equivalent in chips generates a $100 drop with this transaction. If he then makes $1 bets on "red" at (American, or double-zero) roulette he may on the average expect to make some 1,900 wagers, losing some and winning others, before losing his entire bankroll and thereby producing a $100 win for the casino. He may, of course, stop playing before he loses his entire bankroll, and walk away with either more or less than his initial $100 in chips. Collectively, however, players will leave at the tables a percentage of their gross wagering (handle, *not* bankroll) equivalent to the house "edge" or advantage on the bet in question: in this case, for "red" at roulette, 5.26 percent. This edge is the difference between the mathematical probability that red will come up and the amount the house pays when this actually happens. Winning bets on red are paid at even money, so that if the player bets $1 on red and wins he receives $2. There are eighteen red numbers and eighteen black numbers, *and,* unfortunately for the player, two green (zero and double zero) numbers, which means that for each thirty-eight spins of the roulette wheel the player betting $1 on red each spin will, over time, lose twenty bets for every eighteen he wins. This makes roulette unfair, and ensures a casino win of $2 for every $38 bet on red—a 5.26 percent house advantage. All commercial gambling games are in a similar fashion unfair, and the degree of unfairness, expressed as the percentage of gross wagering the operator may expect to retain, is, for players collectively, the price of a particular form of gambling.[56]

The edge, or house advantage, varies from bet to bet. At craps, for example, the edge ranges from 1.402 percent for "Don't Pass" bets to

16.667 percent for "All Sevens," while at blackjack, depending on the number of decks used and the player's card-counting skills and betting strategy, the edge ranges from some negative value (i.e., player advantage) to above 6 percent. The average, or effective, price of gaming is thus the edge for each bet or slot machine weighted by the total handle, or amount wagered, on each bet or slot machine. This average casino edge, which is the price of casino gaming in the sense that retention from lottery sales or pari-mutuel handle is the price of these forms of gambling, is not certainly known. We estimate this average, or effective, casino edge for American casinos in 1983 at 2.6 percent for table games and 11.6 percent for slot machines.[57] Gambling at casino table games, in other words, is cheaper than buying lottery tickets or playing the horses in that the gambler "buys" more gambles for the money he spends, or loses. Slot machines are more expensive than table games but still somewhat cheaper than horse racing and much cheaper than lotteries.[58] Moreover, in contrast to State lotteries, players have some ability to influence the price of casino gaming. As we have seen, some casino games have much higher house advantages than others. If for some reason players were to desert blackjack tables, where the edge is small, and instead bet equivalent sums on big six wheels, where the edge is extortionately high, the price of gaming would rise considerably.[59] The price of lottery gambling, on the other hand, remains fixed regardless of gambling behavior.

Probability of Winning Individual Bets and Payout Ratios: For many players wins are reinforcing. Slot machines and most table games allow players to make bets where the probabilities of winning are relatively high. Generally these frequent wins are at low payout ratios. Gaming activity characterized by frequent wins and low payout ratios is conducive to continuous gambling: the frequent wins encourage further gambles, but the payouts are not sufficiently large in relation to investments to produce significant increases in the player's net worth. It should be understood that games of frequent wins and low payout ratios are played by a variety of gamblers, from persons with modest bankrolls to high rollers. Further, individual gamblers have different views of the optimal relationship between the probability of wins and expected payout ratios; the range of choice available at casino games is an important reason for the wide popularity of this form of commercial gambling.

Credit and Cash: Casino gaming is the only major form of legal commercial gambling offered on a credit basis. In Nevada (where gambling debts are only recently legally collectible) the decision to extend credit is discretionary with the individual casino. In New Jersey (where gambling debts are legally collectible) the State has placed an indirect control on the extension of credit by Atlantic City casinos by limiting to 4 percent of gross win the before-tax adjustment a casino can make for uncollectible patron checks or markers.

Credit play is extremely important in American casino table gaming. Reliable statistics for credit extended by Nevada casinos are not publicly available; the State of New Jersey, however, requires Atlantic City casinos to annually report the dollar amount of the credit they extend. In 1981 the nine operating Atlantic City casinos extended just over $1 billion in credit, only slightly less than (95 percent of) the casinos' gross win for that year ($1,045,070,361 in credit; $1,099,779,177 gross win). Credit policy is perhaps the most important means by which casinos position themselves in the marketplace: a casino seeking a high-roller clientele will extend liberal credit; "grind" houses, which depend upon gamblers of more modest income, normally enforce more restrictive credit policies. Credit as a percentage of gross win for Atlantic City casinos reflects this variation. Among the nine casinos operating in 1981 this percentage ranged from a high of 151 percent at Caesars (which extended $293,855,072 in credit to win $194,094,699) to a low of 42 percent at Harrah's (which extended $59,879,455 in credit and won $142,531,544).[60]

Credit play is often considered to be an incentive or an inducement to excessive gambling that increases the risk of unaffordable losses. Great Britain, for example, forbids its casinos to extend credit in any form other than the acceptance of personal checks, which the casino is required to bank within two banking days.[61] We do not question the importance of credit as a structural characteristic of casino gaming, nor do we wish to minimize the potential dangers credit play creates for individuals who—for whatever reason—gamble excessively. Instances of the abuse of credit in casino gaming and illegal bookmaking, the two forms of commercial gambling that extend credit freely, are well-documented and familiar to everyone with an interest in gambling and gambling behavior.[62]

We do, however, regard credit as only one of many structural characteristics of casino gaming, and we reject the notion that credit, or any other single characteristic, exerts a determining influence over the gambling behavior of most casino patrons. In our view the interaction of gamblers and games is a complex and not a simple function. People who otherwise gamble in a controlled fashion will not, other things being equal, be transformed into uncontrolled, compulsive gamblers if credit is made available. There is an analogy to other forms of consumer credit: a Bloomingdale's charge card does not, for most of its holders, stimulate uncontrolled and unaffordable buying, even from a store that is generally regarded as highly sophisticated in stimulating consumption. This is not to say that Bloomingdale's charge card–holders do not sometimes buy things they would not be able to pay for with the cash in their wallets or purses, or that charge accounts do not sometimes grow uncomfortably, or even unaffordably, large. The relevant issues are incidence and responsibility. The abuse of Bloomingdale's charge cards by a minority is not an argument for abolishing such credit. The majority of customers, and of course Bloomingdale's, which, for better or worse, is a legally and socially approved institution, benefit from charge cards. There is a social assumption of adult responsibility in the use of this form of consumer credit we see no reason to question.

While casinos are not here being equated with department stores, the issues of consumer abuse raised by both kinds of credit differ in degree rather than kind. Credit play may indeed increase the size of wins or losses of conventional gamblers, but we assume the responsibility for such financial consequences resides with the individuals who gamble and approve of it. By the same token there is a public responsibility to regulate documented abuses, such as the extension of credit to compulsive gamblers—a responsibility that in our view devolves not upon the casino but on government. The legalization of casino credit play, or any other form of gambling, adds a clause to the social contract of public responsibility for the consequences of all legal and approved activities; we would all do well to read the fine print in these clauses carefully before signing.

An obvious characteristic of casino gaming that is somewhat related to credit is that unlike lottery or racetrack gambling the usual medium of exchange for table games is not cash but chips or checks. (Slot machines are normally played with coins.) The use of chips contributes to the "unreality" of gaming wins and losses: at least to novice gamblers, a black chip is not the same as its equivalent $100 dollar bill. This, too, may increase the size of wins and losses at casino games.

The Context of Casino Gaming

Place: Casino gaming is limited to two relatively isolated resort areas, the State of Nevada and Atlantic City, New Jersey. In contrast to other forms of legal commercial gambling, therefore, access to casinos remains for most Americans effectively restricted by geography. In large measure this restriction is due to the structural characteristics of gaming. There is a general realization that casinos raise more, and more complicated, social questions than any other form of commercial gambling. States that have authorized lotteries and racetracks have stopped short of casinos: even with the example of the rapid development of an enormously successful casino industry in Atlantic City following the opening of Resorts International in 1978, no further legalizations have occurred.

The unwillingness of both voters and their elected representatives to approve more casinos—even as they authorize other forms of gambling—was confirmed in 1984. In September the Chicago City Council allowed a widely debated proposal to place a casino referendum on the November ballot to die. In the November elections two casino initiatives, one to allow casinos in Garland County (Hot Springs), Arkansas, and the other a constitutional amendment calling for casinos as an aid to economic development for the depressed mining community of Pueblo, Colorado, failed by decisive margins.[63] At the time of writing the only serious remaining interest in legalizing casino gaming is in Louisiana, where the recent $100 million bankruptcy of the New Orleans Fair and a past history of illicit but unofficially sanctioned casinos together with a historically tolerant attitude towards the traditional vices and entertainment generally have combined to persuade some Louisiana politicians that New Orleans should become the next jurisdiction to allow casinos. The possibility of extending their business to New Orleans has attracted the interest of several major U.S. casino firms, including Resorts International; we note, however, in assessing the prospects for legalization in Louisiana that many of the same conditions were present in Miami, Florida, in 1978, when a heavily financed initiative to legalize casinos along the Gold Coast was defeated by a 73-to-27 margin.[64]

The reluctance of voters and legislatures to allow the proliferation of casinos was accurately foreshadowed by the 1976 Federal Commission on the Review of the National Policy Toward Gambling, which concluded that

> densely populated areas are likely to find it much more difficult (than has Nevada) to cope with the effects of overindulgence. If Nevada-style casinos were legalized in heavily urban areas, participation by low-income people can be expected to result in increased social problems and an expanded need for government services, thereby offsetting in whole or in part any advantages derived from the stimulation of local businesses.[65]

For this reason the commission recommended that

> any legalization of casino gambling be restricted by the State to relatively isolated areas where the impact on surrounding populations can be minimized. Although the Commission realizes that such a

principle might not appeal to State policymakers who wish to stimulate existing resort areas, it nonetheless believes that the likely social effects of legalized casino gambling outweigh purely economic considerations.[66]

Situation: Unlike lotteries, casino games are played in a timeless, hermetic environment of elaborate unreality. The larger Nevada and Atlantic City resorts are luxurious fantasies that like Disneyland and similar theme amusement parks are fashioned as vanished or imaginary worlds: Imperial Rome (Caesars Palace, Las Vegas), the Old West (the "sawdust joints" of downtown Reno and Las Vegas's Glitter Gulch), the Nineties of boaters and long dresses and soda fountains (the Golden Nugget, Atlantic City). Casino floors normally have neither clocks nor windows.[67] In contrast to the library-like quiet of the older Continental casinos, where croupiers speak in hushed tones and the fall of roulette balls can be heard across the *salle,* the action at the tables and slot machines is amplified by a show of sound and lights that is a distinctively American contribution to commercial gambling. Alcoholic beverages are freely available, often at no cost, and attractive female staff and showgirls in various costumes of undress contribute to an atmosphere of general license. Environment thus reinforces geography: just as casinos are physically separated from mainstream America the moral constraints that elsewhere govern alcohol, sex, and money end at the casino door. The writ of the domain of work does not run inside these playlands, and the currency of labor, the dollar bills by which Americans measure the success or failure of their lives, is changed at the cashier's cage into chips, a medium of play.

Ownership and Operation: The casino industry is privately owned and operated. In a country that values free enterprise this may seem unexceptional, but the peculiar moral status of gambling throughout American history has produced a situation in which, as gaming finally spreads beyond Nevada, the identity and what John Dennis Dombrink has termed "the character of the primary investors in the legal casino gambling industry"[68] is an evidently insoluble problem.

For many years the American demand for gaming, like the American demand for alcoholic beverages during Prohibition, had no legal suppliers. Like bootleg whiskey in the 1920s, casinos were an illicit business, and with repeal gaming was a natural investment for criminals made wealthy by the Volstead Act.[69] When Nevada decriminalized gambling in 1931 the participation of organized crime in the ownership and operation of legal casino gaming was inevitable. To a far greater degree than any other form of legal commercial gambling casinos have thus confronted American society with a problem that remains intractable: how, within the constraints imposed on lawmakers, law enforcement agencies, and judicial administration by the civil rights of a constitutional democracy, can government distinguish between criminal and legitimate casino owners and operators?

A review of the British experience provides a useful perspective on the seriousness of this problem. The Betting and Gaming Act of 1960 made casinos, in the guise of members' clubs, legal, and allowed relatively free entry to gaming provided that operators conducted their business fairly and honestly.[70] Gaming proved to be enormously profitable. Within eight years Britain had more than a thousand legal casinos, and the industry was, in the words of the 1978 Royal Commission on Gambling, "being infiltrated by criminals and other undesirable characters."[71] Parliament responded to this situation by enacting the Gaming Act of 1968, which made participation in commercial gaming, whether as owner or operator, a privilege to be conceded by a Gaming Board invested with extraordinary powers. These powers were, and remain, extremely broad. The board, "in deciding whether or not to grant a certificate" (of consent to operate a commercial gaming establishment) need "have regard *only* to the question whether, *in their opinion,* the applicant is likely to be capable" of complying with the very stringent Gaming Act and regulations made pursuant to it. Further, "in determining these questions, the Board may take into account *any circumstances which appear to it to be relevant,* but *is required* to consider *in particular the character, reputation, and financial standing*" of the applicant. Further, "the Gaming Act of 1968 gives the Board power to *regulate its own procedure.*" Finally, "*there (is) no legal requirement upon the Board to give reason for a refusal to grant a certificate* or to reveal its sources of information. . . . If the Board follows the procedures (of its own devising, and approved by the Court of Appeal in 1970) . . . and gives no reason for its decision, it is in practice legally impregnable. *There can be no inquiry into whether its decision (to refuse to grant a license) was right or wrong*" (emphasis added).[72]

For all practical purposes these are the powers of a star chamber. The British Gaming Board is a self-regulating authority empowered to decide, as a matter of its opinion based on whatever evidence it chooses to consider, who shall own and work in British casinos. As long as it gives no reasons for denying a license to operate its decision cannot be questioned—and the board is not required to give a reason. By common consent the exercise of these extraordinary powers has enabled the Gaming Board to cleanse Britain's casino industry of criminal elements. The 1978 Royal Commission, however, which inquired into the continued need for such authority, concluded that the danger of the return of these criminal elements to British gaming was sufficiently great to warrant the continued exercise of nearly absolute power by the Gaming Board.

It is obvious that the British solution to the problem of criminal ownership and operation of casinos is not available to American jurisdictions that authorize this form of commercial gambling. The powers exercised by the British Gaming Board are utterly inconsistent with the Bill of Rights and Constitution. Casino gaming, if it is to be allowed in this country, must be regulated with the *limited* powers of constitutional government.[73] This limitation means, in effect, that States contemplating legal gaming face a difficult choice: the revenue and economic, and recreational, benefits of casinos must be weighed against the danger of criminal participation. As in games of mixed chance and skill, the outcome of making this particular decision is uncertain, and depends in part on the behavior of the elected and appointed officials who carry it out. There is a premium on skillful play: sound and effective government can do much to ensure that the potential benefits of gaming are realized at acceptable social costs. But the great attractiveness of casino games[74] and the consequently enormous potential economic and political power of the casino industry inevitably place great stress on governments that attempt to regulate it, and to date these governments have often not been equal to the task. It is a pretty problem. We will return to it in Chapters 5 and 7.

Purpose: In both Nevada and Atlantic City casinos were legalized for the purposes of raising government revenues and promoting economic development. The revenue and economic contributions of gaming are thus convenient measures of the industry's success or failure in achieving society's stated reasons for allowing it.

In calendar 1982 Nevada had a total of 1,587 gaming licenses in force, of which 1,297 were for Restricted Slots (fifteen or fewer slot machines, mostly in supermarkets, restaurants, and other nongambling retail businesses), 62 were for Nonrestricted Slots (sixteen or more slot machines, but no table games), and 228 were for Nonrestricted Games and Slots (unlimited slot machines, games such as blackjack, roulette and so forth, and card games). These 1,587 licensed gaming locations had 87,635 slot machines; 391 craps tables, 210 roulette tables, 3,085 blackjack or "21" tables, 141 keno games, and 247 baccarat, wheel of fortune, bingo, and other games for a total of 4,074 games; and 603 poker and panguingui tables. The State's calendar 1982 gross win (player losses), including money won by sixty-eight licensed bookmakers, was \$2.7 billion, of which \$1.3 billion was derived from slot machines and \$1.4 billion from card and table games and bookmaking.[75]

Direct levies on gaming and casino entertainment taxes supplied $175.9 million, or 52.3 percent, of the State's fiscal 1981/1982 General Fund revenue. Additional gaming privilege and entertainment taxes yielded $21.4 million to local governments, making the total direct revenue contribution of Nevada gaming in fiscal 1981/1982 $197.2 million.[76] Gaming and the associated hotel, tourist, and related trade industries are Nevada's largest employers, providing jobs for 113,900 persons, or 27.5 percent of the State's nonagricultural employment in 1981. Indirectly the gaming, hotel, and tourist industries employ an additional 125,300 persons, bringing the total employment provided by these industries to 239,200, or 58 percent of nonagricultural employment. Salaries and wages paid by the gaming, hotel, and tourist industries in 1981 exceeded $1.2 billion. Capital invested by the gaming industry in Nevada in 1981 exceeded $4.1 billion.[77]

It is reasonably clear from these statistics that Nevada has realized both its revenue and economic goals in legalizing casino gaming. The State is arid and following the exhaustion of its gold and silver mines in the late nineteenth century had little in the way of natural resources. Casinos have provided economic opportunities that in all probability would not otherwise have existed, and generate more than half of the State's governmental revenue needs. The record of Atlantic City casino gaming is altogether less clear. While substantial sums, the revenues generated from gaming privilege taxes levied on Atlantic City casinos are small percentages of the State budget. More seriously in view of the Casino Control Act's purpose of fostering the redevelopment of a badly decayed resort and its urban setting, little development has occurred outside the casino/hotel complexes themselves. For all of the jobs and capital investment generated by gaming the Casino Control Act has so far failed to provide Atlantic City with the kind of economic rebirth casinos have given to southern Nevada. The reasons for this failure are complex, and have less to do with the casinos, which are patently successful, than the inability of the governments of Atlantic City and the State of New Jersey to use casino revenues and the casinos' economic contribution as effective redevelopment tools. In December 1984 legislation that requires casinos to pay 1.25 percent of gross win into a Casino Reinvestment Fund was enacted. This bill will produce a projected $1.6 billion in redevelopment funds over a twenty-five-year period: $754 million for Atlantic City; $474 million for the State's eight southern counties; and $425 million for northern New Jersey. Whether New Jersey governments will spend these funds in an effective manner is a question that remains to be answered. We will return to it in Chapter 7.

Although only seven years old, Atlantic City's casino industry has grown to impressive size and makes large revenue and economic contributions. In calendar 1983 the nine operating casinos had 11,890 slot machines and 871 table games. The gross win (player losses) was $1.77 billion. Tax payments to the State's Casino Revenue Fund, which defrays the property taxes, rentals, telephone bills, and utility bills of senior citizens and disabled persons, totaled $139.5 million. Fixed asset investments before accumulated depreciation by the nine operating casinos were accounted at $1.6 billion. The nine operating casinos employed 30,197 persons and paid salaries and wages totaling $482.6 million.[78]

PARI-MUTUEL BETTING

The invention of the pari-mutuel (from the French *pari,* "bet," "wager," "stake," and *mutuel,* "mutual") method of gambling is generally credited to Pierre Oller, the owner of a Paris perfume shop who devised the system in the late 1860s following a series of losses incurred in betting horses at fixed odds against bookmakers in 1865. Oller accused the bookmakers, who then, in France and elsewhere, monopolized horse-race betting, of secretly owning racehorses and running them in their own interest at odds that made it impossible for the public to win. As an alternative to bookmaking Oller proposed to sell tickets on each horse, or betting interest, in a race, with the proceeds, or handle, going into a single fund, or pool. After deducting 5 percent of this pool for operating expenses the remaining, or live, money was to be divided equally among the holders of tickets on the winning horse.[79] Oller's pari-mutuel system had two important differences compared to bookmaking at fixed odds.

Unlike bookmakers, who bet against their clientele and are at risk when their book is unbalanced (i.e., have unequal amounts of money booked on a particular betting interest), the operator of a pari-mutuel system is guaranteed against loss, since he receives a fixed percentage of handle regardless of which betting interest wins.

In pari-mutuel betting bettors wager among themselves, rather than against a bookmaker. Payouts, or winning prices, are a function of the handle less the operator's percentage divided by the number of winning tickets. The odds paid, in other words, are determined by the bettors rather than the bookmakers.

Unlike lotteries or casino gaming, where the outcome of the gambling game itself decides the bet, the objects of pari-mutuel betting are sporting contests—horse and greyhound races and *jai-alai* matches—that are rigorously separated from the conduct of gambling. Horse racing has been part of American life since colonial times, usually in association with legal or illegal commercial betting. In its several forms—the thoroughbred (flat), standardbred (harness), and quarterhorse (sprint) breeds[80] being the most important—horse racing is perhaps the most ritualized of all major sports, and it has generated a subculture with peculiar values and behavioral norms that are the product of a history antedating the United States. Greyhound racing, while dating back at least to a kind of match[81] racing, or coursing, in Elizabethan England, is in its modern form of a field in pursuit of an artificial lure of much more recent origins. In the early twentieth century an American, Owen Patrick Smith, perfected a mechanical hare as a humane alternative to the killing of live hares in coursing events, and with the assistance of this invention greyhound racing developed into a major betting sport following the pari-mutuel legalizations of the Depression era. *Jai-alai* (Basque for "merry festival") originated in the 1600s among the Basques of the western Pyrenees. Curved basket-like bats, or rackets *(cestas),* are used to play a hard ball, the *pelota,* off the floor and walls of a three-sided court in games contested by eight teams playing as either singles or doubles, with seven points normally deciding the bets on each game. The discussion of pari-mutuel betting that follows concerns horse racing, which is by far the largest and geographically the most widespread of the three pari-mutuel industries. (The gambling activities of all three forms are broadly similar; the few points of significant difference between horse racing and the other two are discussed in the notes to this chapter.)

Entry-level Knowledge: A very considerable knowledge of the sports involved is required for more than casual participation in pari-mutuel betting. This entry-level knowledge requirement distinguishes pari-mutuel betting from lotteries and casinos: anyone can buy a lottery ticket or pull the handle of a slot machine. In comparison pari-mutuel betting presents a "closed" aspect to the uninitiated public; the elaborate, ritualized subculture of horse racing and the considerable special knowledge needed to handicap and bet horses are significant barriers to participation, and cause the pari-mutuel sports to interact with society in ways quite dissimilar to lotteries and casinos.

To begin with, a person encountering this form of gambling for the first time must learn the rudiments of an unfamiliar sport; the meaning of an arcane wagering terminology,[82] the by-no-means obvious operation of the tote board; at least something about the information contained in the race program, if not the vastly more detailed and complicated *Racing Form;* and the business-like, no-nonsense process of transacting bets and perhaps cashing winning tickets at the pari-mutuel windows. This is just for openers: there is as much to learn about horse racing as there is about stock or bond markets, and, for bettors inclined to pursue the sport to its higher levels, intellectual challenges rivaling those of option or commodity trading.[83] The beginner must learn all this in the intimidating environment of the racetrack,[84] where self-absorption is the rule among horseplayers and racetrack personnel alike. One's first encounter with haute cuisine or a foreign country are analogous experiences: even if he or she is familiar with other forms of gambling, the novice trackgoer is in fact entering a highly specialized subculture, and the initial reaction is likely to be culture-shock. This structural characteristic of pari-mutuel racing constitutes a marketing problem of the first magnitude for racetracks that have to compete with more accessible State lotteries and casinos; racing industries in New England and the greater New York metropolitan area are in particular finding it difficult to maintain their market shares for this reason.

Paradoxically, however, the extensive knowledge required for entry into pari-mutuel betting, once acquired, is a powerful inducement to habitual and even obsessive, but not compulsive, gambling. Horseplayers, as well as greyhound racing and *jai-alai* bettors, have made a substantial investment of time, money, and mental application in pari-mutuel betting. In the process they have, further, been socialized into a subculture that extends beyond the betting activity itself. Readers who doubt either of these statements are invited to visit a racetrack or *jai-alai* fronton: we are confident that, without prior familiarity, these places will be confusing and palpably foreign—the natives absorbed in unintelligible rituals, and the betting activities themselves incomprehensible. To initiates, however, racetracks, and frontons and OTB offices, are familiar surroundings. The special knowledge horseplayers have gained and the social behavior they have learned can only be exercised in this setting: in other words, the racetrack—unlike the State lottery and to a far greater extent than a casino—becomes a way of life. For this reason, horse-race betting, more than any other form of gambling, is likely to become habitual behavior.

Intrinsic Interest: To a greater degree than any other form of commercial gambling (including counting cards at blackjack and bookmaking on horse racing and other sports) pari-mutuel betting constitutes an intellectual challenge. There are two distinct elements to this activity: (1) handicapping the sporting event—i.e., the horse or greyhound race or *jai-alai* game—and, once this is done, (2) betting, or choosing from the odds and wagers offered the investment that in the bettor's (personal, and highly subjective) opinion will yield the most satisfactory return.

Handicapping is a time-consuming activity requiring the careful analysis of data concerning (for horse races) the ancestry and past performances of each betting interest (i.e., horse and jockey) in the race and the conditions under which these betting interests are to run (weight allowances, kind of race, weather, track condition, the apparent condition of the horse, and so forth). For serious handicappers these data may be very considerable, and the process of collecting, filing, and analyzing data on horses, jockeys (or drivers for standardbreds) and races becomes largely divorced from betting *per se,* and is conducted, of necessity, as a leisure activity at home or somewhere other than the racetrack grounds.

While engaged in handicapping—especially when this is done away from the track—horseplayers are not, in the sense of gambling, for example, at casino games, *in action.* This characteristic of pari-mutuel betting activity encourages obsessive involvement while at the same time militating against compulsive gambling: the betting process itself requires the horseplayer to reflect upon the probable consequences of his gambles.

Pari-mutuel betting differs from other commercial gambling activities in that the odds on any particular betting interest change continuously during the twenty-to-thirty minute interval between races. These changes are reflected on the tote board, which by recording shifts in odds as wagers are made registers the collective betting market opinion in a manner analogous to the stock market ticker-tape. (Bets involving three or more betting interests are an exception to this statement for the technical reason that the number of betting interests in these pools exceeds the tote board's display capacity.) For example, a horse that opens ("the first flash") at even money to win may actually start its race, some twenty or thirty minutes later, at odds of five-to-one. The interpretation of such changing odds is an important consideration in pari-mutuel betting; many horseplayers defer their bets until a minute or so before *post time,* when the pari-mutuel machines are locked and betting for that race is closed. The point being made here is that the process of pari-mutuel betting, unlike all other commercial gambling activities, is, over its entire twenty-to-thirty minute duration, a competition among the bettors. This competition does not determine the outcome of the gambling event (i.e., the horse race), which, like gambling events in casinos or lotteries, is beyond the bettor's control. (A fixed race is of course a different question. In many jurisdictions owners, and often trainers also, are allowed to bet on their own horse. These exceptions notwithstanding, the betting public is not, generally, in a position to influence the performance of horses.) But the competition among bettors does determine the financial value of successful bets as to this outcome—in other words, the odds at which winning bets are paid. This structural characteristic of pari-mutuel betting adds an element of intrinsic interest, competition, that distinguishes horse racing, greyhound racing, and *jai-alai* from all other forms of commercial gambling.[85]

Frequency of Opportunities to Gamble and Payout Intervals: In contrast to both State lottery "instant" games and casino gaming, pari-mutuel betting is characterized by relatively infrequent opportunities to gamble and more lengthy payout intervals. Racing programs commonly consist of nine races at intervals of twenty to thirty minutes. Payouts, while fairly prompt compared to payouts from illegal bookmakers, are not immediate: successful bettors normally have to stand in line to cash winning pari-mutuel tickets, and, in the not unusual case that the outcome of a race is doubtful or contested, this wait may be prolonged. The relative infrequency of opportunities to gamble and cumbersome payout process reduce considerably the rate at which money cycles through pari-mutuel machines in comparison with slot-machine or table gaming.

Off-track betting is characterized by even longer intervals between gambles. New York and Connecticut OTB offices are designed to service a walk-in trade and generally provide no public seating or other amenities to encourage patrons to spend more than a few minutes there. Many OTB bettors make bets on their way to or from work and cash them, if they win, at the same time the following day. The teletheater operated by Connecticut OTB in New Haven and the experimental live televised harness racing programs ("simulcasting") in four New York OTB offices (located on Staten Island and in Suffolk County) have dramatically altered the nature of OTB betting: with live televised racing available bettors tend to remain in OTB offices for the entire race card, and betting resembles on-track activity, with winnings rewagered, or "churned," through the pari-mutuel machines on successive races.

Probability of Winning Individual Bets and Payout Ratios: In many of the States that allow pari-mutuel betting the available wagers range from place or show bets on favorites to triples and other combinations. The likelihood of winning a place or show bet on a favorite is high (in 1981 the percentage of winning favorites at flat—thoroughbred—race tracks ranged from 12 percent to 54 percent, with the average, for 70,882 races, being 32 percent) and the payout ratio correspondingly low. The likelihood of winning a triple bet (which requires the bettor to pick the first three horses, greyhounds, or *jai-alai* teams in the correct order of finish) is much lower and the payout ratio is higher.

In 1980 Hollywood Park, a major racetrack in Southern California, introduced a "pick 6" wager, in which bettors are required to select the winning horses in six consecutive races; in the first fifty-one days it was offered the "pick 6" produced payoffs averaging $80,400, with four payoffs exceeding $300,000. In June 1983 the California Horse Racing Board allowed Hollywood Park to carry over a "pick 6" pool to the following day in the event there are no winners. This carry-over provision is expected to produce payoffs approaching $1 million, making pari-mutuel horse racing competitive with "progressive" slot machine jackpots and all but the highest State lottery Lotto game prizes. The highest pari-mutuel payout in American history was produced by a carry-over "pick 6" pool at the Palm Beach Jai Alai Fronton in West Palm Beach, Florida, on March 1, 1983, when a bettor, or bettors, won $988,326 on a $2 ticket for correctly picking the winning players in the second through the seventh games of that evening's program.

As with casino gaming, the wide ranges of likelihoods of winning individual bets and payout ratios available in pari-mutuel betting accommodate a wide variety of gambling behavior. Provided the bettor is a relatively astute handicapper, betting favorites to win, place, or show is a relatively low-risk form of gambling. Triples and "pick 6" wagers are conversely difficult or impossible to handicap and put the bettor at much higher risk. The individual pari-mutuel sports themselves strongly influence the bettors' choice of wagers: in high-quality thoroughbred horse racing win, place, and show betting usually constitutes a substantial percentage of total handle even when multiple and exotic wagering is offered; in greyhound racing and *jai-alai* multiple and exotic wagers account for most of the betting.

Price: Takeout Percentages and Kinds of Wagers: The rate at which pari-mutuel operations extract money from bettors is more actively controlled by the States than is the case with any other form of commercial gambling. States exercise this control through two distinct but related mechanisms: takeout percentages, or the gross deduction from pari-mutuel pools before distributions to winners, which are normally statutory, and the kinds of wagers a pari-mutuel operation may offer, which is variously governed by statute or direct State regulation. Wagers and takeout percentages at a typical racetrack appear in Table 2.

TABLE 2
TYPICAL PARI-MUTUEL TAKEOUT PERCENTAGES

Kind of Wager	*Takeout (%)*
Win/Place/Show (regular wagers)	17
Daily Double/Exacta (multiple wagers)	19
Triple/Trifecta (exotic wagers)	25

A State that allows racetracks to offer only win, place, and show betting (relatively easy bets to handicap) at a 17 percent takeout will extract money from bettors at a much slower rate than one allowing exotic wagers (which are much more difficult to handicap) at higher takeout percentages. In win, place, and show betting more money (83 percent of the pool in the example in Table 2) is distributed among a large number of bettors; in triple betting less money (75 percent of the pool) is distributed to far fewer bettors, with the result that unsuccessful bettors are rapidly "tapped out." While bettor behavior obviously contributes to the rate at which money is lost in that bettors may choose not to make exotic wagers even if they are offered, it remains true that the authority to decide the kind and price of pari-mutuel gambles resides with the States, which (usually) exercise this authority in detailed laws and regulations.

In contrast to State lotteries, where takeout percentages, though also statutory, have tended to remain relatively constant over time, pari-mutuel takeout percentages are frequently changed. There has been a general tendency for States to increase takeout rates in efforts to extract more revenues from pari-mutuel betting, for distribution to either government or the racing industry. In 1980 the average effective takeout from thoroughbred racing was about 18.5 percent, nearly double the 10 to 11 percent takeouts common prior to World War II. Coincidentally with these increases in takeout, racetrack handle and attendance, which had grown steadily from the end of the war through the mid 1960s, reached plateaus and then began to deteriorate: attendance (gate) at flat (thoroughbred) racetracks peaked at 44,410,124 in 1977 and had declined to 41,706,915 in 1983, while handle, deflated for increases in racing days and expressed in constant (1967) dollars, after growing rapidly through the mid 1950s leveled off in the next decade and following 1965 steeply declined.[86] By the mid 1970s these trends had caused widespread concern that takeout levels were too high. Several major racing States, notably New York and California, experimented with takeout reductions, and economists produced a small but interesting professional literature on optimal takeout rates and the theory of pari-mutuel taxation.[87] The results of these experimental takeout reductions have been inconclusive. In general, racing interests remain convinced that current takeout levels are too high; State governments, however, responsive as always to immediate revenue needs, continue to resist industry efforts to lower takeouts on a permanent basis.[88] Here as elsewhere the revenue imperative is the predominant influence on gambling policy; because of the financial needs of government and the racing industry horseplayers can look forward to further increases in the price of their chosen gambling activity.

Range of Odds and Stakes: Unlike lottery players or casino gamers, horseplayers, and persons who bet on football games or other sports, are betting on the outcome of events that are not *a priori* calculable:

providing the horse race or football game is honest, there is no absolutely certain way to predict which horse or which team is going to win. The odds on such events—in contrast to the odds or probability that "red" will come up at roulette—are subjective. For commercial gambling purposes these subjective probabilities are determined in one of two ways: arbitrarily, by bookmakers, or pari-mutuelly, by the bettors themselves.

Bookmakers begin with a line, or expert opinion, concerning the likely outcome of horse races or football games, and then (carefully) adjust this line to equalize the betting on these events to produce a balanced book.[89] The line for an NFL football game, for example, might have one team to win by seven points. The usual stake is $11 and the usual payout $10, so that if the line perfectly equalizes the betting (that is, makes the outcome of the game appear to be an even money proposition to the book's clientele) the bookmaker will take in $11 on each side of the game, for a total of $22, and once the game is over pay out $21, for a gross revenue (not a profit, since he must cover his expenses) of $1, or 4.4 percent. If the bookmaker's book is not balanced within this very narrow margin of 4.4 percent he is, in effect, gambling against his customers, or setting his subjective opinion about the outcome of the football game against the collective subjective opinion of his clientele. Unbalanced books force bookmakers to gamble that the short money will win; because the outcomes of football games are uncertain the operator of a consistently unbalanced book runs the unacceptable business risk of gambler's ruin, or losses that exceed his assets: sooner or later he will have to shut down his bookmaking operation.

Pari-mutuel betting substitutes for the fixed odds or line set by bookmakers odds that reflect the collective wagering of the investors in pari-mutuel pools. Pari-mutuel odds are therefore in no sense statistical probabilities: prior to the horse race (or other event) these odds reflect the collective market opinion as to the (uncertain) outcome of the race, and after the finishers are known these odds determine the value of successful investments in the various pari-mutuel pools. For example, if there are ten horses in a race, and sixty people bet $2, or $120, on each of the ten horses to win, the total win pool is 10 × $120 = $1,200. As Table 2 shows, the takeout from win pools is commonly 17 percent, which leaves $1,200 × .17 = $204 for the operator (i.e., the racetrack, horsemen, and government) and $996 for the holders of tickets on the winning horse. A total of sixty $2 bets, or $120, was bet on the horse that won. Each of these sixty winning tickets is thus worth $996 divided by $120 = $8.30 for each dollar bet, or $16.60 for each $2 ticket.[90]

Unlike the fixed odds of lotteries or casino games, pari-mutuel odds do not affect all bettors equally. As we have seen, the fixed odds and narrow range of stakes in slot machine gaming produce rates of change in the slot player's worth that are essentially constant, and predictable, for all players. The variable odds and stakes available at table games allow players to vary the rate of change in their net worth by varying their betting strategies; all players, however, choosing similar strategies[91] will over the long term experience similar changes in their net worth. In other words, all players may avail themselves of the range of odds and stakes offered by a casino on an equal basis, the only inequalities being individual choice (some players, for whatever reason, choose to gamble at poor odds) and the fact that at some games the best strategies require sizable bankrolls for what most players would regard as a meaningful return.

In contrast to casino gaming, the outcome of a given strategy of pari-mutuel betting is not a simple function of odds and stakes. Two additional factors must be considered: takeout percentages, which affect all bettors equally, and handicapping skills, which are very unequally shared among the betting population. The effect of takeout on the outcome of pari-mutuel betting is simple enough: regardless of the odds at which winning bets are paid less money is distributed to winners than was initially wagered. Higher takeouts reduce returns on successful bets. For example, in New York it is currently possible to place a win bet on a horse at Yonkers Raceway, where the takeout from win pools is 17 percent, or, alternatively, to place the same win bet on the same horse off-track, at an OTB office, where the takeout from win pools is also 17 percent but an additional statutory surcharge of 5 percent of the total payout (i.e., the original $2 investment plus the amount won) is levied on winning tickets. The practical effect of the so-called 5 percent surcharge is to increase the takeout from off-track win pools to 21.3 percent.[92] If the horse in question wins successful on-track bettors share 83 percent of the pool. Successful off-track bettors share approximately 78.7 percent of the pool; in other words, the price of identical win bets is 4.3 handle points, or 25.3 percent, higher for off-track bettors. As may readily be imagined, the 5 percent surcharge is wildly unpopular with New York horseplayers. The differential takeout it created has had an important social consequence: a resurgence of illegal off-track betting. The law imposing the surcharge in effect established a statutory price advantage for illegal bookmakers, who customarily pay track odds. As a result, small "handbooks" specializing in horse-race bets, whom OTB had largely driven out of business, unexpectedly found their market restored by the New York legislature.[93]

The relation of handicapping skills to pari-mutuel odds, stakes, and takeout percentages is complex. Unlike lotteries or gaming, where similar choices of odds and stakes will over time produce similar outcomes, two horseplayers may bet identical stakes at similar pari-mutuel odds and, depending on their respective handicapping skills, with significantly different results. Expert handicappers will, other things being equal, cash a higher percentage of winning tickets than less astute horseplayers, and, as we can attest from personal experience, persons with no handicapping skills can make a great many bets without winning at all. In comparison with gaming or lotteries, where "red" at roulette or winning lottery prizes appear with calculable frequency regardless of the gambler's skill, pari-mutuel odds and stakes are distinctly undemocratic. Pari-mutuel horse racing includes an aristocracy of horseplayers: the ones who can pick winners.

New York provides some convenient evidence of the practical consequences of the importance of handicapping skills. OTB and New York racetracks combine on-track and off-track wagers on identical betting interests into common pools, which, after the deduction of takeout percentages, are distributed to the holders of winning tickets. As a result of this procedure a steady, continuous transfer of dollars from off-track to on-track bettors occurs: for reasons that certainly include the facts that, first, due to the surcharge no knowledgeable horseplayer would bet at OTB if he could get to the track; second, more current and complete racing information (track conditions, the appearance of the horse, and so forth) is available on-track; and third, consequently the strong probability that the on-track betting population are on balance more accurate handicappers than their off-track counterparts, on-track bettors win disproportionate amounts of combined on-track and off-track pools. OTB bettors, in other words, subsidize the better-informed and more expert on-track horseplayers.[94]

The degree to which skill is a factor in pari-mutuel betting outcomes has already been touched upon in connection with odds and stakes. A different perspective on the efficacy of skill in pari-mutuel betting is provided by professional economists. In the 1960s and 1970s the vogue for the efficient market theory associated with the Center for Research in Security Prices at the University of Chicago produced several analyses of pari-mutuel betting markets designed to answer the question of whether these markets are efficient, i.e., whether all information affecting pari-mutuel odds is discounted and reflected so quickly on racetrack tote boards that at the close of betting the subjective probabilities of (or odds on) each betting interest conform closely enough to empirical results that no individual investor (or bettor) in this market can consistently obtain an edge, or advantage—or, in horse-racing parlance, find and profit from "overlays," or undervalued horses.[95] We find the evidence for weak efficiency—or limited opportunities for superior betting performance—fairly convincing. Not surprisingly, this conclusion agrees with our observations over a period of years of an admittedly very small number of highly sophisticated horseplayers who apparently earn substantial incomes from betting. We believe skill at handicapping plays a large enough role in determining pari-mutuel betting outcomes to enable good handicappers to significantly outperform poor handicappers. The question is whether this margin of superiority is sufficient, at all but the highest levels of proficiency, to overcome the high takeout that constitutes the price of pari-mutuel wagers. Without attempting here to quantify our opinion, we tentatively conclude that for the majority of even quite expert handicappers the takeout levels prevailing in modern America pari-mutuel betting do prevent consistent long-term wagering gains. Other things being equal, then, for all but a tiny minority of truly expert horseplayers, increasing levels of financial investment in pari-mutuel betting will result in increasingly heavy losses.

Credit and Cash: In the United States pari-mutuel betting is available only on a cash basis. The problems and potential for abuse associated with credit play at casino games are thus not characteristic of pari-mutuel betting activities. The unavailability of credit at racetracks and frontons—and OTB offices—does however contribute to illegal bookmaking, in that bookmakers customarily allow their regular customers to bet on credit. In the case of on-track betting this is a relatively minor consideration, since on-track pari-mutuel betting and off-track bookmaking are in several other important respects very imperfect substitutes. OTB is a different matter: one of the justifications for legalizing off-track betting was to curb illegal gambling by providing a competitive legal alternative to bookmakers. To the extent that the ability to extend credit constitutes a competitive advantage for bookmakers this structural characteristic of legal off-track betting has impaired OTB's effectiveness in accomplishing one of its statutory purposes. (The 5 percent surcharge is a much more important reason for OTB's limited effectiveness in reducing illegal betting.)

The Context of Pari-mutuel Betting

Place: Racetracks share with casinos, and are distinguished from State lotteries and OTB by, significant geographic and demographic barriers to regular participation in the gambling activities they provide. Pari-mutuel laws typically restrict wagering to the racetrack grounds. This restriction has had several consequences: first, it has limited regular attendance at racetracks to persons living in relative geographic proximity with the financial means and leisure time to make a habit of spending afternoons or evenings at the races. Even today, with some 240 racetracks and frontons operating in the United States, these geographic and demographic barriers to regular pari-mutuel betting remain effective for large numbers of Americans. The inevitable result, when coupled with the widespread popularity of racing and the ever more general American propensity to gamble, has been the creation of substantial demand for illegal off-track bookmaking.

In the absence of effective enforcement of antibookmaking laws illegal bookmaking on horse racing has flourished. Partly in response to this situation, the State of New York authorized in 1970 the first legal off-track pari-mutuel betting operation in modern American history. As originally enacted, the New York off-track betting law's purpose was twofold: to raise government revenue and to reduce illegal gambling on horse races. OTB effectively eliminated the geographic and demographic barriers to horse-race betting. At present six regional public-benefit off-track betting corporations offer pari-mutuel wagers identical to those available at New York racetracks in some 330 neighborhood offices and through telephone deposit account betting services. A single agency of the State of Connecticut operates a similar OTB system. In both States OTB has succeeded in accomplishing its revenue goals: in 1980 New York and Connecticut OTB distributed $161 million to State, county, and municipal governments, and an additional $85 million to the racing industry. As has already been indicated, OTB has been less successful in terms of its second statutory purpose of reducing illegal gambling. The reasons for this failure are examined below.

In an era of widespread commercial gambling legalizations the continuing geographic and demographic barriers (outside New York and Connecticut) to pari-mutuel betting are increasingly anachronistic. Growing competition from other forms of gambling is eroding racetrack handles and attendance in many markets. This erosion is reducing gross pari-mutuel revenues at the same time State and local governments, many of which are experiencing severe financial difficulties, are looking with renewed appetites to gambling as a source of "painless" taxes. The resulting squeeze on pari-mutuel revenue endangers racetracks located in older markets that are saturated with betting opportunities and potentially endangers the vast racehorse breeding industry.

In these circumstances it seems to us inevitable that new pari-mutuel betting operations will be authorized, as the only practical method of relieving the squeeze on revenues many governments consider essential. Five major legalizations have in fact occurred in the past two years: Minnesota and Oklahoma authorized pari-mutuel horse racing in November 1982; Iowa followed suit in June 1983; in June 1984 a local (Jefferson

County) election approved a referendum permitting pari-mutuel horse racing in Birmingham, Alabama; and in November 1984 Missouri voters likewise approved pari-mutuel horse racing. The impending expansion of pari-mutuel betting will take two forms: first, racetracks will be legalized by States that do not now (1983) allow this form of gambling; and second, off-track betting, and live televised racing in conjunction with betting operations (''simulcasting''), will be authorized by jurisdictions in which pari-mutuel betting is presently allowed.

Situation or Environment: Like casinos, and unlike State lotteries, racetracks and frontons—and to a much lesser degree OTB offices—are hermetic environments enclosed by social boundaries that seal their inhabitants, the horseplayers, owners, trainers, jockeys or drivers, and racetrack personnel, off from the real world. The racetrack is an alternative reality. Within it a unique social organization and symbolic systems of meaning are generated from the game of pari-mutuel racing. This form of gambling is, in Goffman's terms, a ''world-building'' game: its formal rules and structural characteristics generate a closed and internally consistent society. Entering this society the bettor sheds his real-world self and assumes a new identity: that of *horseplayer.* In this role he is integrated into the racetrack-world as a respected member of this gambling-generated subculture.

Ownership and Operation: The depression-era legalizations that are the origin of modern pari-mutuel racing and *jai-alai* essentially enabled existing, privately owned sports (horse racing, greyhound racing, and *jai-alai*) to conduct legal pari-mutuel betting in exchange for a revenue contribution to government in the form of pari-mutuel tax. The States assumed a regulatory responsibility for pari-mutuel betting, but declined operational roles or equity participation in the commercial gambling industries they authorized. While not wholly free of criminal elements pari-mutuel racing and *jai-alai* were never dominated by organized crime, and, while lightly regulated in comparison with casino gaming, have not posed intractable problems of criminal ownership and operation.

For both economic and political reasons, however, the pari-mutuel industries appear to be evolving from purely private enterprise into quasi, or even outright, governmental entities. Along the eastern seaboard and in parts of the Middle West pari-mutuel horse racing is a mature and perhaps a declining industry. A consolidation involving the closing of smaller, uneconomic tracks has been underway since the mid 1970s, and appears likely to continue. In these circumstances new racetrack construction cannot be funded by the private sector. The States' needs for pari-mutuel revenues are however more pressing than ever, and these needs are reinforced by pressure from breeding interests for additional racing opportunities. In 1976 the combined operation of these factors produced the Meadowlands, a major harness- and flat-racing facility financed by the State of New Jersey, which is using the pari-mutuel revenue generated from the Meadowlands's racing operations to pay the capital construction costs of the stadium and arena operated by the New Jersey Sports and Exposition Authority. In New York State political factors have combined with the racing industry's economic problems to produce similar results: the major thoroughbred racetracks, Belmont Park, Aqueduct, and Saratoga, are operated by the non-profit, State-franchised New York Racing Association (NYRA), and when the legislature, in response to one of New York City's periodic fiscal crises, legalized off-track betting as a means of raising municipal revenues it created a governmental public benefit corporation to conduct this form of commercial gambling.[96] It appears certain that this shifting of segments of the pari-mutuel betting industries from the private to the public sector will continue.

Purpose: Unlike State lotteries, which initially were authorized solely to raise government funds, pari-mutuel betting serves both revenue and economic purposes. Following the legalization of pari-mutuel betting by a number of States during the Depression[97] racetracks—and in Florida *jai-alai* frontons—enjoyed an effective monopoly on legal commercial gambling outside Nevada for three decades. With the statutory right to exploit sizable geographic markets free of legal competition the racing industry assumed impressive dimensions, which, despite some contraction in the increasingly competitive environment of the late 1970s and 1980s, are largely preserved today.[98]

In 1983 pari-mutuel betting was legal in 34 States with 73 percent of the total population. Pari-mutuel racing was conducted at 112 flat (thoroughbred and/or quarterhorse) racetracks, 67 harness (standardbred) racetracks, 7 off-track betting operations, 48 greyhound racetracks, and 13 *jai-alai* frontons. Attendance at these facilities in 1983 totaled 98.6 million. Handle, or gross wagering, was $14.6 billion. Retention, or gross win (bettor losses), was approximately $2.8 billion. Of this amount, $854.9 million, or 30 percent, was distributed to State and local governments. The balance, $1.97 billion, was shared among racetrack, OTB, and fronton operators, horse owners and breeders, dog owners and breeders, and others working in the pari-mutuel industries.[99]

The Horse Industry

Like casino gaming, which in Nevada makes a large indirect contribution to the economy by stimulating a massive tourist industry, pari-mutuel betting supports a major economic activity not directly involved with gambling: the racehorse industry, an important component of American agribusiness. The horse industry comprises two overlapping but broadly distinguishable interests: breeders, whose farms produce thoroughbred, standardbred, and quarterhorse foals; and owners and trainers, who purchase these foals as yearlings, race them as two-year-olds, three-year-olds, and so forth, and, in the event a horse establishes breeding value by winning races, close the cycle by returning it, for a financial consideration that in the case of a major stakes winner may be very substantial, to a farm for breeding purposes.

Owners and trainers share directly in pari-mutuel retention through purses, which in most States are distributed to the first three finishers and averaged 5.9 percent of handle, or approximately $706 million, in 1983.[100]

Breeders likewise share directly (though to a much lesser extent) in pari-mutuel retention in the form of distributions to State breeding funds, which subsidize State breeding industries. In 1982 distributions from pari-mutuel wagers to breeding funds in twenty-two States totaled an estimated $42 million, or approximately 0.35 percent of handle.[101] Horse breeding is a major industry, directly employing eighty thousand people and representing (in 1981) estimated invested capital of $10 billion.[102] The breeders' principal interest in pari-mutuel betting is however indirect: the value of the agricultural commodity they produce, thoroughbred, standardbred, and quarterhorse foals, is predicated on the continuing opportunity to enter horses in races on which pari-mutuel betting is allowed. In macro-economic terms, racetracks are the breeding industry's showcases and pari-mutuel betting is the activity that supports the value of racehorses.[103]

During the 1970s the revenue and economic purposes of pari-mutuel betting laws began to come into serious conflict. The States, responding to their own and the racing industry's revenue needs, continued to raise effective takeout rates while diverting hundreds of millions of dollars in pari-mutuel taxes to racetracks and horsemen. The allocation of pari-mutuel revenue between public use and racing industry interests is a fairly straightforward question of public policy that legislatures are, presumably, equipped to answer in the public interest. The economic consequences of high takeout levels are somewhat more complex. As a method of taxation, pari-mutuel commission (the State tax component of takeout) has a peculiar characteristic: because it is a percentage of the *gross* wagering dollar this tax may be exacted from the bettor without regard to the cost to racetracks of producing it. In other words, government can, literally, raise takeout levels to the point where pari-mutuel betting becomes completely uneconomic, for operators and bettors alike, without feeling the adverse effects of declining sales (or in this case handles) and rising operator costs that normally act as a brake on excessive taxation. If the revenue needs of government, or even of a segment of the racing industry itself, are allowed to dominate pari-mutuel tax policy to the exclusion of other considerations the enormous economic contribution made by pari-mutuel betting will be endangered. The self-defeating parallel is clear: these same short-term revenue considerations have been allowed to frustrate an important social purpose of New York off-track betting by imposing a surcharge on off-track payouts that created a statutory price advantage for illegal bookmakers.

We began this chapter with the observation that while not all games are gambling all gambling is fundamentally a game. All gambling entails financial risk on an event of uncertain outcome, with, usually but in varying degrees, the attendant possibility of ruin. There the similarity among the various forms of commercial gambling ends. To gamblers each game presents a set of distinguishing characteristics and contextual variables that constitute a unique activity. The implications of this for understanding individual gambling motivations and behaviors are profound, and will be the subject of the next chapter.

The unique character of lotteries, casinos, and pari-mutuel betting has equally important implications for public policy. Gambling is a matter of personal choice, but the business of risk—the conduct of legal commercial gambling—is governed, at least *pro forma* and usually in fact, by State governments that for better or worse exercise considerable control over the social outcome of these rapidly expanding enterprises. Privately owned commercial gambling businesses have a fairly narrow responsibility: to maximize returns to shareholders within the constraints of enabling gambling laws. The situation with respect to State-operated commercial gambling is less clear. Government bears a much larger and more complex burden. It must ensure, to the best of its sometimes limited abilities and always finite resources, that commercial gambling is conducted in the public interest. Leaving aside for the moment the question of what exactly the public interest in commercial gambling is, we can examine, briefly, the basis for government's authority in this area and some principles by which that authority can most effectively be exercised.

The fundamental principle upon which government control of commercial gambling rests is that the conduct of a gambling business is a privilege and not a right. This is the true significance of statutory and constitutional prohibitions: commercial gambling is still generally illegal *except* when States specifically authorize it. In exchange for granting a commercial gambling franchise the States may bind the franchisee to public purposes and establish procedures to make sure these purposes are realized. That is, in theory; in practice, as has been indicated in this chapter and will be demonstrated at greater length below, the purposes

for which States have made exceptions to gambling prohibitions are often contradictory, and the regulatory mechanisms of gambling control very often leave much to be desired. It may be that some of the problems raised by the acceptance of commercial gambling in mainstream America will prove to have no clear solutions, but this review of the structures and contexts of lotteries, casinos, and pari-mutuel betting provides us with some general conclusions regarding the interactions between gambling and society.

First, and perhaps most importantly, the revenue imperative emerges as the single most powerful influence on the evolution of commercial gambling. Time and again—in horse racing, where revenue needs have pushed takeouts to economically destructive levels; in State lottery numbers games and governmental off-track betting, where these same revenue needs outweigh the social consideration of curbing illegal gambling; in gaming, where revenue and economic contributions made by casinos legitimate organized crime interests and objections to the licensing of patently unfit operators are ignored by corporations grown powerful enough to have their way with self-proclaimed "stringent" government regulators—the revenue imperative is for all practic[al] purposes governing. There is no reason to suppose this will chang[e]. American jurisdictions that allow commercial gambling will do s[o] regardless of stated purposes and justifications—primarily to gene[rate] revenues. Even where longer-term economic considerations exist and recognized by enlightened governments and voters, money—and us[ually] money in the short-term, money to close this election-year's b[udget] gap—will continue to dictate gambling policy.

Second, the "pariah" label that has been affixed to gamblin[g] longer accurate. Lotteries and OTB are owned and operated by g[overn]ment, and can hardly be called pariahs. Pari-mutuel horse [racing,] especially thoroughbred racing, is conducted by the American e[stablish]ment. Government is the principal beneficiary of pari-mutue[l] revenue and the sole beneficiary of lottery gambling, and it is [...] continue to regard either of these commercial activities as [...] beyond the pale of the normal economy. The casino gaming [...] increasingly dominated by publicly held corporations such as [...] Holiday Inns with credentials indistinguishable from the ge[neral] American business, and, while the tainted character of [...] involved in gaming is still an issue, casinos are now just an [...] provided by diversified leisure conglomerates. Commerci[al] no longer a pariah. It is a legitimate business.

Third, the excessive attention paid to such "human-i[...] as overnight lottery millionaires, compulsive gamblers, a[...] stories of organized crime's involvement with legal and [...]

continues to obscure the tremendous social and economic implications of widespread legalization. The jobs, general economic contributions (and sometimes attendant dislocations), and cultural and subcultural changes now taking place as the result of enabling laws are by and large either ignored or disposed of with lip service. The legalization of OTB in New York is a prime example. As originally enacted, the off-track betting law returned only 1 to 1.5 percent of handle to the racing industry at the same time OTB was drastically restructuring the market for horse-race wagering. Had the State—with OTB's support—not increased the industry's claim on off-track handle a serious contraction of New York's racetrack operations would almost certainly have occurred, with ripple-through effects on horse owners, trainers, breeders, backstretch personnel, and the State itself, which enjoys large percentages of on-track handle dollars. Gambling legalizations are not simple laws. They have manifold and sometimes unforeseeable consequences, and deserve the most informed and disinterested scrutiny.

Finally, the nature and seriousness of the dilemma posed by organized crime's participation in the gaming industry is not widely enough understood. The problem is not bad men with guns; it is that tainted corporate interests, able to command the finest managerial, financial, and legal talent in the world, have been grandfathered by gaming laws into the American economic system and are becoming indistinguishable from legitimate businesses. The only bar to the entry of these profoundly criminal interests into the mainstream American economy is an ill-paid and in terms of native talent and ability often disastrously overmatched bureaucracy appointed by elected officials who are themselves vulnerable to the political pressures all corporations, good and bad, can so effectively bring to bear on government's decisionmaking process. As with other gambling issues, the problem of organized crime in the gaming industry resists simple solution, but perhaps if the intractible nature of the difficulty is more widely perceived politically motivated rhetoric about "tough" casino control laws will no longer be mistaken by the public for an answer.

NOTES

1. "Teletrack," a trademark of General Instrument Corporation, which operates is unique facility for the State's off-track betting system.

2. From an August 1982 Gallup poll commissioned by *Gaming Business Magazine.* ward J. Klein and Gary Selesner, "Results of the First Gallup Organization Study of lic Attitudes Toward Legalized Gambling," *Gaming Business Magazine,* July 1983, 19–21. A national sample of 1,564 persons 18 or more years of age were interviewed

by telephone. The figure of 66 million adults is apparently understated by the omission of persons who bet greyhounds but not at least one of the following: horses, *jai-alai,* professional sports, casinos, or lotteries.

3. This figure is *handle,* or gross amount wagered. The collective *bankroll* of these 66 million gamblers, or the disposable income put at risk, was considerably less and may very roughly be estimated at $4.1 billion for pari-mutuel betting, $18 billion for casinos, and $5 billion for State lotteries for a total collective bankroll of $27 billion. For a more complete discussion of the concepts of handle and bankroll see Appendix.

4. See Appendix, Table A-1.

5. For the role of the Progressive reform movement in the enactment of Prohibition see James H. Timberlake, *Prohibition and the Progressive Movement, 1900–1920* (Cambridge, Mass.: Harvard University Press, 1963).

6. Illegal numbers are distinguished from legal numbers by the fact that winning numbers are not determined by the lottery operator; three digits of the day's pari-mutuel handle at a designated racetrack are commonly used for this purpose. State numbers games make their own determination of winners, often promoting the game by turning these drawings into evening television shows or other media events. In either case, the chance of winning is independent of player skill.

7. Arizona (1981), Colorado (1982), Connecticut (1971), Delaware (1973), Illinois (1974), Maine (1974), Maryland (1972), Massachusetts (1971), Michigan (1972), New Hampshire (1963), New Jersey (1970), New York (1967), Ohio (1973), Pennsylvania (1971), Rhode Island (1974), Vermont (1977), and Washington (1982). On November 6, 1984, four more State lotteries were authorized. Voters in California, Missouri, Oregon, and West Virginia approved constitutional amendments that either mandate or authorize State-operated lotteries. Dates indicate when lotteries were authorized; in some States the date of implementation is later.

8. Blakey, *Development of the Law of Gambling,* p. 224. See also R. Clay Sprowls, "On the Terms of the New York State Lottery," *National Tax Journal* 23 (March 1970):74–82, for an analysis of the original New York lottery in terms of price (expected value), probability of winning any prize, prize structure, changes in these terms made in 1969, and a comparison with two French lotteries and the Irish Sweepstakes.

9. Only 240 prizes were awarded for each one million tickets purchased in the original New York lottery. Sprowls, "New York State Lottery," pp. 75–76.

10. Council of State Governments, *Gambling: A Source of State Revenue* (Columbus, Ohio: Council of State Governments, 1973), p. 16; Weinstein and Deitch, *Impact of Legalized Gambling,* pp. 60–61.

11. The role of government-authorized private lotteries in colonial and earlier United States history is reviewed in some detail in G. Robert Blakey, "State Conducted Lotteries: History, Problems," *Journal of Social Issues* 35 (Summer 1979):62–71. Robert R. Kinsey, "The Role of Lotteries in Public Finance," *National Tax Journal* 16 (March 1963):11–19, explores the revenue potential of a national lottery along the lines of British soccer pools, and estimates the resulting net federal lottery revenues at $1.75 billion.

12. Skolnick, *House of Cards,* pp. 333, 344–46. Skolnick's insight involves two separate considerations: *government revenues* and *economic contribution.* These imperatives may conflict: a State may tax legal gambling at excessively high rates in response to immediate revenue needs to the point of making gambling operations unprofitable, thereby endangering their economic (jobs, capital spending, etc.) contribution.

13. New Jersey State Lottery, *Annual Report* (1980), p. 4.

14. Weinstein and Deitch, *Impact of Legalized Gambling,* p. 61.

15. Blakey, *Development of the Law of Gambling,* p. 227.

16. New Jersey State Lottery, *Annual Report* (1980), p. 4.

17. Ibid., p. 5.

18. By commentators, not by the vendors who design lottery games. Lottery tickets are highly evolved products that incorporate sophisticated marketing techniques and state-of-the-art security and production technology. Like other characteristics of State lotteries, tickets are dynamic: the ones in use today bear little resemblance to those sold by the New Hampshire Sweepstakes in 1964. As discussed in the text, many of the present functions of lottery tickets may in the next few years be transferred to video gaming devices, which would then become the medium through which players interact with lottery games.

19. Illinois State Lottery, *Third Annual Report* (July 1, 1976–June 30, 1977).

20. Vermont Lottery Commission, *Annual Report* (1978).

21. New Jersey State Lottery, *Annual Report* (1980), p. 5.

22. Ibid. (1977), p. 2.

23. *New York Daily News,* "City to Get Video Poker," August 19, 1981.

24. *New York Times,* "New State Gaming Plan Runs into Legal Tangle," August 20, 1981. The attorney general subsequently informed the lottery director that "in my opinion, the specific games described to us are prohibited by both the Constitution of the State of New York and by its statutory law." Letter from Robert Abrams, attorney general, State of New York, to John D. Quinn, director, New York State Lottery, September 8, 1981.

25. Irwin I. Kimmelman, attorney general, State of New Jersey, Formal Opinion No. 5—1982, June 22, 1982.

26. *Atlantic City Press,* "Kean's Pen Stroke Zaps Video Lottery," March 2, 1983. This newspaper reported the investigation of the lottery commission chairman, Reese Palley, in very complete fashion.

27. John J. Easton, Jr., attorney general, State of Vermont, Opinion No. 83-9, September 13, 1982.

28. *Gaming Business Magazine,* August 1982, p. 39.

29. Public Gaming Research Institute, *Public Gaming Newsletter* 11 (August 1983).

30. Terri La Fleur, "GB Lottery Report: The VLT Phenomenon," *Gaming Business Magazine,* June 1984, pp. 11–12.

31. Claudia Waterloo, "Video Lottery Test in Illinois Attracts Players—and Critics," *Wall Street Journal,* August 24, 1984.

32. Much larger prizes have been awarded in lotteries in other countries. On December 22, 1983, the national lottery of Spain in the Christmas drawing awarded $73 million as the first prize ("El Gordo"—"the Fat One"). Full tickets in this drawing cost approximately $158 and are divisible into 10 parts, which are in turn often shared out among numerous players; the $73 million first prize was paid out to holders of 46 tickets with the five-digit winning number, 53288. *New York Times,* "Lottery's 'Fat One' Showers Cash on Spain," December 23, 1983. A prize of $40 million was won by Michael Wittkowski, a printer, in an Illinois Lottery Lotto drawing on September 3, 1984.

33. Or, in the case of the Washington, D.C., Lottery, of the District of Columbia.

34. The off-track betting system of Connecticut and the public benefit off-track betting corporations in New York are the other contemporary instances of government ownership and operation of commercial gambling.

35. This statement is true as a practical matter for all games currently offered by State lotteries. It would not necessarily be true of some other forms of commercial

gambling. Bets on single football games at fixed odds—"head-to-head" betting against bookmakers—produce narrow gross margins, perhaps less than 2 percent and not more than 4.5 percent, and would be highly risky businesses for States, or anyone else, to operate. Legally as well as practically, risk was a factor in the decision of the Delaware State Lottery to cancel its December 12, 1976, multiple-choice fixed-odds sports card game, "Touchdown II." The betting line established by the lottery varied from the line offered by local bookmakers, and this difference was widely publicized by the sporting press. A large amount ($95,929, compared to $33,134 in the previous week's game) was wagered against the lottery, reportedly by professional gamblers; the lottery and the State of Delaware became nervous about the outcome. "Touchdown II" was cancelled because of this nervousness, and the lottery attempted to refund the bets on this game. In the event had "Touchdown II" been played the lottery would have won: Delaware's attorney general ruled that the State was required to pay the advertized prizes, which totaled $67,000, or 70 percent of the $95,000 wagered. This exceeded the statutory maximum 45 percent return to winners in Delaware lottery games and did not allow the lottery to make statutory distributions to the State General Fund (30 percent) and lottery agents (5 percent). Partly for this reason "Touchdown II" was declared to be in violation of Delaware's lottery law (29 Del. C. Sections 4805(a)(11) and 4815) by the United States District Court for the District of Delaware. See Marvin R. Brams and Harmon Carey, "The Delaware Lotteries: From Failure to Success" (paper presented at the Third Annual Conference on Gambling, University of Nevada, Las Vegas, December, 1976); and Opinion, Civil Action No. 76–273, United States District Court for the District of Delaware, Wilmington, Del., August 11, 1977, Stapleton, District Judge.

36. Frederick D. Stocker, "State Sponsored Gambling as a Source of Public Revenue," *National Tax Journal* 25 (September 1972):437–41.

37. The disposition of lottery gross wagering, or handle, is statutory. On average, these laws allocate 54 percent of the handle dollar to expenses and government revenue and 46 percent to prizes. See the Appendix for a comparison of these distributions to those in other forms of gambling.

38. By the same token there is a cultural dimension to what is usually regarded as the exclusively economic question of whether lotteries are fair. For a representative statement of the narrowly economic view of the fairness of lotteries, and by extension of all commercial gambling, see Sprowls, "On the Terms of the New York State Lottery," p. 75. "In order for a lottery entrepreneur to cover costs and make a profit, the lottery must be unfair. The total paid out in prizes must be less than the total revenue derived from tickets, and the ratio of these two totals is the expected value—a measure of the worth of an individual ticket or of the fairness of the lottery. . . ." Sprowls, unlike many critics of gambling, realizes that "the fact that lotteries are unfair is trivial."

39. Kallick, "Survey of American Gambling," in *Gambling in America,* Appendix 2, pp. 104–14.

40. Michael H. Spiro, "On the Tax Incidence of the Pennsylvania Lottery," *National Tax Journal* 27 (March 1974):57–61.

41. Roger E. Brinner and Charles T. Clotfelter, "An Economic Appraisal of State Lotteries," *National Tax Journal* 28 (December 1975):395–404.

42. Scientific Games, *Washington State Lottery: Preliminary Analysis of Lottery Players* (Norcross, Ga.: Scientific Games, Inc., 1983), Version I. Of those questioned about household income 22.7 percent did not respond. This was the highest incidence of nonresponse in the survey. In general, the survey results indicate persons with very low education and income did not participate in the lottery at above average (in proportion to their representation in the general population) rates and suggest above average participa-

tion by persons with annual incomes of $25,000 to $35,000. See as well "Washington State Keeps Demographic Tabs on Instant Lottery Players," *Public Gaming Magazine,* February 1982. Scientific Games is a subsidiary of Bally Manufacturing Company and the Washington lottery's vendor.

43. The chairman of the New Jersey State Lottery Commission, Reese Palley, pleaded not guilty to a thirteen-count indictment alleging forgery, conspiracy, and the fabrication of evidence to cloak conflict of interest charges arising from Palley's relationships with Syntech International Inc., a vendor which had bid on a proposal to provide the lottery with one hundred video lottery devices. The grand jury that indicted Palley found nothing illegal concerning the apparent conflicts of interest Palley allegedly tried to cover up. "Palley Pleads Innocent at Brief Arraignment," *Atlantic City Press,* May 10, 1983. This newspaper provided very complete coverage of the New Jersey Lottery video game episode.

44. With the exception of Washington State.

45. This revenue is, of course, used for various purposes by individual lottery States. New York's constitution requires lottery revenues to be used in aid of education, while Pennsylvania State lottery revenues are earmarked for the benefit of Pennsylvania senior citizens, and so forth. Some States have established lotteries for special interests. In 1979, for example, Massachusetts created the Massachusetts Arts Lottery, which, after some initial difficulties, generated $10 million in the first half of 1983 for the support of local arts projects in Massachusetts. "Gambling Foots the Bill for Massachusetts Arts," *New York Times,* July 17, 1983.

46. For the history of numbers or policy consult Lawrence J. Kaplan and James M. Maher, Economics of the Numbers Game," *American Journal of Economics and Sociology* 29 (October 1970):391–408; Sullivan, *By Chance a Winner;* Ezell, *Fortune's Merry Wheel;* Bender, *Tickets to Fortune;* Mark H. Haller, "Bootleggers and American Gambling 1920–1950," in *Gambling in America,* Appendix 1, pp. 102–43.

47. Zvi Adar, "Efficiency and Equity of State Lotteries," in *Gambling in America,* Appendix 1, pp. 789-804, discusses the poor substitutability of State lottery games for illegal numbers.

48. The combined vote on November 6, 1984, on constitutional amendments mandating or authorizing State lotteries in California, Missouri, Oregon, and West Virginia was 7,343,122 *For* and 4,812,541 *Against.* By State the voting was California: 5,248,052 *For* and 3,812,402 *Against;* Oregon: 740,940 *For* and 379,995 *Against;* Missouri: 1,354,120 *For* and 620,144 *Against;* and West Virginia: 424,965 *For* and 215,006 *Against.* (Returns were supplied by the various secretaries of state.)

49. *Pai gow* is dealt in a number of Nevada casinos because of its popularity with the Oriental community. The interested reader may consult Michael J. Musante, *Pai Gow* (Las Vegas: MJM Enterprises, 1981). There is a computer-aided mathematical analysis of *pai gow:* John M. Gwynn, "An Optimal Strategy for the Game of Pai Gow," in *The Gambling Papers,* ed. Eadington, 13:28–45.

50. In American casinos roulette wheels normally have double zeros, making their odds less favorable than the single-zero wheels used in most European casinos. Keno, bingo, *pai gow,* bookmaking, and pari-mutuel *jai-alai* are legal in Nevada but not in Atlantic City.

51. The law of independent trials states that the outcome of an event in a series is independent of preceding events. For example, in a game consisting of bets on successive tosses of a coin the outcome of a particular toss is not affected by preceding tosses in the series; because "heads" comes up fifty times in a row does not mean "tails" is more likely than "heads" on the fifty-first toss. Many card games violate this law. In blackjack,

for example, the likelihood of drawing an ace is dependent on the number of aces already dealt; in single-deck games the task of keeping count of how many aces, and other cards, have been dealt is not difficult, and this count can be used to advantage by a fairly large number of players. As a result single-deck blackjack games are rarely encountered.

52. The clearest conveniently available description of such *player rating systems* is Bill Friedman, *Casino Management* (Secaucus, N.J.: Lyle Stuart, 1974), pp. 113–47. *Rouge et Noir News* and *Rouge et Noir Resort Management Report,* gaming industry newsletters published monthly, regularly evaluate casino-player rating systems from both the player's and the casino's perspective.

53. This account simplifies the Resorts, Merck, and Casino Control Commission staff table minimum proposals, which provided for different percentages of tables to post varying minimums at different times of day and on weekends and holidays. For a more detailed account see *Rouge et Noir News* 10 (June 15, 1978):2–10, and subsequent issues, especially September, October, and November 1978. There is a short summary of this episode in Gigi Mahon, *The Company That Bought the Boardwalk* (New York: Random House, 1980), pp. 160–62.

54. New Jersey does set a minimum price for slot-machine gaming by requiring slot machines to pay back a minimum 83 percent of handle. Casino Control Act, Article 7, S. 5:12–100 (e). Nevada operators are free to set their own slot payback percentages, which appear to range from 85 percent to 97 percent. We have used 14 percent as the average Nevada operator retention from slot handle. For a more detailed discussion of slot-machine handle and retention see the Appendix.

55. Atlantic City casinos are required to report slot handle. Handle statistics are not publicly available for Nevada slot machines. Nevada slot handle is estimated in the Appendix, Table A-2.

56. The standard work on the mathematics of games of chance and skill is Richard A. Epstein, *The Theory of Gambling and Statistical Logic* (New York: Academic Press, 1967), which assumes a knowledge of basic calculus. Of many popular treatments Allan N. Wilson, *The Casino Gambler's Guide* (New York: Harper & Row, 1970) is clearly written and widely available.

57. See the Appendix for a more detailed discussion and the derivation of these numbers.

58. The price of casino gaming, and of other forms of gambling, may alternatively be considered to be the percentage of the players' collective *bankroll* left in the casino, racetrack, or lottery. In the case of casinos this is typically 18 percent to 20 percent. The estimation of the collective bankroll of horseplayers depends on the "churn factor" one assigns to pari-mutuel handles. Racetrack operators commonly estimate churn at from three to five times bankroll. A recent theoretical mathematical analysis suggests a much lower factor of 1.7 percent. Killingsworth, Liddy & Co., *The Impacts of Reducing the Takeout* (Arlington, Mass.: Killingsworth, Liddy & Co., 1980), Appendices, pp. A1–A6. We do not have a high enough degree of confidence in any of these estimated churn factors to make a comparison of the price of gaming and pari-mutuel betting through bankrolls worthwhile. See the Appendix for a further discussion.

59. The price sensitivity of casino players would make an interesting study. It seems clear that the tremendous increase in the popularity of blackjack is due to the publicity given to card-counting systems, which reduce the house edge, and hence the price, of this game. European or single-zero roulette wheels, which cut the price of American or double-zero roulette in half, have been introduced in Atlantic City, and a comparison of the drop and win at these wheels compared to double-zero wheels would perhaps yield some useful information about price elasticities of table games.

60. Annual reports for the year ended December 31, 1981, filed with the Casino Control Commission of the State of New Jersey: Caesars Boardwalk Regency Hotel/ Casino and Harrah's Marina Hotel Casino, Schedule of Accounts Receivable (schedule 11), Undeposited Patron Check Activity, line 20.

61. Section 6 of the Gaming Act of 1968.

62. A convenient review of the problems associated with casino credit is provided by four days of hearings before the New Jersey State Commission of Investigation on Atlantic City casino credit practices from March 1 through 4, 1983. The hearings are reported in the *New York Times,* March 5, 1983, and the *Atlantic City Press,* March 5, 1983. The SCI hearings documented four distinct classes of credit-related issues in addition to abuses leading to unaffordable losses by compulsive gamblers or by persons who are encouraged to gamble beyond their means by the extension of credit: (1) The provision of the Casino Control Act allowing casinos to deduct 4 percent of uncollectible debts reduces State gaming privilege tax collections. (2) The extension of credit to "criminal elements" or undesirable persons, who, in the SCI's view, may thereby obtain ninety-day interest-free loans from the casino, use money thus obtained for loansharking, drug trafficking, or other illegal purposes, and, with or without the collusion of casino personnel, defraud the casino of funds extended in the form of credit. (3) The related problem of depositing illegally held cash (that is, cash derived from illicit activities, such as drug traffic, that is not reported as taxable income) with casinos ostensibly to establish credit to be subsequently drawn upon for gambling but in fact for the purpose of "laundering" such funds. Arthur S. Lane, chairman, *Recommendations on Casino Credit Controls* (Trenton: State of New Jersey Commission of Investigation, 1983), with specific recommendations for statutory and regulatory changes concerning casino credit practices. The issue of the use of casinos to launder illegally held cash is created in part by the omission of casinos from the U.S. Treasury Department regulation requiring banks and other financial institutions to report transactions involving more than $10,000. The laundering issue has been exacerbated by the very large amounts of illicit cash generated from the cocaine trade. *Wall Street Journal,* "Using Loophole in Treasury Rule, Casinos Said to Help Launder Illegal-Drug Money," March 17, 1983.

63. The results were: Arkansas (to approve legal casinos in Garland County), 236,937 *For* and 554,729 *Against;* Colorado (to approve a constitutional amendment calling for casinos on a 4,300-acre site in Pueblo), 406,637 *For* and 816,816 *Against.* For a valuable analysis of the issues raised by the Pueblo, Colorado, and Hot Springs, Arkansas, casino initiatives in the context of their historical background, see William N. Thompson, "Casino Drives in Colo., Ark. Likely to Die," *Gaming & Wagering Business,* October 1984, pp. 43–46.

64. For an exhaustive analysis of the 1978 Florida casino initiative, see Dombrink, "Outlaw Businessmen," pp. 183–253.

65. *Gambling in America,* p. 102.

66. Ibid.

67. The Playboy Casino in Atlantic City is an exception to the latter statement in that windows provide a view from the casino floor across the boardwalk to the Atlantic Ocean.

68. Dombrink, "Outlaw Businessmen," p. 129. This is the most thorough discussion of organized crime and the casino industry, with an exhaustive bibliography. A more accessible and indispensible study is Skolnick, *House of Cards.* For illegal gambling generally see as well the Appendix.

69. The best study of the relation between Prohibition and criminal participation in American commercial gambling is Haller, "Bootleggers and American Gambling," in

Gambling in America, Appendix 1, pp. 201–43, with an excellent bibliography. Haller makes the points that organized crime's investments of capital derived from illegal alcohol began almost as soon as bootleg profits started rolling in, and that syndicated illegal gambling existed long before Prohibition. It is nevertheless true that many of the founding investors of the Las Vegas casino industry, including Benjamin (''Bugsy'') Siegel, Meyer Lansky, Frank Costello, Hyman Abrams, Moe Dalitz, and their associates had amassed fortunes from bootlegging. The tainted character of Nevada gaming and State licensing requirements that effectively precluded public corporate ownership of Nevada casinos limited the industry's access to capital markets until the enactment of Nevada's Corporate Gaming Acts of 1967 and 1969 and made less legitimate sources of investment important to the industry through the 1960s. See William R. Eadington and James S. Hattori, ''A Legislative History of Gambling in Nevada,'' *Nevada Review of Business and Economics* 2 (Spring 1978):13–17, and Eadington, ''The Evolution of Corporate Gambling in Nevada,'' *Nevada Review of Business and Economics* 6 (Spring 1982):13–22.

70. In effect, the 1960 act made it possible for anyone to run a casino as of right. Royal Commission on Gambling, The Lord Rothschild, chairman, *Final Report,* 2 vols. (London: Her Majesty's Stationery Office, 1978), pp. 268, 286, 315.

71. Ibid., p. 315.

72. Ibid., pp. 315–19 (emphasis added).

73. Skolnick's *House of Cards* is the definitive study of the difficulties experienced by Nevada in attempting to separate criminals from legitimate operators in its casino industry.

74. Ibid.

75. Nevada, State Gaming Control Board, *Quarterly Report for the Quarter Ended December 31, 1982 and Calendar Year to Date January 1, 1982, through December 31, 1982.*

76. Nevada, State Gaming Control Board, *Direct Levies on Gaming in Nevada: Fiscal Year Ended June 30, 1982;* Economics Research Associates, *The Role of Gaming in the Nevada Economy: An Update* (San Francisco: Economics Research Associates, 1983). This report was prepared for the Gaming Industry Association of Nevada and Nevada Resort Association (January 1983).

77. Economics Research Associates, *Role of Gaming in the Nevada Economy.*

78. New Jersey Casino Control Commission, ''Employment and Payroll Summary,'' Schedule 44, in 1983 *Annual Report* and annual reports filed by each casino for the year ending December 31, 1983. A discussion of the impact of casino gaming on Atlantic City may be found in George Sternlieb and James W. Hughes, *The Atlantic City Gamble* (Cambridge, Mass.: Harvard University Press, 1983).

79. There is a good general account of the origins and early history of pari-mutuels in Rienzi Wilson Jennings, *Taxation of Thoroughbred Racing* (Lexington, Ky.: University of Kentucky Press, 1949), pp. 22–27. This book remains one of the best studies of pari-mutuel taxation. Jennings's discussion of Oller's invention is based on Frank G. Menke, *Down the Stretch: The Story of Colonel Matt J. Winn* (New York: Smith & Durrell, 1944), a history of Churchill Downs and Kentucky racing and breeding that contains much valuable information about bookmaking and pari-mutuel betting between the 1870s and World War II.

80. Thoroughbreds are ridden from standing starts by jockeys around oval, flat, turf, or dirt tracks. Standardbreds are driven from moving starts by drivers of light carts, or sulkies, harnessed to the horse, around dirt tracks. Quarterhorses are ridden from standing, explosive starts down straight tracks, often the stretch or straight segment of flat

tracks used for thoroughbred racing, in high-speed sprints that are the equine equivalent of automobile drag races.

81. Match races are between two animals, or betting interests, and while common enough in earlier times are today rarely scheduled, or *carded,* for modern betting purposes.

82. Common pari-mutuel bets include, besides the familiar win, place, and show, daily doubles (the winners of two consecutive races), exactas (the first two finishers, in order, in one race), quinielas or quinellas (the first two finishers, in any order, in one race), trifectas (the first three finishers, in order, in one race), superfectas (the first four finishers, in order, in one race), wheel bets (one horse, or betting interest, in combination with every other horse or betting interest in the pool), box bets (three horses or betting interests in every possible winning combination), and many variations on these kinds of wagers.

83. The most successful horseplayer we know is, in fact, a retired options trader who, being now of independent means, finds racetracks to offer similar opportunities and a more relaxed environment for the exercise of his skills. A less expensive education in the complexities of handicapping than betting oneself can be acquired from Andrew Beyer, *Picking Winners* (Boston: Houghton Mifflin, 1975); this is perhaps the most thought-provoking of all the myriad studies of the subject. The clearest introduction to handicapping and betting horses is Tom Ainslie, *Theory and Practice of Handicapping* (New York: Trident Press, 1970). Much useful information is contained in *Ainslie's Complete Guide to Thoroughbred Racing* (New York: Simon and Schuster, 1979), and *Ainslie's New Complete Guide to Harness Racing* (New York: Simon and Schuster, 1980). *Ainslie's Encyclopedia of Thoroughbred Handicapping* (New York: William Morrow, 1978) is a convenient reference. Of the enormous literature on horse-race betting E. R. DaSilva and Roy M. Dorcus, *Science in Betting: The Players and the Horses* (New York: Harper & Brothers, 1961) presents empirical results of extended trials of basic pari-mutuel betting strategies.

84. Or, in New York and Connecticut, in the somewhat less intimidating local OTB office.

85. Poker and related card games are of course also competitive; these games are, however, in comparison with casino gaming, lotteries, pari-mutuel betting, and illegal bookmaking, of relatively minor commercial importance. Most poker is played as a social as opposed to a commercial activity.

86. Attendance is the *gate,* or turnstile count, and is from the National Association of State Racing Commissioners, *Annual Reports* (Lexington, Ky.: National Association of State Racing Commissioners, 1950–1982). Total North American (including the United States, Canada, and Mexico) thoroughbred handle for the period 1950–1973 is adjusted for increases in racing days by dividing the annual number of races (62,264 in 1973) into annual gross handle ($4,880,412,330 in 1973) and the resulting average annual wager per race ($78,000 in 1973 dollars) deflated by the Consumer Price Index (1967 = 100, or $57,000) in David Novick, "Economic Outlook of the Racing Industry," in *The Blood-Horse,* July 22, 1974, pp. 2760–66 (this periodical has been published weekly in Lexington by the Thoroughbred Owners and Breeders Association since May 11, 1929). Despite the moderating inflation of the last two years the downward trend in deflated thoroughbred handle per race has continued. In 1982 the average amount wagered per thoroughbred race in the United States, Canada, and Puerto Rico (excluding Mexico) was $94,000 in 1982 dollars but only $33,000 in 1967 dollars. For trends in pari-mutuel economics between 1950 and 1979, see Novick, "Economics of the Thoroughbred Industry" (or similar title), annual article from 1965 through 1979,

generally in the July issue of *The Blood-Horse*. These articles, together with Novick, *An Economic Study of Harness Horse Racing* (Santa Monica, Calif.: David Novick Associates, 1962) and Novick, *Economics of the Pari-Mutuel Business* (Santa Monica, Calif.: David Novick Associates, 1963) are valuable for the study of pari-mutuel horse racing in the postwar period. In the last few years pari-mutuel economics has received considerable attention. See in addition to Novick, Pugh-Roberts Associates, Inc., *The Future of Thoroughbred Racing in the United States* (Cambridge, Mass.: Pugh-Roberts Associates, 1975), an econometric model of the pari-mutuel thoroughbred racing industry commissioned by the Jockey Club, and since 1976 numerous contract research studies of aspects of pari-mutuel economics by Killingsworth, Liddy & Co., Inc. (now Killingsworth Associates, Inc.).

87. Studies with continuing relevance include Sanford V. Berg and Emery Jay Yelton, "Profits, Payments, and Complementary Products: Additional Ways to Improve Pari-Mutuel Taxation," *National Tax Journal* 22 (June 1976):191–99; Richard P. Brief, Samprit Chatterjee, Stephen Figlewski, Jay-Louise Weldon, and Joel Owen, *A Study of the Economic Impact of the Change in the Pari-Mutuel Tax on the Pari-Mutuel Industry in New York State Mandated by Chapter 576 of the Laws of 1978: Final Report* (New York: New York University, Graduate School of Business Administration, 1980); John H. Ciccolo, "Taxation of Earnings from Parimutuel Betting," "Optimal On-Track and Off-Track Takeout Rates," with a "Note on Bookmaking," "Taxation of Earnings from Parimutuel Horse Betting," "The Impact of New York City Off-Track Betting Activity on the Revenues of New York State and the Thoroughbred Racing Industry," and "The Impact of Increasing Racing Days: Some Preliminary Empirical Results," all in *Gambling in America,* Appendix 1, pp. 818–85; Charles W. deSeve, "Improved Pari-Mutuel Taxation," *National Tax Journal* 26 (December 1973):591–96; Arthur Gruen, "An Inquiry into the Economics of Race-Track Gambling," *Journal of Political Economy* 84 (November 1976):169–77; W. Douglas Morgan and Jon David Vasché, "Horseracing Demand, Parimutuel Taxation and State Revenue Potential," *National Tax Journal* 32 (June 1979):185–94; Donn R. Pescatrice, "An Interstate Off-Track Betting System," *National Tax Journal* 32 (June 1979):209–13; and Daniel B. Suits, "Gambling Taxes: Regressivity and Revenue Potential," *National Tax Journal* 30 (January 1977):19–35. As noted in the text, the results of these studies are inconclusive as regards demand elasticities for pari-mutuel horse-race wagering and optimum takeout rates. A fundamental problem is that a snapshot approach—i.e., a detailed analysis of takeout and demand within a short period—cannot by definition identify or predict long-term effects, while attempts to model wagering demand using long-time series data must take into account so many variables, some of them, such as quality of racing in both the jurisdiction studied and in competing jurisdictions, difficult or impossible to quantify, that results are dependent on whatever *arbitrary* values the analyst assigns to these variables.

88. The argument for reducing *total effective takeouts* is that at present levels racing is not competitive with other forms of commercial gambling. For a comparison of the price of pari-mutuel betting with other commercial games see the Appendix. While total effective takeout levels have tended to increase in the last ten or fifteen years there are some noteworthy counterveiling trends within pari-mutuel tax structures. Several major racing States, including California and New York, have reduced takeouts from win/place/show pools in an attempt to make these usually low-payout ratio bets more competitive with other forms of gambling. Takeouts from "exotic" or multiple-horse pools such as triples and pick-6s have on the other hand frequently been raised, on the theory that these high-payout ratio bets are less price-sensitive. A second major trend has been to reallocate pari-mutuel revenues from government to racetracks and horsemen. Essentially, State

governments, recognizing the increased financial needs of mature or declining racing industries, have adjusted pari-mutuel tax structures to provide tax relief to their racing industries. In 1970, for example, State and provincial governments in the U.S. and Canada received 8.01 percent of thoroughbred handle; and in 1981 this percentage was 4.26 percent; Killingsworth Associates, *Trends in Pari-Mutuel Taxation of Thoroughbred Racing in the United States and Canada* (Lexington, Mass.: Killingsworth Associates, Inc., 1983), p. 1. Most of this reduction in State and provincial pari-mutuel tax went to racetracks and horse owners, trainers, and breeders; the percentage difference between government's claim in 1970 and 1981, 3.75 percent, amounted to about $292 million in 1982 alone. In other words, by reducing their claim on pari-mutuel revenue and increasing the racing industry's claim by a roughly equivalent percentage State and provincial governments have in effect transferred sums currently approaching $300 million annually from public to racing-industry use over the last twelve years.

89. For the last decade the most important line has originated in Las Vegas. By reputation the most important oddsmaker during this period was Robert ("Bob") Martin. For professional football, for example, Mr. Martin would devise a weekly line, privately allow some ten or twelve "respected bettors" to bet (perhaps heavily) into this line, and adjust the line by giving or taking points until this private betting was equalized on either side of the coming week's games. The result, a set of point spreads for each game scheduled to be played that week, was then made available to Nevada's legal bookmakers. The making of lines for betting team sports at fixed odds is perhaps the most difficult entrepreneurial decision in commercial gambling.

90. The calculation of pari-mutuel payouts is not usually this simple. First, if payouts work out to more or less than a dime (or in some jurisdictions more or less than a nickel or, for multiple horse bets, a quarter), the odd cents are rounded down as *breakage* and retained by the operator. A payout of $16.64, for example, would be paid at $16.60, with 4¢ breakage added to the takeout. Breakage produces substantial revenues: in 1980 breakage from U.S. thoroughbred racing, which was shared among racetracks, horse owners, breeders, and government, amounted to $53 million, or 0.75 percent of total handle; Horsemen's Benevolent and Protective Association, *Racing Statistics* (Rockville, Md.: Horsemen's Benevolent and Protective Association, 1980). Secondly, horses are not equally bet, since some are considered much more likely to win than others. For example, if the *favorite* attracts most of the betting and a *dark horse* wins the payout for win, the value of winning tickets will be much higher because the win pool is shared among fewer successful investments. Conversely, if a very heavily bet favorite wins the money remaining in the win pool after the takeout is removed, there may not be enough to pay all the winning tickets at the statutory minimum: in most States, either $2.05, $2.10, or $2.20 for a $2 ticket. This condition is known as a *minus pool,* and as a rule the racetrack is required by law to supply enough money from its share of the takeout to pay every winning ticket presented at the pari-mutuel windows at the minimum price. In practice minus pools are rare occurrences in pari-mutuel betting.

91. For example, $10 bets on "don't pass" at craps. Blackjack is an exception to this statement, where similar betting strategies will produce results that vary with the individual player's card-counting skills and the casino's willingness to let skilled counters play.

92. The 5 percent surcharge is calculated on the live money, or, in the example, 83 percent of the pool: $83 \times .05 = 4.15$ handle points. Both takeout and surcharge are, however, normally somewhat higher than the statutory percentages due to breakage.

93. On the surcharge see Eugene Martin Christiansen and Michael D. Shagan, "The New York Off-Track Betting Law: An Exercise in Selective Decriminalization," *Connecticut Law Review* 12 (Summer 1980):854–69.

94. For a detailed analysis, see Stephen Figlewski, ''Subjective Information and Market Efficiency in a Betting Market,'' *Journal of Political Economy* 87 (1979):75–88.

95. The more interesting of these studies include Mukhtar M. Ali, ''Probability of Utility Estimates for Racetrack Bettors,'' *Journal of Political Economy* 85 (August 1977):803–15, an analysis of subjective and ''estimated objective'' winning probabilities obtained from 20,247 harness horse races that concluded horses with low subjective winning probabilities are overbet while horses with high subjective probabilities of winning are underbet. Ali alternatively explains this finding by (1) supposing bettors are risk-neutral and not sophisticated, or (2) sophisticated and risk-loving, with a tendency to increase risk as bankroll diminishes. Ali finds the second hypothesis more persuasive. See as well Ali, ''Some Evidence of the Efficiency of a Speculative Market,'' *Econometrica* 47 (March 1979):387–92, which finds the market for win bets to be efficient. Wayne W. Snyder, ''Horse Racing: Testing the Efficient Markets Mode,'' *Journal of Finance* 33 (September 1978):1109–18, analyzes data published in six previous studies for 312,000 entries in 35,285 races and finds a marked difference between the entries' subjective (i.e., pari-mutuel odds) and objective (empirical) probabilities of winning; consistent with Ali's findings, Snyder's analysis shows favorites are underbet and longshots are overbet, which Snyder explains by attributing to the betting public a preference for long-odds bets, i.e., that bettors are risk-loving. Weak, semistrong, and strong efficiency tests are applied to horse-race betting markets: the weak and strong tests fail while the semistrong test is inconclusive, and Snyder concludes that unlike the securities market horse-race odds are not determined in an efficient market. Jack Dowie, ''On the Efficiency and Equity of Betting Markets'' (paper, analyzing a sample of all races run at British courses in 1973, presented at the Second Annual Conference on Gambling, Lake Tahoe, Nev., 1975). Dowie and Burton P. Fabricand, *The Science of Winning* (New York: Van Nostrand Reinhold, 1979), conclude that present pari-mutuel horse-race betting markets are weakly efficient. Donald B. Hausch, William T. Ziemba, and Mark Rubinstein, ''Efficiency of the Market for Racetrack Betting,'' in *The Gambling Papers,* ed. Eadington, 12:109–35, confirm the findings of earlier studies that inefficiencies exist for underbet favorites and overbet longshots, but conclude that at present takeout levels these inefficiencies are not sufficient to produce profits from betting overlays. Place and show pools at Santa Anita and Exhibition Park are analyzed, and evidence of weak efficiency in these markets is presented. Figlewski, ''Subjective Information and Market Efficiency in a Betting Market,'' pp. 75–88, analyzes 189 races at Belmont Park in June and July 1977 and concludes that track odds discount expert handicappers' information efficiently, but that the OTB betting population makes less efficient use of this information. See as well several older studies: M. Friedman and L. J. Savage, ''The Utility Analysis of Choices Involving Risk,'' *Journal of Political Economy* 56 (August 1948):279–304; R. M. Griffith, ''Odds Adjustments by American Horse-Race Bettors,'' *American Journal of Psychology* 62 (April 1949):290–94; R. N. Rossett, ''Gambling and Rationality,'' pp. 595-607; R. Isaacs, ''Optimal Horse Race Bets,'' *American Mathematical Monthly* (May 1953):310–15. These studies of market efficiency in football betting are relevant: Lyn D. Pankoff, ''Market Efficiency and Football Betting,'' *Journal of Business* 41 (April 1968):203–14, concludes that the market for betting National Football League games at fixed odds against bookmakers is efficient. Vernon L. Smith, ''Economic Theory of Wager Markets,'' *Western Economic Journal* 9 (September 1971):242–55, examines eight propositions regarding fixed odds betting markets in a theoretical fashion; this thought-provoking paper is too little known. Michael E. Canes, ''The Market for Pro Football Betting,'' in *Gambling in America,* ed. Eadington, pp. 108–37, concludes that the market for football betting at fixed odds is efficient.

96. On the origins of off-track betting see Christiansen and Shagan, "The New York Off-Track Betting Law." The advent of OTB in New York is discussed, in popular fashion, in terms of the application of game theory to business decisions in John McDonald, *The Game of Business* (Garden City, N.Y.: Anchor Press/Doubleday, 1977), pp. 246–65.

97. The legalization of pari-mutuel betting is discussed in a historical context in Chapter 5.

98. From the 1930s until 1979 pari-mutuel betting, in both handle (or gross wagering) and retention (gross revenues, or operator win or bettor losses) was the largest form of legal commercial gambling in the United States. In 1979 the combined gross win of Nevada and Atlantic City casinos ($2.45 billion) for the first time exceeded pari-mutuel retention ($2.39 billion): State Gaming Control Board, *Nevada Gaming Abstract* (1979); New Jersey Casino Control Commission, *Annual Report June 30, 1979;* National Association of State Racing Commissioners, *Pari-Mutuel Racing 1979 Statistical Summary.* Since 1979 gaming, driven by the explosive growth of Atlantic City casinos, has decisively surpassed pari-mutuel betting (and by our estimate illegal bookmaking as well) to become the largest commercial gambling game in the United States.

99. These data are derived from National Association of State Racing Commissioners, *Pari-Mutuel Racing 1983 Statistical Summary;* American Greyhound Track Operators Association, *1983 Summary of State Pari-Mutuel Tax Structures* (North Miami, Fla.: American Greyhound Track Operators Association, 1983); Harness Tracks of America, Inc., Morristown, N.J.; United States Trotting Association, Columbus, Ohio; the American Horse Council, Washington, D.C.; and various State racing commission and pari-mutuel regulatory agency 1983 annual reports.

100. This $706 million was derived directly from pari-mutuel betting and constituted about 93 percent of all purses paid in 1983. The remaining 7 percent consisted principally of stake and entry fees paid by horsemen to racetracks and supplementary distributions from breeding funds, which in most cases are also derived from pari-mutuel betting. Total purses won by horsemen at U.S. tracks in 1983, from all sources, amounted to $758.9 million. National Association of State Racing Commissioners, *Pari-Mutuel Racing 1983 Statistical Summary.*

101. American Horse Council, surveys of thoroughbred and standardbred breeder incentive programs. The estimate of $42 million was derived by applying statutory breeding fund claims on handle to State flat and harness handles reported by the National Association of State Racing Commissioners.

102. American Horse Council, Inc., Washington, D.C., R. Richards Rolapp, president, "Statement in Support of H.R. 4592," U.S. Congress, House Ways and Means Committee, 97th Cong., 2d sess., *Hearings Before the Subcommittee on Select Revenue Measures,* March 16, 1982.

103. Primary or yearling racehorse markets, especially the select summer sales held in Kentucky and Saratoga, N.Y., have for the last six or seven years been dominated in their (rapidly escalating) upper price ranges by speculation not directly related to the pari-mutuel economy. Syndicated British gambling and Middle Eastern petrodollar interests are attempting to corner certain breeding lines, and competitive bidding between these groups has driven some yearling prices far above any possible return in purses won in even the most successful racing career. At the 1983 Keeneland Select Summer Sales, for example, a yearling was purchased by Sheikh Mohammed bin Rashid al Maktoum of Dubai for $10.2 million. The Sheikh and his brothers spent $54.5 million at the 1983 Keeneland, Fasig-Tipton (Ky.), and Saratoga select summer sales; Robert Sangster, the head of syndicated international breeding interests based in the British Isles, spent $17.9

million at the 1983 Keeneland sales; and Prince Khaled Abdullah of Saudi Arabia spent $10.3 at Keeneland, Fasig-Tipton, and Saratoga, for a total expenditure by these three interests of $82.7 million for American yearlings in 1983. (These expenditures were in addition to substantial purchases at European yearling sales.) These three buyers race for the most part in Britain, Ireland, and France. In 1982 total purses paid in these three countries were in American dollars valued at approximately $70 million. Even were the yearlings purchased by these three groups to win *all* the purses generated from pari-mutuel betting in France and the British Isles their owners would not recover their investment: "What's Going On Here" (editorial), *The Blood-Horse,* October 15, 1983, p. 7289.

Essentially the payers of such yearling prices are speculating as to future breeding values rather than expected returns from purses derived from pari-mutuel betting and are willing to make very large capital investments in first-quality American bloodstock for offshore breeding purposes. In their middle and lower ranges, however, American yearling prices are more directly related to the expected return in purses won in racing careers, with syndication rights in any winner of a graded stakes race and the federal tax treatment of horsebreeding being important additional factors in determining racehorse and broodmare values. For an analysis of recent trends in purse distributions by an economist see Robert G. Lawrence, "All About Purses" (annual article), *The Thoroughbred Record,* especially April 29, 1981, pp. 1915–22; May 12, 1982, pp. 2509–18; and June 8, 1983, pp. 2806–18. See as well David L. Heckerman, "The Economics of Selling," *The Blood-Horse,* July 18, 1981, pp. 4120–22. These two periodicals provide detailed coverage of yearling sales and other racehorse and broodmare markets.

4

An Explanation of Gambling Behavior

> Once engrossed in the action, a man can ignore the rest of the world.
>
> —Jay Livingston, *Compulsive Gamblers: A Culture of Losers*

Society has an immense stake in commercial gambling. Americans are wagering more money in casinos, at pari-mutuel betting, and on lotteries than at any previous time in history. Unfortunately, many of the issues raised by the legalizations of recent decades have been poorly framed, and any understanding of the social implications of the business of risk remains rudimentary.

This is particularly true of gambling behavior. In focusing attention on the compulsive acts of a small minority of individuals society has lost sight of the heterogeneity of gambling. From Sunday supplements to learned journals, this indigenous variety of risky play has been subjected to a psychological reductionism that makes no distinction between sober horseplayers and junkie gamblers. The parallel with drug-addiction is not accidental. Underlying the prevailing views of both gambling and the recreational use of drugs is a peculiarly American fear: fear of pleasure for its own sake and a distrust of play that finds expression in gambling prohibitions and a rationale in theories of gamblers as faulty-state mechanisms—sick or potentially sick.

Unlike heroin addiction and similar afflictions with demonstrable physiological causes, gambling should not be seen as the result of some latent urge residing in the individual psyche, waiting like some unsprung booby-trap for the opportunity to emerge and devour the rest of the gambler's personality.[1] Such thinking is not likely to lead to a balanced understanding of something as varied and complex as gambling behavior. Yet the idea that gambling is some kind of interior devil that must be suppressed or denied the opportunity to tempt people to destruction continues to infuse the nation's thinking about gambling even as Americans flock to the lottery ticket vendor and the casino door.

One of the purposes of this book is to provide an alternative perspective on this aspect of the business of risk. Just as we have substituted a view of commercial gambling in the real world for the myth of monolithic gambling, we now examine gamblers as social role players, interacting with one another and with specific games in real-world situations. We believe that, except for compulsive gamblers, very little gambling behavior can be explained by resorting to psychological reductionism. Symbolic interaction, within the sociological perspective, enables us to see how important actual experiences acquired over time are in determining most gambling behavior.

Like gambling games, gambling behavior is not monolithic.[2] "Gambling" is a word that covers a variety of behaviors and activities, some of which bear little resemblance to compulsive self-destruction or even to "inherent riskiness." Indeed, the role of gambler is usually both conventional and situational. Most gambling behaviors are influenced greatly by interactions between gamblers and particular gambling games. The source of these behaviors—whether the game itself, the player, or a combination of player and game—determines different patterns of gambling that in turn lead to different outcomes, the majority of which do not entail unaffordable losses.

Individuals learn gambling behavior in two ways: by interacting with formal rules or structures and, in a socializing process, by taking into account the gambling behaviors of others through symbolic interchange of shared responses. In some cases gambling may become progressively more intense, and it is possible to speak of gambling careers and gambling identities. In short, gambling behavior is determined by the gambling game itself, by the context in which that game is conducted, by the personality of the gambler, and, in most cases, by the interaction of the gambler with the characteristics of that particular game.

The initial stimulus to gamble is either generated from an individual's personality or is the product of totally random circumstances. It is always socially motivated—even in the case of individuals who ultimately exhibit compulsive gambling behavior. Contrary to the belief of many psychologists, gambling careers cannot be predicted at the outset with any certainty. It is not possible to say that a particular individual will, as an inevitable result of an initial encounter with gambling, exhibit a particular type of gambling behavior. Such predictions can, however, be made for populations in terms of statistical averages derived from actual gambling behaviors exhibited by similar populations with similar opportunities to gamble. In other words, it is possible to roughly predict the incidence of gambling behaviors. For example, two American populations, each with similar lottery games as their sole form of legal commercial gambling, will exhibit similar percentages of different (casual, occasional, risky, compulsive, and nongambling) behaviors. This has important implications for gambling policy.

GAMES, PERSONALITY, AND GAMBLING BEHAVIOR

Gambling behaviors arrange themselves along a spectrum of increasing (but not necessarily progressive) involvement. The definition of behavioral categories is, to some extent, subjective: by making fine distinctions and proceeding on a game-by-game basis, the number of possible categories of gambling behavior could be made very large. In deciding on the classification presented here we have observed three criteria: first, examples of the behavior must be observable in all forms of gambling; second, the behavior must be readily distinguishable, even to untrained observers, in real-world gambling situations; and third, the categories must be sufficiently general so that their total number is not unusable for analytical purposes.

This classification is summarized in Table 3. Identifiable types of gamblers—casual, occasional, and so forth—are classified in terms of the three sources of motivations and behaviors: *gambler-generated, interactional,* and *game-generated.* An example of game-generated behavior is found in the expert nonprofessional horseplayer. The more he learns about the game, the more skills he acquires at handicapping, the more the game takes over and generates its own unique set of behaviors and motivations. There is a true progression, or behavioral career, that corresponds more and more closely to the formal structures of the game until, in the extreme example, gambling ceases to be interactional and a near-identity of structure and behavior, game and gambler, is reached, with gambling and game constituting two sides of a single coin. Interactional behaviors are midway between game-generated and personality-generated gambling. An example is the professional gambler. He is deeply knowledgeable about the particular game, but is using it for his own purposes. Gambler-generated behavior is best exemplified by the compulsive gambler. His behavior is the expression of personality traits that is manifested in gambling situations but is not really a function of the structure and context of any particular game.

TABLE 3
A CLASSIFICATION OF GAMBLING BEHAVIORS

Type of Gambling	*Gambler-Generated Behaviors*	*Interactional Behaviors*	*Game-Generated Behaviors*
Casual	L		
Occasional	L		
Risky	L—H*		
Professional		H	
Habitual		L	
Serious		M ←	M
Obsessive		L—M →	H
Compulsive	H →	→	H
Non-Gamblers:			
Would-Be	N/A	N/A	N/A
Anti-	N/A	N/A	N/A
Not Interested	N/A	N/A	N/A

* Risky gambling is highly variable in terms of involvement. Individual risk-seeking gamblers may, for example, gamble casually on one occasion and—perhaps at a different game—intensely on another. In contrast to other gambling behaviors, the sporadic nature of risky gambling makes predictions about any risk-seeking individual's *next* gambling session highly uncertain.

Identifiable types of gamblers—casual, occasional, and so forth—are defined in terms of their motivation and broadly distinguishable nature. Typical, or characteristic, degrees of involvement, as measured by the expenditure of time, money, and energy on the activity, are expressed in Table 3 by the symbols "H" (high), "M" (medium), "L" (low), and "N/A" (not applicable). Typical behavioral careers are indicated by arrows. We emphasize that the categories of casual, professional, obsessive, and so forth are *types* and not *identities;* for example, an individual might be a professional poker player and an occasional sports bettor and exhibit entirely dissimilar gambling behaviors when engaged in these respective gambling activities.

Casual gambling is conducted on impulse or happenstance. Curiosity and social reasons are common motivations of casual gambling; the decision to gamble casually is nearly always the product of a specific social context. The structural characteristics of particular gambling activities discussed in the preceding chapter—odds, payout ratios, price, and so forth—are unimportant to casual gamblers, most of whom know little or nothing about the games they play. Uninformed gambles are a hallmark of casual gambling: hitting blackjack hands of eighteen or better when the dealer must take another card or betting two dollars on a horse because the gambler likes the horse's name are typical examples. The proportion of casual gambling to other gambling behaviors is roughly constant from game to game with the exception of racetracks and *jai-alai* frontons, where the requisite entry-level knowledge discourages casual betting. Casual gambling may be the start of a gambling career or may simply be an unrelated episode in the lives of individuals who never will gamble on a regular basis.

Occasional gambling is a determined act. Common motivations of occasional gambling are escape or a special occasion such as a birthday, holiday, or celebration. A less common but significant motivation is hope. The usual stimulus is an extraordinarily large payoff, of which multi-million dollar State lottery Lotto prizes are the best current example. Such enormous payoffs encourage nongamblers to take an unusual chance—to risk a small sum in the hope of winning great wealth.

In all cases, however, the motivation of occasional gambling is idiosyncratic and, as with casual gambling, does not derive from the gambling game *per se.* Unlike casual gambling, however, occasional gambling may entail measurable expenditures of time and money. A vacation in Las Vegas, for example, usually lasts several days and involves considerable expense aside from gaming losses, which, even for individuals who do not ordinarily gamble, may easily run in a casino environment to several hundred dollars. At other commercial games occasional gambling losses are likely to be smaller, due both to the slower rate of change in net worth typical of these games and to the occasional nature of the behavior. For the most part, occasional gambling resembles analogous nongambling behaviors, such as a trip to Disneyland or a fling at some form of recreation, more closely than it resembles the more committed types of gambling. As is true of casual gambling, occasional gambling may or may not be the start of a gambling career; in the affirmative case this behavior ceases to be occasional, and the individual's subsequent gambling falls into one or more of the following categories.

Risky gambling behavior is also gambler-generated. These gamblers seek risk rather than a particular gambling activity: for them, risky nongambling activities, such as sky-diving or mountain climbing, are more likely to be acceptable substitutes than low-risk forms of gambling. It is important to distinguish between true risk-seeking and various self-destructive behaviors. Technical rock climbers, for example, systematically try to minimize the very considerable dangers inherent in their chosen sport: skill and proficiency rather than reckless or foolhardy actions are the measures of status among this fraternity of risk-seekers, who derive satisfaction from success in a risky endeavor as opposed to morbid thrills from courting self-destruction. Risky gambling is a similarly controlled behavior that should not be confused with uncontrolled, self-destructive, compulsive gambling. Because by definition risky gambling is for meaningful stakes and frequently at poor odds, it may produce large wins or losses, but it is usually not prolonged. Levels of involvement in risky gambling are highly variable. Depending on circumstances and the particular game, gambling for risk may be trivial or intense, even for successive gambles by the same individual. A disinclination to "play it safe" may prompt risk-seekers to spice a normally nongambling activity—a friendly bridge game, for instance—with a wager; the same individuals may on an irregular basis gamble considerable amounts of money at commercial games for no other reason than the risk involved. High-stakes baccarat is the classic example: a significant percentage of the $441 million baccarat drop reported by Atlantic City casinos in 1982 was gambled by a small number of very wealthy gamblers whose patronage is based on the casinos' willingness to play this game for enormous sums.[3] Whatever their means, risky gamblers are essentially gambling for entertainment; as we have already noted, the self-destructive, uncontrolled qualities of compulsive gambling are not characteristic of risky gambling behavior.

Professional gambling is unique in that it is productive of economic gain. The professional gambler turns the leisure world into work; he is not, however, a worker but a true professional in the vocational sense of the word. Contemporary professional gamblers are the surviving remnants of a class of itinerant individual entrepreneurs that prior to the organization of gambling as a business by bookmaker-politicians in the second half of the nineteenth century constituted American commercial gambling.[4] The gambling behavior of a professional is interactional and highly controlled and is usually the result of a studied approach to his chosen game. Professional gamblers are, for obvious reasons, concentrated in games where the element of skill is sufficient to produce a player advantage; blackjack and pari-mutuel betting are the most popular choices.[5] Professional gambling behavior is recognizable to trained observers, a circumstance that has led card-counters to adopt disguises and elaborate strategems in efforts to escape detection by blackjack pit bosses and casino security personnel.[6] At racetracks professionals are noticeable by their deliberate, sometimes infrequent, sizable bets.[7]

For successful professionals, gambling produces financial gains, which both removes this behavior from the category of play and distinguishes it from other gambling behaviors. A precise quantitative measurement of the proportion of professional gamblers to the gambling population as a whole is not possible, but the standards for success are high, and we believe that these individuals represent a tiny minority of gamblers. This minority, however, puts disproportionate amounts of money into action in selected gambling situations.

Habitual gambling is interactional, and normally it is integrated into the gambler's "real" life. For most habitual gamblers, gambling is incidental to other activities and is not a focused behavior in its own right. There is a minimal investment of time, money, or deliberate effort in this activity, which may be of no more importance to the individual than buying a daily newspaper. Habitual horse-race betting is a partial exception to this statement in that habitual horseplayers may devote some measurable portion of their day to a perusal of the *Racing Form* or some other aid to handicapping. Horse-race betting aside, habitual betting involves little thought or conscious decisionmaking. The games most closely associated with habitual gambling are State lotteries and legal and illegal numbers. Habitual players of these games may not even define themselves as "gamblers," so completely integrated into everyday work and living are these activities.

Serious gambling resembles the serious pursuit of a hobby. In contrast to casual or occasional gambling—and like obsessive gambling—the game itself is of considerable intrinsic interest. Serious gambling is interactional but predicated on a particular gambling game; other games, even if they offer similar odds, frequency of gambles, payout ratios, and so forth, are rarely acceptable substitutes. Unlike obsessive gambling behavior, however, the serious gambler's involvement with his chosen game is not progressive beyond objectively determinable limits. As is true of hobbies generally, once serious gambling reaches a level that is satisfactory to the gambler it stabilizes and is relegated to a delimited niche. It does not spill over the bounds of leisure play into the gambler's real life. Serious gambling is controlled behavior, but depending on the choice of game and the gambler's means may entail significant losses.

Only games of mixed chance and skill become objects of serious gambling. There are two reasons for this. First, only games of mixed chance and skill have sufficient inherent complexity to sustain serious interest. Secondly, serious gamblers are generally both intelligent and knowledgeable about gambling, and other things being equal they prefer to gamble at games where they have at least a theoretical chance of winning.[8]

The serious gambling game *par excellence* is sports betting. Nearly all sports bettors maintain a hobbylike interest in football, baseball, basketball, and so forth that is amplified by wagers on the outcomes of these games. Sports betting resembles horse-race betting in that the act of betting and the gambling event are separated, with the gambling event—the horse race or football game—something in which it is possible to have a nongambling interest. Serious sports betting, however, is more easily integrated into everyday life than serious racetack betting, for the simple reason that football games and other sports events of interest to gamblers may be seen on television in the bettor's home. Serious gambling may also be noncommercial. "Friendly" but relatively serious bets between amateur golf players are common, and similar betting is characteristic of many amateur athletic contests.

Obsessive gambling is the end result of a progressive involvement with a particular game that transforms conventional, interactive gambling into an obsessional activity. To a greater degree than any other gambling behavior, obsessive gambling is the product of socially conditioned careers. Nearly always, obsessive gamblers are seeking escape. Typically, they find the real world in some respect unsatisfactory and perhaps intolerable: work or personal relationships may create uncomfortable levels of stress, or—and this was a finding we found particularly interesting—the ambiguity and uncertainty inherent in society may produce disturbing feelings of insecurity. It is not unusual for Americans to feel adrift in a world in chaos; anomie, that chestnut of the behavioral sciences, does, in fact, rob many lives of meaning. Certain forms of gambling offer such individuals a way out. Like occasional and risky gambling, obsessive gambling is, very often, an escape—but not from boredom, and not for thrills or excitement. The attraction of obsessive gambling is not risk but certainty: it is an escape into order.

Obsessive gambling behavior is very unevenly distributed among the different commercial gambling games. There are few obsessive lottery players, for example. The intrinsic interest of lottery games is too easily exhausted, and the environment in which these games are played generally too prosaic, for this form of gambling to become the object of obsession with any frequency. To supply the needs of potential obsessive gamblers a gambling activity generally has the following characteristics: first, it is world-building—that is, capable of generating the rituals and rules of an internally consistent subculture; second, it is conveniently available; third, it constitutes a separate alternative reality complete with satisfying gambler roles; and fourth, as a game, it possesses intrinsic play interest and complexity.

Racetracks and, to a lesser extent, casinos are the forms of commercial gambling that satisfy these criteria. As we noted in the preceding chapter, on entering a racetrack the gambler sheds his real-world identity and assumes a new persona—that of *horseplayer.* The complex social structure of the racetrack-world includes among its many specialized roles a central position for horseplayers. It also provides an occupation: betting. For the obsessive gambler, escape into the order of the racetrack-world becomes entrapment. Initial contact with this form of gambling starts a career that progresses through stages of normal interactional gambling behavior into a spiral of increasing obsession. The better turns for more and more of his emotional and social needs to the subculture of the track. This obsession is not uncontrollable: the normal division of time into work and leisure worlds is preserved. But the obsessive gambler finds it increasingly difficult to alternate between these worlds—his compensatory identity of horseplayer loses its efficacy outside the racetrack grounds; consequently he leaves only to return.

By any definition obsessive gambling is nonconventional behavior. At the least this kind of gambling takes on far more importance than American society conventionally assigns to play. When it becomes obsessive, gambling ceases to be a free and limited recreation; it is then a perversion of play and far more than a game to the gambler.

Obsessive gambling, while nonconventional behavior, is not compulsive. As the following discussion shows, obsessive and compulsive gambling behaviors have almost no points of resemblance beyond a high level of involvement. The obsessive gambler is not sick in a clinical sense. Control is a fundamental characteristic of *all* obsessive behavior, whether the object of the obsession is horseracing or jogging. The obsessive horseplayer stops betting before he loses everything. This appears to be due in large measure to the fact that racetrack gambling generates a set of internal controls that act as a brake on excessive or unaffordable losses. The subculture of the track reserves its greatest contempt for the horseplayer who allows himself to go broke. The cultural norms that legitimatize obsessive betting condemn spontaneous, uncontrolled betting that ignores the discipline of handicapping. Unknowledgeable persons who bet large sums are objects of ridicule; likewise, the uncontrollable, compulsive, gambler is regarded with contemptuous pity.

The question of motivation is important here. The aim of professional gamblers is to make money, and successful professionals—blackjack card-counters and truly expert handicappers—achieve this goal. Because it is productive of regular economic gains, professional gambling qualifies as conventional behavior—like commodity traders, professional gamblers are working at specialized careers.

In some respects obsessive gamblers may be regarded as failed professionals. Like other gambling behaviors, obsessive racetrack betting has, over the long term, a negative expectation of gain due to its high statutory price. Professional bettors are able to overcome this high price through their superior handicapping skills and their deliberate and extremely disciplined betting, which is always systematic and usually limited to infrequent but highly favorable opportunities. It is not unusual, in our observation, for professional bettors to come to the track for the purpose of making a specific bet only to encounter some new conditions—a late jockey change, for example—that makes the bet less favorable and then to leave without betting at all. In contrast, obsessive horseplayers tend to bet every race on the card. The analysis of gambling games in Chapter 2 has shown that this behavior must result in loss. The competitive nature of pari-mutuel betting activities ensures that favorable betting opportunities are relatively rare;[9] when combined with the high takeouts prevailing at American racetracks, this means that continuous betting is an inherently losing strategy.

Obsessive gambling, therefore, is not productive of economic gain and hence does not constitute work. Essentially, obsessive gamblers are spending money at what, in conventional terms, is play. But the very high level of involvement—the large expenditures of time, money, and energy—characteristic of obsessive gambling is wholly inconsistent with conventional meanings of play. Obsessive gambling is no longer, in the sense of conventional gambling behaviors, purely interactional. The gambling behavior now conforms so closely to the structures of the game that game and behavior are nearly indistinguishable. Obsessive gamblers are absorbed into gambling games; what began as conventional interactive behavior takes on the attributes of a new persona and an alternative life. In contrast to the genuinely conventional gambling behaviors previously discussed, *the game itself* is now generating its own motivation: obsessive betting is its own reward. Unlike the occasional gambler, who gambles for entertainment, or the professional, who gambles for profit, the aim of obsessive horseplayers is simply to stay in the game. This aim, which is reinforced by all the rituals and social values of his chosen subculture, enjoins the obsessive horseplayer from incurring unaffordable losses. Financial ruin would deny him access to the object of his obsession; thus, the very forces that set him spiraling into obsessive behavior place a floor under his descent.

Compulsive gambling is a step beyond obsession into personality disorder. The defining characteristic of compulsive gambling is that it is uncontrollable. Like obsessive gamblers, compulsive gamblers want to keep playing; but unlike *all* other gambling behaviors, compulsive gambling is not constrained either by the characteristics of the gambling games themselves or by the prospect, or even the actual fact, of unaffordable losses.

As in the case of obsessive gambling, the question of motivation is crucial. Although at the outset of obsessive gambling careers the gambler may gamble for entertainment or other innocuous reasons, there is a progressive involvement with the activity that eventually transforms an interactional behavior into behavior that is almost wholly generated by the game itself. Casual, occasional, risky, habitual, and serious gambling are play behaviors—voluntary activities that occupy circumscribed areas of the gambler's life and do not effect permanent changes in the gambler's personality. When gambling becomes obsessive the game, and not the gambler, is controlling. His search for certainty in an uncertain world has led the obsessive gambler into paradox: security in a risky occupation. Unlike the larger, real, world upon which individual actions appear to have no impact, the results of gambling activities are both predictable and immediate. Far from being psychologically pathological, the obsessive gambler's escape into the order of subcultures that are generated by gambling games is an understandable response to the social pressures that bear in varying degrees on all Americans.

Compulsive gambling careers, in contrast, are radically different from those typical of other gambling behaviors. Properly speaking, compulsive gamblers do not have careers in particular gambling games. Once established, this behavior is motivated by internal psychological needs that are not social in origin. Compulsive gambling is not conditioned by the ritualized order of gambling subcultures that is so important to obsessive gamblers. The game itself and the gambling environment are of secondary importance. Compulsive gambling is escape, but not, as is true of occasional and risky gambling, from boredom to excitement, or, as with obsessive gambling, from chaos into order: compulsive gambling is an escape into the psyche. Compulsive gamblers are not playing games; rather, in an existential sense, they are simply playing.

Even cursory observations of compulsive gambling will confirm these statements. The compulsive gambler gambles without regard to normal gambling considerations. His primary concern is a single characteristic of gambling activities: *action.* In its purest form compulsive gambling is simply this: action without end or limit. The activity becomes progressively all-absorbing: distinctions between work and leisure worlds are erased; personal relationships are sacrificed; eventually even the game itself is obliterated, and the activity becomes irrational in terms of the internal logic of all forms of gambling. Thus, the "best" gamble becomes the next one; all normal criteria—odds, prospective return, probability of winning, and so forth—are irrelevant to the compulsive gambler. Control vanishes, and his gambling becomes essentially infantile: a simple form of immediate stimulus-response gratification. Compulsive gambling is one of the most purely solipsistic of all behaviors.

Some forms of commercial gambling satisfy the needs of compulsive gamblers much more completely than others. Racetrack gambling, for example, is a world-building game that generates an internally consistent subculture. For obsessive gamblers, who seek annihilation of self in preexisting worlds of meaning, this subculture is a primary attraction. Compulsive gamblers have a diametrically opposed aim: they seek to annihilate the world. Rules, behavioral norms, specific characteristics of particular gambling games, and even other individuals that impede the compulsive gambler's quest for action are alike ignored or actively avoided. For this reason compulsive gamblers appear crazy, even in most gambling environments; as the previous discussion demonstrates, gambling is, normally, social, and the social anarchy represented by the compulsive gambler's single-minded pursuit of action is perceived by conventional gamblers as an unpleasant and disruptive influence.

The only form of commercial gambling that encourages action without limit is casino gaming. The gambler is sealed off from the real world and enclosed within fantasy surroundings in which every detail is conducive to gambling. Table games, as Chapter 3 explains, are characterized by high frequency of gambles and are extremely player-active, and the wide range of odds and stakes available facilitate rapid changes in net worth. In short, to a greater degree than any other commercial gambling game, table gaming offers action. Normally, these characteristics would constitute an automatic brake on excessive loss: continuous action at games with negative expectations of gain ''tap out'' gamblers quickly. Unlike the racetrack patron, however, who has little or no credit available to him,[10] and the lottery player, who has none, the casino gambler, especially if he is a heavy player, may have almost unlimited credit and consequently total financial exposure to the gaming tables. The rapid rate of change in net worth possible at table games can, when combined with uncontrolled gambling on credit, in even a single session of play produce a disastrous financial loss.

For all of these reasons compulsive gambling is more commonly observed, and probably more commonly occurs, in casino gaming than in any other form of commercial gambling. The only other gambling game that in our experience attracts compulsive gamblers in significant numbers is sports betting. This appears to be because this form of gambling is normally on a credit basis and may be played for very high stakes. Sports betting, because it is illegal (except in Nevada) and usually transacted over the telephone, is inherently the most private of all commercial gambling activities; consequently it is extremely difficult to discuss in quantitative terms.

Nongamblers by definition do not exhibit gambling behavior. The motivations of nongamblers are nevertheless of some interest in the context of the present discussion. *Antigambling* sentiments are commonly religious or moral (and sometimes political) in origin, and have had enormous consequences for the relationship of gambling to American society. By labeling gambling immoral, irreligious, or deviant the opponents of gambling have profoundly influenced all kinds of gambling behavior. *Would-be* gamblers presumably would exhibit gambling behaviors in approximate statistical correlation to the behaviors of actual gamblers. The number of would-be gamblers is substantial: many parts of the United States have little or no commercial gambling, and, should one or another form of gambling be introduced into these areas we would expect the resulting gambling behaviors to closely resemble the foregoing classification. *Ignorant* persons have no practical knowledge of or experience with gambling. *Uninterested* persons are, statistically speaking, a small minority of the population: these are individuals who are unknowledgeable about gambling but derive no value from it. For uninterested persons gambling is neither fun nor a meaningful activity, and therefore cannot be play. In some cases there is decided antipathy: gambling is distasteful, not for moral or religious reasons, but because of some characteristics of the gambling activities themselves.

AN EXPLANATION OF GAMBLING BEHAVIOR

We have seen that gambling motivations are extremely varied. They are obviously important in determining an individual's first gambling experiences, and they influence, in widely varying degrees, the subsequent development of a gambling career. The widespread popularity of gambling is, in fact, due in no small measure to its capacity for appealing to many different motivations. It is important to understand that gambling motivations change, both over time and from game to game; they are not, as many psychologists have claimed, unvarying personality traits.

Gambling careers are likewise very diverse. Casual and occasional gamblers may gamble so infrequently that specific gambling activities never attain any relevance to their gambling behavior. More usually gambling becomes a truly interactive behavior, in which individuals engage in particular gambling activities, producing identifiable patterns of gambling. For habitual and serious gamblers, gambling remains interactional: a delimited activity, of greater or lesser significance, in the gambler's leisure world. In gambling careers that end in obsession these limits are erased. Gambling ceases to be interactive; the person submits wholly to the game, and the individual assumes the new persona of *gambler.* Only gambling subcultures provide respected social roles for gamblers, and at this point the obsessive gambling career entraps the gambler. His gambling stabilizes at a heavy, but controlled and affordable, level and takes on the permanence of a life-style. Diametrically opposed to obsessive gambling is the pseudo-career of the compulsive gambler: in this case personality dominates from the outset until, in the final stages, the gambler is reduced to a simple craving for action that may not even require socially structured gambling situations for its satisfaction.

Gambling Behaviors and the Choice of Game

The existence of distinct gambling behaviors implies that the relative attractiveness of the different forms of commercial gambling is variable over a wide range, that is, over time and among games for any gambler confronted with more than one gambling option. Where only one form of gambling—for example, horse racing—is available, gamblers are confronted with a classic monopoly. If they choose to gamble, they must patronize the only game in town. This has, in fact, been true of horse racing in many areas since the 1930s. Racetracks had monopolies on legal gambling, which they were thus able to exploit in relative freedom from competition. In these circumstances the appeal of racetrack gambling was maximized; at the same time there were segments of the gambling market—that is, would-be gamblers—for whom racetrack gambling simply had no attraction. The legalization of lotteries, numbers, OTB, and casino gaming has broken the monopoly once held by horse racing, and making gambling a competitive business in many States has made the relative attractiveness of different gambling activities of great significance to society.

Because each gambling game is characterized by a menu of activities that interact with motivations to produce distinctive gambling outcomes and gambling behaviors, in authorizing a particular form of gambling a State is, in effect, creating the gambling behavior characteristic of that form. For example, the citizens of a State that allows only lottery games will exhibit markedly different gambling behavior than the citizens of a State that allows lottery games, horseracing, OTB, and casino gaming.

While satisfying on one level, it would be simplistic to present a single measure of the relative attractiveness of each commercial gambling game by ranking and summing numerical values assigned to their structural characteristics. Weinstein and Deitch attempted to profile games in terms of a number of structural characteristics and concluded that "the important structural differences between forms of gambling indicate that each form must be considered separately."[11] We agree. Gambling games can be compared through particular characteristics (i.e., relative price or frequency of gambles), but they cannot be compared across characteristics. There is no meaningful way to compare price vs. frequency of gambles; these are qualitative variables, not quantitative ones. It is important to recognize that, except at the extremes of gambling behaviors, games are not substitutable.[12] The obverse is likewise true: gambling behaviors are not substitutable among games. The obsessive horseplayer, for example, has learned a set of skills and routines that are not useful in playing a lottery.

While a single figure representing the relative attractiveness of gambling games cannot be generated, it is possible to compare attractiveness through particular characteristics and particular types of gamblers. It is important to understand that a form of gambling may present different aspects to novices and to initiated gamblers. The high entry-level knowledge required for racetrack betting, for example, discourages participation by novices, even novices with knowledge of other forms of gambling; to horseplayers, however, these same requirements are a powerful inducement to betting. In comparison, casino gaming has both wide appeal and the ability to stimulate high levels of gambler involvement. Bookmaking ranks next in these respects, even though in many other ways it does not resemble casino gaming. Racetracks, *jai-alai*, OTB, lotteries, and numbers follow. If casinos are introduced into the geographic market area of a racetrack gaming will not immediately constitute a more attractive gambling activity for confirmed horseplayers. For novice gamblers, on the other hand, casinos are significantly more attractive, meaning that the introduction of casino gaming into racetrack market areas will, over the long term, erode racetrack attendance and handle.[13]

The structural characteristics of commercial gambling games are not the sole factors determining a given game's gross win, or collective player losses. The contextual variables of place and situation are of major importance in this regard. Numbers games, for example, despite their widespread popularity, rank at the bottom: numbers are a very high-priced, extremely simple game characterized by infrequency of gambles, a very narrow range of odds and stakes, no (objective) skill, limited player participation,[14] a low probability of winning, and payout ratios of windfall proportions—a profile that prevents numbers from extracting money from the population at high rates, even in areas where the game is almost universally played.[15] The widespread availability of numbers, coupled with their popularity, produces a substantial gross win—some $2.5 billion in 1983—despite the low extractive capability of numbers games. Although currently perhaps the most dynamic form of commercial gambling, State lotteries similarly—and notwithstanding their very high price—extract money at comparatively low rates. It should, however, be pointed out that State lotteries are rapidly changing in this respect.[16] Prior to the introduction of "instant" and player-active "pick-it" and legal numbers games, State lotteries were much more benign—in other words, much less attractive to the practicing and would-be gambling population. Should the vendors of video gaming devices succeed (with the help of State lottery administrators) in introducing these devices into lottery operations, this form of gambling will, we expect, become fully competitive with racetracks in extractive capability.

Gambling Behaviors and Patterns of Loss

The obverse of the gambling-game profiles just discussed is the emergence of clearly identifiable patterns of loss. As has already been remarked, each commercial gambling game produces distinctive gambling behaviors. Numbers games, for example, create high percentages of habitual gambling relative to other games, and, as far as we are able to determine, no professional gamblers; blackjack, on the other hand, has produced the new profession of card-counting. In general, highly extractive games produce highly motivated gambling behaviors—in other words, professional, serious, obsessive, and compulsive gambling. The correlation of game profile and gambling behavior is not perfect: casual and occasional gambling, which are characterized by low levels of involvement, occur at racetracks and in casinos, and obsessive and compulsive lottery gambling is not unknown. But the correlation between extractive games and high levels of involvement is strong enough to yield a useful result: gambling games interact with collective gambling behaviors to produce identifiable, and predictable, patterns of loss.

State lotteries offer perhaps the clearest example. Lottery games rank fairly low in extractive capability. These games, however, are easy to play, offer an enormous range of odds, and are widely available. The States' ingenuity in making lottery games competitive in nearly all segments of the gambling market has made lotteries the game of choice for casual, occasional, and many habitual gamblers. It is probable that today more people gamble at lottery games than any other form of commercial gambling, including pari-mutuel racing. Lottery gambling is characterized by small stakes; variable, but generally high, odds; and very high price. The participation of large numbers of casual, occasional, and habitual gamblers in such gambling activities means that most players will lose small amounts of money. Some occasional purchasers of lottery tickets will win modest sums, and a few individuals will win more substantial amounts, including the multi-million dollar prizes that have recently become a leading element in the profile of lottery games.

In other words, the State lotteries' $3 billion 1983 gross win ($5.6 billion sales) is extracted in small amounts from large numbers of people. Using the results of a 1975 survey of American gambling behavior commissioned by the federal Commission on the Review of the National Policy Toward Gambling, the Survey Research Center of the Institute for Social Research at the University of Michigan estimated the average loss per lottery player in 1974 at $13.89. Gross lottery sales in 1974 (in eleven States) were $681 million, with a gross win (assuming an average takeout of 55 percent) of approximately $375 million.[17] Since 1974 lottery games have evolved into a more extractive form of gambling. The effect of this is clearly evident in per capita lottery sales (in States with lotteries only), which have grown from $12.71 in 1974 to $58.17 in 1983, an increase of 358 percent. Since average takeouts from lottery games remain at 55 percent, the 1974 average annual per capita loss estimated by the Survey Research Center would likewise have increased by 358 percent, from $6.99 in 1974 to $26.55 in 1983. The increase in average annual loss per player is more difficult to estimate, due to changes in the rate of participation that have produced the enormous growth in lottery sales since 1974.

In contrast, pari-mutuel betting is more extractive, and more highly motivated gambling behaviors are observable at racetracks and *jai-alai* frontons. Professional, serious, and obsessive betting accounts for the bulk of pari-mutuel handles. Stakes are higher than in lottery gambling while the price, although still high, is somewhat lower. Pari-mutuel betting is widely available and, despite the entry-level knowledge required for participation, remains fairly competitive with the even more extractive illegal bookmaking and casino games.

Gross attendance at U.S. racetracks and frontons in 1983 was 105,123,799.[18] Per bettor wagering in 1983 on racing and *jai-alai* programs ranged from less than $100 to more than $300, with the average being $139. The 1975 SRC survey estimated average annual horse-race bettor losses at $85, by applying a 16.6 percent takeout to an average annual wager per bettor of $512.70.[19] Considering that the average per bettor wager on racing programs in 1974 was $100 and that the average number of visits to horse tracks was (according to the Survey Research Center's own findings) seven, this loss estimate appears to be too low. Even using the center's own methodology the 1974 average annual wager per bettor would be $700 and average annual bettor losses $116. If these figures are updated to 1983—by substituting an average wager per racing program of $139 and multiplying this by seven visits—the average annual per bettor wager becomes $973, with the average annual loss per bettor of $183 (using an average takeout of 18.8 percent).

Whatever the exact average annual per bettor loss, racetracks and *jai-alai* frontons without question produce heavier losses than lottery and numbers games. Moreover, the range of loss is greater, due to more variable odds and stakes and the redistributive effect of the exercise of handicapping skills. Highly motivated racetrack bettors, especially obsessive horseplayers, may incur annual losses much larger than the average.

An estimation of per bettor wagering and losses at OTB offices is difficult because OTB does not record admissions. There is no doubt, however, that the habitual nature of OTB betting, coupled with the higher price (effectively 23.6 percent in New York, where approximately 89 percent of all legal off-track bets are handled) exacted from substantially the same wagers available at racetracks, make OTB a more extractive form of gambling than its structural characteristics alone suggest. The crucial variable is contextual. Like lotteries, OTB offices are nearly ubiquitous and are completely integrated into neighborhood, work, and residential life. The configuration of OTB offices is designed to facilitate participation on a daily basis, and this, combined with the inherently involving nature of pari-mutuel betting, means that OTB will inevitably produce large numbers of habitual gamblers. Only lotteries and numbers games are comparable in this respect. Professional gamblers usually do not bet through OTB because of both the absence of much current racing information and (in New York) the surcharge; obsessive horseplayers by definition frequent the subculture of the track; and casual and occasional gambling behavior is deterred by the barrier of entry-level knowledge characteristic of all pari-mutuel betting. OTB remains the special preserve of the habitual gambler.

Bookmaking on team sports creates gambling behaviors broadly similar to those created by pari-mutuel betting. The differences are that casual and occasional betting is almost unknown, and the serious and professional gamblers who bet team sports are frequently even more highly involved than horseplayers in the sports events that are the object of this form of gambling. Bookmaking is highly extractive, due to the facts that sports bets are usually large and, more importantly, are customarily accepted on credit. In spite of the low price and generally good (subjective) odds characteristic of sports betting, the losses, while variable, are often large. The 1975 University of Michigan survey estimated average per capita losses (per sports bettor) at $28, an estimate we find extremely low, even for 1974.[20] While we recognize that illegal activities are notoriously difficult to study, based upon our own observations of sports-betting behavior we are confident that this form of gambling produces large losses for many players. In number and amount these losses are second only to those produced by casino table games and State lotteries.

Casino gaming is the most extractive of all forms of commercial gambling, a statement amply supported by the fact that although confined to just two jurisdictions (one of them isolated from major population centers) in 1983 casinos won $4.6 billion from gamblers. Moreover, casinos are unique in that they stimulate the full spectrum of gambling behaviors. American casinos (in contrast to those in London) are actually two forms of gambling: slot machines and table games; and each form appeals to easily distinguishable segments of the gambling population.

Of all gambling games, slot machines are the easiest to learn. They require no skill, but some participation, on the part of the player; they have high intrinsic play value on a mechanical level; they have very high frequency of gambles; and they offer great ranges of odds, probability of wins, and payout ratios. In short, these devices are almost perfectly calculated to stimulate highly motivated gambling behaviors in individuals who may know nothing about the more complicated games.

Table games add to the attractions of slot machines the structural characteristics of skill, a great range of stakes, and, most importantly, credit play. Every gambling behavior—casual, occasional, risky, professional, habitual, serious, obsessive, and compulsive—at every level of motivation is accommodated by table gaming. In combining table games with slot machines modern American casinos have created the most nearly universal gambling opportunity in history. No other form of commercial gambling is comparable.

The resulting patterns of loss are also unique. The Survey Research Center estimated the average annual bet per casino gamer for 1974 at $448. By applying an operator takeout, or price, of 15 percent to this figure the center arrived at an average annual loss per casino gamer of $67.[21] As was stated in Chapter 3, a price of 15 percent for casino gaming is, by any reasonable calculation, too high. The center arrived at it by substituting casino *drop* for gross wagering, or *handle*. Drop is much smaller than handle. The application of reported losses to casino drop produces a high—and erroneous—takeout, or price; this is the error into which the center fell.[22]

In any case, in comparison with all other forms of gambling, casinos extract larger losses from a larger percentage of the population. That large losses will result from table gaming should be obvious from the description of the structural characteristics of these games presented in Chapter 2. Slot machines, however, are often assumed to be a less extractive form of gambling. This assumption is erroneous. By way of illustration, consider that in 1983, 340,248 buses carried 10,970,551 passengers to Atlantic City.[23] If these passengers were primarily slot-machine players[24] and contributed only half of the casinos' $867 million slot win,[25] the average per player slot loss per visit was $39.51. Atlantic City bus passengers are normally repeat visitors, often on a regular, and even weekly, basis. It is a fair assumption that per capita average annual slot losses were much higher than $39.51. Assuming the 10,970,551 bus passengers comprised approximately 1.8 million individuals making an average of six visits a year, the average annual per player slot loss of bus passengers was $237. For the overwhelmingly blue-collar population who use bus transportation an annual expenditure on slot gaming of $237 is high—more, for comparison, than a family of three with an annual income of $15,000 spent on alcoholic beverages in 1981.[26]

Conventional and Nonconventional Gambling Behaviors

At the beginning of this chapter we stated that gambling behaviors arrange themselves along a spectrum of increasing but not necessarily progressive involvement. At the lower end is casual gambling, where involvement is minimal; the opposite extreme is compulsive gambling, where involvement is total. In between is a graduated range of behaviors resulting from the interactions, in particular social contexts, of gamblers and gambling games. There is a natural division of this spectrum into conventional and nonconventional types of gambling. Casual, occasional, habitual, risky, and serious gambling behaviors all are located along the conventional side of this division; professional, obsessive, and compulsive gambling behaviors are located along the nonconventional side. This division is categorical: instances of any given gambling behavior are always either conventional or nonconventional, depending on the location of that behavior along this spectrum.

Conventional gambling behaviors fall into the realm of leisure and constitute play. Gambling behaviors labeled nonconventional fall outside this realm. There is thus a perfect correspondence both between gambling as play and conventional behavior and between gambling that does not conform to cultural definitions of play and nonconventional behavior. (It is, in fact, this correspondence that is the basis for the cultural distinctions between gambling behaviors made in Table 3.) Play is superfluous in that it serves no economic purpose; is never imposed by physical, moral, or psychological necessity; is done at leisure; may be begun and suspended at will; contains its own internal course and meanings; and is distinct from "ordinary" life both as to locality and duration. Play is not, however, trivial; it is fundamental to social life. In play, one's personality is fully and freely expressed, and this expression is made absolutely necessary by the anomie and meaninglessness of so many modern careers. Without play American life would lose essential meanings; society would indeed conform to the dehumanized economic mechanism Marx predicted. More and more the domain of work constricts the promises of childhood and the cultural inheritance from past generations; increasingly, only at play, in the domain of leisure, are Americans free.

Conventional gambling behaviors are examples of such liberating play. Casual, occasional, habitual, risky, and serious gamblers gamble freely at games that structure a portion of their leisure time. The various compulsions so frequently cited by psychologists as the motivations for gambling are not characteristic of these behaviors. Conventional gambling serves no purposes other than those common to other forms of play. It does not intrude itself into "ordinary" life nor does it impair the conventional gambler's ability to function in the domain of work or to carry out personal responsibilities. It is voluntary behavior.

Losses incurred as a result of conventional gambling are voluntary expenditures for a particular leisure activity. They do not differ in sociological meaning from expenditures for movie or theater tickets, pleasure travel, an evening at Carnegie Hall, a night's dancing at a discotheque, or a day's amusement at Disneyland. The risk, diversion, excitement, temporary escape, immediate gratification of individual decisions, possibility of financial gain, and multitude of similar satisfactions that conventional gamblers derive from gambling are values received in exchange for gambling losses. The cultural, legal, moral, ethical, religious, and economic meanings of these expenditures are not relevant here. To individual gamblers and to society these expenditures are, in sociological terms, normative behavior; conventional gambling losses are discretionary and affordable payments for play.

Professional, obsessive, and compulsive gambling are perversions of activities that in normative terms are play, and as such are nonconventional behaviors. As was noted earlier, professional gambling serves an economic purpose and therefore constitutes work. Obsessive gambling is an escape from societal or personal pressures into the order of gambling-generated subcultures that transcends the realm of leisure and intrudes upon the "ordinary" world. It is a self-annihilating behavior that ultimately conforms so closely to the game's formal structures that the interactional nature of conventional gambling is transformed: conventional gambling motivations are replaced by motivations generated from the game itself. Compulsive gambling is a manifestation of personality disorder. This behavior is not, in its final stages, interactional at all. In contrast to obsessive gambling it is world-annihilating, wholly solipsistic, and actively destructive of the personality, which ceases to gamble with any other purpose than the stimulus/response gratifications of the activity itself. Alone among gambling behaviors and in contrast to normative play and to work as well, compulsive gambling is infantile and completely uncontrolled.

The involuntary nature of compulsive gambling, the excessive importance of obsessive gambling, and professional gamblers' extraction of economic gains from activities that are normatively play raise some difficult questions regarding the valuation of losses resulting from these nonconventional behaviors. First, the "values" received in exchange for these losses, arguably, corrupt both individuals who exhibit nonconventional gambling behavior, and society itself. Unlike a casual or risky gambler, the compulsive gambler derives no benefit from gambling but rather the reverse: certain financial loss and probable ruin, the sacrifice of personal relationships, responsibilities, work, and ultimately self. The obsessive gambler escapes pressures that in varying degrees bear upon everyone; but in contrast to the temporary escape of conventional gambling, which may leave the conventional gambler refreshed and, thus, better able to deal with these pressures, the obsessive gambler's escape is more or less permanent. The problems that prompt obsessive behavior, which are in some objective sense "real," are made worse by gambling instead of being resolved.

Alone among nonconventional gamblers, the professional realizes objective gains from gambling. We can think of no sociological consideration that would deny him his profits. Professional gamblers are generally exceptionally free individuals, and it is hard to impute some social ill to their gambling activities. The classic objection to professional gambling is that it violates the work ethic: the card-counter or poker player is "getting something for nothing," the corollary being that these gamblers profit from the weaknesses of others. Of course, these arguments may be used against any gambling behavior; to the extent that they reflect moral and religious or even ethical views they are essentially matters of belief and, as such, unanswerable. It should be clear from the analysis of gambling games provided in Chapters 2 and 3, however, that successful professional gamblers will always be a tiny minority of the gambling population. The casinos that offer blackjack are not charitable institutions, and the highly competitive nature of poker and pari-mutuel betting ensures that the number of exploitable gambling situations will remain small and the standards of success in these professions high. In other words, inherent structural characteristics protect both the operators and the patrons of commercial gambling games from excessive exploitation by professionals. (Informal poker and bridge games are another matter. We are convinced that substantial amounts of money are extracted by professionals from these activities.) Commercial gambling games that offered significant professional gambling opportunities would quickly cease to be commercial; the measures taken by casinos to limit the winnings of blackjack card-counters are a good example of the change in gambling structures that in such cases naturally occurs.

Conventional gambling losses represent discretionary consumer spending for values received in leisure pursuits. They are expenditures, voluntary and generally harmless, for a variety of needs subsumed under the general category of play. But losses incurred in the course of *nonconventional* gambling are not harmless. This is widely understood as far as compulsive gambling losses are concerned, but the identification of this comparatively rare behavior with all kinds of gambling by antigambling reformers and their witting or unwitting allies in the fields of medicine and psychology has robbed this indisputable fact of much of its credibility with policymakers and the public. Once it is realized, however, that "harmful" gambling is not one but several distinct behaviors and is the product of interactions between particular games and individual gamblers in highly variable social contexts—once it is realized, in short, that nonconventional gambling is not an identity trait but a behavior that, in a given set of circumstances, may be exhibited by normal people—the entire issue becomes clearer. Casual, occasional, risky, habitual, and serious gambling are limited by the general bounds that circumscribe all leisure play. These gambling behaviors are, in a sense, self-regulating: conventional gamblers will only gamble, and consequently will only lose, so much before turning to other activities.

Obsessive and compulsive gambling are qualitatively different. The downward spiral into obsessive gambling can absorb large portions, and even all, of the gambler's disposable income. The uncontrolled nature of compulsive gambling entails the possibility of unlimited loss. Both behaviors are easily exploitable, and we have serious reservations about gambling laws that contain a statutory motivation for government, either directly or through franchised operators, to increase losses incurred from obsessive and compulsive gambling.

In asserting these reservations we do not suggest a return to blanket prohibition. Rather we wish to elucidate an important public issue that is usually "debated" in the language of emotional polemic. The existence of nonconventional gambling behaviors poses a problem that in some ways parallels the problem posed by criminal participation in the casino gaming industry. It is not difficult for informed observers to identify criminal elements, but it appears impossible, within the constraints of constitutional government, to devise laws and law enforcement procedures that bar these criminals while at the same time admitting legitimate operators. Similarly, the identification of nonconventional gambling behaviors is relatively easy, but there seem to be no criteria for predicting "harmful" gambling careers. Nor is there, in our view, any more or better justification for efforts to deny nonconventional gamblers access to public gambling than there would be for attempts to deny potential or practicing alcoholics access to bars or liquor stores.

NOTES

1. We take no position in the debate as to whether compulsive gambling should be classified as a disease. There are complex medical and legal matters at stake in this debate, including the use of public funds for compulsive gambling study and treatment, the question of whether compulsive gambling may be used as a defense in legal proceedings where the responsibility for gambling-related debts or crimes is an issue, the responsibility of casino credit managers where compulsive gamblers are concerned, and the respective liabilities of casinos and self-described compulsive gamblers for bad credit resulting from willful attempts to defraud casinos. Two recent and widely publicized examples, both involving credit, are the extension of more than $4 million to David Zarin in 1980 by Resorts International (Atlantic City) and the suspension of Art Schlichter in 1983 by the National Football League for betting on professional football games. In May 1981 Zarin was charged with ninety-three counts of theft by deception, and, upon admitting to compulsive gambling, was accepted in a pretrial intervention program. Resorts was fined $75,000 in settlement of charges of violating laws and regulations governing casino credit, acknowledging "that its pre-existing credit practices and policies were insufficient to prevent it from being defrauded by one of its casino patrons." Daniel Heneghan, "Resorts Agrees to Fine in $4 M. Zarin Case," *Atlantic City Press,* September 8, 1982. In March 1983, Schlichter, a quarterback for the Baltimore Colts, admitted to losing a sum which was eventually reported to exceed $750,000 to Baltimore bookmakers and following his suspension by the NFL was admitted to an undisclosed center for treatment of compulsive gambling: Douglas S. Looney, "A Big Loss for a Gambling Quarterback," *Sports Illustrated,* May 30, 1983, pp. 30–31. Schlichter's suspension received extensive media coverage, prompting the academic authors of a recent book about Thomas Szasz, a critic of the psychiatric profession, to remark in the *Los Angeles Times* that "There is not the slightest shred of evidence that gambling can be pathological, or actually disease-related. Moreover, there is no evidence that it is any less controllable than any other human temptation. How can psychiatrists persuade the public that gambling is a disease when it isn't and why would they want to mislabel it in this fashion?" Richard E. Vatz and Lee S. Weinberg, quoted by Andrew Beyer, "Psychiatrists Ill-Advised on Gambling," *Washington Post,* July 3, 1983.

2. John Koza, "Who Is Playing What: A Demographic Study," *Public Gaming Magazine,* March, April, May, June 1984, empirically supports our view that gambling games are not generally substitutable one for another. For example, regular horse players tended not to be regular lottery players in Koza's study. (Koza is one of the founders and the present chairman and chief executive officer of Scientific Games, Inc., a wholly owned subsidiary of Bally Manufacturing Company, that is the largest vendor of games to State lotteries.)

3. Baccarat odds are among the most favorable of all commercial gambling games, the average house "edge," or advantage, being approximately 1.2 percent of handle. These low odds combined with the characteristic betting of very high stakes risky baccarat players explain the great volatility of baccarat win-to-drop *(hold)* percentages in comparison with other table games. In the second half of 1982, for example, five of the nine Atlantic City casinos reported monthly losses at baccarat: Resorts International, a loss of $1,179,768 for September; the Sands, a loss of $177,287 in August; Playboy, losses of $94,363 in August and $34,051 in October; Caesars, a loss of $1,405,910 in November; and the Tropicana, a loss of $97,879 in October: State of New Jersey, Casino Control Commission, *Monthly Reports of Casino Revenues and Estimated Tax on Gross Revenues.* These losses are produced by player strategies of making comparatively few bets of enormous size, which, in effect, allow the baccarat player willing to put such amounts at risk to escape the "grind," or relentless operation of the house edge against player bankrolls that over a sufficient number of gambles at all casino games produces the house win, or player loss. Collectively, of course, baccarat players lose because this game, while offering high stakes at low odds, remains unfavorable to players. Overall the nine Atlantic City casinos won $54 million at baccarat in 1982. The monthly losses incurred in the second half of 1982 do, however, indicate the invited presence in Atlantic City casinos of some successful risky baccarat players—high rollers are avidly sought by American casinos that seek to position themselves at the high end of the market. No monthly losses were reported for other table games, where the odds and characteristic betting of smaller stakes preclude such results.

4. There are three good accounts of the transformation of professional gambling from the occupation of talented entrepreneurs to organized businesses in the late nineteenth century: David R. Johnson, "A Sinful Business," in *Police and Society,* ed. Bayley, pp. 17–47; and Haller, "Changing Structure of American Gambling"; Haller, "Bootleggers and American Gambling," in *Gambling in America,* Appendix 1, pp. 102–43.

5. Poker is at its higher levels dominated by professional gamblers, but, as has previously been noted, this game is of relatively minor commercial importance. An excellent recent profile of professional poker players is A. Alvarez, "A Reporter at Large: Poker World Series," *New Yorker,* March 7, 14, 1983.

6. Ken Uston and Roger Rapoport, *The Big Player* (New York: Holt, Rinehart and Winston, 1977) is an entertaining account of the adventures of a team of blackjack card-counters.

7. Of the large number of books by or about professional horseplayers, Beyer, *Picking Winners,* may be recommended for the insights it provides into a highly specialized profession.

8. Serious and knowledgeable readers may be tempted to cite European roulette as an exception to these statements. While relatively unpopular with Americans, roulette historically has been the principal game in casinos on the Continent, particularly in France and along the Mediterranean. Many Europeans play roulette seriously and to the exclusion of other games—in other words, in a manner corresponding to the authors' definition of *serious* gambling. The basis for this interest in roulette is the belief, or superstition, that the *next* turn of the wheel can somehow be predicted by analyzing the results of previous turns. More precisely, serious roulette players do not believe this game is subject to the law of independent trials; they are encouraged in this illusion by European casinos, which allow roulette players to keep elaborate records of the results of successive trials of their roulette wheels, with some casinos going so far as to provide computer-generated print-outs and/or video displays of these results at their roulette

tables. Attentive readers of the preceding chapter know that roulette is a game of pure chance and will realize that serious roulette players are in fact exercising a *pseudo-skill.* Attempts to win at roulette by finding clues to future trials in past results are a species of numerology; the "dream books" perused by players of inner-city numbers games are like cultural artifacts of American commercial gambling.

9. That is, pari-mutuel betting markets are at least weakly efficient.

10. Pari-mutuel betting in the United States has historically been on a cash basis. In recent years, however, racetracks in several eastern States have allowed banks to install cash machines activated by bank credit cards. Holders of such cards have access to credit to the limit of their card account through these machines. This credit is extended by the bank, and not the racetrack, in contrast to the credit extended directly by casinos and illegal bookmakers.

11. Weinstein and Deitch, *The Impact of Legalized Gambling,* p. 150.

12. The compulsive gambler is an exception at one extreme: he will gamble on anything. The game is irrelevant. His motivations (from Table 3) are not game-generated. Casual gamblers are exceptions at the opposite extreme, and the particular game for these individuals is also more or less unimportant.

13. Somewhat different conclusions regarding the consequences of introducing casinos into racetrack market areas are reached by Killingsworth, Liddy & Co. (Killingsworth Associates) in "The Nature of Wagering Markets and the Implications for Pari-Mutuel Regulation and Taxation" (Arlington, Mass.: Killingsworth, Liddy & Co., 1981): "The impacts on racing, should casinos be introduced to most areas, would be relatively severe. . . . The fan base for racing contains a substantial number of persons who would bet at casinos, if casino gamble were made more accessible to them. . . . Survey data indicate that current casinos in the vicinity of a racetrack appeal to about *sixty percent* of the track patrons. . . . These fans are more likely to *substitute* visits to the casino for visits to the track . . . because this group contains a significant number of fans who tend to visit the track as often and wager as much as their 'wagering budgets' will allow." The adverse impact of the introduction of casinos on racetrack handles and attendance would certainly be more severe in markets saturated with gambling opportunities; in any case, however, we believe the immediate effects will be less severe than the long-term effects as current gamblers die out and new gamblers mature into the market.

14. Though limited—to the choice of the number played—this is the game's main attraction.

15. Numbers games would extract money at even lower rates were it not for the fact that numbers gambling is, par excellence, the example of habitual behavior.

16. State lotteries (inclusive of legal numbers games) won $2.2 billion in 1982, due principally to the fact that approximately 42 percent of the nation's population had easy access to lottery gambling.

17. Kallick, "Survey of American Gambling," in *Gambling in America,* Appendix 2, pp. 93–96.

18. National Association of State Racing Commissioners, *Pari-Mutuel Racing 1983 Statistical Summary.* This figure is the *gate,* or number of paid admissions. The number of individual patrons was of course much smaller, reflecting the tendency of pari-mutuel bettors to gamble on a regular basis.

19. Kallick, "Survey of American Gambling," in *Gambling in America,* Appendix 2, pp. 93–96.

20. For a discusison of this and other estimates of illegal gambling, see the Appendix.

21. Kallick, "Survey of American Gambling," in *Gambling in America,* Appendix 2, pp. 93–96.

22. For a more complete discussion of casino handle and drop, and of alternative methods of arriving at the price of gaming by employing each of these statistics, see the Appendix.

23. Atlantic City Casino Hotel Association, *Fact Sheet Prepared January 1984,* p. 14.

24. Atlantic City casinos maintain bus fleets that are for the most part used in slot gaming promotions.

25. Bus passengers almost certainly contributed more than half of the 1983 Atlantic City slot win.

26. U.S. Department of Labor, Bureau of Labor Statistics, *Consumer Expenditure Survey: Diary Survey, 1980–81,* Bulletin 2173 (Washington, D.C.: U.S. Department of Labor Bureau of Labor Statistics, 1983), p. 20.

5

Commercial Gambling as a Social Institution

Remember just 20 years ago a meeting to discuss casino gambling might well have been held in a back room in Appalachia, not at the Waldorf-Astoria in the public eye.

—James E. Ritchie, *First Annual Gaming Conference (1979)*

The history of gambling in America is the history of a contradiction: from colonial times Americans have enthusiastically bet on horses and bought lottery tickets, all the while condemning gambling as vice. The censure of racetracks, lotteries, cards, dice, and so forth is among the most enduring of American social mores; few activities have been so widely and consistently regarded as wrong. Today society is in the midst of a historic change: the acceptance of gambling in mainstream America. Fiscal pressures, social change, the scale of modern commercial gambling operations, and the accelerating pace of legalization are transforming the older, relatively small-scale games that were organically related to American culture into a new and qualitatively different entity: the leisure institution of Big Gambling.

Gambling is news. Hardly a day goes by without a newspaper story about the latest lottery millionaire; and the run-up in gaming company stock prices following the spectacularly profitable debut of casinos in Atlantic City[1] made this formerly obscure corner of American business front-page material for the financial press, from the *Wall Street Journal* and the *New York Times*[2] to smalltown papers. However, the social implications of institutionalizing commercial gambling in American society are, unfortunately, not news. The *personal* tragedies and triumphs of gamblers are being transformed into *social* issues,[3] but this transformation has gone largely unnoticed by policymakers and by the media, and its implications, though profound, have not previously been analyzed. There are two principal reasons for this.

First, like psychologists fixated on the compulsive gambling of individuals, the news media have found the personal triumphs and tragedies of gamblers make much better copy than the social issues raised by Big Gambling. Overnight lottery millionaires, $100,000 baccarat plaques and the high rollers who use them, "junkie" gamblers, the exclusion of card-counters by casinos, and the lurid but superficial details of the very real problem of organized crime's participation in the gaming industry are far more newsworthy than, for example, the transformation of American values by the institutionalization of a business our parents considered vice. Second, unlike special interests, at the institutional level of society social interests have no constituency. Large corporations generate revenues and create jobs. They have access to the media through their public relations offices and influence government through a variety of means, of which political action committees (PACs) and lobbyists are only the most obvious. The public has none of this apparatus of institutionalized power. It has two, and only two, representatives in the social process at the institutional level: government and the media.

As a representative of the public interest in commercial gambling, government has two disadvantages. To begin with, it is itself a principal beneficiary of gambling revenues. The revenue imperative has given the States, as well as many counties and municipalities, a vested interest in the legitimation and development of commercial gambling. When revenue and social considerations conflict the natural tendency of government is to compromise—meaning, inevitably, to compromise the public interest. Second, government reacts most effectively to constituent pressure. Between elections this means, for all practical purposes, pressure from interests sufficiently organized to lobby effectively. Only at the polls does the public constitute an effective pressure group. By voting the public is able to address social issues, including social issues raised by commercial gambling. But these issues are, as we have pointed out, complex and widely misunderstood.

Commercial gambling is not something most people are familiar with, nor is it, because of its ambiguous moral status, a subject that is easy to discuss or consider dispassionately. What information voters have about commercial gambling is, for the most part, derived from the media, especially from newspapers. It is, thus, of the utmost importance that press coverage of commercial gambling be informed, thorough, accurate, and impartial: absent these qualities, gambling policies and laws will be the result of a tug-of-war between the fading authority of moral and religious antigambling sentiment and the burgeoning power of institutionalized commercial gambling interests. In these circumstances it is not difficult to predict the outcome. Gambling law and policy will be dictated by gambling interests, and the public be damned.

As a consequence of the institutionalization of commercial gambling an enormous responsibility has devolved upon the news media: the guardianship of the public interest in an aspect of American life that is undergoing rapid and radical change. It is, however, a fact of life that human- (and not social-) interest stories sell newspapers. Casinos and State lotteries naturally attract coverage: like the president, gambling is news. Gambling interests make effective use of this advantage. On the infrequent occasions[4] when public attention is directed to the more fundamental issues raised by large-scale gambling operations the industry is quick to divert the media to more "newsworthy," and, for the industry, more comfortable, subjects. In practice this strategy has served gambling interests extremely well: the industry avoids conflict on issues where unfavorable public opinion might lead to adverse decisions involving legalization or licensing and instead maneuvers its adversaries into debates it can afford to lose. The 1976 campaign to legalize gaming in Atlantic City is a classic example.

Going into this debate the prolegalization forces had at least two major liabilities: first, in 1974 an attempt to bring gaming to New Jersey had failed,[5] principally due to opposition from churches and law enforcement officials, including the State's attorney general;[6] second, the 1976 campaign was largely financed by a corporation, Resorts International, that had past associations with organized crime.[7] Issues, however, do not become social issues unless they are so identified—and the manager of the 1976 prolegalization campaign, a California political consultant named Sanford Weiner, carefully framed the debate to shift the discussion from the possibly adverse social effects of casinos to the economic benefits of legalization.[8] The 1976 referendum limited casinos to a single locality, Atlantic City; revenues were earmarked for the elderly; and casinos were to be privately owned and operated, a provision Weiner used to advantage by emphasizing that the State would not be at financial risk and would, moreover, enact "tough" enabling laws to eliminate the threat of organized crime. Attention was diverted from the issue of organized crime's involvement by an appeal to the public through the revenue imperative: casinos were needed to generate money for an especially deserving group (the elderly) and to redevelop an economically depressed community (Atlantic City). As the closest student of this strategy observes, "Weiner's campaign sold casino gambling to the voters from two angles. It *quieted fears* [of organized crime] . . . through . . . the promise of strict controls . . . [and it] *sold hope*—for jobs, tax relief, and redevelopment for Atlantic City."[9] The industry had chosen the right issues: on November 2, 1976, the public approved casinos by a three-to-two margin.

Usually even this tactic is not required: the economic and political power of Big Gambling gives it considerable ability to set news media agendas. A case in point is a media campaign conducted by Atlantic City gaming interests in the winter of 1980–81 to persuade the public that "over-regulation" by the State of New Jersey was causing the most productive casinos in the world to go broke. The campaign was carefully orchestrated and brilliantly executed: following the release of December 1980 operating results—which showed the six casinos then operating won $48 million, or an average of $8 million per casino, that month,[10] for a total of $624 million in that calendar year[11]—a series of front-page newspaper stories appeared reporting December operating losses for all six casinos, layoffs of casino employees, the delay or shelving of two new casino projects (by Harrah's [Holiday Inns] and Hilton), and industry threats of decreased revenues and capital investment if the State did not relax its "over-regulation."[12]

The press became a forum for the industry's demands: elimination of the authority of the Casino Control Commission (CCC) to review casino advertising prior to publication; elimination of a requirement for each casino to provide nightly nongambling theater entertainment; easing of restrictions on "junkets"—that is, complimentary trips to casinos for preferred customers that have historically posed serious regulatory problems in Nevada, New Jersey, and other jurisdictions: increasing allowable casino space in proportion to noncasino public space inside casino/hotels; elimination of residency requirements for casino and hotel license-holders; repeal of the blanket consent to inspections, searches, and seizures inside casino hotels by the State, required as a condition of licensing; and other demands of a technical nature. An unstated corollary to the industry's position was a *rapprochement* separating the regulation of casino operations from the political and social issue of organized crime's equity and influence in casinos: if the casino companies would submit to a ritual cleansing of tainted stockholders,[13] the State would make a distinction between the corporations, on the one hand, and the actions and organized crime associations of their founders on the other; the companies would be allowed to operate within a regulatory framework conducive to maximum profits—and, hence, maximum capital investment, a maximum number of casino jobs, and maximum State gaming revenues.

Despite some pointed suggestions by former CCC commissioner Albert Merck that the industry—and not the State's regulations—bore much of the responsibility for the December 1980 operating losses and a widely circulated industry newsletter pointing out the "Alice-in-Wonderland" quality of the casinos' argument that "over-regulation" was causing the casinos to show red ink,[14] no articles analyzing the casinos' position appeared in the general press. Relevant facts were ignored or buried in long articles with headlines and lead paragraphs that reflected the industry's propaganda. These facts included the traditionally seasonal nature of Atlantic City's tourist trade (a less attractive place in mid winter is difficult to imagine); the decision of several of the casino companies[15] to build their facilities with money borrowed at rates above the highest prime interest rates of modern times, thereby incurring punitive debt service charges;[16] recognition that three of the six casinos opened late in 1980 and incurred high start-up costs but won relatively small amounts, while all three of the casinos in operation throughout 1980 were highly profitable;[17] the industry's voluntary decision to refrain from junkets (which were one way to get high rollers to Atlantic City in winter) rather than comply with State junket-agent licensing requirements; and the fact that several of the reported operating losses were "paper" deficits created by transfers of large amounts of money from Atlantic City casinos to parent corporations located in other States. The result of the casinos' media campaign was wholly predictable: the State acceded to a relaxation of its more "onerous" regulations, and Caesars and Bally were duly licensed to operate in Atlantic City after Caesars agreed to buy (at an attractive price) the stock held by its founders linked to organized crime,[18] and Bally agreed to sever its ties with its founder and chief executive.[19] The industry's profitability was magically restored. During 1981 three more casinos opened. Despite the high start-up costs and low productivities of these new facilities, the casinos reported 1981 operating income totaling $78.5 million.[20] In 1982, with no new casino openings, the industry's operating income soared to $162 million. Net income for 1982 was $56.7 million.[21] By the third quarter of 1983 all nine casinos were operating in the black. Riding what the *New York Times* now called an "avalanche of casino revenues" the industry's reported *net* income for the first three quarters of 1983 was $145 million.[22] The nine casinos won $1.77 billion in 1983 and $1.95 billion in 1984, nearly surpassing the projected 1984 gross win of the eighty-five large casinos in Las Vegas.[23] The fears of an end to capital investment in Atlantic City so effectively raised by the industry's January 1981 media campaign were, needless to say, groundless. A joint venture of Harrah's (Holiday Inns) and the Trump Organization (a major New York real estate concern) opened a tenth hotel/casino on the Boardwalk in the spring of 1984 and the delayed Hilton hotel/casino in the Marina is now scheduled for completion in 1985, with several other casinos in various stages of planning or construction.

The tendency of gambling interests to camouflage the social implications of Big Gambling is reinforced by the fact that ideas about gambling—and, of course, about other forms of work and play as well—are governed by cultural norms, or ideal standards of behavior. These norms generally lag societal change and may persist long after they cease to reflect the way people actually behave. This is particularly true for gambling. Cards and dice still bear the stigmata of vice and deviance; as an industry, commercial gambling retains the pariah status it acquired in the latter half of the nineteenth century. Privately owned commercial gambling businesses (with the exception of some racetracks) still cannot obtain long-term institutional financing. They must generate capital from operating revenues and/or raise it from public offerings.

This labeling obscures a fundamental and almost certainly irreversible social change. Unlike the sporadic legalizations of earlier centuries, which merely decriminalized activities that remained culturally proscribed and hence were easily and frequently reversed, the wholesale dismantling of gambling prohibitions currently underway reflects a deeper social process. For the first time in our long history of risking money on a chance gambling is being formally legitimated. There is an important distinction to be made here. *Legalization* is something that happens on a given day by the action of a State or its voters. *Legitimation* is conferred by social institutions within a changing cultural context. It is a process, not a discrete act, occurring over years or even generations.[24] But it is happening now. A devil is being exorcised from gambling games, and Americans are granting themselves absolution from a traditional sin. Commercial gambling is entering the American social structure and assuming a place alongside sports, theme amusement parks, television, packaged vacations, and so on as a major leisure-activity institution.

Like other institutions, Big Gambling does not lead an autonomous existence. It acts on and is acted upon by other institutions in a manner analogous to the interactions among individuals and games that is apparent at the micro-level of sociological analysis. Conflict theory is ideally suited to the study of these interactions, especially the legalization process. This approach assumes neither a social consensus of common interests nor a single entity, or process, called "society." There is no consensus of values regarding commercial gambling.

Contemporary gambling industries—whether private, nonprofit, or State-operated—are the result of a history of at least two competing interests, one that would legalize and extend gambling opportunities and one that would curtail gambling or prohibit it entirely. At present the first interest is ascendant and is transforming commercial gambling from a felonious act into a source of government revenue. This transformation raises important social questions in view of the behaviors and losses that are consequences of commercial gambling. The legal status of commercial gambling, which remains a generally proscribed activity allowed by exception, makes the interactions of gambling interests and law-making bodies matters of peculiar importance. Conflict theory, with its assumption that interests rather than individuals define "society" through the exercise of power at the institutional level, provides a special insight into the role of the state in institutionalizing gambling. By applying this theory to the histories of the major forms of commercial gambling we will see that the power of institutional gambling extends beyond its familiar economic and political dimensions to the definition of social values. Power is self-legitimating; might, in other words, makes gambling right.

Social institutions function to provide "firm and reliable programs that individuals can follow at a low level of awareness."[25] People respond automatically to social institutions: these responses are the involuntary behaviors that, like breathing, allow more conscious activities to proceed. Historically the American response to gambling was not automatic. As a socially proscribed activity it prompted conscious attention: one either upheld cultural norms and shunned gambling or violated them and indulged. Today gambling is so commonplace it has become virtually a fact of American life. While a number of factors, including changes in American values that are discussed in more detail in Chapter 6, contribute to this process of institutionalization, none is more important than the role of the state.

Political scientist James O'Connor describes the paradoxical role of modern capitalistic states:

> The capitalistic state must try to fulfill two basic and often mutually contradictory functions—accumulation and legitimation. . . . This means the state must try to maintain or create the conditions in which profitable capital accumulation is possible. However, the state must also try to maintain or create the conditions for social harmony. A capitalistic state that openly uses coercive forces to help one class accumulate capital at the expense of the other classes loses its legitimacy and hence undermines the basis of its loyalty and support.[26]

Twentieth-century America conforms to this description. As contemporary political debate clearly illustrates, the state is in a difficult position: "Every economic and social class . . . wants government to spend more and more money on more and more things. [But] no one wants to pay new taxes or higher rates on old taxes."[27] In these circumstances demand for funding invariably outstrips supply. Further, there is an intensification of the state's fiscal problems and a risk of taxpayer revolt whenever the state is unable to conceal additional expenditures or to justify them ideologically—thus, the search for quick, painless, and "invisible" means of raising revenues to satisfy the insatiable public maw. Economic growth must be stimulated and jobs must be created. The situation is particularly acute in decaying urban areas, such as Atlantic City. For the state these needs take on the nature of an imperative: it must address these issues to preserve or legitimate itself; it must at least appear to offer something to everyone, including those who are cut off from traditional avenues of capital accumulation.

Enter the business of risk. On the surface, commercial gambling appears to be a perfect solution to the state's problems. Revenues are generated from gambling privilege taxes or from the profits of state-run gambling operations. These revenues are "voluntary" taxation: individuals are not forced to pay unless they gamble. To further align gambling taxes with a popular conception of the public interest, the funds generated are often earmarked for conspicuously noble purposes, such as aid to senior citizens, support for the arts, or the revitalization of a dying city. In theory, the people who play are the people who pay, while society as a whole benefits. The state can even claim a social dividend; illegal gambling will be curbed through legal competition.

The record of commercial gambling as a solution to the fiscal crisis of the state is mixed. The political appeal of "voluntary" gambling taxes is undeniable: gambling remains the only traditional vice that legislators can vote for *and* be reelected. Legalizations create an opportunity that many people want, and in this sense gambling authorizations do respond to expressed needs. And gambling does generate revenue, quite a lot of it. In 1983 the government take from lotteries, pari-mutuel betting, and gaming privilege taxes was (very roughly) $3.4 billion.[28] These are direct revenues; the indirect revenue contribution of commercial gambling—in the form of federal, State, and municipal income taxes; property taxes; payroll taxes; and miscellaneous local taxes and license fees—while impossible to estimate precisely, may well have been $1 billion.

Critics of legal gambling are fond of pointing out that except in Nevada,[29] gambling revenues constitute small percentages of government budgets, but this criticism grossly underestimates the political significance of these revenues. The $3.4 billion government derived in 1983 from the direct taxation of gambling translates into thousands of incremental increases in State sales, income, and local property taxes that were not made and filled thousands of budget lines that otherwise would have required funding from other sources. The fiscal crisis of the state is real: at a time when all usual tax resources are being tapped to the point of risking taxpayer revolts the "small" incremental percentages of government budgets supplied by gambling revenues take on the character of political necessities. State lottery or off-track betting dollars that constitute (for example) 8 percent of State aid to education[30] or 5 percent of county or municipal budgets can easily be the equivalent of a 10 percent increase in sales or property taxes. No one should underestimate the political suasion of such calculations on State and local elected officials.

Herein lie the unspoken social implications of using commercial gambling as a solution to the fiscal crisis of the state. These "voluntary" taxes work so well that politicians soon want more of them. Insatiable public needs become a revenue imperative in the formulation of gambling law. The people who voluntarily play are asked to pay more. Government claims on wagering increase, but the cost to the consumer rises. Gambling revenues *may* likewise increase,[31] but at the social cost of making legal gambling more expensive than illegal games, thereby stimulating illegal gambling and so eliminating one of the promised social benefits of legalization.

The internal economic logic of gambling markets forces government to authorize price-insensitive games, of which State lotteries are the preeminent example. While government takes about 6¢ from every dollar bet at racetracks and frontons and about 7.5¢ from every dollar lost at casinos,[32] it keeps from 40¢ to 45¢ of every dollar used to buy lottery tickets. Government's claim on gambling revenue is a powerful reason for it to encourage (or allow private operators to encourage) people to participate in all legal games, but the state's enormous stake in State lotteries is an irresistible temptation. Because the cost to operate a lottery is typically only 8¢ or 9¢ on the sales dollar, *and moreover because the cost falls as sales rise,* the States have every incentive to stimulate lottery gambling. From their point of view lotteries are a perfect deal: for every dollar spent to run a lottery government gets back four or five dollars in "voluntary" taxes—and then government taxes the player's winnings as income. No wonder the state has awarded legitimacy—literally, in the case of lotteries, the State seal of approval—to the forms of gambling that lend themselves to taxation, while continuing to proscribe popular games, such as head-to-head sports betting, which government can neither safely operate nor efficiently tax.

The fiscal crisis of the state, however, is not the only factor contributing to the institutionalization of commercial gambling. Commercialization is an equally powerful force in the transformation of small-scale indigenous social constructions of risk into Big Gambling. In a capitalistic system governments are not the only economic units governed by the revenue imperative. Corporations and large private businesses also generate and disburse revenues on a large scale. In Max Weber's view corporate enterprise performs these functions by rationalizing economic systems for maximum efficiency: beginning with relatively simple manufactures in the nineteenth century rationality and efficiency have transformed an ever-widening range of economic and even cultural activities into modern social institutions.[33] In the twentieth century leisure activities have likewise been subjected to this commercializing process. A range of activities that were formerly thought of as play have undergone an astonishing transformation into major commercial entities. Invariably these transformations are accompanied by great increases in economic scale, and the end result is the addition to the economy of new leisure institutions: prepackaged, standardized activities that substitute for the spontaneous creativity of true play the pseudo-play of built-in responses to programmed experiences. Institutionalized leisure includes such activities and industries as movies, television, theme amusement parks, packaged travel, and professional sports. Even shopping, traditionally a more or less spontaneous activity of going from store to store, has been orchestrated and programmed by shopping malls, self-contained environments combining the visual stimuli, dining and recreational facilities, and other characteristics of theme amusement parks.

All of these different institutionalized leisure activities have an important quality in common: they are the end products of a commercializing process driven by the profit motive. The design of shopping malls serves a purpose beyond utilitarian convenience or even entertainment. Like casinos, these modern versions of the bazaar are fantasy environments that extract more money from shoppers than they would spend walking past a block of similar stores along Main Street. The revenues generated from professional football are enormously greater[34] than the college game from which it is derived—and college football itself was commercialized in the latter half of the nineteenth century.[35] Commercialization substitutes profit for all other values, including the intrinsic values of play. Football, for example, originally played for the sake of the game, has today—especially when "played" or performed for the electronic media rather than for live spectators—in both its collegiate and professional forms acquired an entirely different purpose: winning, at all costs, for the sake of profit.[36]

The following model of leisure transformation summarizes the changes encountered as spontaneous play becomes a leisure institution.

A MODEL OF LEISURE TRANSFORMATION

First, a decentralized, relatively small-scale, spontaneous leisure activity becomes subject to pressures that are usually economic and technological in nature. These pressures act on the leisure activity to change what was true play into a commercial behavior. The interests stimulating this process compete for authority by interacting with society as a whole, using the power they have acquired to legitimate their existence and to conventionalize the behaviors their prepackaged pseudo-play activity stimulates. Eventually the conventional, mass-marketed pseudo-play corrupts the original meaning of the leisure activity. Programmed experiences with built-in responses replace creative play, and the social value of leisure is changed.

Gambling is currently undergoing this process of commercialization and institutionalization. Since the inauguration of the first modern State lottery in 1963, and with accelerating speed in the last decade, spontaneous play at gambling games has increasingly conformed to the programmed experiences[37] provided by America's newest leisure institution. The stakes in this competition, whether measured in dollars, political influence, or the future shape and direction of our society, are large, and it is obvious that gambling competes for these stakes extremely well. The outcome is no longer in doubt: Big Gambling is part of mainstream America. As a step towards understanding the implications of institutionalizing the business of risk we will trace gambling's progress through the model of social transformation outlined above, and then examine in detail recent instances of two peculiarly important stages in this process: the interactions of gambling interests and the state that occur during legalization and licensing of commercial gambling operations.

From colonial times to the Great Depression, gambling remained a social outcast while recording a varied and complicated legal history. During this period American mores were remarkably stable: to gamble was an asocial act, a violation of the Protestant ethic and basic tenets of the American social contract. The number of ills attributed to this single activity is truly impressive. Early on, gambling was blamed for corrupting public morals and damned as sin. It impaired the work ethic and weakened the Puritan virtues of thrift and industry that are the foundation of American capitalism. Even when legal, gambling was associated with criminals and various crimes. It destroyed the bonds of social cohesion, including family, church, and community. It corrupted all three branches of government. Over time, the catalogue of gambling-related social dysfunctions was kept up-to-date: risky chance and sudden wealth unconnected with the production of goods and services violate the principles of rationality and disciplined efficiency that Weber identified as the basis of social institutions;[38] and once the terminology of modern psychology had become current gambling was labeled a stimulus to deviance and clinically pathological behavior.[39]

A more damning indictment is difficult to imagine. Curiously enough, the consistently negative social valuation of gambling is very imperfectly reflected in pre-twentieth-century gambling law, which may accurately be characterized as a series of attempts to alternately banish and allow particular games. As a corpus this law is a hodge-podge. At one time or another various jurisdictions have specifically authorized or tacitly allowed every conceivable kind of gambling, only to ban it again for reasons that range from social considerations to political expediency. Legislatures seem to have responded to more or less fleeting pro- and antigambling sentiments rather than more deeply held cultural values for much of this period; only in the latter half of the nineteenth century was the States' erratic toleration of gambling broadly decreased and the numerous and unsystematic game-specific proscriptions effectively codified into a general gambling prohibition.[40]

Commercial gambling is a relatively recent development. The immediate antecedents of modern gambling industries are the nineteenth-century private lottery companies and the organization of individual gambler-entrepreneurs—riverboat gamblers, bookmakers, and gambling-house owners—into generally illegal but tolerated syndicates that between 1840 and the late 1870s transformed gaming and horse and sports betting from professions into businesses.[41] This Weberian rationalization of gambling services was motivated in part by antigambling laws. The new syndicates were organized for the commercial purpose of generating increased revenues by more efficiently supplying the American demand for gambling opportunities. Gambling prohibitions were an obvious impediment. Instead of trying to legalize commercial gambling, however, the syndicates gained control of political organizations[42] and obtained sufficient influence over municipal and State governments to maintain what were, in effect, government-protected monopolies: antigambling laws were selectively enforced against nonsyndicate operators, ensuring a competition-free market for syndicated bookmakers, race wires, numbers games, and gambling houses.[43] Ironically, these illicit businesses frequently achieved levels of social respectability denied the nineteenth-century political machines: Canfield's elegant Saratoga Club at Saratoga Springs, New York, was patronized by the aristocracy; and the Metropolitan Turf Association of bookmakers, formed upon the demise of pari-mutuel betting at New York tracks in 1888, was a respected business serving a clientele drawn from all strata of society.[44]

The reform that swept many of the most notorious late nineteenth-century political machines from power left in its wake blanket gambling prohibitions in many States. Numbers relapsed into a relatively unorganized inner-city game, only to be reorganized and placed on a sound financial footing by bootleggers made wealthy by the Volstead Act. Bookmaking remained a major commercial business but was driven underground, with the result that between 1900 and World War I some ninety-five racetracks—which had been financially dependent on fees charged bookmakers for the privilege of taking bets on the racetrack grounds—were closed.[45]

The economic crisis within the racing and horse breeding industries caused by the enforcement of antibookmaking laws combined with the fiscal crisis of State governments created by the depression to lay the foundations of the modern legal commercial gambling industries. Following legalizations by Maryland in 1920 and Louisiana and Illinois in 1926 and 1927, respectively, a wave of pari-mutuel legalizations occurred during the depression that firmly established track-operated pari-mutuels as a legitimate form of gambling. In 1931 Nevada, its meager economy threatened, legalized casino gaming.

The revenue needs of the States were thus the primary stimulus for establishing the two industries that were to dominate legal American commercial gambling for nearly half a century. These needs were combined with the appetite for profit that is one of the motivating forces of the American economy to create privately owned and operated pari-mutuel betting and casino gaming industries. These businesses were franchised by the States to conduct commercial gambling on the condition that government derive a "reasonable"—in fact, an extraordinary—revenue from this newly decriminalized activity. As legitimate businesses racetracks and casinos were subject to federal and State income tax; in addition, however, State governments imposed gambling privilege taxes (generally percentages of handle from racetracks and of gross win from casinos). Theoretically, as levies on gross gambling, these privilege taxes are exacted from gamblers rather than operators[46] and are examples of sumptuary taxation, like taxes on alcohol and tobacco.[47]

In other words, private enterprise was allowed to conduct commercial gambling in exchange for a revenue contribution over and above the normal tax liabilities incurred by profitable businesses. The need for revenue, of both government and the gambling industry itself, is thus the first of the forces that brought legal commercial gambling into being and have fueled its development. The revenue needs of private industry are conventional features of our economic system. The extraordinary claim on gambling revenue created by the States as a justification for allowing the conduct of proscribed activities—of allowing commercial sin and deviance—is not. Following Skolnick, we have termed this extraordinary, unconventional government claim on gambling the revenue imperative.[48] This imperative has been the most important single influence on the evolution of gambling laws and policy in the United States because of the unprecedented post-depression demands on State budgets.

The second of the two major forces influencing the evolution of commercial gambling is the American propensity to gamble. This propensity is cultural in origin and of long standing. It gave rise to the often romanticized "professional gambler" who worked the riverboats and cattle towns of nineteenth-century America and to the small-scale, generally quasi-legal, commercial gambling that has always been part of American life. After 1900 prohibition effectively deprived Americans of legal opportunities to gamble, and the resulting unsatisfied demand made the pari-mutuel and gaming industries of the depression era economically viable. Today, unsatisfied demand continues to fuel gambling industries: the anticipated success of newly legalized pari-mutuel racing in Oklahoma and Minnesota and the explosive growth of casino gaming in Atlantic City since 1978 are recent examples of this phenomenon.

Together, the revenue imperative and Americans' propensity to gamble are the engine that is changing a centuries-old form of leisure play into institutionalized gambling. This emerging institution is now exerting unprecedented efforts to stimulate the output of this engine (gamblers' losses) by transforming American gambling behaviors. As in other areas of life, technology is playing an increasingly important role in this transformation. Bookmaking was the first form of gambling to undergo radical technological change: the telephone made illegal betting transactions much harder for police to disrupt; and face-to-face contact between bettor and bookie has been almost wholly replaced by telephone conversation. In an analogous manner video electronics are transforming casino and lottery play. Video versions of poker and blackjack occupy growing space on many casino floors. Prototypes of video gaming devices that combine the elements of arcade games and slot machines are currently available from more than a score of vendors for use both in casinos and in State lotteries. Video lottery devices ("VLTs," or video lottery terminals) are in 1984 in limited use in Nebraska, and in Nevada the Gaming Control Board recently approved the arcade-like "Gold Fever" video game for experimental use in casinos. Most State lotteries now transact wagering through on-line computer systems that facilitate more rapid lottery play and have made player-selected numbers practical to operate. And in a somewhat tardy emulation of illegal sports betting, horse racing is being married to closed-circuit television ("simulcasting") for telephone account betting purposes that effectively extends legal commercial gambling into the home.[49]

The first of these forces, government's need for revenue, is for all practical purposes infinite in a state that promises everything to everyone. This force cannot be exhausted because these needs are insatiable: government spending is limited only by the political process and the relatively untested prospect of State and municipal bankruptcy.[50] From this perspective the laws establishing government's extraordinary claims on gambling revenue have been successful: in 1982 the value of these claims was approximately $3 billion, that being the amount of revenue derived by government from gambling over and above the tax revenues profitable businesses would normally produce.

From the broader perspective of the interactions of institutional gambling and society, however, there is a clear perversion of intent in the laws establishing these claims. If gambling were just another business there would be no basis for the extraordinary taxation of gambling revenues. But gambling is not just another business. Cultural norms, which directly influence legislative actions particularly where normatively unconventional activities like gambling are involved, as a rule make it politically difficult for lawmakers to vote for legalized gambling of any kind. An affirmative vote on such measures can be construed as a vote for legalized vice or sin. Legislatures authorizing gambling, whether in response to revenue needs or political pressures created by gambling interests, need to justify their acts in terms acceptable to the media and the public. The time-honored practice of authorizing gambling as a revenue measure has proven to be the most politically effective "cover" for legalization. By augmenting existing funds with "painless" and "voluntary" gambling taxes such measures acquire universal political, and popular, appeal: no one likes involuntary taxes. Moreover, legislators receive the additional political benefit of the rationale for sumptuary taxation: to discourage gambling on moral or religious grounds by taxing it. The inherent contradiction in these two rationales—of encouraging gambling by authorizing it to raise "painless" revenue, on the one hand, but discouraging gambling by taxing it, on the other—is too subtle to constitute a defect within the generally imprecise nature of legislative discourse, but the government dependency on gambling losses thus created is real and is one of the most important consequences of American gambling law.

Of equal importance is the fact that government has a powerful incentive to alter gambling behaviors so as to increase gambling losses, either directly (through its lotteries and OTB operations) or indirectly (through the gambling privilege taxes exacted from franchised private racetracks and casinos).[51]

The geographically isolated racetracks and illegal numbers and bookmaking of earlier generations satisfied what might be termed the "naturally occurring" (or, in British legal usage, "unstimulated") demand for gambling opportunities. This spontaneous gambling constitutes true, voluntary, nonobsessive play and is, therefore, a conventional leisure activity. There are natural limits to the losses that can be generated from such spontaneous, unstimulated, gambling. These limits, however, conflict with the dictates of the revenue imperative. The small scale and ambiguous legal status of the gambling operations of earlier generations tended to resolve this conflict in the players' favor: even the rationalization of gambling services in the nineteenth century was no more than an attempt to supply a naturally occurring demand.

Today, however, the power to determine the shape and dimensions of gambling markets is shifting from consumers to suppliers: for the first time in history, the institutionalization of the business of risk has made it possible for commercial operators to erase the natural limits to losses imposed by spontaneous play by effecting wholesale changes in gambling behaviors. If, for example, State lotteries are found in practice to extract revenues at too slow a rate, the wide geographical dispersion and large scale of lottery operations, coupled with modern gambling technology and the authority of the state, can rapidly and easily alter the game's characteristics to stimulate gambling behaviors that produce larger losses and, hence, larger lottery revenues. The point is that there is no longer a consensus, or community of interest, between institutional gambling and those members of society who choose to gamble. Riverboat gamblers and the members of the Metropolitan Turf Association had no need to promote their services: both were called into being to satisfy existing appetites. Today this relationship is reversed: the institutionalized business of risk seeks to substitute the built-in responses of programmed gambling experiences designed to produce maximum losses for the limited, naturally occurring demand for gambling opportunities inherent in the American character.

It is at this point that American gambling policy diverges from that of most other industrialized countries. There is a fundamental difference between allowing gambling to the extent of satisfying unstimulated demand and actively promoting gambling, using all the resources and advertising techniques of modern commercial enterprise, as though it were soap or some sort of passive entertainment, like movies or television. There are natural limits to consumer spending on most leisure activities: people can buy only so many television sets, attend only so many movies, visit Disneyland only so many times, and spend only so much money while they are there. None of these activities involves a realistic risk of financial ruin. But the more aggressive forms of gambling stimulate behaviors that progressively extend these limits and may, for some percentage of the population, erase them entirely. The amount of money gamblers can spend on gambling is (at least theoretically) unlimited, and all gambling games entail (at least theoretically) the possibility of ruin.

For these reasons many industrial countries allow commercial gambling only to the extent of supplying spontaneous, or unstimulated, demand. Great Britain's casino gaming policies and law are an example. The British Gaming Act of 1968 allows casinos "only on the scale needed to meet the unstimulated demand for them." "The principle of satisfying unstimulated demand is the connecting thread which runs through the whole fabric of gaming control."[52] To this end the Gaming Act imposes a number of restrictions on casino operations: casinos are proprietary clubs, in which members may gamble provided they were admitted to membership forty-eight hours after making a personal application in writing on the premises;[53] junkets, a mainstay of many U.S. casinos, are banned by the British Casino Association, a trade association of casino operators that requires its members to conduct gaming with regard to the spirit and intent, as well as the letter, of the Gaming Act;[54] each casino may install a maximum of only two slot (fruit) machines;[55] no singing, dancing (either among members or by performers), or other entertainment may be provided; alcohol may be served with meals but not at the gaming tables; casinos may not advertise themselves;[56] tipping (dealer tokes) is forbidden; and credit, other than personal checks that may not be postdated and must be exchanged for cash or chips in their full amount and banked by the casino within two banking days, is not allowed.[57]

These restrictions are intended to ensure that British gaming serves primarily social rather than economic purposes. As enunciated by the chairman of the Gaming Board of Great Britain, the Lord Allen of Abbeydale, the Gaming Act of 1968 was intended

> to purge gaming of its criminal elements, to cut out excessive profits, to ensure that gaming was honestly conducted in decent surroundings, and to reduce drastically the number of commercial clubs [casinos]. . . . Operators . . . were to be strictly controlled in such a way as to discourage socially-damaging excesses and to prevent the incursion of crime. . . . [Regulatory] procedures were drawn on the basis that the loss of a license by an operator who misbehaved could be

> looked on by the authorities with equanimity. . . . It was not a basic purpose of the act to raise revenue for the state. . . . There can certainly be no doubt that the aim in [Nevada and New Jersey] differs a great deal from what Parliament intended for Great Britain.[58]

Unlike Nevada, where the prime purposes of allowing gaming are to generate income for government and to stimulate tourism, and New Jersey, where casinos were legalized to create jobs, a different social philosophy underlies the entire British Gaming Act: "The principle on which [the Act] proceeds is that no one can claim a right to provide commercial gaming; it is a privilege to be conceded [by the Crown] subject to the most searching scrutiny, and only in response to public demand."[59]

These are not idle words. In December 1979, following investigations[60] of fraud, theft, and various illegal practices including junket operations, the illegal extension of credit, and skimming from the gaming tables at the Victoria Sporting Club,[61] the London Metropolitan Police and the Gaming Board instituted proceedings (in March 1980) to cancel the club's gaming license. In retaliation, Victor Lownes, the head of Playboy Ltd., the Victoria Sporting Club's new owner, supposedly suggested to the police that other London casinos were engaged in illegal practices, particularly in soliciting business by illegal means. The devaluation of the pound and the enormous flood of petrodollars into oil-producing Middle Eastern states triggered by the rise in oil prices in 1973 had combined to make the London casino market perhaps the most lucrative in history.[62] In the late 1970s Ladbroke's and Playboy's London casinos had become the principal rivals for the patronage of wealthy Middle Eastern gamblers; in the words of a former Playboy executive, the two companies "were playing for keeps in the high stakes game of wooing and winning the sheiks."[63] This patronage had become particularly important to Ladbroke. The Saudi Arabian Adnan Khashoggi and his entourage were the Ladbroke Club's single largest source of casino win, reportedly losing £250,000 nightly for two or three years in what was probably the largest single game in the world. Khashoggi eventually quit gambling with Ladbroke, and the firm, in an effort to maintain its revenues, expanded a marketing program begun in 1976 to include the systematic identification of high rollers patronizing other London casinos and lavish efforts to recruit these very desirable players for Ladbroke's casinos.[64] In April 1979 the police filed objections against the license renewal of three of the four casinos operated by Ladbroke Group Ltd.;[65] in July 1979 the licensing magistrates refused to renew the licenses of the three Ladbroke casinos; and that December, following two unsuccessful appeals of this decision, the casinos were closed. Shortly thereafter (in July 1980) Ladbroke relinquished the license for its fourth London casino and retired from the London gaming industry.[66]

The Gaming Board and the police continued their efforts to force London casinos into compliance with the Gaming Act. On November 3, 1979, Gaming Board inspectors and more than four hundred police made a dawn raid on the four casinos operated by Coral Leisure Group Ltd. The following April the board and the police asked the South Westminster magistrates to cancel the licenses for three of the Coral casinos,[67] citing violations of the Gaming Act including the requirement that checks exchanged for chips must be banked within two banking days. Still unsatisfied, in February 1981 the Gaming Board and the London Metropolitan Police raided the administrative offices of two of Playboy Ltd.'s three London casinos[68] and in April filed objections to the renewal of the licenses for all three London casinos. Playboy Enterprises Inc. (USA) reacted by dismissing Lownes, chairman and general manager of the supposedly independent, wholly British-controlled Playboy Ltd., together with William Gerhauser, his assistant managing director, and several Playboy Ltd. trustees and directors, thereby demonstrating a degree of foreign control over British Playboy apparently violating the Gaming Act requirement that casino licensees be resident or incorporated in Great Britain.[69] In October 1981 the Licensing Magistrates for South Westminster ruled that Playboy was "not a fit and proper body to hold such licenses," citing among other violations of law serious infractions of the Gaming Act's credit restrictions and the solicitation of business by illegal means.[70] In November 1981 Playboy announced the sale of its British gambling operations to Trident Television Ltd. for $34.1 million;[71] the sale was consummated in January 1982.[72] The Victoria Sporting Club was allowed to remain open, but in February 1982 the Clermont and the Playboy Club of London were closed. The independently owned Olympic Club was also raided in July 1981 and closed at the same time as the Clermont and Playboy clubs.

This upheaval within the London gaming industry reduced by one-third the number of casinos operating in London, from twenty-three in 1978[73] to sixteen in March 1982.[74] Despite the great profitability and considerable economic significance of the closed casinos, the Gaming Board, at the annual licensing sessions for 1982, took the position that the gaming facilities provided by the reduced number of clubs operating as of November 1981 were sufficient to meet unstimulated demand.[75] In May 1982 when the board gave this advice to the licensing magistrates eight applications by apparently qualified operators[76] for additional London casino licenses were pending. After hearing each of these applications four additional licenses were granted, with the remainder denied on the grounds of insufficient unstimulated demand.[77]

Both this policy and its rigorous enforcement are unimaginable in an American jurisdiction. Today American commercial gambling is not merely supplying the naturally occurring demand for gambling opportunities, it is creating that demand. Even if this were being done solely by private operators under effective state regulation it would raise serious questions of social policy in view of what we have learned about gambling behaviors. But this demand is also being created by the States themselves—by governments that in the area of gambling policy are, for all practical purposes, sovereign.[78] This fact adds a specifically political dimension to the issues raised by the institutionalization of commercial gambling in America.

In common with other commercial enterprises, gambling interests compete for economic power. Unlike most businesses, however, gambling operations strive—at times desperately—for two things that are normally matters of course: the legal right to do business and social legitimacy. Prior to the nineteenth-century rise of private lottery companies and some locally influential syndicated bookmaking operations, commercial gambling had essentially no legitimate institutional power. Illegal operators were able to exercise power by illegal means, including the corruption of government and law enforcement officials and the threat and use of violence. Gambling-related corruption is an enduring theme in American history, but it is only in the last half-century that the business of risk emerged as a legitimate competitor for power at the institutional level.

Legal or illicit, commercial gambling stands in a different relationship to the state than do other economic activities. Unlike its competitors for the leisure dollar, gambling requires special dispensation from State constitutional and statutory proscriptions. At first this might seem to simplify matters: the state has the legal right to decide what forms of gambling shall be allowed and who shall conduct them. In practice, however, this power has had the paradoxical result of greatly impairing government's ability to cope with commercial gambling. At every point of contact between gambling and the state—legislation, regulation, law enforcement, tax collection, and the delivery of social services—unusual or unique problems occur. While these problems are manifold they share a common origin in the fact that commercial gambling is allowed by exception to general constitutional and/or statutory prohibitions.

Prohibition was the original sin. It removed gambling from the realm of legitimate economic endeavor but failed to eliminate, or even to measurably decrease, the American propensity to gamble. The inevitable result was the creation of vast markets for commercial gambling which had no legal supplier. These proscribed markets in turn created a number of intractible problems. First, bookmakers, numbers banks, and casino operators made determined, persistent, and successful attempts to enter these markets illegally. The practical result of prohibition was thus to establish these forms of commercial gambling as the business of organized crime; this continuing criminal presence is perhaps the most lasting legacy of late nineteenth-century gambling law.

It is worth remarking this unintended consequence of well-meaning but misguided antigambling laws in the context of contemporary legislation. The stated purposes of gambling initiatives—revenues, economic development, and so forth—are expressions of intent, nothing more. The enactment of these intentions makes them law, but the extent of their subsequent enforcement depends largely upon their degree of correspondence to social and economic reality. The gambling prohibitions succeeded as therapy but failed as laws: they were reflections of the morals and emotions of reformers, not measures that could be realistically applied to American society. The enactment of such prohibitions assuaged sensibilities offended by the spectacle of Americans playing with money and inflicted upon society a problem in the form of organized criminal influence in commercial gambling that remains insoluble. Ironically, this history has a useful moral: the stated purposes of gambling legislation should be evaluated in terms of the proposed law's probable effects in the specific social and economic circumstances in which it would be applied.

A second result of prohibition was to divert the resources of law enforcement and judicial administration to generally futile efforts to keep the lucrative but proscribed gambling markets unsupplied. Third, illegal commercial gambling operators (who, like the owners of legitimate enterprises, wish to secure continuing business) made systematic efforts to disarm prohibitory laws by applying a portion of illegal gambling revenues to the corruption of law enforcement agencies. For the illegal operator these expenditures are simply a cost of doing business, a cost offset by his negligible tax liability. The end result is that criminal organizations have established relatively secure positions in important gambling markets, from lottery games (numbers) to horse-race and sports betting to gaming. The occasional arrest and very infrequent imprisonment of operating or even upper-level employees amount to no more than forced personnel changes in these illegal businesses, and such actions have virtually no impact on the stability or growth of illegal gambling. Even when a form of gambling dominated by criminal elements is legalized, illegal operators often continue in business, either as a better-paying tax-free alternative to legal games, as in the case of off-track betting and State lottery numbers, or by being "grandfathered" into legitimate industries created by enabling laws, as has occurred with casino gaming.

Finally, prohibition has limited legal entry to gambling markets to those suppliers chosen by State legislatures. The revenue potential of proscribed gambling markets is enormous; thus, legislatures are able to create major gambling industries by statute. The pressures to do so and to do so in an unwise manner are great; and while these pressures are strong when they originate in private interests they are even stronger, because harder to recognize, when they come from government itself. A recent New York case study shows how pressures arising from conflicting interests were resolved in the legislature to produce a new legal gambling industry, governmental off-track betting.

LEGALIZATION AS THE RESOLUTION OF INSTITUTIONAL CONFLICT: OFF-TRACK BETTING IN NEW YORK

Pari-mutuel betting was introduced into American horse racing in 1877 at Morris and Jerome Park in New York and at Churchill Downs in Kentucky the following year. The new machines threatened both the monopolies of newly syndicated bookmakers and the morals of the growing reform movement in American politics. Acting in their respective interests, the Tammany Hall–supported bookmakers and their reform movement adversaries combined to halt the spread of track-operated pari-mutuels. By the turn of the century the reformers had emerged victorious from the three-way conflict, and, in a parallel to the contemporary antilottery laws, horse race betting, whether at fixed or pari-mutuel odds, was generally illegal.

The gambling prohibitions damaged horse racing economically, but the sport survived. In many jurisdictions antibookmaking laws were not rigorously enforced and betting at fixed odds was tolerated at a number of major racetracks.[79] This accommodation, typical of contradictory American attitudes toward gambling, gave reformers the satisfaction of prohibiting bookmaking and gave the racing industry the betting revenue it needed to survive. As with other games, the American propensity to gamble began, slowly at first, to erode the nineteenth-century proscription of horse-race betting. But instead of decriminalizing bookmakers, twentieth-century initiatives sought to authorize the track-operated pari-mutuel systems that are the economic basis of the modern racing industry. In 1906 Kentucky legalized pari-mutuel betting at racetracks;

Maryland followed suit in 1920; and a general movement to legalize on-track pari-mutuels began to coalesce as the earlier wave of antigambling reform receded. The debate over pari-mutuel horse racing intensified as the 1920s wore on. Opposition came principally from Protestant churches and retail businessmen, as well as from the entertainment industry. Support for legalization came from racing and breeding interests and from the States themselves, which viewed widespread illegal horse-race betting as an untapped source of revenue.

The State's revenue needs proved to be the decisive factor. In 1926 Louisiana acted to license pari-mutuel horse racing.[80] Illinois authorized pari-mutuel racing in 1927. The onset of the depression plunged many States into fiscal crisis, and the pace of legalization accelerated: Florida legalized pari-mutuel horse and greyhound racing in 1931 and pari-mutuel *jai-alai* in 1935. New Hampshire, West Virginia, Ohio, and Michigan legalized pari-mutuel horse racing in 1933; Massachusetts and Rhode Island in 1934; and Maine, Delaware, and Arkansas in 1935.

Pari-mutuel betting on horse races was legalized in New York in 1939 by the State's voters, who in November of that year approved an amendment to the constitution, which generally prohibits gambling, authorizing the legislature to permit this form of commercial gambling. In 1940 enabling legislation was duly enacted, legalizing pari-mutuel horse-race betting for the purposes of providing a "reasonable revenue for the support of government" and promoting "agriculture generally and the improvement of breeding of horses particularly" in New York State.[81] Both purposes were substantially realized in the following decades: between 1940 and 1970 the State derived $2.3 billion from pari-mutuel betting,[82] and New York developed a major standardbred breeding industry.

The 1940 act created three distinct interests in pari-mutuel betting: the racetracks, which operated the pari-mutuel machines and thereby added the conduct of commercial gambling to their horse racing business; horse owners, trainers, and breeders, who were dependent on pari-mutuel revenue for their livelihoods; and the State treasury, which had a statutory claim on varying percentages of the pari-mutuel handle. A fourth interest, the bettors whose gambling losses must satisfy the revenue needs of racetracks, horsemen, and government, was not recognized in the 1940 act except to the extent of provisions intended to guarantee that betting was honestly conducted.[83]

These interests shortly began to come into conflict. The tax structure originally applied to pari-mutuel betting was weighted in favor of State government. Takeout from pari-mutuel pools was set at 10 percent plus breakage, with 6 percent of the pool and 50 percent of breakage payable to the State as pari-mutuel tax and 4 percent of the pool plus the remaining 50 percent of breakage retained by the racing industry. This distribution reflected the two statutory claims on pari-mutuel revenue: the State, which had granted itself a claim to a "reasonable revenue" from pari-mutuel racing, and the racing and breeding industries, which the State sought to promote through legal gambling. New York State benefited substantially from its claim, extracting some $436 million from pari-mutuel betting between 1940 and 1954.

After World War II, a third claimant appeared. In 1946 New York City enacted a local law whereby the city received an additional 5 percent of handle on horse races run within the city's borders. (The measure was known as the "O'Dwyer bite," after Mayor William O'Dwyer.) This action subsequently was extended by the State legislature to other local governmental units in which racetracks were located.[84] The city's claim on pari-mutuel revenue was satisfied at the expense of the bettors, whose financial interest in betting, it should be recalled, was not recognized in New York's pari-mutuel law. Effectively the takeout from pari-mutuel pools on races run within New York City was now 15 percent plus breakage—a 50 percent increase both in the price of horse-race wagering and in the amount of money extracted by government from this form of legal commercial gambling.

The respective claims of New York City and New York State to pari-mutuel revenue set the stage for a classic intergovernmental conflict. Driven by the revenue imperative, the State, in a series of legislative acts between 1951 and 1955, gradually absorbed New York City's 5 percent takeout. In 1956 the legislature completed this process by reducing the municipal tax on pari-mutuel revenue to zero and abolishing it, thus depriving New York City, Nassau County, and Saratoga County of a revenue source that had yielded $135.6 million between 1946 and 1954.[85] These governments, and especially New York City, began to cast about for some way to restore their gambling revenues. The eventual solution to this problem was to permit more commercial gambling in the form of municipally operated off-track betting.

Coincidentally with the intergovernmental conflict over pari-mutuel revenue a crisis was developing within the State's thoroughbred racing industry. Initially profitable as a result of its near-monopoly[86] on legal commercial gambling, the private thoroughbred racing associations conducting meetings at Jamaica, Aqueduct, Belmont Park, and Saratoga began to encounter financial difficulties in the early 1950s. The associations' net earnings declined rapidly after 1952, due (according to both the associations and the New York State Racing Commission) to the deteriorating condition of the flat tracks' aging plants and to competition from other jurisdictions for the top-quality racing that traditionally had been the special preserve of New York racetracks.

Thus by 1955 the pari-mutuel industry created by the State sixteen years earlier had entered a crisis. The State saw the source of substantial revenues—that is, pari-mutuel betting on thoroughbred racing—endangered by the apparent inability of the privately operated racing industry to maintain its preeminent position. New York City and other local governments had seen their share of pari-mutuel revenues absorbed by the State and, in light of the racing industry's financial needs, had no realistic prospects of restoring these revenues from on-track wagering. And the racing industry held steadfastly to its position that the capital needed to rebuild its physical plant could not be raised in the usual financial markets. Each of these three interests—the private racing associations and the Jockey Club, a private organization established in the nineteenth century that exercises a stewardship over the conduct of thoroughbred racing and breeding; the State Racing Commission; and New York City—went separately to the legislature seeking a resolution of this crisis on satisfactory terms. The legislature, then, became the arena in which these separate interests disputed the future of the State's pari-mutuel industry.

The first interest to obtain a resolution of its difficulties was the thoroughbred racing industry. In September 1954 the chairman of the Jockey Club, John W. Hanes, and two of the club's members, Christopher T. Chenery and Harry F. Guggenheim, proposed in a letter addressed to Ashley T. Cole, chairman of the State Racing Commission, a plan to revitalize New York flat racing. The Jockey Club plan proposed to merge the privately owned corporations operating Belmont Park, Jamaica, Aqueduct, and Saratoga racetracks into a new, non-profit racing association, to be called the Greater New York Association. The New York Racing Association, as it eventually came to be called, was to be debt capitalized through long-term borrowing secured, both as to principal and interest, by a first charge against all association income. Ownership of the association, and of the real properties the association proposed to acquire with part of its debt capitalization, was to be vested in the Jockey Club through nondividend-paying common stock.[87]

The Jockey Club plan aroused immediate opposition within the racing industry and the legislature. Cyrus S. Jullien, president of the Queens County Jockey Club, which operated Aqueduct, and James Butler, one of Aqueduct's major shareholders,[88] claimed that the plan would amount to socialized racing and would destroy incentive and the competitive nature of the industry.[89] One feature of the plan, the closing of the Jamaica racetrack, was opposed by horsemen as likely to result in fewer racing opportunities.[90] A member of the racing commission, William C. Langley, opposed the plan,[91] and Assemblyman James J. McGuiness charged that it would constitute the subsidization of private enterprise by the State. New York City, which was actively trying to restore its claim to a share of pari-mutuel revenues, made its support for the plan contingent upon legislative assurance that city revenues from thoroughbred racing would not be adversely affected.[92]

Supporters of the Jockey Club plan prevailed. On April 2, 1955, legislation enabling the Greater New York Association passed the assembly by a vote of 78–62 (76 votes needed for passage) and the senate by a vote of 31–23 (with 30 votes needed for passage). In May Gov. Averell Harriman signed the bill into law, and the following month the racing commission approved the GNYA's incorporation, with common stock valued at $1,000 to be held by the members of the association's board of trustees.[93] The framework thus established for New York State thoroughbred racing has been continued to the present.

New York City was initially less successful in its efforts to obtain from the legislature a renewal of its direct claim on pari-mutuel revenue. In 1954, the year in which the Jockey Club proposed the transfer of thoroughbred racing from the private sector to the non-profit Greater New York Association, the legislature appointed a seven-member committee (known as the Wicks committee) to study off-track betting. Six of the seven members had previously announced their opposition to off-track betting, and the committee recommended against off-track betting in any form by a vote of 6–1, citing abuses of this form of gambling in other countries. Following the report of the Wicks committee, however, the city's budget director, Abraham Beame, began to study off-track betting as a replacement for the city's vanished "O'Dwyer bite"—5 percent of the pari-mutuel handle of races run within the city. In October 1958 a Mayor's Citizens' Committee on Off-Track Betting was established by Robert Wagner, who proposed to raise $80 million to $100 million for the city's 1959–60 budget from this form of gambling. The citizens' committee voted four to two in favor of off-track betting. Based on this vote legislation to authorize off-track betting was introduced in the legislature in 1959; it failed. Similar legislation was introduced in 1960, 1961, and 1962; these bills also failed.

Opposition to OTB came from two quarters: the racing industry, which feared dilution of its monopoly on pari-mutuel betting, and persons opposed to commercial gambling, generally on moral, ethical, religious, or social grounds. These interests combined to block off-track betting. In general, the public debate over legalization weighed New York City's financial needs against the presumed adverse social consequences of off-track betting: the poor would bet, and moreover would bet disproportionate amounts of money; minors would be introduced to gambling; family life would be disrupted as fathers left their homes for off-track betting parlors; crime would increase; and public morals would be fatally impaired. In 1963 Mayor Wagner sought to reply to these arguments by obtaining permission from the Court of Appeals for a nonbinding voter referendum on off-track betting.[94]

The referendum was approved by a three-to-two margin, and in December 1963 and January 1964 the citizens' committee issued reports that included a comprehensive Plan for Legal Off-Track Betting in the City of New York. Enabling legislation based on this plan, and limited to New York City, was introduced in 1965, 1966, 1967, 1968, and 1969; all of these bills failed. Then, in 1970, an unusual set of political circumstances suddenly shifted the balance of political power in favor of off-track betting. The new mayor, John V. Lindsay, faced a $300 million budget gap. Municipally operated off-track betting, so long sought by the city, offered a partial solution. The racing industry, however, remained adamantly opposed. Normally these industry interests controlled the legislative process where pari-mutuel horse racing was concerned. (The industry's ability to create the New York Racing Association in just six months in 1954–55 and its success in preventing off-track betting initiatives actively supported by New York City, a powerful force in the legislature, are ample testimony to that fact.) But racing interests were unprepared for the political circumstances in which the issue of off-track betting had become embroiled.

Gov. Nelson A. Rockefeller was financially, socially, and politically independent of the interests comprising horse racing and breeding. In 1970 the governor's command of both the State's executive branch and its Republican Party was unchallenged, and when off-track betting became politically expedient Rockefeller did not hesitate. On April 16, 1970, without prior discussion between city and State representatives, Lindsay and Rockefeller incorporated off-track betting into a package of revenue aids intended to close the city's $300 million budget gap for fiscal 1971. None of the arguments, either pro or con, that had formed the substance of the eighteen-year-long public debate were factors in this decision. The moral, ethical, religious, and social arguments against OTB were rendered moot by the abbreviated timetable and the quasi-dictated manner of the decision to legalize. Public opinion simply had insufficient time to register on the legislative process. Three days after the agreement between the mayor and the governor a State-wide, local-option off-track betting bill, with a companion bill creating a New York City Off-Track Betting Corporation, was sent to the legislature under a message of necessity from the governor. On the following day, April 20, the bill was passed, and it became law two days later, on April 22, 1970, with Governor Rockefeller's signature.[95] After eighteen years the city of New York had succeeded in getting into the commercial gambling business.

The advent of off-track betting was a milestone in a conflict among complex social, economic, and political interests that had extended over a period of thirty years. The wellspring of this conflict was not moral or political but social and cultural: the enduring propensity of large numbers of New Yorkers to bet horses, within or outside the law. Frustrated by a bookmaking prohibition wrung from the State by antigambling reformers this propensity found expression in the depression-era movement to legalize pari-mutuel betting. In the 1930s pari-mutuel machines—the iron men—were the focus of a four-way struggle for the New York horseplayer: bookmakers opposed a new competitor; the racetracks seized upon track-operated pari-mutuels as a means of taking horse-race betting revenue from the bookmaking ring; antigambling interests saw in the machines a new threat to public morality; and the State, which derived no revenue from bookmaking, saw in pari-mutuels a new revenue source and a stimulus to the development of a horse-breeding industry. The voters resolved the conflict by approving pari-mutuel betting in the 1939 general election, and the following year the legislature established a new context for the tug-of-war over horse racing by enacting the State's pari-mutuel racing law. The focus of conflict was now pari-mutuel revenue. By 1950 five interests had established pari-mutuel claims: the State; county and municipal governments, of which New York City was the most important; the racetracks; horsemen; and (indirectly) the breeding industry. The State and thoroughbred racing interests won the first round: by 1955 the State had absorbed the city's share of pari-mutuel revenue and acceded to the formation of a non-profit association of thoroughbred racetracks that over the next quarter century required for its maintenance an ever-increasing share of pari-mutuel revenues.[96] In the conflict's second phase both the NYRA and New York City prevailed: the NYRA by doubling its share of pari-mutuel handle, at the expense of the State and the horseplayers, from 4 percent to 8 percent,[97] and the city by winning the authority in 1970 to conduct off-track betting, from which it derived $572.4 million between the start of OTB operations in April 1971 and June 30, 1982.[98]

Off-track betting was precipitated by two forces: New York City's chronic revenue needs and political expediency. Neither the economic well-being of the racing industry, which was one of the statutory purposes for the 1939 exception to the State's constitutional prohibition of commercial gambling, nor any moral, religious, and social objections to off-track betting were factors in the decision to legalize. Revenue and political considerations have likewise governed the development of New York's off-track betting industry, and of the pari-mutuel racing industry generally, since 1970. The legislature justified legal off-track betting with two statutory purposes: "to derive from such betting . . . a reasonable revenue for the support of government, and to prevent and curb unlawful bookmaking and illegal wagering on horseraces."[99]

Initially off-track betting (or OTB as the New York City Off-Track Betting Corporation immediately came to be called) accomplished both of these purposes. In its first twenty months of operation OTB handled $568.9 million and distributed $30 million to the State and to New York City. Small bookmakers specializing in horse-race betting ("handbooks") were driven from the market. The racing industry, however, fared less well. Overnight, off-track betting had broken the tracks' monopoly on legal pari-mutuel wagering. OTB drew handle from racetrack pari-mutuel windows as well as from illegal bookmakers, while at the same time attracting some new bettors to pari-mutuel racing. The overall market had been increased, but the tax structure initially applied to off-track handle favored government at the expense of the racetracks and horsemen. The industry's share of OTB's first twenty months' handle was $13.9 million, less than half the amount distributed to government and not enough to make up for OTB's impact on track handle and attendance.[100]

The restructuring of the market for pari-mutuel wagering effected by OTB and the government-weighted tax structure that was applied to off-track handle combined to produce a crisis in New York's racing industry. In bowing to the revenue imperative and creating a new commercial gambling industry without sufficient regard for the probable effect of its action on an existing industry, the legislature had inadvertently endangered the revenue and economic contributions of the racing and breeding industries that it had originally sought to encourage by enabling pari-mutuel betting in 1939. Economic reality, in the form of the evident distress of the racetracks, forced the State to reconsider. In 1972 and again in 1973 it increased racing's claim on off-track handle, enlarging upon the statutory purposes of off-track betting by adding to the off-track betting law "the intention [that] off-track betting is conducted in a manner compatible with the well being of the horse racing and breeding industries in this state, which industries are and should continue to be major sources of revenue to state and local government and sources of employment for thousands of state residents."[101]

In just twenty-one months, the immediate impact of off-track betting on the racing industry was clearly evident from declining racetrack handles and attendance.[102] This illustrates a general truth about gambling legalizations: the economic consequences of commercial gambling can be reduced to statistics, measured, and used as a comparatively reliable basis for making needed changes in gambling policy and laws;[103] the social consequences of commercial gambling, legal or not, are much less apparent. The second statutory purpose of off-track betting, to curb illegal bookmaking, provides a case in point.

Until 1974 OTB, the tracks, and illegal bookmakers paid identical winning prices, enabling OTB to attract significant amounts of business away from bookmakers. In 1974, however, the legislature imposed a 5 percent surcharge on legal off-track payouts. The surcharge is an example of the revenue imperative in gambling law, a measure intended to increase OTB's financial contribution to municipal and local governments. Currently this tax yields about $65 million annually—a quantifiable result that has made an indelible impression on legislators. The surcharge, however, has much less easily quantified but disastrous consequences for OTB's ability to compete with illegal bookmaking. It makes OTB's payouts lower, often much lower, than illegal payouts.[104] In effect the surcharge is a statutory price advantage for illegal bookmakers. The inevitable result was a resurgence in illegal horse-race wagering. Despite objections from law enforcement officials and annual OTB-sponsored surcharge-reform bills, the legislature, weighing the bird in the hand of $65 million against the unquantifiable benefits of lifting the surcharge,[105] have done the predictable thing and continued this socially indefensible tax.

With the legalization of off-track betting the conflict among the various interests in New York's pari-mutuel racing industry entered a third phase. A new and essentially political interest had entered the struggle: local government. A majority of New York State's municipal and county governments are directly involved in the operation of off-track betting—a unique development in the history of American commercial gambling. OTB was not the only supplier to enter the New York gambling market in the 1970s. Coincidentally with the introduction of off-track betting a profound change in the market economics of pari-mutuel racing began. Throughout the eastern States, racetracks, which had enjoyed nearly uninterrupted growth in handle and attendance since the end of World War II, started to feel the effects of competition from other forms of legal commercial gambling. Unsatisfied with their substantial pari-mutuel revenues, the eastern States authorized lotteries, *jai-alai*, OTB, and, in Atlantic City, casinos. An eroding patron-base forced racetracks into the destructive competition for horses, purse money, and horseplayers that is today forcing weaker tracks to close.

This internecine competition among States for pari-mutuel revenues is particularly severe in the New York and Philadelphia metropolitan areas.[106] In 1976 New Jersey completed the first stage of a $450 million sports complex funded by revenues derived from flat and harness racing at the Meadowlands, a new racetrack located across the Hudson River opposite midtown Manhattan. The tax structure applied to Meadowlands' handle distributes only 0.5 percent to the State; the bulk of net revenue from racing operations, totaling $41.5 million in 1982, is used to service bonds for the sports complex.[107] Essentially the Meadowlands is an example of state capitalism in commercial gambling: the State of New Jersey elected to forgo its revenue claims in the interest of economic development. Its unusual tax structure has enabled the Meadowlands to offer attractive purses, and the resulting high-quality racing, together with its new facility and proximity to New York City, have made the track—especially its harness meeting—enormously successful. The impact of the Meadowlands on the four New York metropolitan area racetracks, coming on top of the economic restructuring produced by OTB, was very serious, particularly for the harness tracks, Roosevelt and Yonkers raceways.[108]

Today the conflict over New York pari-mutuel betting remains unresolved. OTB is firmly established as a social institution, with the legitimacy of a governmental operation and the street-level character of State lotteries. It is a local gambling business: part of hundreds of New York neighborhoods and scores of New York governments. But the revenues that OTB generates, and the economic needs of the racing industry that grow more acute as the industry's economic crisis deepens, have perpetuated the struggle over off-track betting. On taking office in January 1984, Gov. Mario Cuomo announced a review of the State's six regional off-track betting corporations, with specific consideration given to three possible arrangements: a single State-operated system; private ownership and operation; or operation by the New York Racing Association.[109] OTB, a commercial gambling industry created to serve both revenue and social purposes, has become the object of a power struggle at the institutional level of society. The State, large private interests, and the thoroughbred racing industry wish either to acquire or increase a vested interest in off-track betting. OTB and its constituent county and municipal governments is a fourth interest in this competition, which will be played out and resolved in the New York legislature.

It is a high-stakes game. For New York City and local governments throughout the State a claim on pari-mutuel revenue worth some $125 million a year is at risk. The State itself has the prospect of equivalent revenue gains, while to the NYRA control over OTB represents a solution to the chronic financial weakness that threatens the State's thoroughbred economy. Overriding these parochial interests is the general economic crisis racing in New York shares with that in other eastern States. OTB, augmented by State-wide simulcasting, is the key, providing a means of generating sufficient revenues to restore horse racing to economic health. Finally, there is the even larger, but more diffuse, public interest in commercial gambling. What are the social costs of the surcharge, and how are these costs to be measured against the revenue that the surcharge yields? How are the interests of horseplayers, whose losses fund the entire pari-mutuel economy (and significant percentages of New York government budgets), served by legal off-track betting that pays poorer odds than illegal bookmakers? Does OTB add or subtract from the sum total of true leisure play in New Yorkers' increasingly regimented lives? What is the public interest in off-track betting or State lotteries or Atlantic City casinos?

COMMERCIAL GAMBLING AS A SOCIAL INSTITUTION

The variety of interests in commercial gambling make objective answers to these questions impossible. Conflict and uncertainty are inevitable: as a social institution gambling is an inherently risky business. It is nevertheless possible to identify some of the social—as opposed to the special—interests in gambling as an institutional component of society.

Historically, the social value of gambling was a unique form of leisure play. Gambling supplied Americans with a combination of circumscribed risk, temporary escape from the workaday world, internally consistent subcultures, a variety of self-actualizing acts that (at least momentarily) restored to the individual the feeling of mastery over fate, and the opportunity to play with money instead of being dominated by it. This combination of values was not duplicated by any other leisure activity.

The labeling of gambling as deviance and vice, while preventing some of its true social values from being generally recognized, also kept gambling within specific social limits. Now these limits are being erased, and the social values of some unique games, which were the common property of American society, are being sacrificed to the special interests of institutional gambling. The business of risk is replacing naturally occurring gambling behaviors with stimulated responses to programmed experiences designed to produce maximum losses from the maximum number of people. Gambling interests are thereby served, but at the cost of increasing the personal and social risks of gambling. For individual gamblers, as well as for society as a whole, the price of institutionally stimulated gambling is rising as the revenue imperative forces government to extract more and more money from gamblers to satisfy the state's insatiable revenue needs. Moreover, the public funds raised through government's extraordinary claim on gambling revenue are not derived from the creation of wealth (as they are from other taxes); they are derived from gamblers' losses, causing the economic interests of government and players to be diametrically opposed. Government, which bears the primary responsibility for the social consequences of economic activity, has a vested interest the losses of a large and unprotected body of consumers.

These facts should be highly disturbing to the public. The role of government in the interaction of institutional gambling and society is crucial. To produce general benefits, conflicting interests must compete for power before a strong, impartial, and competent referee. Because gambling is, for most practical purposes, an area reserved to the States, the role of referee has fallen to State government. In practice, this has proven to be an unhappy choice. With a few notable exceptions, State governments have failed to meet the criteria of strength, impartiality, and competence in representing the public interest in commercial gambling.

Instead government has been a weak and divided advocate, further crippled by its lack of any clear conception of the public interest it is supposed to represent. The underlying reason for this is that the interactions of legal commercial gambling with society conform to the conflict model of sociological analysis. It is an inherent quality of conflict models that only interests represented in the model are considered in the model's operation. For this model to serve public interests, these interests must be represented at the institutional level of social interaction. Unfortunately, the public interest is not an effective institutional presence in the conflicts that are now transforming American commercial gambling.

There are several reasons for this failure. First, as has been shown, government is itself an interested party by virtue of its extraordinary claim on gambling revenue. Second, government is a divided institution. Legislatures and executive chambers are directly responsible for funding government operations and, as a result, are most sensitive to the revenue imperative. More specific constituencies are represented by various predominantly bureaucratic agencies: the poor and disadvantaged by welfare, housing, and economic redevelopment agencies; compulsive gamblers by public health departments; law enforcement by police departments and attorneys general; regulatory authorities by commissions usually located within the executive branch; community and real estate interests by planning boards or commissions at various levels; and so forth. Finally, a real understanding of gambling is rare outside the gambling industries themselves, and legislators, who deal with the range of society's concerns, have as their primary interests raising sufficient revenue for their constituents' needs and ensuring their own reelection.

None of the deficiencies in government's qualifications as referee are easy to remedy. It is, therefore, understandable that government has generally proven to be weak in withstanding the pressures of special gambling interests, especially when the pressure of revenue and economic imperatives is brought to bear upon legislatures and governors, where power is concentrated and responsibilities are unmanageably diverse. New York State had ample warning of the possibly adverse effect on its valuable racing industry of legalizing off-track betting with a tax structure favoring government; it did not listen. Many of the well-publicized difficulties encountered by New York, New Jersey, and other States in trying to reconcile legal commercial gambling with the public good are explainable in these terms. Virtually without exception, these States came under great pressure to grant the right to conduct gambling operations as a special dispensation. In assessing these experiences, it is not really material whether this pressure came from the Establishment, government, legitimate businesses, or organized crime. Regardless of their identity, the special gambling interests were satisfied, and the public interest, however defined, came off second best. Experience so far seems to indicate that there is no simple mechanism for granting the right to conduct commercial gambling that includes the public interest in the decisionmaking process.

As long as a day at the races or an hour at some quasi-legal casino tables was still genuine leisure play, defining the public interest in gambling was relatively simple: to obtain the social benefits of betting on horses or dice—temporary escape, self-actualization, and so on—with minimum social risk and at the least possible cost to consumers. The rise of gambling to institutional status has altered the social meaning of this increasingly important leisure activity beyond recognition, and the definition of the public interest in this area of American life is no longer simple.

NOTES

1. Gaming company stocks appreciated enormously in the twelve months following the opening of Resorts International's Atlantic City casino in May 1978. Resorts A and B common, which traded for \$2 and \$3 in the middle 1970s, had risen to \$190 by September 1978. There is an entertaining account of this speculative flurry in Mahon, *The Company That Bought the Boardwalk,* pp. 163–73. More detailed coverage of gaming

company securities during this period can be found in *Rouge et Noir News* and *Rouge et Noir Resort Management Report* for 1978 and succeeding years.

2. Neither paper approves of gambling. The *New York Times* has in recent years run dozens of editorials against gambling of one kind or another: "The Betting Addiction," a two-part piece condemning Atlantic City gaming and various forms of commercial gambling in Connecticut, which was occasioned by the publication of *The Atlantic City Gamble* by George Sternlieb and James Hughes and appeared in the December 28, 1983, issue, is a recent and representative example. The same day the *Wall Street Journal* used the same excuse for a very negative editorial evaluation of the Atlantic City casino experience, "A Bad Bet," December 28, 1983. Despite these views, both newspapers provide extensive coverage of the financial aspects of commercial gambling. The *New York Times* additionally devotes some space to gambling-related social issues, or, more accurately, to gambling-related social problems; the *Wall Street Journal* has for some years set a journalistic standard for analytical reporting on the involvement of organized crime in casino gaming, with numerous articles by Jonathan Kwitny and Jim Drinkhall being particularly valuable.

3. The transformation of personal experiences into social phenomena is discussed in C. Wright Mills, *The Sociological Imagination* (London: Oxford University Press, 1959), where a public or social issue is defined as the perception things should be better, or different, with the further implication that society can do something about the issue so perceived.

4. Usually preceding legalization and during licensing proceedings, hence the peculiar importance of these stages in the institutionalization process.

5. A 1974 referendum that would have allowed State-owned and operated casinos throughout New Jersey, with the revenues going to the State's general fund, failed by a vote of 1.2 million to 800,000. New Jersey Election Law Enforcement Commission, "Special Report of Contributions and Expenditures Re Public Question #1, 1976 N.J. General Election—Authorizing Casino Gambling in Atlantic City" (1977).

6. An exhaustively researched account of the 1974 and 1976 New Jersey casino initiatives is provided in Dombrink, "Outlaw Businessmen," pp. 152–82.

7. For a detailed examination of the associations of Resorts International with organized crime see State of New Jersey, Department of Law and Public Safety, Division of Gaming Enforcement, Robert P. Martinez, director, *Statement of Exceptions and Investigative Report Re the Casino License Application of Resorts International Hotel, Inc.* (Trenton: Division of Gaming Enforcement, 1978). See also Mahon, *The Company That Bought the Boardwalk,* for an entertaining account by a knowledgeable financial journalist.

8. Dombrink, "Outlaw Businessmen," pp. 175–76.

9. Ibid., p. 176.

10. By comparison the 125 largest Nevada casinos won $3.2 billion, or an average of about $2.1 million per casino per month, during the fiscal year ending June 30, 1979. State of Nevada, *Nevada Gaming Abstract* (Carson City, Nev.: Gaming Control Board, 1979).

11. State of New Jersey, *Monthly Reports of Casino Revenues and Estimated Tax on Gross Revenues* (Trenton, N.J.: Casino Control Commission, 1981).

12. Donald Janson, "Jersey Casinos Expect First Monthly Deficits Since Their Openings," *New York Times,* January 14, 1981; "Resorts International Laying off up to 400 at Atlantic City," *Wall Street Journal,* January 12, 1981; "N.J. Dec. Casino Revenue off 19.3%," *Newsday,* January 14, 1981; Ronald Alsop, "Casino Glut in Atlantic City Brings Intense Competition," *Wall Street Journal,* January 14, 1981;

"Hilton Delays Work on N.J. Casino," *New York Daily News,* January 16, 1981; Peter Mattiace, "Casinos Lobbying for Less State Controls," *Bergen County* (N.J.) *Record,* January 16, 1981; Daniel Heneghan, "Casinos' Lament: December Win Just Not Enough to Pay Bills," *Atlantic City Press,* January 14, 1981; Heneghan, "Codey: Alter View of Casinos," *Atlantic City Press,* January 16, 1981, reporting the chairman of the New Jersey Assembly's State Government Committee's announcement that he was "reviewing a list of more than 25 possible changes to the Casino Control Act recommended by industry executives to . . . ease unnecessary burdens on the casino industry." Heneghan reports this exchange between a casino executive and chairman Codey: "We told him [Codey] that development here has come to a screaching [sic] halt because the industry can't make money here. . . . [Unless] the [control] commission and the Legislature . . . back off . . . no one is going to bring any more money" into Atlantic City. Heneghan, "Hilton Shelves $250M. A.C. Casino Plans," *Atlantic City Press,* January 17, 1981; "Harrah's Cites N.J. Rules in Delaying Plan for Casino," *Newsday,* January 20, 1981, reporting Harrah's announcement it would delay plans to build a casino on the Boardwalk "while it tries to determine whether New Jersey's tight casino regulations are worth the expense"; "Atlantic City's Red Ink Chasing Casino Builders," *New York Post,* January 20, 1981; "Atlantic City Gambling Loses Its Glow," *Business Week,* January 26, 1981, pp. 85–90.

13. The examples to date being William T. O'Donnell, formerly president and chairman of the board of Bally Manufacturing Corporation, and Clifford S. and Stuart Z. Perlman, formerly chairman and vice chairman of Caesars World Inc., who divested themselves of their holdings in these companies as conditions for the companies' licensing in Atlantic City. The first and precedent-setting decision was concerning the Caesars license application; the evidence for the Perlmans' relationships with organized crime is presented in State of New Jersey, Department of Law and Public Safety, Division of Gaming Enforcement, *Report to the Casino Control Commission with Reference to the Casino License Application of Boardwalk Regency Corporation* (1980), and John J. Degnan, attorney general of New Jersey, and Robert P. Martinez, director, Division of Gaming Enforcement, "Statement of Issues," *In the Matter of the Casino License Application of Boardwalk Regency Corporation: Casino License Application Proceeding* (Trenton: New Jersey Casino Control Commission, 1980). See as well *Rouge et Noir News,* September 30, 1980, pp. 3–40, which reprints the results of a 1976 audit of Caesars World Inc., Dennis C. Gomes, chief, Audit Division, Nevada Gaming Control Board, *Investigation of the Background of Alvin Ira Melnick and His Financial Relationship with Caesars World and/or Its Stockholders and Executives,* March 5, 1976.

14. *Rouge et Noir News* and *Rouge et Noir Resort Management Report,* January 1981.

15. Resorts, Harrah's (Holiday Inns), and Golden Nugget were exceptions.

16. Bally reported $36,341,286 and Caesars $13,673,380 in 1980 interest expenses, a total of $50 million in debt service for these two facilities alone. State of New Jersey, *1980 Annual Reports* filed by these companies with the Casino Control Commission, Schedule 2, "Statements of Income."

17. The Sands (Greate Bay), Harrah's, and Golden Nugget opened in 1980. The combined reported 1980 win for these three facilities was $40,043,352, slightly more than 6 percent of the $642,673,245 won by Atlantic City casinos that year, while their reported 1980 expenses were $74,346,789, or 11 percent of the industry's $673,959,609 total reported 1980 expenses. The three casinos in operation *throughout* 1980—Resorts, Caesars, and Bally—reported 1980 operating income of $96,266,730 and 1980 net income of $46,982,582. None of these three established casinos reported 1980 losses. In

other words, the industry's 1980 operating results were distorted by the high costs and low productivities of three new casinos, an elementary financial consideration ignored by the general press. State of New Jersey, *1980 Annual Reports* filed by the six Atlantic City casinos with the Casino Control Commission, Schedule 2, "Statements of Income."

18. The Perlmans received $20 a share, or approximately twice the current market value, for 4.84 million shares in a settlement valued at $99 million. Stockholder suits forced the Perlmans to refund $7 million of this amount; Daniel Heneghan, "Perlmans Resign from Caesars," *Atlantic City Press,* December 30, 1981, and Heneghan, "Perlmans to Refund $7 Million," ibid., April 1, 1982.

19. William T. O'Donnell. At the time of writing, O'Donnell's divestiture of his equity in Bally Manufacturing Corporation and Bally's Park Place, its Atlantic City subsidiary, had not been completed. In January 1984 Bally announced it would purchase 690,000 shares of Bally Manufacturing common owned by O'Donnell for $25 a share, representing a 16 percent premium over the current market price of about $21.50. In 1979 O'Donnell owned 1.8 million shares. Daniel Heneghan, "Bally to Buy Former Chairman's Stock," *Atlantic City Press,* January 10, 1984.

20. Four casinos (three of them—Playboy, Tropicana, and Claridge—newly opened; the fourth was the Sands) reported operating losses totaling $67.4 million. Due to these start-up-related financial results the industry reported an after income tax (net income) 1981 loss of $11.8 million. State of New Jersey, *1981 Annual Reports* filed with the Casino Control Commission, Schedule 2, "Statements of Income." The CCC subsequently reported larger 1981 net losses for the Claridge and Playboy; by this accounting the industry's 1981 net loss was $19.7 million. State of New Jersey, Casino Control Commission, "The New Jersey Casino Industry's Net Income: 1978 through 1982," April 5, 1983.

21. State of New Jersey, *1982 Annual Reports* filed with the Casino Control Commission, Schedule 2, "Statements of Income."

22. Donald Janson, "Revenues Soaring at Jersey Casinos," *New York Times,* November 20, 1983.

23. These estimates are H. Steven Norton's, executive vice president of Resorts International, as reported in the *Atlantic City Press,* January 11, 1984.

24. The distinction between the legalization and the legitimation of casino gaming is cogently drawn by Stephen A. Wynn, chairman and president of Golden Nugget, Inc.: "The legalization of gaming is an event that takes place at a specific moment in time, as it did in New Jersey on November 8, 1976. But the legitimization of gaming is something else. That happens over a period of time, when gaming is assimilated into a community and completely accepted by that community. That will involve a resolution of all the opposing forces that are created by gaming. Legitimization will arrive when the industry is completely accepted by the institutional financiers—when you see Equitable and Prudential making 25-year term loans for constructing casino/hotels." Wynn, "Expansion of Legalized Gaming and Factors That Will Influence It" (speech presented at Laventhol & Horwath Second Annual Gaming Conference, Waldorf-Astoria, New York City, October 1, 1980).

25. Peter L. Berger and Hansfried Kellner, *Sociology Reinterpreted: An Essay on Method and Vocation* (Garden City, N.Y.: Doubleday/Anchor, 1981), p. 155.

26. James O'Connor, *The Fiscal Crisis of the State* (New York: St. Martin's, 1973), p. 6.

27. Ibid., p. 1.

28. By game, the amounts were: State lotteries, $2.2 billion; pari-mutuel horse racing, greyhound racing, and *jai-alai,* $855 million; and casino gaming, $350 million. For the sources of these statistics see Chapter 3 and the Appendix.

29. Where direct levies on gaming and casino entertainment contributed more than 50 percent of the State's fiscal 1982 General Fund. State of Nevada, Gaming Control Board, *Direct Levies on Gaming in Nevada: An Analysis of the Rates and Structure by All Levels of Government,* for the fiscal year ended June 30, 1982.

30. New York State's fiscal 1983 budget included $4.221 billion for "General Support for Public Schools," equivalent to roughly one out of every four dollars collected by the State. The State lottery, whose revenues are for the support of education, was budgeted to contribute $195 million, or 4.6 percent, of this $4.2 billion appropriation. The lottery's fiscal 1983 contribution exceeded this estimate: $262,376,000, or 6.2 percent, of the $4.2 billion budgeted State aid to education was generated from lottery gambling. This sterling performance had a predictable effect: in his fiscal 1984 budget Gov. Mario Cuomo proposed to increase the State's aid to education to more than $5 billion, with the increased expenditure to be funded in part by a new lottery game, multiple-choice pool cards on professional team sports, that the governor estimated would generate an additional $100 million in lottery revenues. *This $100 million in sports betting revenues is the largest single new revenue source in the State's fiscal 1984 budget,* and, if in fact such betting proves to be legal under New York's constitution (the State's attorney general is reported to doubt this) and lives up to expectations, the lottery's fiscal 1984 contribution to the State's aid to education will exceed $400 million, or 8 percent, of budgeted expenditures. In the *political* terms of marginal increases to tax rates already stretched to the point of taxpayer revolts, 8 percent of a major and sensitive budget item such as aid to education is very serious money. State of New York, Executive Chamber, Hugh L. Carey, governor, *Executive Budget for the Fiscal Year April 1, 1982 to March 31, 1983,* pp. 55–57; New York State Lottery, "Composition of Revenue and Revenue Allocations," *Annual Report 1982–83,* p. 10; Mario Cuomo, "Excerpts From Governor Cuomo's Budget Message to the State Legislature," *New York Times,* January 17, 1984; Edward A. Gargan, "[Attorney General] Abrams Aide Casts Doubt on Legality of Betting Plan," *New York Times,* January 17, 1984.

31. The relation of gambling tax rates to revenue yields is dependent on price and demand elasticities for particular gambling opportunities that remain very poorly understood. For a recent brief discussion of the subject, see Donn R. Pescatrice, "The Inelastic Demand for Wagering," *Journal of Applied Economics* 12 (March 1980):1–10, and the discussion of the literature in ch. 3, nn.80,81.

32. The government percentage of casino *handle* is less than 1 percent. For comparisons of lottery sales, pari-mutuel handle, and casino gross wagering, drop, and win, see the Appendix.

33. Max Weber, *Theory of Social and Economic Organization,* trans. A. M. Henderson and Talcott Parsons (1925; New York: Free Press, 1957). For readers intimidated by this formidable work an example may be helpful: there is a powerful tendency for activities that acquire a commercial purpose to be rationalized. The reason is simple: rationalization increases profit. Widgets, for example, might be made for their own sake as well as a livelihood, in the manner of handicrafts such as Oriental rugs or fine English shotguns. This method of manufacture will not produce many widgets, however. From a commercial point of view this is a defect. By rationalizing every step in the production of widgets every element in their manufacture that does *not maximize* profit can be eliminated. The commercial goal (profit) is then perfectly served by the (now rational) process of widget-making.

34. The contract between the National Football League (NFL) and the television networks covering the 1982-85 seasons was valued by the NFL at $1 billion, or about $8 million per member club annually for the life of the contract, at the time of its negotiation.

35. For an account of the commercialization of college football from published and unpublished sources see David L. Westby and Allen Sack, "The Rationalization and Commercialization of College Football in the Late Nineteenth Century," *Journal of Higher Education* 47 (November/December 1976):625–48.

36. Ibid., pp. 626–27.

37. With the introduction of video gaming devices into casinos and State lotteries this becomes literally true.

38. To provide an alternative to rationality and discipline is, of course, one of the social functions of play; see the discussion of the sociology of games and play developed by Huizinga and Caillois in Chapters 2, 3, and 4.

39. For examples of antigambling views see Russ Coggins, ed., *The Gambling Menace* (Nashville, Tenn.: Broadman Press, 1966); Walter Wagner, *To Gamble, or Not to Gamble* (New York: World Publishing Co., 1972); and ch. 1, n. 5.

40. Cornell, *Development of the Law of Gambling*. The social and economic history of the States' ambivalent attitude toward gambling is summed up by Dombrink as "the political economy of tolerated vice" ("Outlaw Businessmen," p. 57); we have remarked in Chapter 1 the parallel "moral economy of vice," in which gambling was, and remains, essential to some deeply rooted currents of American social and political reform.

41. This evolution of gambling from a profession of talented individuals into organized business reflects the operation of the Weberian principles of rationality and efficiency, which, in addition to the usual economic benefits of increased volume and profits, provided syndicates with protection from antigambling law enforcement through police corruption and political connections. For histories of lotteries in America see ch. 1, n. 12. The best history of the origins of American commercial gambling is Johnson, "A Sinful Business," in *Police and Society*, ed. Bayley, pp. 17–47.

42. The most thorough historian of late nineteenth- and early twentieth-century commercial gambling remarks that from the 1880s to about 1905 "gamblers, and vice entrepreneurs generally, exercised an influence on local politics and law enforcement that has seldom been equaled since that time. In many neighborhoods, it was not so much that gambling syndicates influenced local political organization; rather, gambling syndicates *were* the local political organizations." Haller, "Changing Structure of American Gambling," p. 88. See as well the discussion of the "political economy of tolerated vice" in Dombrink, "Outlaw Businessmen," pp. 49–62.

43. For example, in New York a law enacted in 1887 granted members of the Metropolitan Turf Association special immunity from the bookmaking law for thirty racing days a year. Cornell, *Development of the Law of Gambling*, p. 178.

44. For a brief account of the career of Richard Canfield see Chafetz, *Play the Devil*, pp. 318–39. Steve Thomas, "The Iron Men," *The Thoroughbred Record*, June 17, 1981, pp. 2586–89, provides a good history of New York bookmaking.

45. Haller, "Bootleggers and American Gambling," in *Gambling in America*, Appendix 1, pp. 102–43.

46. Gambling taxation is more complex in practice. Pari-mutuel retention and casino win are, on one hand, gamblers' losses and, on the other hand, constitute operators' gross revenues, or the equivalent of *sales* to a retail business. For gamblers, the exaction of privilege taxes amounts to the double taxation of gambling activities, since the *price* of gambling includes the privilege tax, while payouts are subject to federal and (usually) State income taxation. Operators are affected by privilege taxes in that these levies are deductions from gross revenues. If they rise beyond a given level the residue will be insufficient for expenses, profit, and normal business tax liabilities. Because privilege taxes are exacted from gross gambling State governments are not sensitive to operator

costs; a State could in theory raise privilege taxes to levels that *increase* government revenues while forcing operators to incur losses and eventual bankruptcy.

47. For a discussion of gambling privilege taxes as sumptuary taxation see George Ignatin, "Taxing Peter to Spite Paul: The Effects of Taxes and Regulation on Sports Gambling," in *The Gambling Papers: Proceedings of the Fifth National Conference on Gambling and Risk Taking,* ed. William R. Eadington, 13 vols. (Reno: Bureau of Business and Economic Research, College of Business Administration, University of Nevada), 9:92–126.

48. Skolnick, *House of Cards.*

49. See "Nebraska VLTs: Taking Root or Just a Flash in the Cornfield?," *Gaming Business Magazine,* November 1983, p. 6; and Andrew Pollack, "Electronics Invades Gambling," *New York Times,* January 21, 1984.

50. O'Conner, *Fiscal Crisis of the State,* p. 1.

51. Private operators have, of course, similar interests and motivations.

52. Royal Commission on Gambling, *Final Report,* pp. 270, 290; see as well the discussion of casino gaming in Chapter 3.

53. Section 12 of the Gaming Act of 1968. *Bona fide* guests of members who meet this requirement may also gamble *immediately.* This loophole in the forty-eight-hour rule was allegedly utilized by casinos operated by Playboy Ltd., which allegedly enrolled porters of leading London hotels as members who then brought foreign gambles to Playboy's casinos as their "guests." For a succinct account of Playboy Ltd.'s alleged violations of the Gaming Act, see Maurice Barnfather, "Is Playboy's Luck Running Out?," *Forbes,* May 11, 1981, pp. 58–59.

54. The British Casino Association's (BCA) code of conduct includes rules that are more rigorous than those contained in or made pursuant to the Gaming Act, with the aim of ensuring a sufficient degree of self-regulation to forestall even stricter statutory or regulatory controls.

55. Section 31 of the Gaming Act of 1968. As a consequence of this restriction British casinos depend almost entirely on table games. In 1981–82 the industry's drop was distributed as follows: American roulette (confusingly, as played in Britain "American" roulette wheels have only one zero), 61 percent; punto banco, 20 percent; blackjack, 17 percent; craps, 1 percent; French roulette, 1 percent. The Monopolies and Mergers Commission, *Report on the proposed merger of Pleasurama PLC and Trident Television PLC and on the merger situation between Grand Metropolitan PLC and Trident Television PLC,* presented to Parliament by the Secretary of State for Trade and Industry (London: Her Majesty's Stationery Office, December 1983). By comparison, slot machines accounted for $4.3 billion, or 36.4 percent, of the $11.8 billion drop reported by Nevada casinos in calendar 1983.

56. Section 42 of the Gaming Act of 1968. This restriction applies to British media. Casinos may advertise in publications that circulate mainly outside Britain, and casino hosts may make visits to clients overseas.

57. Section 16 of the Gaming Act of 1968. Such checks are collectible at law.

58. The Lord Allen of Abbeydale, "Some Reflections on the British Gaming Scene," in *Laventhol & Horwath Second Annual Gaming Conference* (Philadelphia: Laventhol & Horwath, 1980).

59. Home Office, "Introduction to the Gaming Act 1968," in Royal Commission on Gambling, *Final Report* (London: Her Majesty's Stationery Office, 1978), p. 270.

60. Culminating in a raid of the Victoria Sporting Club premises by two hundred police and Gaming Board inspectors in November 1978.

61. Owned by Norwich Enterprises Ltd., which was then negotiating its sale to Playboy Ltd. Playboy acquired this property together with two provincial casinos and some sixty betting shops for $13 million in October 1979, before the institution of

proceedings before the South Westminster Licensing Court (then comprised of five licensing magistrates) for cancellation of the Victoria Sporting Club's gaming license. Following the sale, and despite Playboy's installation of more rigorous gaming controls, the club's license was canceled. Playboy was subsequently successful in its appeal of the magistrates' decision to the Crown Court, and the club was reopened in 1980.

62. The oil shock of 1973 and the resulting tremendous increase in Middle Eastern petrodollars likewise transformed thoroughbred yearling markets, particularly the U.S. select summer sales at Keeneland, Kentucky, and Saratoga, New York, by enabling Middle Eastern interests to engage in bidding wars with the syndicate headed by Robert Sangster, the owner of Vernons Pools, a large operator of soccer betting pools, Greek shipowner Stavros Niarchos, the Aga Khan, Texas oilman Nelson Bunker Hunt, and others for certain breeding lines. For Sangster's reaction to the influence of Middle Eastern oil fortunes on yearling prices see Steven Crist, "Sangster's Boast Ruffles Bluegrass," *New York Times,* July 23, 1982; the relationship of yearling markets to the pari-mutuel economy is discussed in Chapter 3.

63. Gary Selesner, "U.K.'s Ladbroke: Betting on and Betting the U.S.," *Gaming Business Magazine,* June 1982, pp. 4–49.

64. There were extensive disclosures of Ladbroke's methods of soliciting business in the London press. This so-called "Unit Six" operation utilized a private detective agency, as well as cabdrivers and luxury hotel staff, to identify and trace high rollers belonging to casinos owned by Playboy and other companies; a policeman was paid for supplying names and other information contained in police car license registration files. For these and other details in the context of a concise and accurate summary of the entire episode see David Miers, "The Mismanagement of Casino Gaming," *British Journal of Criminology* 21 (January 1981):79–86. Miers adds a cogent analysis of the episode's implications for British gaming policy and law.

65. The three casinos were the Hertford, the Hyde Park Casino, and the Ladbroke Club. Lownes joined with the police in opposing the renewal of the Ladbroke licenses, and reportedly infuriated the police for taking credit for the Westminster magistrates' refusal to renew them. See Daniel Heneghan, "British Test for Playboy is Starting," *Atlantic City Press,* September 14, 1981.

66. Monopolies and Mergers Commission, *Report on the proposed merger of Pleasurama PLC and Trident Television PLC and on the merger situation between Grand Metropolitan PLC and Trident Television PLC,* p. 12.

67. Coral's four London casinos were the International Sporting Club, the Palm Beach, the Curzon, and Crockford's. The first three, following the takeover of Coral by Bass Ltd., were sold to Lonrho Ltd. (the International Sporting Club), Grand Metropolitan (the Palm Beach), and Aspinall's Club Ltd. (the Curzon), but notwithstanding these sales the casinos were closed in March 1981. Lonrho successfully appealed the closing of the International Sporting Club and reopened this property in June 1981. Grand Metropolitan obtained a license for the Palm Beach, which also reopened in June 1981. The objections to Crockford's, also purchased by Lonrho, were eventually withdrawn, and this casino remained open. The Curzon was closed; it opened in May 1984 as the Aspinall Curzon. Ibid., pp. 12–16.

68. The Clermont Club and the Playboy Club of London.

69. On June 6, 1981, the Gaming Board added to its objections the allegation that the Playboy casinos were being controlled from outside the United Kingdom.

70. Some idea of the scale of the high roller gambling at London casinos may be formed from the disclosure during these license hearings that Playboy had accepted worthless checks from a Qatar merchant totalling $4 million *after this player had written*

$32 million in good checks. Terri Minsky, "Playboy Enters British Court Today on License Renewal," *Wall Street Journal,* September 14, 1981; Daniel Heneghan, "British Test for Playboy Is Starting," *Atlantic City Press,* September 14, 1981; "Playboy Empire Shaken as British Lift 2 Licenses," *Atlantic City Press,* October 6, 1981; Lloyd Shearer, "The Gamble Playboy Lost," *Parade,* December 13, 1981. For Lownes's view of these events see Victor Lownes, *The Day the Bunny Died* (Secaucus, N.J.: Lyle Stuart, 1982).

71. In addition to the three London casinos these properties included Playboy Club casinos in Manchester and Portsmouth, eighty-one betting shops, and a 50 percent interest in two other provincial casinos. In fiscal 1981 the three London casinos alone reported operating profits of $38.8 million; Playboy's British gambling operations were estimated to be worth "under normal circumstances" at least $300 million. Anthony M. Hoffman, a vice president of A. G. Becker, Inc., quoted by Norman Peagam and Frederick Kempe, "Playboy to Sell British Casinos for $31.4 Million," *Wall Street Journal,* November 4, 1981. See as well Sandra Salmans, "British Casino Sale by Playboy," *New York Times,* November 4, 1981; Heneghan, "Playboy to Sell British Casinos," *Atlantic City Press,* November 4, 1981. Trident eventually (January 1982) paid $26 million for Playboy's British gambling properties; Playboy Enterprises (USA) said it expected to realize "a little under $50 million" from the sale. "Playboy Wraps up Deal to Sell Trident Its U.K. Holdings," *Variety,* December 23, 1981; "Trident Holders Back Purchase of Playboy's Casinos in the U.K.," *Wall Street Journal,* January 6, 1982.

72. The loss of its British gaming licenses was particularly serious for Playboy, which by the late 1970s was deriving most of its net income from its London casinos: for the year ending June 30, 1981—before the sale of its British gambling operations to Trident Television Ltd. for a reported $34.1 million—Playboy's London casinos generated pretax earnings of $38.8 million; its British gambling operations produced 85 percent of the company's fiscal 1981 operating revenues. Leonard Downie, Jr., "London Court Strips Playboy of Licenses For 2 Casinos," *Washington Post,* October 6, 1981; "Playboy in London Loses Casino Fight," *New York Times,* October 6, 1981; Heywood Klein and Ronald Alsop, "Playboy Loses 2 London Casino Licenses, Clouding Plan for Atlantic City Operation," *Wall Street Journal,* October 6, 1981.

73. A twenty-fourth London casino was then licensed but did not begin operating until August 1979. There were of course additional casinos located within the United Kingdom; as of December 31, 1976, there were 24 casinos operating in London, 81 elsewhere in England, 4 in Wales, and 12 in Scotland, for a total of 121 casinos. Royal Commission on Gambling, *Final Report,* Annex F, pp. 518–19.

74. The number of London casinos had increased to nineteen by June 1983.

75. The board conceded that due to the then-recent closures (February 1982) of the Playboy casinos and the probability that existing clubs would not appeal equally to all classes of players there might be room for one or two additional casinos. Monopolies and Mergers Commission, *Report on the proposed merger of Pleasurama PLC and Trident Television PLC and on the merger situation between Grand Metropolitan PLC and Trident Television PLC,* p. 13.

76. The Gaming Board made no objections to any of these eight applications. Ibid., p. 14.

77. Licenses were granted to the Trident Clermont, the Stakis Regency (owned by Stakis PLC), the London Park Tower (owned by Zealcastle), and the Aspinall's Curzon. An addition license, for the independently owned Knightsbridge Sporting Club, was canceled in the course of these hearings. Ibid.

78. The single important exception to this statement is the tax treatment of winnings. Alone among major industrial nations, the United States considers legal winnings to be

taxable income. This creates an obvious incentive to illegal gambling, where winnings produce no tax liability. To the extent that this federal tax policy impairs the States' ability to combat illegal gambling by authorizing competitive legal alternatives, Congress has limited the States' responsibility for gambling policy. In general, however, the States may act autonomously in this area. For the federal tax treatment of winnings see ch. 1, n.22.

79. New York, traditionally the premier thoroughbred racing State, is an example. All forms of commercial gambling are prohibited by the constitution of 1894 (Article I, section 9), including bookmaking, which the legislature strengthened by repealing the special immunities for politically connected on-track bookmakers and imposing statutory penalties in 1895. To circumvent these provisions the tracks developed a system of oral betting, which in a 1909 court decision *(People ex rel. Lichtenstein v. Langan)* was held to be exempt from the antibookmaking law. Cornell, *Development of the Law of Gambling*, pp. 200–201.

80. In an exception to the general rule, *not* for revenue reasons. Louisiana apparently licensed on-track betting to encourage participation in the sport of horseracing as a martial skill; in other words, as a defense measure. Ibid., p. 287.

81. Act of March 31, 1940, ch. 254, section 2, 1940 N.Y. Laws 861; *N.Y. Unconsolidated Laws* section 7952 (McKinney 1979).

82. New York, State Department of Taxation and Finance, *Annual Statistical Review of Pari-Mutuel Tax Operations for the Racing Season of 1982*, p. 3.

83. The legislature's consideration of the public interest in the pari-mutuel betting it authorized was limited to the exclusion of minors from betting and the restriction of the racing season to eight months of the year, these considerations being, of course, additional to the State treasury's "reasonable revenue" from bettor losses, which constitutes public funds.

84. Approximately three-quarters of the city's pari-mutuel receipts were derived from Aqueduct and Jamaica racetracks, which were located wholly within the city, with the remaining quarter contributed by Belmont Park, which, although located principally in Nassau County, extends across the county line into the borough of Queens.

85. New York, New York State Racing Commission, *Annual Report for 1954*, p. 10.

86. New York also had, and has, major pari-mutuel harness racing.

87. The Greater New York Association was chartered under Article 7501 of the New York Unconsolidated Laws. Although not specifically stated in the plan, the contemplated borrowing was predicated on the new association's receiving—from, of course, the State—an exclusive franchise to conduct pari-mutuel flat racing. Upon the receipt of this franchise and the subscription of the GNYA's bonded debt the plan envisioned the sale of Jamaica Racetrack and the discontinuation of racing there; the reconstruction of Belmont Park "at a cost of $15,000,000 more or less" (the eventual cost was $41.9 million, expended in installments of $7.4 million between 1955 and 1959 and $34.5 million between 1964 and 1968); the eventual reconstruction of Aqueduct, which "might cost from $35,000,000 to $45,000,000 (actually $32.9 million, between 1955 and 1959, with an additional expenditure, for winter racing, of $8 million in 1975); and capital improvements to Saratoga, "at a cost of $3,000,000 more or less" ($1.1 million was expended for this purpose between 1955 and 1959).

The justifications advanced by the Jockey Club for this arrangement are worth enumerating. As given in the 1954 letter to Ashley Cole, these were as follows:

1. "Flat racing must be in the hands of responsible members of the community."

2. "Flat racing in [New York] State has up to now been kept free from political consideration and it must continue to be kept free."

3. Franchises to conduct pari-mutuel racing "granted . . . by the State are valuable concessions carrying high obligations to the public."

4. "The State is entitled to adequate taxation from racing operations. The proposed plan would eliminate private profits, and would include incentive payment plans and adequate salaries to professional managers to assure the most efficient operation of the race tracks. Last year the State received from flat racing 32 million dollars. Our [the club's] plan should make it possible to increase attendance, increase income to the State, and decrease tax to the public. This would make it possible for the State again to compete successfully with other States which exact a smaller percentage from their racing associations and their patrons."

5. "Racing has become in recent years the most popular spectator sport in the United States, measured by paid attendance. As a result, the facilities now provided in New York are wholly inadequate for the needs and enjoyment of the public. With the successful consumation of this plan, we could have facilities second to none, which would include ample parking and rapid transportation facilities with convenient terminals; sufficient good-vision seating capacity with protection from the elements; adequate catering facilities; arrangements for ample circulation and escalator facilities."

The Jockey Club letter, from John W. Hanes, Christopher T. Chenery, and Harry F. Guggenheim, to Ashley Trimble Cole, chairman of the New York State Racing Commission, dated September 20, 1954, was reprinted in the New York State Racing Commission's *Annual Report for 1954* (pp. 18–20).

There are several points concerning these justifications worth noting. First, the Jockey Club neglected to mention that its members, and the constituency it represents, breed, own, and race thoroughbreds. As the reader may recall from the structural analysis of the pari-mutuel betting industry in Chapter 3, racetracks, and particularly the New York racetracks that have historically offered the country's premier quality racing, function, in economic terms, as the showcases for the products of breeding farms. Some recent speculation by off-shore syndicates aside, the value of racehorses, and hence the *raison d' etre* of the entire racehorse industry, is predicated on continuing opportunities to enter these horses in races on which pari-mutuel betting is allowed. It was thus in the interest of the Jockey Club to see first-quality racing continue in New York, and, as importantly, continue under the control of the club or its constituency.

Secondly, the Jockey Club plan sought to maintain the supremacy of New York racing against challenges from less highly taxed, modern racing plants in other States. The most important of these competing racetracks, southern California's Santa Anita and Hollywood Park, were in 1954 and remain today privately owned and operated—and extremely successful—businesses that at the time of writing (1983) are, by the New York Racing Association's (NYRA; the Greater New York Association adopted this name on April 8, 1958) own admission, a serious threat to the primacy of New York racing. The Jockey Club plan did not explain why private enterprise should have been unworkable in New York.

Thirdly, the plan's intention of keeping New York racing "free from political consideration" implies that political considerations in commercial gambling are not in the public interest; and while this is not an unreasonable assertion it is difficult to square with the conversion of a private industry to a quasigovernmental nonprofit operation.

88. All four racetracks were closely held.

89. Leo Egan, "Strong opposition to 'Dream' Track," *New York Times*, March 26, 1955. Butler and Jullien further (and accurately, as things turned out) asserted that the Jockey Club's estimate of $45 million to acquire and rebuild the State's flat racing plant was far too low. A memorandum filed by Butler and Jullien with the New York State Senate and Assembly rules committees made several additional points (as reported by

Frank M. Blunk in the *New York Times,* "Aqueduct Head Steps up Attack on Jockey Club's 'Dream Track,'" March 28, 1955):

1. "It [the Jockey Club plan] definitely puts the State of New York into the business of running a racetrack."

2. "It seeks special legislation [the charter of the nonprofit association and the grant of an exclusive pari-mutuel racing franchise to this association] so that a group may then borrow money, which cannot be borrowed until and unless it is enacted."

3. "It requests the freezing of this group into a twenty-five year monopoly of thoroughbred racing in New York State."

4. It would politicize racing by giving the state tax commission "a strong incentive for questioning purses, operating expenses, salaries and other items and subject the [new nonprofit] association to political control."

90. Alexander Feinberg, "State Racing Unit Aids Supertrack," *New York Times,* June 22, 1955.

91. "Cole Backs Plan for Super-track," *New York Times,* February 16, 1955.

92. Egan, "Strong Oppostion to 'Dream' Track," *New York Times,* March 26, 1955. This opposition produced a counter-proposal for the rehabilitation of the State's flat racing industry whereby Jullien and Butler would retain Aqueduct, rebuild it, and operate it as a profit-making business. According to the *New York Times,* Jullien "asserted that new tracks with all modern facilities could be constructed if the state allowed the thoroughbred organizations the same [more generous; in 1955 thoroughbred associations retained 4 percent of a $600,000 daily handle while standardbred (or harness racing) associations effectively retained 7.5 percent of a $600,000 daily handle] participation in mutual [*sic*] revenues that the harness tracks enjoy" (March 26, 1955).

93. Not, in one of the enabling legislation's few significant departures from the Jockey Club plan, vested in the Jockey Club itself. In September the GNYA was authorized by the State Racing Commission to acquire the Queens County Jockey Club (Aqueduct), the Westchester Racing Association (Belmont), the Metropolitan Jockey Club (Jamaica), and the Saratoga Association (Saratoga and Jamaica) for a total of $32.6 million. The racing commission granted to the association twenty-five year franchises to conduct racing and pari-mutuel betting at its tracks, and on October 1, 1955, the association negotiated a credit agreement with Guaranty Trust and twelve other banks for $47 million, at 4.5 percent interest, to be repaid over a period of ten years.

94. The text of this referendum reads: "A Local Law to amend the Administrative Code of the City of New York, in relation to establishing and providing for the expenses of a committee to formulate a plan for the conduct of off-track betting on horse races." The results were:

Borough	*Yes*	*No*
Manhattan	175,380	59,295
The Bronx	178,840	46,939
Brooklyn	285,130	86,617
Queens	286,550	95,055
Richmond	32,446	12,404
Total	958,346	300,310

95. New York State Off-Track Pari-Mutuel Betting Law, chapter 143, *1970 N.Y. Laws 900.* For the history of the implementation of New York's off-track betting law, see Howard J. Samuels, "The Off-Track Betting Experiment in New York," *Howard Law Journal* 17 (1973):731–57; and Christiansen and Shagan, "The New York Off-Track Betting Law," pp. 854–69. A more entertaining account of OTB's early years is McDonald, "Off-Track Betting on Horseracing," pp. 246–65.

96. "[There has been] a continuing increase in NYRA's share of the takeout over the years. The purpose of this increase was to enable NYRA to meet its debt obligations. In effect, NYRA's participation of the pari-mutuel takeout [handle is meant] approximately doubled from 4% in 1955 to 8% in 1975. Over this same period, the State's share declined from 11% in 1955 to 9% in 1975. The additional two percent inuring to the benefit of NYRA resulted from an increase in gross takeout from 15% to 17%." State of New York Commission of Investigation, David Brown, chairman, *Review of the Financial Condition of the New York Racing Association* (1976), pp. 47–50. The troubled financial history of the NYRA can be traced through New York State Department of Audit and Control, *Audit Report* (#NY-35-64), March 9, 1964; *Audit Report* (#NY-St-14-72), December 31, 1971; *Audit Report* (#NY-AUTH-2-78), January 18, 1978; and Audit Report (NY-AUTH-1-79), December 26, 1979; State of New York, Commission to Study and Investigate the Thoroughbred Industry in New York State, Robert J. Morgado, chairman, *Report* (Albany: Executive Chamber, 1977); and Joint Legislative Task Force to Study and Evaluate the Pari-mutuel Racing and Breeding Industry in New York State, Jon J. McCloskey, executive director, *A Discussion Paper on the New York Racing Association,* March 1, 1980.

97. Each handle point was worth from approximately $5 million to $7.5 million a year over this twenty-year period, making the aggregate value of NYRA's increased claim somewhere between $300 million and $600 million.

98. New York City Off-Track Betting Corporation, *1983 Annual Report,* p. 6. The city's Off-Track Betting Corporation distributed more than $1.3 billion during this period: $623.1 million to New York City; $200.1 million to New York State; $79.8 million to various local governments within New York State; and $418.4 million to the racing industry.

99. *N.Y. Unconsolidated Laws,* section 8062 (McKinney 1979).

100. Racetracks have two major sources of revenue from racing operations: pari-mutuel commissions and attendance-related and other non–pari-mutuel revenues, consisting of admissions, concessions, television rights (these rights are currently being disputed between racetracks and horse owners), and so forth. While non–pari-mutuel revenues are normally much smaller than pari-mutuel commissions they are not subject to pari-mutuel taxes, and may be significant to track profitability out of proportion to their amount.

101. *N.Y. Unconsolidated Laws* section 8062 (McKinney Supp. 1973–1974). This amendment was enacted with the New York City Off-Track Betting Corporation's support.

102. That OTB caused a reduction in track handle and attendance is not disputed. The extent of this impact is however a matter of debate. Contemporary published analyses purporting to determine the handle and attendance reductions attributable to OTB were in fact funded by the racing industry for use in legislative contexts. Christiansen and Shagan, "The New York Off-Track Betting Law," p. 859.

103. The financial results of legal gambling—gross wagering and revenues—are of concern to tax authorities and are reported as a matter of public record. Gambling's impact on the economy—jobs, income and property taxes, the stimulation of nongambling industries such as tourism or horsebreeding, changes in the markets of competing gambling and nongambling businesses and so forth—while not usually the subject of regular reporting, are likewise measureable, and can be quantified by a number of generally accepted techniques.

104. Bookmakers customarily pay track odds. In New York the on-track takeout from win/place/show pools at the time the surcharge was imposed was 17 percent. The surcharge raised OTB's effective takeout from these pools to 22 percent (actually to 23.6

percent because of double breakage), a percentage increase of 38.8 percent in the price of legal off-track betting. Christiansen and Shagan, "The New York Off-Track Betting Law," p. 867.

105. These include, in addition to reduced illegal horse-race betting, a corresponding increase in legal OTB handle.

106. For evidence of this destructive competition and the role of the revenue imperative in creating it in areas outside the market of New York tracks, see "Tracks: Too Many Purses," *Philadelphia Daily News,* October 25, 1983; "Brandywine to Give Way to Mall," *Philadelphia Inquirer,* October 29, 1983; "Ky. Bill Would Raise State Racing Taxes," *Daily Racing Form,* December 3, 1983, p. 3. The first two articles chronicle the saturation of the Philadelphia racing market and the exacerbation of this problem by the high takeout rate. The *Inquirer* article, in discussing the closing of Brandywine Racetrack, quotes Joseph Longo, Brandywine's treasurer: "The so-called monopoly that the race tracks had 15 years ago just isn't there anymore, because there's just so many of them [racetracks] and they're running [open] all the time." In 1982–1983 Brandywine had 139 racing days, with an average attendance of 4,623 and an average handle of $312,625. In 1970, over 100 racing days, attendance averaged 9,466 and handle $621,963. The *Daily News* article discusses the problems that have beset Atlantic City Race Course since the opening of Atlantic City casinos and the start of the New Jersey Lottery: "Atlantic City Race Course opened in 1946 with a 42-day meet and averaged 13,402 fans and $1,205,764 in betting. It reached its peak in the mid-1950s but still was a very strong track through 1974. Then the bottom fell out. There came a state lottery for the dreamers to chase. Never mind that the takeout was a killing 50 percent or more, this gambling gimmick replaced the racetrack as the place to strike it rich with a minimum investment. The Meadowlands opened in 1976, and the high-rolling casinos opened next door in Atlantic City. Within three years the [Atlantic City] track went from a 12,322 attendance, $1,386,401-betting revenue average to 7,101—$619,429. State revenue dropped from $8,238,651 (1972) to $599,234 (1979)." The following remarks about Atlantic City Race Course are attributed to Sam Anzalone, general manager of the Meadowlands racetrack, see "Ky. Bill Would Raise State Racing Taxes," *Daily Racing Form,* December 3, 1983, p. 2: "It got so bad that Levy [president of Atlantic City Race Course] was going to close the track a week ahead of schedule if not given relief in the form of an inter-track wagering bill. . . . An average of about 1,500 fans have turned out to make more than $200,000 in nightly bets, watch the races on closed-circuit television, then cash their tickets on the spot and go on to the next race. In this new gimmick Atlantic City's plant acts as a betting parlor for the Meadowlands racing." The *Daily Racing Form* suggests further trouble for the racing industry in the form of a new revenue measure: "The bill would increase the pari-mutuel takeout at Keeneland and Churchill Downs by 1½ per cent, to 17½ per cent. The state's portion would be increased at these two tracks by 1 per cent. Currently the state gets 4¾ per cent of the handle. The bill would also put a sales tax on all horses sold at public auction with a rebate for out-of-state residents. Initial reactions to the bill by industry leaders were negative."

107. The Meadowlands racetrack is part of the New Jersey Sports and Exposition Authority, an instrumentality of the State created by acts of the legislature in 1971 and 1973. The sports complex, which includes, besides the racetrack, a stadium and an arena, was constructed through a series of bond issues that are being repaid from pari-mutuel revenue. New Jersey Sports and Exposition Authority, "Statements of Revenues and Expenses" and "Notes to Financial Statements," in *1982 Annual Report.*

108. This impact is summarized by a New York State legislative task force: "In 1976, Nassau and Suffolk [Long Island] OTB Regions experienced their first full year of

operations and in September, the Meadowlands opened. This had a negative impact on Yonkers attendance and handle inasmuch as average daily attendance declined 11.8 percent and handle declined 12.4 percent. The full impact of this new competition was realized in 1977 when Yonkers experienced a 27.7 percent decline in average daily attendance and a 25.2 percent decline in average daily handle.'' State of New York, Joint Legislative Task Force to Study and Evaluate the Pari-mutuel Racing and Breeding Industry in New York State, *First Interim Report,* July 1, 1978, pp. 80–81.

109. Miriam Pawel, ''NY Racing Assn. Asks to Run OTB, Vows Higher Take,'' *Newsday,* January 24, 1984; ''Cuomo Aide Advocates Privately Run N.Y. OTB,'' *Daily Racing Form,* January 11, 1984; Michael Oreskes, ''Cuomo Studies Restructuring of State OTB,'' *New York Times,* January 25, 1984.

6

Commercial Gambling and American Values

> When you're counting on a killing
> Always count me in
> Talk me into losin' just as long as I can win
> I want the easy
> Easy money
> I want the good times
> Oh, I never had
>
> I want the easy
> Easy money
> I want the good life
> I want it bad
>
> —Billy Joel, "Easy Money"

In *1984* George Orwell included gambling, in the form of a lottery administered by the Ministry of Plenty, among the instruments of social control employed by his totalitarian state. The lottery's players are for the most part "proles," a semiliterate proletariat obsessively interested in the game's weekly award of enormous prizes. Orwell is careful to show that this obsessive play serves the players as well as the state: his lottery is the one public event capable of engaging the proles' attention. It is "their . . . delight, their folly, their anodyne, their intellectual stimulant"[1]—in a word, *meaning* in an otherwise purely biological existence. This is a bit too good to be true, of course: the lottery is fraudulent, its largest prizes awarded to imaginary persons. Chance and hope are alike illusory. The "gambling" of Orwell's proles is a manipulated response to counterfeit stimuli provided by Big Brother, and what normally would be the social utility of lottery play—hope, equality, escape, and dreams—is perverted into a mechanism of social and political control.

Comparisons of Orwell's mechanistic society with the real world have been staples of popular and academic writing since the publication of *1984* thirty-five years ago. The opposition of totalitarian order and humanist values is irresistible: no matter which side of the argument one finds congenial the conflict is the moral tale of our times. Like sociological theories of human behavior, moral tales are susceptible to differing interpretations, morality being relative to cultural frames of reference. Parallels to convenient moral parables are easily drawn; nevertheless, now that 1984 has come and gone there are certainly points of correspondence between Orwellian lotteries and American commercial gambling. Hope, emotional and mental stimulation, and the anesthetizing qualities of ritualized order are recognizable gambling motivations, and the proposition that these motivations are especially powerful among the poor and disenfranchised has been endorsed by many observers. More generally, there are obvious similarities between Orwell's totalitarian state and an increasingly bureaucratic American society. One after another, work and leisure pursuits that for earlier generations were matters of personal choice and effort have been taken over by social institutions and made routine; and it is tempting to see in this process an Orwellian transformation of American communities of free individuals into an institutional society.

Among the activities that have in this way been institutionalized the vices have been the most difficult to assimilate into cultural patterns. Some vices, notably nonsanctioned sexual behavior, appear to be inherently resistant to bureaucratic control. Others have been integrated into mainstream American popular culture, the turbulent history of the manufacture and consumption of alcohol being the best example. It is important to understand that while economics is a powerful motivating force in this process, it is not controlling. The use of "recreational" drugs remains proscribed—actively in the case of "hard" drugs such as heroin and passively regarding less dangerous substances such as marijuana—despite the enormous costs of enforcing this proscription and the tremendous potential value of recreational drug markets to both the state and legitimate suppliers.

Gambling is the great exception among the vices. This activity, which in 1900 stood in much the same relation to American society as other illicit pleasures, has been subjected to the same forces that have institutionalized work and play. A status quo in which Americans gambled with the conviction that gambling was wrong was upset by the financial stress placed upon State governments by the depression. The first modern gambling industries were legalized for the purpose of alleviating this stress through the creation of a government claim on legal gambling revenues, a claim that has remained a unique source of State and local government funds. Driven by this revenue imperative, by the historic American propensity to gamble, by economic shifts in postindustrial society, and finally by changes in American culture itself, legal gambling has grown during the past fifty years into a leisure institution, the only one of the traditional vices to achieve this status. As such, Big Gambling has become an important and increasingly visible component of American popular culture.

Popular culture is one of the most powerful myth-makers of our democratic society. The United States has no state-sanctioned religion or mandatory course of instruction to indoctrinate its citizens in approved mores and beliefs. Instead Americans are socialized by the culture that surrounds us: the examples of elders and peers we observe, the media that informs us, the stories we are told, the objects we cherish, and the games we play. Popular culture reflects, teaches, and creates the very myths that hold society together through rituals, beliefs, icons, and heroes. In contemporary American society popular culture articulates, transmits, and reinforces values in a manner similar to the role traditionally played by religion. It is therefore important to see commercial gambling in its cultural context. Big Gambling reflects the cultural evolution of mainstream America while it is simultaneously one of the forces shaping that evolution.

THE CHANGING CULTURAL CONTEXT

Contemporary American culture has changed dramatically since the days of the first settlements and, for that matter, since the beginning of the present century. Originally individuals were imbedded in the life of the "community"; they were tied to common traditions, a religious context, and some sense of transcendental (or *a priori*) values. When a person made a decision about whether an action was right or wrong he resolved a more or less clear-cut dichotomy. His choice followed or rejected cultural values based on clearly established foundations that gave life its meaning. Culture clearly distinguished between good and evil, success and failure, work and leisure. Choices today are not so clear. Values have become relative, and their meaning has become ambiguous. Often the person finds himself in a vacuum created by the loss of clearly defined authority structures, and so he retreats into himself as arbiter. But within the anomic (atom-like) person there are no anchors of unchanging principles, and he returns to the social group to help him find meaning. Within modern, "rationally organized" society, the state, the media, and corporate institutions assume the role of a power elite and create societal values in the absence of family, church, and tradition. Social institutions create self-legitimating values.[2]

There is an important paradox in this change. On the one hand, the individual would appear to be freed from ancient tyranny—free from the demands of tradition, church, family, and other authority figures. He is not bound by a rubric that predetermines everything from his station in life to his behavior. He seems to be free to create his own meanings. On the other hand, the person is incapable of responding to this freedom without the reassurance of a stable value system. He looks for signals from the surrounding society, and therein lies the problem: in looking to society for affirmation of his worth as an individual, he actually comes under the tyranny of new forces that are just as demanding as the old. The media and government or commercial bureaucracies are anonymous and impersonal trend-setters, as far beyond the control of an individual as were the shapers of the earlier, discarded, transcendental values. Freedom without values, then, becomes just a different kind of slavery.

According to the historian David Potter, one of the most salient characteristics of the American character and American culture is abundance.[3] If America itself is the result of a massive collective gamble the payoff is a society shaped by its material wealth. Other nations may scorn American materialism for all its negative qualities, but at the same time they strive to match our standard of living. From the outset, American government attempted to deny special privilege and to bring material well-being to its people. Democratic capitalism evolved as the means to this end, but, as Wendell Wilkie noted, the American economy could not prosper unless ''Americans regard as necessities what other people look on as luxuries.''[4] Such expectations continue to shape our values and chart our destiny.

From the very beginning of American civilization our forefathers believed in the work ethic, but this basic principle began to change because of the unprecedented material abundance offered by a new land. God was seen as the great governor of the country. He had not only ordered the Great Chain of Being, but He also arranged the various stations and vocations of mankind in the way best suited to His divine will and the comming of His kingdom. Originally, the Protestant ethic emphasized man's accountability to God. Man's duty was to prepare the way for God's kingdom by his life on earth. An individual had the obligation to discover his calling and to work at it to the best of his ability. Christian character was measured by the diligence of man's efforts to live up to his particular calling: energy was the index of his goodness. In one sense, this mythology could be said to keep people of low station content in their place; conversely, it could also be seen to bestow dignity and a sense of intrinsic worth upon the lowly. The opportunities offered by a new land and an emerging civilization spawned an evolution of these principles. Our Puritan ancestors worked diligently to follow God's commandments, and in a land that rewarded such labor they became prosperous. At the same time, gambling was shunned as the work of the devil, tempting God's children to waste their time. Within the space of three generations, however, Puritan ideals began to wane under the pressure of material success. A pilgrim's progress toward a heavenly kingdom was not forgotten, but life in America was rapidly becoming anything but a vale of tears.

The work ethic was firmly planted in the American psyche. As the Age of Reason dawned, Benjamin Franklin articulated the new ideals. Man could earn rewards in an afterlife through honest labor, but he could also expect a measure of earthly reward. Satisfaction in a job well done was still prized in Franklin's philosophy, and wealth, as long as it was honestly earned, was respected as a sign of God's blessing of man's endeavors. Franklin's autobiography and *Poor Richard's Almanac* became popular, and Franklin himself became a genuine American hero, because the ideas he expressed so accurately reflected the popular mind of the emerging nation. By the early nineteenth century, Alexis de Tocqueville observed that money and popular favor were the measure of worth in American society.[5] After all, money can be counted; it is neutral; and in a democracy it is theoretically equally available to all. As long as America offered an expanding frontier and a multitude of opportunities for those willing to take a chance and to work hard, money was a fair measure of a man's worth. Risk in the new republic took the form of pulling up stakes and heading for the frontier.

During the period of industrialization in the mid and late nineteenth century, the secularized work ethic reached a kind of maturity in the heroes of Horatio Alger's stories. Ambitious boys who worked hard and lived decent lives were rewarded with social respectability and the accompanying material rewards. Their rise from poverty to (at least middle-class) riches was the result of their ambition, honesty, diligence, and frugality—in short, all the virtues that Franklin had preached a century earlier. America still offered an abundance of opportunities, though their locus had shifted from the geographic to the commercial frontiers. Material gain was portrayed as the almost inevitable consequence of hard work, and thus it became the new measure of success. Gradually idealism was overshadowed by materialism, and Americans began to seek fulfillment in purely secular terms.

The Alger heroes offered a sharp contrast to the real-life industrial barons of the same era. For although men like Andrew Carnegie and

John D. Rockefeller had worked their way to the top and were personally pious and "well-intentioned," they were also highly competitive and professionally ruthless. When David Potter examines the American character, he notes that a common denominator among the anthropological, sociological, and psychological interpretations of the American experience is the notion of material competition.[6] In fact, the American character may be seen as a unique set of responses to an unusually competitive situation. Emerging business thrived on an economic version of social Darwinism: competition for the survival of the fittest, with money, power, and social prestige for the victors. According to Carnegie's "Gospel of Wealth," equal abundance implied an almost savage existence with no chance for progress.[7] But eighteenth-century thought had posited a belief in social and economic progress for mankind, and such progress implied that there would be those who could take the initiative and lead the way.

Equality, in the American interpretation, was never meant to imply that all people should occupy roughly equivalent stations in life. Puritan John Winthrop had noted that there would always be those who were powerful and wealthy as well as those who were less fortunate.[8] In a democratic society, equality meant parity in competition—the means to the end of material abundance. Universal opportunity, an important part of the American dream, places the onus on the individual. He is expected to achieve, to run the gamut from "rags to riches," on the strength of his willingness to work and his competitive spirit. He is not satisfied to be on par with everyone else; he wants more. Laissez-faire government allowed the cadre of robber barons to rise to power on the labor of the working classes. The gap between the haves and the have-nots widened, but this was a natural result of the competition. When the ranks of "polite society" were assaulted by the *nouveau riche,* the sheer force of money won the day.

Clearly, some Americans were conspicuously "more equal" than others; in 1899 Thorstein Veblen noted the importance of material consumption and the display of status in his *Theory of the Leisure Class.* Even though America had an egalitarian society, class distinctions remained; and while not the result of a caste system, these distinctions evolved in an arbitrary manner. Status, a sense of self-worth, no longer was achieved by virtue of belonging to a community, performing work, and taking pride in a job well done, no matter how humble the task. As Veblen noted, status was now bestowed only on members of the top class of economic achievers and displayed through the consumption of material goods. Status is conferred through invidious comparison with others in terms of the possession of materially quantifiable objects, status symbols.[9] This shift from a productive to a consumptive ethic propelled America into the twentieth century and set the stage for the rise of the institution of perfect consumption, Big Gambling.

For the first third of this century competition for the material abundance of this country went unchecked. American culture became ever more commercialized through the rise of what David Potter calls "the institution of abundance"—that is, advertising.[10] By the 1920s Americans were promised every conceivable material comfort on easy payment plans, and luxuries such as the automobile became part of what Americans defined as a decent standard of living. Sinclair Lewis's George Babbitt was a middle-class product of this culture. Babbitt was never able to be satisfied in the materialistic cocoon of Floral Heights, because no matter how completely he conformed to the social standards of his class, no matter how many artifacts of the American dream he bought, he still longed for self-fulfillment. As a culture, Americans faced a peculiar dilemma: our aspirations were fueled by advertisements, but they led only to higher plateaus of dissatisfaction. The only threat to the spiral of abundance was the depression of the 1930s. This economic catastrophe produced little cultural stock-taking, although Americans realized that there were forces in the economy beyond the control of an individual. Nevertheless, with the coming of the Second World War and recovery underway, the industrial complex again boomed. Wartime sacrifices heightened the demand for consumer goods, and postwar Americans had great expectations for the last half of the century.

In 1942, the anthropologist Margaret Mead posed questions that probed these expectations.

> Has the American scene shifted so that we still demand of every child a measure of success which is actually less and less possible for him to attain? . . . Have we made it a condition of success that a man should reach a position higher than his father's when such an achievement . . . is dependent upon the existence of a frontier and an expanding economy?[11]

Postwar American culture reinforced the urge toward material advancement through advertising and television, the new addition to institutional media. The message was that by consuming particular products or living the life of Ozzie and Harriet perfection (and happiness) could be achieved. Americans became collectively more greedy, like children whose Christmas list continually grows, and at the same time there was less and less chance to ever be satisfied because accomplishments could never keep pace with aspirations.

In the midst of the materialistic binge of the 1950s, sociologists David Riesman and William Whyte saw something amiss.[12] They noted that the person caught up in commercial society was alienated from traditional work values and had become "other-directed." Instead of being oriented toward the production of wealth, as in the earlier versions of the work ethic, organization men strove to fit in with their peers by consuming status symbols.

As the postindustrial age began, Riesman argued, the emphasis in society shifted from production and work to consumption and leisure. This was accompanied by a shift in American values away from traditional sources of direction to the influence of peers and the expanding mass media. A person was judged not on his ability to produce but on his choices as a consumer: "On the side of leisure and consumption, there is the compulsion to prove oneself a good, normal American by acquiring the 'standard package of consumer goods.'"[13] The person looked to the society around him as the measure of his success, and, like Babbitt a generation earlier, he measured success in terms of how much he could surpass previous accomplishments (both his own and others'). But he knew more than Babbitt; the economic catastrophe of the depression and the precarious state of the cold-war world in the atomic age caused him to doubt. Deprived of any firm idealism to direct his aspirations, he derived his dreams from the media and other external authorities, even though he was beginning to suspect that they were as empty and meaningless as he.

During the 1960s and 1970s, Americans began to question the materialistic urge of previous decades. In *The Image: A Guide to Pseudo-Events in America,* historian Daniel Boorstin notes that the new authority figures offer only illusions that leave us fundamentally dissatisfied with reality. Further, there seems to be no real basis for social cohesion; the specialized bureaucracies of modern civilization have cut individuals off from binding ties. Interestingly enough, both conservative and liberal observers decry this situation. The sociologist Robert Nisbet argues that the individual has no independent values and strength to resist the pseudo-community of cults or political Big Brothers,[14] while Philip Slater, a social scientist and observer of contemporary American culture, contends that individuals need the community and a sense of social connection in order to be truly free to create personal meaning.[15] The historian Christopher Lasch observes that Americans have become increasingly alienated from their own history; like children they live only in a narcissistic present without past experience or future goals as guides.[16] Americans no longer work in the hope of a future spiritual or earthly reward, they only consume—and take less and less satisfaction from that consumption. This description mirrors the true gambler's state, except that he may, in fact, derive some satisfaction from his play. Despite the fads of self-help and pop-psychology, attempts to reach self-understanding yield only emptiness. A continuous stream of new fads, new products, appears, but there will always be newer fads and newer products to take their place.

Loosed from the traditional moorings of idealism, contemporary culture is in a state of flux. Clark Kerr, a former president of the University of California, suggests that the traditional work ethic contained the seeds of its own destruction:

> Hard work leads to affluence; affluence leads to new life-styles; new life-styles diminish the work ethic. But what seemed like affluence yesterday tends to become for many people the minimum acceptable standard of living today, and affluence remains somewhere ahead.[17]

Compounding this problem is what the pollster Daniel Yankelovich calls a "psychology of entitlement."[18] Many Americans have withdrawn emotional involvement from their work and at the same time insisted upon steady increases in pay and fringe benefits. Success symbols of the past—a stable nuclear family, certain key possessions such as a single family home in the suburbs and an appropriate automobile, and the visible symbols of respectability reinforced through the media (a well-kept house, well-scrubbed children, and even "saving for a rainy day")—were accessible to the average American during times of economic expansion, and moreover they were concrete. In the absence of higher ideals, it was of some comfort to know where one stood in society—and to let others know as well—through these symbols. Yankelovich summarizes the significance of the postwar era through 1970 in this way:

> Individual aspirations for success and the socioeconomic trajectory of the society toward ever greater growth fitted together harmoniously. The individual wanted what the society was prepared to reward. When people worked hard, earned money, and spent it unstintingly on consumer goods, it brought them self-esteem and the approval of others as well as material comfort. Crucially important, people were able to feel that they were advancing the goals of the larger society as well as fulfilling themselves.[19]

But today America is in the midst of a change in cultural values that includes a revision of the traditional symbols of success. The ability of institutions to deliver the goods and the ability of the economy to live up to people's expectations are no longer taken for granted: are the values of a consumer society worth a nose-to-the-grindstone way of life? If they are not extinct, the work ethic and traditional symbols of success have been changed significantly. Americans want to fulfill the dream of a "full rich life, and . . . see the building of an ethic built around . . . obligations to self, rather than obligations to others."[20] Work and family responsibilities have declined in importance as leisure has assumed a higher value. The sociologist Amitai Etzioni notes, "The diligent labor and monetary frugality of past generations [are] paying off, and the new generation, less concerned with self-discipline, the future, or transcendental values, [is] more eager to enjoy the available goods and services immediately."[21]

Much of contemporary popular culture, including the institution of commercial gambling, reflects and stimulates this change in values. Commercial institutions have substituted manufactured images for reality to such an extent that it is difficult to discern authentic experiences. The spectacle of a Super Bowl game, played as much for profit as for the championship, bears only incidental resemblance to the *game* of football. Pulp romance novels substitute for genuine emotion. Mass-produced, celebrity-endorsed toys program the play of children, and disaster or horror films package and manipulate feelings of terror and anger. Commercial airlines and Americanized hotel chains make it possible to circle the globe without ever leaving the safety of familiar surroundings. Although free from old restrictions, the possibility for genuine experiences is stifled by new, equally impersonal, institutional masters.

GAMBLING AND CULTURE

In December 1982 a success story of sorts—perhaps a recession-influenced version of the American dream—was reported on the front page of the *Philadelphia Inquirer.*[22] Donald Bakley, a systems analyst for a utility company, had joined the ranks of the wealthy. However, unlike the Alger heroes of a century ago, Bakley had not earned his success through hard work, ambition, and prudent investment. Instead, he simply was lucky and chose six numbers, winning a New Jersey lottery prize of over $4 million. Every week in several States, would-be winners line up to purchase Lotto tickets. They choose their six numbers, often settling on birthdays, anniversaries, or lucky numbers.

Journalists can speak of "lofty visions" as they quote a player who dreams that he will some day hit the number.[23] Is such a dream real? Boorstin suggests that real dreams can serve as behavioral guidelines for future goals and help the individual and the culture move toward them.

Illusions, on the other hand, are counterproductive because there is nothing that an individual can do to make them come true. The get-rich-quick dreams of the individual lottery player are largely an illusion. He lives in irrational hope for salvation—the instant success of being a winner. There is nothing the player can do to influence the outcome but buy tickets. His chances for winning are real but remote and certainly are not due to any personal qualities. Thus, the lottery winner becomes a celebrity, but he is not a hero. Moreover, the player's hopes are centered on individual, or at most familial, benefits. A laid-off steelworker dreams of a new car, travel, and the ability to provide for his family; but winning the prize will not earn him his job back, nor will it improve the economic slump that has caused his lay-off. He will be lucky if he wins, and to that extent he will be successful, but he will not have earned his reward:

> [H]e is successful not because of his own personal abilities so much as because he "got the breaks." The whole competitive struggle is presented as a lottery in which a few winners, no more talented or energetic than any one else, drew the lucky tickets. The effect on the masses is at once consoling (it might have been me) and deadening to effort, ambition (there are no rules, so why struggle?).[24]

The culture and the social structure are absolved of their sins by the promotion of instant millionaires. It does not matter if State lotteries are among the most regressive taxes pushed on the many who can afford them least.[25] "Mathematically a lottery or sweepstake is a bad bet, but the adventurer is not concerned with the odds, the appealing fact is that one ticket has as much chance as another, and one ticket must draw the big prize."[26] Lotteries fit neatly into our democratic, egalitarian culture—everyone has an equal chance for the unequal outcome. But as Roger Caillois points out, there is nothing a person can do to increase the chance of success but buy additional tickets.[27] Lasch has labeled our cravings limitless and our psyches restless, dissatisfied, demanding instant gratification;[28] if the culture has worked itself into such a desperate state, entrepreneurs oblige by offering long-odds payoffs for small bettors.

Whether the culture actively promotes this type of gambling or whether it flourishes because of conditions within society is a moot point. It is clear that certain aspects of commercial gambling reflect changes in the culture. If the laid-off steelworker's Protestant ethic had not been eroded enough already, how hard would he look for work after winning an instant fortune? In such a situation, people either become disillusioned or must go to great lengths to maintain their illusions; and since the state has a vested interest in preserving social stability it will cooperate with the image-makers. Social systems, however, need to motivate and sustain individual effort through rewards and sanctions. But winnings from gambling, rewards for "luck," will not encourage people to learn skills or to be productive in any sustained fashion.

Nevertheless, commercial gambling institutions are among the image-makers, and they are replacing the spontaneous play that earlier generations engaged in—at racetracks, in sawdust casinos, or with the neighborhood numbers runner—with slick advertising campaigns that encourage packaged gambling experiences. Such changes are simply part of the general transformation of American life and leisure. The growing influence of bureaucratic institutions over the working lives of nearly all Americans has made escape from routine a more pressing need than ever before. America is still a society of abundance, and our affluence affords us increasing amounts of leisure time and disposable income. Yet we remain unsatisfied. The cause of our dissatisfaction may not be due to some failing of our creativity: American culture is vital enough to be imitated throughout the world. The search is not necessarily for a new Beethoven but for an escape from the ordinary, for some alternative to the predictability of the workaday world.

Leisure play should provide this escape; and gambling games would appear to be an appropriate form. However, as we have seen, the growth of institutional leisure has drastically reduced the opportunities for engaging in genuine creative play or risk. This is a true measure of America's cultural predicament: play, the traditional restorative for the mental, physical, and emotional stresses of the real world of work and personal relationships, is becoming just another routine. Few leisure activities are free expressions of the individual, and there are few genuine games. Their place is being taken by programmed behaviors that generate profits for leisure institutions.

The erosion of the cultural norms that had prohibited gambling permitted a much-needed and unique form of leisure play to enter mainstream America. Historically, the impetus for this occurred at a time of general cultural reevaluation, as it became clear that resources and opportunities were limited after all. The irony is that the mechanism responsible for this change, the revenue imperative, is rapidly transforming gambling into a social institution. The very qualities that gave gambling a unique social value—excitement, safe risk, escape—are being changed into yet another set of rote behaviors that serve institutional purposes rather than individual needs.

True play is liberating; it is an antidote to despair and a wellspring of hope. When gambling is genuine play it fulfills all these functions. It is unfortunate that in the history of gambling in America attention has mostly been focused on the pathological behavior of a minority of gamblers, leading to the conclusion that gambling itself was the cause of their hopelessness. As a society Americans have always been distrustful of play and pleasure, perhaps placing too much value on industry and work. For this reason, Orwell's parable of a work-ordered social order in which spontaneous behavior is a major crime should have a special relevance for Americans. The political predictions of *1984* have not come true, at least in the Western hemisphere; they did not need to. Stronger forces than politics—economic, technological, and cultural forces—are reconstituting American society in an insitutional form that Orwell would surely recognize. The balance of power is shifting away from the state, and corporations and civil bureaucracies are ascending to social power. Orwell correctly ascribes liberating qualities to the proles' lottery play, but a repressive state could never successfully use these qualities to subjugate the behavior of its citizens to routine. Only by making play itself a routine and destroying its liberating qualities could a society or social institution turn a lottery or any other game into a means of social control.

THE NEW GAMBLING IDEOLOGY

As we write in 1984 Big Gambling is firmly established as a potent social and economic institution. The interests that make up the commercial gambling institution (especially State lotteries and casino gaming corporations) are replacing negative images of games of chance with what amounts to a new ideology of gambling. This ideology is created by interactions of gambling interests with legislatures and regulatory agencies, and it is ultimately packaged and disseminated by the media for popular consumption.

Popular attitudes toward gambling are being changed in several ways. One of the most basic changes involves the way in which the public perceives gambling losses. Under old norms losses were considered socially unjustifiable as well as harmful to individuals.

The values of thrift and prudence were incompatible with wasting money by gambling. In addition, because much gambling was illicit, losses were equated with revenues to illegal operators, who were usually identified by law enforcement spokesmen with organized crime. The new gambling ideology, however, terms a portion of operator win (or retention) public revenue, without mentioning the fact that it is generated from the public's gambling losses. The social cost of public revenue generated by commercial gambling is hidden by the phraseology. Further, there is the unstated assumption that this public revenue is derived from those who can afford to gamble, like the revenue from a luxury tax, or from those who shouldn't, and therefore deserve to be penalized and, if possible, discouraged from gambling. Although rarely articulated, this attitude is a vestige of a moral and religious antigambling bias, an unwritten subtext to much gambling law.

Second, the new ideology posits that legalization rather than enforcement of antigambling laws will eliminate illegal gambling. The elimination of illegal gambling is a recurring theme in American enabling law and, in the abstract, is a long-standing policy goal. This idea has received a new and wider currency in the last twenty years, notably as a statutory purpose of legal off-track betting and State lottery numbers games. As has been previously noted, this is a reasonable policy provided the legal games are competitive in price with illegal numbers and bookmaking. But this concept has been extended to casino gaming and lotteries, neither of which are major illegal activities. It is illogical to assume that either casinos or lotteries will divert substantial amounts of existing wagering from illegal channels: the overwhelming volume of illegal gambling is booked on football and other sports (including horse racing) or bet at illegal numbers games. In addition, the profits of the bookmaker have been overestimated.[29] For similar reasons attempts to characterize casino and lottery revenue as money recovered from organized crime are either misinformed or misleading;[30] these revenues are unlikely to be affected by the introduction of legal lotteries or gaming into their markets.[31]

A corollary is the exaggeration of the dollar handle and retention of illegal gambling.[32] "For 30 years, agencies of the Departments of Treasury and Justice have supplied a succession of congressional committees and Presidential commissions with seemingly 'hard' estimates of illegal gambling that have failed to stand up to the scrutiny of qualified independent analysts."[33]

In 1979 Internal Revenue published FBI estimates of illegal wagering in the United States in 1976 ranging from $45.2 billion to $56.4 billion, with revenues (losses) of from $9.8 billion to $12.4 billion.[34] In 1983 the IRS published its own estimates of illegal wagering for 1979. These were considerably lower than the FBI's estimates for 1976: revenues of $2.96 billion and (by extrapolation from Internal Revenue's "higher estimates" of unreported income) handle of about $16 billion.[35] Roughly half of this handle ($7.6 billion) is illegal sports bookmaking, which has a gross retention of approximately 4.5 percent. Even if Internal Revenue's estimate of illegal sports book handle was only one-third of the actual amount of illegal sports book wagering in 1979 was only $22.8 billion, with illegal revenues from this source totaling only $1 billion, from which, of course, bookmakers would have to deduct expenses. While still enormous sums, these estimates are far lower than those commonly cited by commercial gambling interests, which start at $50 billion (handle) and range upwards. These wildly overstated and unsupportable estimates are part of the new gambling ideology and only serve to obscure the true dimensions of the problem.[36]

The third aspect of the new ideology is the current assumption that legal gambling can stimulate economic development or, in the case of Atlantic City, redevelopment. This is a principal statutory justification for casino gaming and an important one for pari-mutuel horse racing, upon which the horse-breeding industry depends. The economic benefits that have been realized from gaming and pari-mutuel betting are both real and quantifiable, and consequently they have become an important part of the new gambling ideology. These benefits however are endangered by the revenue imperative, which has forced pari-mutuel takeouts to uneconomic levels and may, in time, lead to the excessive taxation of gross gaming win. An economic benefit, then, accrues from gambling only if public revenues are limited, and the necessity for this limitation is usually not recognized.

Because compulsive or pathological gambling is an uncomfortable, though relatively safe, subject for gambling interests, the new ideology minimizes this issue and portrays all gambling games as equally harmless forms of entertainment. While it is certainly true that compulsive gambling has received considerable attention from the opponents of gambling, it is equally true that, as Chapter 4 shows, particular gambling games stimulate markedly different gambling behaviors—some of which produce much higher losses and more rapid rates of loss than others. This fact, which should be a fundamental consideration in formulating gambling law and policy, is often discounted or ignored by gambling interests for the obvious reason that its admission would lead to difficult questions concerning the social consequences of making the more aggressive games widely available.

It is worth remembering that the pleasurable aspects of gambling are not given much emphasis in the new gambling ideology. Only rarely does a gambling industry spokesman claim the entertainment value of gambling is a justification for allowing it. To our knowledge, the provision of public entertainment has never been a statutory purpose of enabling legislation. This appears to be a lingering effect of the Puritan ethic, which found the pleasures of vice, including gambling, worthy of particular damnation. It seems that Americans may now gamble, but they still ought not to enjoy it.

The aspect of gambling most often emphasized by the industry's advertising and promotion is the possibility of winning. Casinos, racetracks, and State lotteries make extensive use of this theme in virtually all of their newspaper, billboard, and television advertisements. But as has been shown, the public cannot win in the long term at lotteries and casino games; and the high takeouts prevailing in pari-mutuel betting have considerably reduced the chances of winning at racetracks and frontons. In promoting gambling games the real chances of winning are virtually ignored. The mathematical probabilities of winning a particular bet are stated only to the extent of compliance with statutory or regulatory requirements. State lotteries, for example, are generally required to state the probabilities of winning a given prize; they do so in paragraphs of microscopic print in booklets available at sales outlets. The probabilities of winning the larger prizes are invariably extremely low—on the order of millions-to-one for multi-million dollar lottery and Lotto games. The amount of the prize, not the probability of winning it, forms the basis for lottery advertising. Lotteries, and casinos paying million-dollar slot-machine jackpots at similar odds, are aided in promoting these games by the print and electronic media, which feature the biographies of winners as real-life rags-to-riches soap operas. Essentially, the media's treatment of large wins amounts to free promotion of the most unfavorable of all commercial gambling games, and lottery sales and slot play tend to soar after such publicity.

The deemphasis of pleasure in the new gambling ideology extends to the other social values of gambling. Escape from deadening routine, the mental and emotional stimulation of circumscribed risk and the definite and immediate nature of gambling decisions, the opportunity to play with money instead of being dominated by it, and the ritualized order and fraternity of gambling subcultures are only some of these social values; none of them figure in the formal or informal public statements of industry officials or government representatives. Casinos are partial exceptions, in that individual operators sometimes base marketing strategies on entertainment and vacation possibilities. Even in these cases, however, the emphasis is on nongambling activities, such as performing talent and recreational facilities, rather than on the casino games themselves. Racetracks frequently adopt the analogous marketing approach, stressing the sport of horse racing rather than pari-mutuel betting.

Even more surprising is the failure of this new ideology to attempt to establish the individual's right to gamble. This failure probably derives in part from the legal status of commercial gambling, which is a matter of privilege rather than right. A more fundamental reason is gambling's ambiguous cultural status. A comparison with alcoholic beverages shows how uncertain this status is: some religious beliefs aside, fifty years after the repeal of Prohibition an adult's right to drink is unquestioned. In contrast, a bet on an NFL game—a natural accompaniment to a few beers for millions of Americans—is illegal outside of Nevada. Proposals to legalize sports betting appear regularly, but always as revenue or antibookmaking measures. To our knowledge, the argument that Americans have a right to wager on the outcome of these games has never been used to justify sports betting initiatives, even though this would appear to be a logical and forceful argument in a democracy that places a high value on the freedom of individual choice.

As in so many other respects, American attitudes toward what might be termed the individual's right to gamble contrast with those of other societies. Great Britain, the society that is perhaps closest to our own, had made this right a fundamental principle of its gambling policy. The 1978 Royal Commission on Gambling, following the views of the previous (1949–51) Royal Commission, stated its "general beliefs about the aims and proper limits of legal control over gambling in a society such as ours" as three broad principles.[37] The first speaks directly to this individual right:

> (i) To interfere as little as possible with individual liberty to take part in the various forms of gambling but to recommend the imposition or continuance of such restrictions as are desirable and practicable to discourage socially damaging excesses and to prevent the incursion of crime into gambling.[38]

The Royal Commission's philosophy (the commission's word; it is difficult to imagine its use by an American governmental body) is completed in two similarly forceful affirmations of an impartial and disinterested concern for the public interest in commercial gambling:

> (ii) To support broadly the principle that the [gambling] facilities offered should respond only to "unstimulated demand." This is a principle about which it is not easy to be specific. . . . It implies, for instance, the maintenance of curbs on certain forms of advertising, and it has up to now been taken to imply the limitation of amenities in betting shops. . . . The principle applies in different degrees to different forms of gambling. . . . People should not be pestered; they should not be distracted from their real work, even if betting at appropriate times boosts the morale of those engaged in repetitive or otherwise uncongenial tasks. . . .

> (iii) There is another important feature of the Royal Commission's philosophy: it is that gamblers should invariably be made aware of what they are letting themselves in for when they gamble—in other words what they may lose. (Gamblers usually know, or think they know, what they may win.) The reader will find in this Report that we have made a major effort in this field.[39]

It is interesting to compare this philosophy with the new gambling ideology being established as an American cultural norm.

GAMBLING IN MAINSTREAM AMERICA

In many ways, the play of the gambler is similar to other forms of popular culture, entertainment and recreation, in America. Big Gambling is certainly as much a commercial institution as other recreation and entertainment industries. The values of a materialistic industrial society have shaped contemporary leisure and the institutions that provide leisure opportunities, and as long as gambling remains in the realm of leisure activity it does not directly conflict with cultural values. Indeed, it reflects and reinforces them in the same way other cultural rituals do.

Until recent times, the Protestant work ethic stood as the most important value in the myth of American capitalist enterprise. Thrift and industry held the keys to material success and spiritual fulfillment. The self-made man, the archetypal embodiment of the American dream, owed his success to habits of industry, sobriety, moderation, self-discipline, and prudent investment. These qualities may still be seen in the successful recreational gambler, but they are caricatured in that he invests in the present—a chance for immediate reward in a culture characterized by self-indulgence. The traditional Horatio Alger–hero and his descendants lived for the future, shunning self-indulgence in favor of slow investment, self-improvement, and a painstaking climb up the ladder of success. A gambler hopes to compress and intensify this experience.

In the contemporary age of diminishing opportunities, the Protestant ethic has been critically eroded. Americans tend to live for the moment in an unpredictable world and, unlike past generations, are quite willing to consume wealth in immediate gratification. Gamblers bet on a quicker future to test their ultimate fate. The pseudo-event of gambling yields an instant measure of success in its own context; it is not as ambiguous as most of life has become. In earlier times, an individual's self-interest was thought to be a rational pursuit of gain and the accumulation of wealth;

today it is a search for fulfillment and psychic survival. Workers are consumers, even in their leisure, and their consumption feeds the social and industrial complex. Having great expectations but few real opportunities to reach his goal, contemporary man is perpetually bored, dissatisfied, and looking for safe risks. Commercial gambling is glad to oblige.

NOTES

1. George Orwell, *1984* (1949, 1961; reprint, New York: New American Library, 1981), p. 73.

2. These changes in the relationship between the person and society, parts of the modernization process, are certainly not sudden. Since the work of the earliest postrevolutionary French sociologists Comte and Durkheim, the underlying theme of much of sociology has been the search for the bases of social order and new sources of cohesion.

3. David M. Potter, *People of Plenty: Economic Abundance and the American Character* (Chicago: University of Chicago Press, 1954).

4. Wendell Wilkie, quoted in Alistair Cooke, *Alistair Cooke's America* (New York: Alfred A. Knopf, 1977), p. 372.

5. Alexis de Tocqueville, *Democracy in America* (New York: Random House, 1954).

6. Potter, *People of Plenty,* pp. 59–60.

7. Andrew Carnegie, "Wealth," *North American Review,* June 1889, reprinted in *An American Primer,* ed. Daniel J. Boorstin (New York: New American Library, 1968), pp. 519–30. Carnegie states, "The price which society pays for the law of competition . . . is . . . great; but the advantages of this law are . . . greater still, for it is to this law that we owe our wonderful material development."

8. John Winthrop, "A Modell of Christian Charity," in *An American Primer,* ed. Boorstin, pp. 28–41. Winthrop told his Puritan followers, "God Almightie in his most holy and wise providence hath soe disposed of the Condicion of mankinde, as in all times some must be rich some poore, some highe and eminent in power and dignitie, others meane and in subieccion. . . . Noe man is made more honorable than another . . . out of any perticuler and singuler respect to himselfe but for the glory of his Creator and the Common good of the Creature, Man."

9. Philip E. Slater, *The Pursuit of Loneliness: American Culture at the Breaking Point* (Boston: Beacon Press, 1970).

10. Potter, *People of Plenty,* pp. 166–88.

11. Margaret Mead, *And Keep Your Powder Dry* (New York: William Morrow, 1942), pp. 68–69.

12. See David Riesman, *The Lonely Crowd* (New Haven, Conn.: Yale University Press, 1961), and William Whyte, *The Organization Man* (New York: Simon & Schuster, 1956).

13. David Riesman, *Abundance for What? and Other Essays* (Garden City, N.Y.: Doubleday, 1964), p. 107.

14. Daniel Boorstin, *The Image: A Guide to Pseudo-events in America* (New York: Atheneum, 1972); Robert Nisbet, *The Quest for Community* (New York: Oxford Univer-

sity Press, 1953); Nisbet, *The Twilight of Authority* (New York: Oxford University Press, 1975); and Nisbet, *Prejudices: A Philosophical Dictionary* (Cambridge, Mass.: Harvard University Press, 1983).

15. Slater, *Pursuit of Loneliness.*

16. Lasch, *Culture of Narcissism.*

17. Clark Kerr, "Introduction: Industrialism with a Human Face," in *Work in America: The Decade Ahead,* ed. Clark Kerr and Jerome M. Rosow (New York: Van Nostrand Reinhold, 1979), p. xx.

18. Daniel Yankelovich, "Work, Values, and the New Breed," in *Work in America,* ed. Kerr and Rosow, pp. 3–26.

19. Ibid., p. 9.

20. Ibid., pp. 10–12.

21. Amitai Etzione, "Work in the American Future: Reindustrialization or Quality of Life," in *Work in America,* ed. Kerr and Rosow, p. 31.

22. "Six Numbers Add up to $4.2 Million," *Philadelphia Inquirer,* December 18, 1982.

23. "$15 Million up for Grabs: With Lottery Prizes at Record Levels, Lines Are Long and Visions Are Lofty," *Philadelphia Inquirer,* December 2, 1982.

24. Dwight MacDonald, "A Theory of Mass Culture," in *Mass Culture: The Popular Arts in America,* ed. Bernard Rosenberg and David Manning White (New York: Free Press, 1957), p. 67.

25. See the Appendix for a discussion of the relationship of illegal gambling to the selective decriminalization of gambling games.

26. Ewen, *Lotteries and Sweepstakes,* p. 368.

27. Caillois, *Man, Play, and Games.*

28. Lasch, *Culture of Narcissism.*

29. In "Fact, Fancy, and Organized Crime," pp. 45–67, Peter Reuter and Jonathan B. Rubinstein argue that the FBI and other government agencies use "bureaucratic puffery" to inflate the threat posed by organized crime and illegal gambling in order to commandeer bigger staffs and budgets for themselves.

30. See the Appendix for a discussion of illegal gambling.

31. See the Appendix for a discussion of this argument.

32. See the Appendix.

33. Eugene Martin Christiansen, "The Gross Annual Wager of the United States (calendar 1982)," *Gaming Business Magazine,* April 1984, 49, and "The Gross Annual Wages of the United States (calendar 1983)," *Gaming Business Magazine,* 5 May 1984.

34. United States, Department of the Treasury, Internal Revenue Service, *Estimates of Income Unreported on Individual Income Tax Returns,* Publication 1104 (9–79) (Washington, D.C.: Internal Revenue Service, 1979), pp. 133–37.

35. United States, Department of the Treasury, Internal Revenue Service, Office of the Assistant Commissioner (Planning, Finance and Research), Research Division, *Income Tax Compliance Research: Estimates for 1973–1981* (Washington, D.C.: Internal Revenue Service, 1983), pp. 198–211.

36. See Appendix for a detailed discussion of problems in estimating illegal gambling.

37. Royal Commission on Gambling, *Final Report,* Comnd. 7200.

38. Ibid.

39. Ibid.

7

The Public Interest and a New Gambling Policy

The larger the economic interest of the state in casino gambling, the greater the outside pressure to erode the mechanisms of control.

—Jerome Skolnick, "The Social Risks of Casino Gambling"

The '84 elections were a watershed in the evolution of U.S. commercial gambling. Actions by various elected officials and the November elections confirmed that lotteries, as they had been prior to the 1890s, have once again become an accepted method of public finance. These same actions and elections reinforced historic public doubts about casinos. While pari-mutuels extended their old-fashioned (and expensive) racetracks into five new jurisdictions, this expansion did not constitute the structural changes in a traditional game that would enable horse racing and *jai-alai* to better survive in the rapidly changing American commercial gambling marketplace.

The five pari-mutuel horse-racing legalizations since 1982 would seem to be a sign of renewed vigor in the betting game that dominated U.S. commercial gambling from the depression into the 1970s. These legalizations add a traditional recreation to some midwestern areas and one State of the Deep South and open important new markets for the produce of American breeding farms; but whether the diverse interests that make up the U.S. racing industry will be able to resolve their internal differences and make effective use of the new tools of simulcasting and off-track betting to regain a measure of their diminishing appeal in markets transformed by State lotteries and casino gaming is a question that remains to be answered. At stake are the livelihoods of hundreds of thousands of individuals now employed at racetracks, in OTB systems, and in the breeding industry. But perhaps more importantly to society at large, that significant part of American culture bound up in the horse, which the pari-mutuel economy has done so much to preserve in an increasingly technological world, is threatened by the dramatic changes now transforming the business of risk.

The failure of numerous casino initiatives since 1976 despite the overwhelming financial success of gaming in Atlantic City is conclusive evidence that the historic questions about casino gaming—the continuing participation of organized crime in the casino industry, the impact on the political process of such concentrated (and in some cases unethical) economic power, and the social and psychological implications of highly extractive casino games—still weigh strongly with mainstream America. The public approval of pari-mutuel betting and State lotteries does not yet extend to the glittering gambling halls now concentrated in isolated communities at either end of the continent.

The decisive step taken by mainstream America in 1984 was toward lotteries. By approving State lotteries in California, Oregon, Missouri, and West Virginia the electorate extended this form of gambling to a majority of the U.S. population and effectively completed the evolution of State lotteries from a dubious and initially unsuccessful experiment in public finance to a normal function of State government.

We are now convinced that the adoption of lotteries by all but a handful of States is inevitable within the next few years. The addition of California alone will be sufficient to pull lottery gross revenues ahead of casino win to make State governments the operators of the largest commercial gambling game in the United States, perhaps as early as 1985. What is happening is that lotteries—this time operated by the States themselves—are assuming the position private lotteries held in colonial America: a normal, accepted tool of public finance. This cyclical history raises the old questions about the wisdom of funding government expenditures from commercial gambling losses, and should remind us that the nineteenth-century State-franchised and State-regulated private lotteries ended in scandals and disaster. State operation has not prevented some historically familiar problems: questions concerning the New York Lottery's integrity forced New York to suspend drawings from October 1975 to September 1976; more recently actions of the chairman of the New Jersey State Lottery Commission have resulted in serious allegations of conflict of interest, and the administration and private vendors of the District of Columbia's lottery have become embroiled in lawsuits amid charges alleging a variety of misconduct.

One thing, however, is certainly new: the lottery games themselves. The evolution of lotteries from passive monthly drawings into complex gambling operations offering full menus of increasingly aggressive player-interactive games promoted by the States is profoundly altering

American gambling behavior and the place of gambling in American life. For good or ill the 1984 elections made the "lotterizing" of the United States a *fait accompli*. Mainstream America has embraced State lotteries, but the larger social consequences of this acceptance, and particularly its implications for American leisure, are unresolved.

Past American experience with gambling would suggest that if we are going to gamble, and from all the evidence it appears inevitable that at some time most of us will, then we should gamble in our own interest. But as the preceding chapters have shown, the majority of Americans, including those who make or influence gambling law and policy, do not agree on what that interest is. Our investigation of commercial gambling has taken us through the published literature on the subject, to the gambling conferences where professionals and scholars confront regulators and members of the gambling industry, to legislative committee hearings where we were asked to testify, to the offices of control commissions, and finally to the gambling establishments themselves. One common idea emerges from these diverse experiences: there may not be a single public interest at all. In any case, it is clear that the collective public interest is not necessarily synonymous with the interests of the institutions directly engaged in gambling or those that benefit financially from gambling revenues.

The public good should be the first and overriding consideration of gambling policy. As we have seen, this never has been the case, nor is it the case today. Prior to the rise of the modern gambling industries, traditional, repressive cultural norms prevented Americans from analyzing gambling dispassionately. These norms also made it difficult to recognize the social and psychological functions of gambling. Instead, by internalizing these repressive norms and then enacting a general legal prohibition, Americans managed to create the worst of all possible worlds: we gambled, illegally, for most of our history. This illegal gambling helped give birth to the institutionalized presence of organized crime that is an undeniable force in America today.

Now the pendulum is swinging in the opposite direction, and for the first time gambling is being accepted into mainstream America. But it is entering society in the form of a powerful leisure institution composed of both private corporations and State gambling operations. This institution is transforming the old gambling activities into more aggressive, commercially profitable games that maximize losses; and gambling itself is being changed into routine behaviors that serve economic ends for the operators and the state, rather than leisure purposes for the individual.

In these rapidly changing and complex circumstances, it is difficult to discover exactly where the public good lies. Yet the relative benefits and costs of commercial gambling must be identified so that they can be considered in the decisions that will determine the future of gambling in America. The preceding chapters have presented a comprehensive look at gambling from a sociological perspective. From this vantage point, we now examine the key elements of the public interest.

Losses and Public Revenue

A distinction should be made between the losses that, by definition, must be incurred for commercial gambling to constitute an on-going business (that is, to cover its costs) and those (additional) losses extracted to satisfy government claims on gambling revenues. The public cannot win in the long term at any commercial gambling game. However, the transmutation of losses, which are the one objective and quantifiable social risk of commercial gambling, into public revenue by the alchemist's stone of "painless taxation" is by far the most intractible issue raised by legalization. The revenue needs of government are pressing and insatiable, and government's extraordinary claim on gambling revenues is so firmly entrenched in State constitutions and statute law that it would be pointless to try to repeal it. The issue thus becomes how to devise effective restraints against the presently irresistible force of the revenue imperative.

If this force is not restrained, if governments continue to extract, either directly or indirectly, more and more revenue from gambling, all of the actual or potential benefits of gambling will eventually disappear. Specifically, the price of gambling will rise, with games becoming more aggressive and extractive. Both per capita and per gambler losses will likewise rise, thus increasing the social and personal risks of commercial gambling. Legal gambling will be increasingly noncompetitive with illegal games. Legalized numbers and off-track betting, as well as sports betting (when and if it becomes legally available outside Nevada), will be unable to eliminate the massive amount of illegal gambling that presently afflicts society. In addition, the economic contributions of commercial gambling will be endangered—first, because government will drain excessive amounts of money from gambling economies and, second, because government's revenue demands will drive the price of legal gambling to the point where it will no longer be able to compete in the leisure marketplace.

Finally, without such restraints, gamblers, as an unprotected body of consumers, will bear a disproportionate share of the common tax burden. Tax equity or fairness is a subjective concept. The current practice of taxing individual gamblers at punitive levels for the right to gamble at certain specified games implies that government fundamentally disapproves of their activity. Nevertheless, government attempts to stimulate gambling, at least in those games it directly controls, in order to increase State revenues, which are derived from player losses. It is difficult to reconcile the fact that gambling is still generally proscribed—and allowed only by exception—with the States' sanction of and stake in the continued growth of commercial gambling. The State finds moral justification for increasing legal commercial gambling by tying it to various entitlement programs, paying no attention to the interests of gamblers.

Maximum Economic Benefit

The economic benefits to be derived from commercial gambling are diverse. They include the stability of the horse-racing and breeding industries supported by pari-mutuel betting and the economic contributions of casino/hotels and related tourism to resort areas in Nevada and New Jersey. They also include the funding of increasingly costly public entitlement programs. These benefits should be encouraged to the extent consistent with minimizing the social risks of gambling. But gamblers should not be held hostage to the economic interests of others in society. The risk of gambler losses should be considered both in the initial decision to allow specific forms of gambling and in the operation of those industries once authorized. In the case of casinos a second social risk is the possibility of, in effect, sanctioning organized crime through the continuing criminal participation in this industry.

The Elimination of Illegal Gambling

The elimination of illegal gambling is clearly in the public interest. Just as clearly, it is apparent that the enforcement of prohibitory law has failed to eliminate illegal numbers and bookmaking. (Casino gaming is a different matter, for while illegal casinos exist, they do so on a small scale; large-scale casino operations can effectively be eliminated by the application of existing law enforcement resources.) But there are two impediments to the elimination of illegal numbers and bookmaking: the first is the absence of legal alternatives in most jurisdictions; and the second is the noncompetitive nature of the legal alternatives that do exist, such as State lottery numbers games and OTB, because they are not perfect substitutes for the illegal games. The most important parameter of substitutability is price; but tax-free winnings, credit, anonymity, community acceptance, and even the "good will" of traditional consumer/supplier relationships enter into it. Yet none of these impediments to substitutability are insurmountable. Before October 1981 Great Britain, for example, allowed virtually all forms of gambling and effectively did not tax legal payouts. As a result, that country did not have a significant illegal gambling problem.

Low Consumer Price

The price of legal gambling should be as low as is consistent with other elements of the public interest. This should be a positive principle of gambling taxation, rather than a laudable goal to which idle lip service is paid. Sumptuary taxation of gambling is not in the public interest.

Maximized Leisure Benefits of Gambling

The social benefits of gambling as genuine leisure play—escape, the enjoyment of circumscribed risk, the spontaneous and voluntary pleasure of making decisions under conditions of uncertainty with immediate and definite results, the intellectual stimulation of handicapping or card-counting—are positive and needed additions to modern life and should be recognized as such. The corruption of these benefits by institutional gambling is part of the general commercialization of American leisure activity.

Minimized Social Risks of Gambling

It is a truism to say that the public good is served by minimizing the social risks of gambling, and this notion frequently passes for policy in legislative debate. However, the minimizing of social risks should be as serious and as specific a statutory purpose of enabling law as are revenue or economic considerations. Excessive losses on the part of the great majority of players who are not compulsive gamblers, as well as losses caused by psychological pathology, are obvious social risks. Increases in illegal gambling, the involvement of organized crime in gaming, increased street crime, and changes within the community itself are among the other social costs of commercial gambling, though these are usually harder to quantify. One difficulty in turning the principle of minimizing these risks into effective policy is finding a way to measure their seriousness. Statutory recognition of the existence of these risks and statutory designation of independent governmental responsibilities for their measurement and correction are two approaches to this problem that remain largely untried and might improve the situation.

Conventional Gambling and Culture

Along with the institutionalization of gambling has come a change in its cultural meaning. Traditional norms relegated gambling to a circumscribed world of nonconventional behavior; gambling was tolerated but not regarded as just another business or behavior. But while gambling was frowned upon, society generally looked the other way when men dared to take a risk. The prescribed male role often encouraged proscribed behaviors. However, as we have seen, commercial gambling today bears the State seal of approval, and this endorsement has profound implications for the meaning of gambling. At the present time, this conventionalization is allowing the pent-up demand for gambling opportunities to rapidly expand the gambling market. But at some time in the future conventionalization could dilute some of the traditional appeals of gambling. No longer is gambling an arena of masculinity enclosed in its own special place. No longer is gambling so magnetically naughty.

Conventional gambling in its most popular forms also reflects a societal shift away from the beliefs, first, that the individual can influence his destiny by his own efforts and, second, that a person is rewarded with what he deserves or what he has earned. Perhaps contemporary Americans have less confidence in their ability to control their destiny. As a people we may have become fatalistic, superstitious, and content to accept unearned rewards bestowed by chance. A civilization cannot survive for very long, however, on wishful thinking and illusions.

Honest Games and Clean Gambling Industries

The integrity both of the commercial gambling games, which directly affect individual players, and of the commercial gambling businesses and industries, which affect society as a whole, are central considerations of the public interest. This conception of the public interest reflects our analysis of a very complex set of activities. However, even the most perfect principles remain abstractions unless translated into policy and laws. Gambling does not take place in an ideal world. It is an extremely practical enterprise, and attempts to improve it must also be practical if they are to be fruitful. Accordingly there follow some practical suggestions for policies to preserve and extend the public interest.

A NEW GAMBLING POLICY

The Role of Government

There is no practical alternative to government as a representative of the public interest at the institutional level of society. As we have pointed out, however, government's qualifications for this role are less than ideal.

Government is an interested party—both because of its extraordinary claim on gambling revenues and because it directly operates lotteries and off-track betting. Paradoxically, typical gambling legislation appears to restrain gambling through the selective decriminalization of particular varieties of games while it simultaneously and aggressively encourages participation in State-run commercial gambling with massive advertising campaigns. Further, government is a divided institution, and in its legislative and executive branches it is often incapable of resisting pressures applied by gambling interests. Finally, government's power to regulate certain aspects of gambling, notably the presence of organized crime, is severely limited by the Bill of Rights. We do not advocate any abridgement of civil rights, for their value to society outweighs any conceivable public interest in gambling. Nor do we propose to reform government in any significant respect. If it were possible to turn the clock back to 1963, we feel the public would have been better served by forbidding direct government operation of commercial gambling, thus avoiding the present conflict between government's roles as a public representative and a gambling operator. This scenario is, however, impossible; government is firmly entrenched in the operation of gambling and is likely to become even more entrenched in the future.

The practical policy question, then, is how to improve government's ability to regulate all gambling operations—its own and those of private interests—impartially, competently, and with the public interest as its first consideration. Within the framework of existing law, there are several changes that can be made in the regulation of gambling at the State level that would markedly increase government's representation of the public interest.

First, the salaries of regulators should be made equivalent to the salaries of their counterparts in the gambling industry. In many cases such salaries would far exceed those paid to the State's highest elected officials, including governors. Unfortunately, there is no substitute for financial independence as a safeguard of administrative integrity in the regulation of gambling.

Second, the manner of appointment to policymaking regulatory positions should be insulated as completely as possible from politics. Both conflict theory and empirical experience have shown conclusively that special interests, especially gambling interests, are far more successful in influencing relatively invisible actions such as executive appointments to racing or casino control commissions than is the general public. With a few exceptions the present methods of appointment have not secured truly independent and knowledgeable regulators. A different method is needed, perhaps one similar to the process used for appointments to the federal judiciary.

Third, laws forbidding gambling regulators from moving rapidly into the industry they regulate should be enacted and rigorously enforced. A sensible additional safeguard of the public interest is the extension of these provisions to other groups, including legislators involved in the enactment of enabling law, members of state executive chambers involved with gambling, members of planning or zoning boards with jurisdiction over racetracks or casinos, and any other public officials whose duties give them the power over gambling operations or vendors.

These measures would not resolve all of society's problems with gambling, but they would do much to restore government's integrity in this area. Legalization has let a powerful genie out of a centuries-old bottle; if commercial gambling is to work for the public good, regulatory agencies and commissions must be made equally powerful in their relations with gambling interests. As things stand now, regulators are sadly overmatched; almost all the cards are in the operators' hands.

Recognition of the Expressed Gambling Desires of the Majority

Much of the difficulty that society has with gambling today derives from a denial of the expressed gambling desires of a majority of Americans throughout our history. It has been true for generations that most Americans gamble. Yet traditional cultural norms and the distorted view of the nature of gambling behavior fostered by studies of compulsive gamblers have combined to frustrate the desire of most Americans for legal gambling opportunities. This has deprived society of many possible social benefits and has inflicted upon all Americans the modern industrial world's most serious illegal gambling problem.

Specifically, if millions of Americans bet on NFL games and other sports illegally that is sufficient evidence of a social need for opportunities to make such bets legally. In this sense individuals should have a right to gamble. There is an exact parallel in America's unhappy history with alcohol. Prohibition frustrated the clearly expressed desire of a majority of Americans to drink. The principal results were to turn over the alcoholic beverage industry to organized crime and to deprive society of the possible benefits of beer, wine, and whiskey without improving in any way the lot of that minority of the population disposed to excessive consumption. The lesson should be clear: if significant numbers of people want to engage in an activity that does not harm significant numbers of other people, there are inevitable serious social penalties for prohibiting—or trying to prohibit—this behavior.

The State has not established the individual's right to gamble; instead it operates from the premise of selective decriminalization which makes sense only in terms of the revenue imperative. Perhaps the reason for this policy lies in the fact that if all gambling were made *legal* there would be no way to justify punitive taxes on commercial gambling, and these extraordinary revenues would disappear. The question remains whether gambling is wrong because it is illegal, or illegal because it is wrong.

Even when government does allow gambling, however, it does not respond appropriately to society's desire to gamble. Instead, legal commercial gambling games are often not indigenous to the population; they are usually the most costly games; and they require the least individual effort from the players. Lotteries, for example, are legal in twenty-one States and are the most artificial and contrived form of commercial gambling, but lotteries serve the revenue imperative. The indigenous game of sports betting, on the other hand, is (on a commercial basis) legal in only one State although the game reflects the spontaneous desire of people to wager on sports events. In a similar fashion, modern corporate casino/hotels are not genuine substitutes for the gambling rooms that were run by entrepreneurs in western mining or cattle towns, in urban centers, or in resort areas, because casino/hotels now must stimulate gambling rather than simply satisfy an indigenous need.

Consideration of Different Gambling Games, Motivations, and Behaviors

In making the decision to legalize a particular form of commercial gambling, the fact that the more aggressive games stimulate higher per capita and per gambler losses should be taken into account. Casino gaming in a major urban center would extract money from the population at unprecedented rates, especially if it were advertised with all the sophistication and resources now being employed to promote Atlantic City casinos. Similarly, the evolution of initially passive games, such as the State lotteries, into the extractive equals of casino slot machines raises serious questions about the consistency of this evolution with the original intent of lottery initiatives.

It is important to realize that the two forms of commercial gambling with the most vigorous growth today—casinos and lotteries—are the most extractive, and as Chapter 4 shows, they have the potential to encourage the most harmful kinds of gambling behaviors. Indeed, the decline of the racing industry and pari-mutuel wagering since the widespread introduction of other legal gambling alternatives may be a significant signal. Player skill and participation are less valuable in the emergent gambling institution: a lottery player cannot exercise a handicapper's knowledge, experience, and judgment—he has only superstition to guide his choices.

Therefore, to ensure that gambling lives up to its statutory purposes or justifications, we suggest the inclusion of a periodic, statutorily mandated review by a politically independent and competent body—preferably including informed members of the public with no vested interest in gambling—to monitor the actual consequences of legalized gambling in all enabling legislation. This suggestion, which presents no great problems of implementation, would increase the importance of the statutory language used to justify legalization. For example, it would become much more difficult to ignore the failure of New York OTB to fulfill its statutory purpose of curbing illegal bookmaking, a failure clearly due to the legislature's subsequent imposition of a surcharge on off-track winnings. Nor could we turn away from the unfulfilled statutory purpose of redeveloping Atlantic City after the legalization of casino gaming. (It is, however, unclear why casinos themselves should be required to cure Atlantic City's urban blight any more than they should be required to pay sumptuary taxes to conduct their business.) If gambling really has become conventional behavior endorsed by the State, then why must casinos justify their existence by solving a community's problems?

In fact the evidence suggests that when casinos enter an existing resort area—whether urban, as in the case of Atlantic City, or rural, as in the proposed cases of Pennsylvania's Poconos or New York's Catskills—the nature of the resort will change qualitatively. Whatever local appeals (climate, setting, or facilities) existed prior to the arrival of casinos will become secondary to the lure of gaming. The indigenous population will suffer some measure of displacement, and the community will undergo a substantial reorganization. What may result is virtually a "company town"—a result very different from that envisioned by enabling legislation. The fact is that casinos compete too well in a capitalistic society. Land values are inflated by speculation; skyrocketing real estate taxes prey on locals who do not sell out to speculators; and existing institutions and recreation facilities cannot match the attraction and economic clout of the casinos.

Finally, we come to the issue of selective decriminalization of gambling and the rationalizations that justify it. Perhaps society would have benefited from a completely different approach. Instead of looking for reasons to decriminalize certain forms of gambling, which ultimately prove to be unsupportable, perhaps the question should be reversed: why should not all commercial gambling be made legal and controlled in the manner of all other legitimate enterprises? The burden of proof would then rest with those who would make a particular gambling activity illegal.

To analyze commercial gambling in a comprehensive fashion it has been necessary to reframe several traditional issues. First, we have shifted the focus from gambling's impact on the individual to its even more crucial impact on social institutions and on American culture. Second, we have shown that gambling is not a homogeneous entity: it is actually a variety of games, each with its own structure and context.

The differences among games have real and predictable consequences for players in terms of motivation, type of play, and outcome. The history of commercial gambling shows its evolution into a social institution and shifts attention from the well-documented dangers of illegal gambling to the less-documented, but no less real, problems surrounding institutional gambling. American culture has contributed to the growth of commercial gambling while making it more difficult for Americans to come to terms with gambling as an activity. Yet Big Gambling reflects and influences the culture that sustains it. The problems and issues surrounding commercial gambling do not have easy or complete solutions that will satisfy all the interested parties; but it is necessary to rationally examine the business of risk because the issues are too important to leave to chance.

Appendix

GROSS WAGERING AND REVENUE

Definitions of columnar headings in Table A-1 (see following page) are discussed here as an aid to the reader.

Number of States Legalized: States in which a particular form of commercial gambling was legal in 1983, regardless of whether such gambling was actually conducted. *Jai-alai,* for example, was legal but not conducted in the State of Nevada in 1983.

Gross Wager ($): The gross amount wagered by bettors and handled by operators. ''Handle,'' ''turnover,'' and ''gross wagering'' are synonymous. ''Drop,'' in casino revenue accounting cash and cash equivalents exchanged for chips, represents the collective bankrolls of players and is not comparable to handle. Except for Atlantic City slot machines, however, handle is neither accounted nor reported for casino games, and drop statistics are often substituted by default for purposes of comparing gaming to other forms of gambling.

Public reporting for commercial gambling generally conforms to the requirements of tax authorities. Pari-mutuel betting is taxed on gross wagering, or handle, which is counted by computerized totalizator betting systems. Similarly, State lottery laws usually specify percentages of sales (or gross wagering or handle) for prizes, State revenues, and operating expenses. In contrast, casino gaming is *not* taxed on the basis of gross wagering, or handle, but on win, which is equivalent to pari-mutuel retention or the percentage of gross lottery sales not distributed to players as prizes. Handle and win are not comparable statistics. Drop, the second statistic used to report casino gaming, is unique: no other form of commercial gambling reports a comparable number. In other words, while the amount of money (or bankroll) gamblers are prepared to bet against casinos—the sums exchanged for chips and dropped into lockboxes—is known, the amount of money horseplayers are prepared to bet against each other at pari-mutuel tracks can only be estimated. Drop and handle, like handle and win, are *not* comparable statistics.

TABLE A-1
GROSS ANNUAL WAGER OF THE UNITED STATES (CALENDAR 1983)*

Game	Number of States Legalized	Gross Wager ($)	Percent Retained by Operators (%)	Operator Revenues (Gamblers' Losses) ($)
Casino Gaming	2			
Slot Machines	2	$ 20,311,000,000	11.6	$ 2,357,000,000
Table Games	2	87,199,000,000	2.6	2,252,000,000
Total		$107,510,000,000	4.3	$ 4,609,000,000
State Lotteries	18	5,600,000,000	54.0	3,024,000,000
Pari-mutuel Betting				
Horseracing	34	9,932,179,426	18.7	1,857,000,000
Off-Track Betting (OTB)	2	1,715,985,659	23.4	402,000,000
Greyhounds	15	2,325,846,934	19.5	454,000,000
Jai-alai	4	619,804,391	18.0	112,000,000
Total		$ 14,593,816,410	19.4	$ 2,825,000,000
Legal Bookmaking	1	852,344,944	5.1	43,513,799
Card Rooms (excluding Nevada)	8	1,052,000,000	5.0	52,000,000
Bingo	45	3,070,000,000	26.0	798,000,000
Charitable Gaming (excluding bingo)		1,400,000,000	33.0	464,000,000
Total Legal Gambling		$134,078,000,000		$11,816,000,000
Illegal Gambling				
Book/Sports/Cards/Horses		23,900,000,000	N/A	2,520,000,000
Numbers		4,890,000,000	51.0	2,490,000,000
Other		100,000,000	17.0	17,000,000
Total		$ 28,890,000,000		$ 5,027,000,000
GRAND TOTAL		$162,968,000,000		$16,843,000,000

SOURCE: Eugene Martin Christiansen, "The Gross Annual Wager of the United States: 1983," "Part I: Handle Trends," "Part II: Revenues," *Gaming Business Magazine*, June, August 1984.

* Readers interested in a more detailed analysis of U.S. gross wagering and revenue should consult the source articles.

Handle, drop, and win are essential concepts for comparisons between different businesses within a single form of commercial gambling—for example, pari-mutuel racetracks and pari-mutuel OTB systems, or casinos in Las Vegas and Atlantic City. Because they are not comparable, however, these concepts must be used with care in comparing different *forms* of gambling, as racetracks and casinos. A comparison of casino win to racetrack handle—a common newspaper practice—grossly understates the volume of gaming compared to pari-mutuel betting, since for every dollar won by the casino very many dollars are wagered. Handle, drop, and win are important to gamblers also. The odds quoted by casinos are generally the percentages of handle, or gross wagering, the casino can expect to win. Players, however, do not as a rule have any clear idea of their gross wagering at table games or slot machines. They are much more likely to know the size of their bankroll, or, from the casino's point of view, the drop they generate. While casinos accurately state that, for example, craps offers bets where the house advantage is as low as 1.4 percent, this percentage is of handle, or gross wagering, not drop or bankroll. Craps commonly wins 16 percent of drop, or the bankrolls of players (see Table 3)—far more than the 1.4 percent of his money the player may think he is losing. At pari-mutuel betting, on the other hand, the amount taken out of gross wagering or handle is nearly universal knowledge: for example, even novice horseplayers know that the takeout, or retention, from win pools at Heartbreak Downs is (say) 17 percent. The point is that horseplayers and casino gamblers are likely to have dissimilar and noncomparable notions of the price they pay for playing their chosen game. Similarly, a frequent confusion in writing about gambling is the use of gross wagering or handle to describe the value of gambling markets. Handle is a measure of the velocity of dollars through gambling games. The amounts that fall out of this flow of handle dollars in the form of operator revenues (player losses) are the best measure of the size or value of gambling games, gambling business, and gambling markets. We have attempted to provide a common basis for both the volume (gross wagering) and price (gross operator revenues or gamblers' losses) of the major forms of commercial gambling in Table A-1. This table is as accurate as we can make it and is, moreover, unique as far as published information available to the general public. It should, however, be used with care and with due attention to the source materials and definitions that follow.

The largest handles in Table A-1 are for casino table games and illegal bookmaking. Both statistics are estimated. These estimates are discussed in some detail below. It should be noted here that while these estimates are the best available, each depends upon unverifiable assumptions that introduce a very large measure of uncertainty into the resulting handle figures. No one *knows* how much is wagered across casino tables or with illegal bookmakers. Statements to the contrary in "official" government reports, sometimes carried out to one or two decimal places to emphasize their impressive but spurious degree of precision, have, through their repetition in the media, done much to confuse the social and revenue implications of commercial gambling. The estimates of gross wagering at table games and with bookmakers given in Table A-1 and discussed in this Appendix are not offered as hard, "officially" reported statistics. Our intention is rather to provide the interested reader with a factual basis for evaluating statements involving gaming and bookmaking handle and revenue figures when they are encountered in newspaper articles or legislative hearings. When asked to legalize sports betting because it will generate "billions of dollars in profits," or support a tax increase for efforts to control the organized crime that is funded by these same "billions of dollars in illegal gambling revenues," or approve some change in the taxation of legal gaming the public should at least be in a position to understand the basic gross wagering and revenue concepts on which such arguments largely depend.

Percent Retained by Operators: The percentage of gross wagering or handle or sales retained by operators, inclusive of all money bet that is not returned to gamblers in the form of winnings. In pari-mutuel accounting "takeout" and "retention" are synonymous terms for this percentage. This number does *not* represent profit. The profitability of any commercial gambling operation, or any other business, is a function of the expenses or other charges against gross revenues.

Operator Revenues (Gamblers' Losses): The gross dollar amount of gross wagering retained, or won, by operators and lost by gamblers, including money used for gambling privilege taxes, operating costs, normal business tax liabilities, and profit. In casino accounting "win" and "gross gambling revenue" are synonymous terms for these dollar amounts. For many purposes operator revenues are a better basis for comparisons between different forms of gambling than handle, since these revenues for the most part either are precisely known[1] or can be estimated with a good degree of certainty.

CASINO GAMING

The estimated gross wagering (handle) and reported operator revenues (player losses) for casino gaming shown in Table A-1 are derived from Table A-2.

TABLE A-2
REPORTED WIN AND ESTIMATED HANDLE FOR UNITED STATES CASINOS (CALENDAR 1983)

Game	Reported Win ($)	"Odds" or House Advantage (%) (Expected Value)	Estimated Handle ($)
		Nevada	
Black Jack	$ 635,873,993	2.4	$ 26,495,000,000
Craps	321,431,346	2.7	11,905,000,000
Roulette	63,886,664	5.3	1,205,000,000
Baccarat	124,652,341	1.2	10,388,000,000
Big Six (Wheel of Fortune)	8,086,747	16.1	50,000,000
Keno	137,670,585	28.8	478,000,000
Bingo	2,600,000	5.6	46,214,380
Pai Gow	1,336,182	6.0	22,000,000
Other	437,276	——	——
Total Games	$1,301,552,487	2.6	$ 50,589,000,000
Card Tables			
Poker	56,519,143	5.0	1,130,000,000
Panguingui	1,796,508	5.0	36,000,000
Total Card Games	$ 58,315,651	5.0	$ 1,166,000,000
Total Games	1,359,868,138		51,755,000,000
Slot Machines	1,490,222,734	11.0	13,547,000,000
GRAND TOTAL	$2,850,090,872		$ 65,302,000,000
		New Jersey	
Black Jack	$ 405,240,780	2.4	$ 16,885,000,000
Craps	327,803,608	2.7	12,141,000,000
Roulette	76,001,424	5.3	1,434,000,000
Baccarat	57,924,440	1.2	4,827,000,000
Big Six (Wheel of Fortune)	25,235,769	16.1	157,000,000
Total Games	$ 892,206,021	2.5	$ 35,444,000,000
Slot Machines	866,715,677	12.8	6,764,380,905
GRAND TOTAL	$1,758,921,698		$ 42,208,380,905

TABLE A-2 CONTINUED

Game	Reported Win ($)	Estimated Handle ($)
	United States	
Black Jack	$1,041,114,773	$ 43,380,000,000
Craps	649,234,954	24,046,000,000
Roulette	139,888,088	2,634,000,000
Baccarat	187,576,781	15,215,000,000
Big Six (Wheel of Fortune)	33,322,516	207,000,000
Keno	137,670,585	478,000,000
Bingo	2,600,679	46,214,380
Pai Gow	1,336,182	22,000,000
Other	437,276	——
Total Games	$2,193,758,508	$ 86,033,000,000
Card Tables		
Poker	56,519,143	1,130,000,000
Panguingui	1,796,508	36,000,000
Total Card Games	$ 58,315,651	$ 1,166,000,000
Total Games	2,252,074,159	87,199,000,000
Slot Machines	2,356,938,411	20,311,000,000
GRAND TOTAL	$4,609,012,570	$107,510,000,000

SOURCES: For Nevada: Economics Research Section, Nevada State Gaming Control Board. For New Jersey: 1983 annual reports filed with the New Jersey Casino Control Commission by Atlantic City casino/hotels.

The gross wagering (handle) estimates for table games used in Tables A-1 and A-2 will seem improbably large even to many persons familiar with gaming. The explanation for the magnitude of these handle figures is essentially the rapid frequency of gambles and the wide range of stakes at craps, blackjack, roulette, and baccarat.[2] While the house advantage for any particular bet at table games is small, generally 3 percent or less, these bets are transacted so rapidly that the ebb and flow of money or chips across the tables before it is finally won or lost results in enormous aggregate gross wagering. Except for Atlantic City slot machines, casino handles are not reported, nor, to our knowledge, have estimates of these handles previously been available to the public. Some explanation of how they are derived is therefore in order.

Nevada win statistics are reported by the Economic Research Section of the Nevada State Gaming Control Board.[3] Atlantic City win and slot machine handle statistics are from annual reports filed by Atlantic City casinos with the New Jersey Casino Control Commission.[4] Table game handles are estimated by dividing each game's expected value (the estimated average "edge" or house advantage, expressed as percentages of handle) into reported win. The expected values follow.

Craps: The figure used in Table A-2, 2.7 percent, is higher than the average edge of 1.92 percent estimated by Dennis Gomes from a record of actual craps play at a major casino on the Las Vegas Strip[5] and somewhat higher than the expected craps values used in many player rating systems. Particular bets at craps have house advantages ranging from 1.402 percent to 16.667 percent. The average edge, or expected value (to the operator, who wants to know how much he can expect to win from his tables) of the game, depends on the average dollar volume of each craps bet over time. Individual casino managements variously calculate this average edge. We have found in actual use for player rating purposes average craps edges as low as 1.4 percent and as high as 3.0 percent. Since the average edge is a function of player choice among craps bets any of these average edges may accurately reflect particular casino craps games. The application of the 2.7 percent average craps edge used in Table A-2 to the reported United States craps win involves an unverifiable assumption concerning craps bet choices by all craps players. It is a reasonable assumption and a conservative one for the purpose of estimating U.S. craps handle, but the reader should understand that small changes in the average edge used for this estimate will produce very large increases or decreases in estimated craps handles. An average edge of 1.4 percent would produce estimated U.S. craps handle of $44.5 billion, compared to the $24 billion estimate used in Table A-2. An average edge of 3.0 percent would, conversely, produce estimated U.S. craps handle of $21.6 billion.

Blackjack: The house advantage at blackjack varies from a negative value (positive player expectation) for skilled card counters in favorable playing conditions to approximately 0.6 percent for basic strategy players in six deck games to above 6.0 percent for players who know little or nothing about blackjack. The calculation of an average U.S. blackjack edge by empirical observations is essentially impossible, since any such observations would record data that are functions of the skills of a particular set of players. The average blackjack edge used in Table A-2, 2.4 percent, is higher than the 1.7 percent derived by Gomes by analogy to craps through known drop/win percentages,[6] but it is essentially the same as the 2.5 percent advantage used by many casino managements. We have found average blackjack edges ranging from less than 1.0 percent to 2.8 percent in actual use by individual casinos. Any of these average edges may accurately reflect blackjack play in these casinos. The application of the 2.4 percent average edge used in Table A-2 to reported U.S. blackjack win to estimate blackjack handle involves unverifiable assumptions about the skill of blackjack players in U.S. casinos. As is true with craps, the use of higher or lower average edges would produce very large changes in estimated blackjack handles. An average edge of 1.0 percent produces estimated blackjack handle of $104 billion, compared to the $43 billion estimate used in Table A-2. An average edge of 2.8 percent produces estimated blackjack handle of $37.2 billion.

The average U.S. craps and blackjack edges used in Table A-2 are conservative for the purpose of estimating craps and blackjack handles. The actual average edges, or expected values, of these two games in casinos catering to sophisticated high rollers are certainly lower than 2.7 percent and 2.4 percent, reflecting the more knowledgeable bet choices of this clientele. Lower expected values for all U.S. craps and blackjack games would produce higher estimated craps and blackjack handles, and it is possible that the actual amount wagered at these games in 1983 was greater than the $67 billion estimate in Table A-2. This figure, $67 billion, is a conservative one; we are confident that at least this amount was wagered at craps and blackjack.

Roulette: The house advantage for all bets at American roulette is 5.26 percent except one (the five-way bet on 1-2-3-0-00) where the advantage is 7.89 percent. For all practical purposes the expected value of roulette in American casinos is 5.26 percent; this has been rounded to 5.3 percent in Table A-2.

Baccarat: Bets at baccarat in U.S. casinos have house advantages of approximately 1.16 percent and 1.37 percent. While player skill is a factor in baccarat outcomes, an average edge of 1.2 percent is reasonable for this game as dealt in Nevada and Atlantic City.[7]

Big Six Wheels: The average edge of this game is approximately 16 percent.

Keno: The reported drop for keno, $478,486,486 in 1983, is synonymous with handle. By applying this drop to the reported win of $138,061,019 this game's expected value is 28.8 percent.

Bingo: The reported drop for bingo, $46,214,380 in 1983, is synonymous with handle. Bingo is offered by many Nevada casinos as a loss leader, hence the much lower operator retention from this game in Nevada (5.627 percent in 1983) than elsewhere.

Pai Gow: A rotating-bank game played with Chinese dominoes. Nevada casinos collect a 5 percent commission from winning hands; approximately 60 percent of hands produce a winner (and a 5 percent house commission) while approximately 40 percent of hands are played with no money changing hands (and no house commission). Player skill affects pai gow outcomes; the dealer strategies employed in Nevada casinos increase the house's retention to more than its 5 percent commission from winning hands. As currently dealt in Nevada casinos the house advantage at pai gow appears to be at least 6 percent.[8]

Other Games: The win from sic bo, faro, chuck-a-luck, and other table games was not large enough in 1983 to be significant in the Table A-1 handle estimates. Handle for card games in Nevada casino card rooms is estimated from the assumption that the reported win from poker and pan represented a rake (a deduction by the house before distribution to winners) of 5 percent of the pot, or total money bet.

Slot Machines: Slot handle is reported by Atlantic City casinos, and the Atlantic City win, handle, and operator retention percentage (12.8 percent) statistics used in Table A-2 are actual numbers. Nevada slot handle is estimated from reported slot win on the assumption that the average operator retention from Nevada slot machines was 11 percent. This figure is somewhat higher than the 8 percent to 10 percent of handle Nevada slot machines are commonly supposed to retain, and it was derived by applying retention percentages obtained from Reno, Las Vegas Strip, and downtown Las Vegas casino slot operations to slot wins for comparable operations throughout the State by extrapolation from the 1983 Nevada *Gaming Abstract*. Like the relatively high expected values used for U.S. craps and blackjack, our figure of 11 percent retention for Nevada slots is conservative for the purpose of estimating Nevada slot handle. The actual percentage retained from Nevada slots in 1983 may well have been lower, and the actual Nevada slot machine handle consequently higher than $13.5 billion. If 8 percent was retained, Nevada slot handle was $18.6 billion; if 10 percent was retained, slot handle was $14.9 billion.

Reported drop and win for United States table games in calendar 1983 is given in Table A-3. As mentioned above, drop is the collective bankroll of players. The portion of this bankroll lost to casinos constitutes win, or gross gambling revenue. From Table A-3 it may be seen that in 1983 gamblers at table games lost 19.1 percent, or $2.2 billion, of their $11.5 billion bankroll. This percentage is sometimes considered to be the price of gaming. The difficulty with this is that drop is not reported for other forms of gambling. The price of lotteries, bookmaking, and pari-mutuel betting is usually expressed as the percentage of handle, or gross wagering, retained by operators. Table A-1 allows comparisons among all forms of gambling, including gaming, on this basis. The reader who pursues the study of gambling will, however, frequently encounter drop and win-to-drop (hold) percentages; we therefore provide them here.

TABLE A-3
REPORTED DROP AND WIN FOR THE MAJOR UNITED STATES TABLE GAMES (CALENDAR 1983)

Game	Drop ($)	Win ($)	Ratio Win to Drop (%) (Hold)
		Nevada	
Black Jack	$ 3,483,953,345	$ 635,873,993	18.25
Craps	1,747,826,372	321,431,346	18.39
Roulette	241,531,074	63,886,664	26.45
Baccarat	569,161,760	124,652,341	21.90
Big Six (Wheel of Fortune)	16,353,582	8,086,747	49.45
Total	$ 6,058,826,133	$1,153,931,091	19.05
		New Jersey	
Black Jack	$ 2,373,564,013	$ 405,240,780	17.07
Craps	2,248,959,284	327,803,608	14.58
Roulette	301,996,920	76,001,424	25.17
Baccarat	442,423,366	57,924,440	13.09
Big Six (Wheel of Fortune)	52,075,073	25,235,769	48.46
Total	$ 5,419,018,656	$ 892,206,021	16.46
		United States	
Black Jack	$ 5,857,517,358	$1,041,114,773	17.77
Craps	3,996,785,656	649,234,954	16.24
Roulette	543,527,994	139,888,088	25.74
Baccarat	1,011,585,126	187,576,781	18.54
Big Six (Wheel of Fortune)	68,428,655	33,322,516	48.70
Total	$11,477,844,789	$2,193,758,508	19.11

SOURCES: For Nevada: Economics Research Section, Nevada State Gaming Control Board. For New Jersey: 1983 annual reports filed with the New Jersey Casino Control Commission by Atlantic City casino/hotels.

One further comment concerning drop may be useful. Gaming is one of two forms of commercial gambling that involve significant recycling of dollars. The other is pari-mutuel betting. Pari-mutuel handles have a significant component of such recycled dollars, referred to as "churn." The churn in pari-mutuel betting is far less significant than in gaming due to the far lower frequency of gambles in pari-mutuel betting: nine or ten races per program at twenty-five-minute intervals, compared to fifty to sixty-five hands an hour at blackjack or roulette. A recent analysis of actual horse-race betting performed by Thomas Aronson of the American Horse Council produced a churn factor of 3.51 percent.[9] At this track for the period analyzed a collective bankroll of $2.5 million was churned into a handle of $8.6 million. In other words, this pari-mutuel handle, $8.6 million, was generated from a "drop" of $2.5 million. The application of this churn factor to the reported 1983 horse-race handle of $10 billion would produce an estimated "drop," or collective horseplayers' bankroll, of approximately $2.9 billion.

These very rough figures may be of interest to persons wishing to compare gaming and pari-mutuel betting.

Upper and lower ranges for reasonable estimates of U.S. casino handle may be established in the following manner. The slot handle estimate used in Table A-1, $20.3 billion, consists of $6.8 billion handle reported by New Jersey and $13.5 billion estimated for Nevada slot machines. Even if the operator retention from Nevada slot machines is 2 percent more or less than our estimate—that is, 9 percent or 13 percent—the resulting change in estimated slot handle would not be significant within the inherent range of uncertainty in the estimates of craps and blackjack handles. As noted above, combined craps and blackjack handle might reasonably be estimated, using defensible assumptions concerning player skill and bet choice, anywhere from less than $60 billion to well over $100 billion, compared with the $67 billion combined craps and blackjack handle used in Table A-1. Even at the lower estimate of $60-plus billion, U.S. table game handle would amount to more than $87 billion. This $87 billion figure is used in Table A-1 and represents in our judgment the lower end of the range of reasonable estimates of 1983 U.S. table game handle that are derivable from available data. At $80 billion handle, the reported 1983 U.S. table game win of $2.25 billion represents gross retention from handle of 2.6 percent. By comparison, in 1976 the British Casino Association estimated the average edge or expected value of British gaming at 2.5 percent of handle.[10] The lower end of the range of reasonable estimates for combined U.S. table game and slot machine handle is therefore more than $100 billion. At even half this figure—an estimate that would require assumptions about player skill and bet choice we consider indefensible—casino gaming, as measured by gross wagering, is the largest commercial gambling game in America.

STATE LOTTERIES

The tally of State lotteries in 1983 includes Washington, D.C., which began its lottery on August 23, 1982, the State of Washington, which began its lottery on November 15, 1982, and Colorado, which authorized a lottery in April 1982 that began in January 1983. The gross wager (or sales in lottery accounting) of $5.6 billion is for the twelve months ending June 30, 1983.[11] The percentage retained by operators of 54 percent is a weighted figure derived from a comparison of State lottery laws and reported sales and gross revenues.

PARI-MUTUEL BETTING

The number of States allowing particular forms of pari-mutuel betting is from the National Association of State Racing Commissioners (NASRC).[12] The number of States allowing various kinds of pari-mutuel betting tallies jurisdictions allowing such betting in calendar 1983 whether or not such betting was actually conducted. Handles and percentages retained by operators are variously derived:

1. Horse-racing handle was supplied by the American Horse Council. Percentage retained by operators is from the Horsemen's Benevolent and Protective Association (HBPA), *1980 Racing Statistics*,[13] which reflect thoroughbred and quarterhorse racing, as adjusted for subsequent changes in statutory takeouts from wagering on such racing

since 1980 and takeouts from harness racing. The effective percentage retained by operators from racing, 18.75 percent, is inclusive of commissions and breakage and is approximate.

2. Off-track betting (OTB) handle is tabulated from the State of New York Department of Taxation and Finance and statistics supplied by the State of Connecticut's Division of Special Revenue.[14] The effective retention from New York off-track betting is 24 percent due to a statutory surcharge of 5 percent of payouts.

3. Handle and retention percentages for greyhound racing are from the American Greyhound Track Operators Association.[15]

4. *Jai-alai* handle is tabulated from statistics supplied by the State of Connecticut's Division of Special Revenue, the Rhode Island Horse Racing and Athletics Commission, and the Florida Division of Pari-Mutuel Wagering of the Department of Business Regulation. Retention percentages are estimated from a weighted comparison of State *jai-alai* laws and reported handles and gross revenues.

LEGAL BOOKMAKING

Gross wagering, retention, and gross operator revenues as reported by the Nevada State Gaming Control Board, Economics Research Section, Carson City, Nevada. This statistic includes $160,325,188 bet on racing, from which bookmakers retained an average of 15.13 percent (or $24,262,825), and $692,019,756 bet on sports, from which bookmakers retained 2.78 percent (or $19,250,974). The effective retention, weighted by dollars bet on sports and racing, was, in 1983, 5.11 percent.

CARD ROOMS

The number of States allowing card rooms in 1983 is reported by *Gaming Business Magazine.*[16] There are no reliable estimates of gross wagering, or losses, in United States card rooms. Both figures are certainly substantial; poker and pan games generated $58.6 million for Nevada operators in 1983, and since these revenues generally represent a maximum 5 percent rake from the pot (or the amount wagered) at least a billion dollars was bet at these games. Card room operators outside of the State of Nevada generally have no stake in the money bet at card games, but derive revenues from the rental of seats at card tables. For example, in California seats at card tables rent from $2 to $30 per hour. There were approximately 2,200 legal poker seats in southern California card rooms in 1981. Very rough calculations of hands per hour and estimates of average size pots can be applied to the number of legal tables in California and the other States excluding Nevada that allow card rooms to produce an equally rough idea of the gross wagering at these games. The result is too uncertain to be called an estimate, but undoubtedly exceeds a billion dollars.[17]

BINGO

There has been a considerable expansion of legal bingo in recent years. In 1974 bingo was legal in thirty-four States.[18] By 1983 bingo was legal in forty-five States[19] and, as a consequence of a 1981 Supreme Court decision upholding a federal appellate court ruling effectively barring local law enforcement officials from regulating bingo on the

Seminole reservation in Florida, is conducted by some forty to sixty Indian tribes around the United States.[20] Unfortunately for analytical purposes, bingo, like charitable gaming, is generally legalized either on a local option basis or by laws that do not include the State regulation and financial reporting required for gaming and pari-mutuel betting. As a result reliable statistics for U.S. bingo games are not easily obtainable. The survey conducted for the Federal Gambling Commission estimated gross wagering (handle) on bingo of $1.7 billion in 1974, with, assuming operator retention (takeout) of 33 percent, gross revenues (player losses) of $551 million.[21] The most recent estimate, consisting of projections from reported handles and retention from those States that require these statistics from bingo operators, is that $3.8 billion was wagered (handled) on bingo in 1982.[22]

Our estimated bingo handle of $3.07 billion in 1983 was arrived at by applying the SRC survey's participation rate (19 percent of respondents in 1974, which the survey projected to 27.3 million Americans) and average annual bet per player ($74)[23] to the population (estimated from the 1980 census) of jurisdictions allowing bingo in 1983 and comparing the result to projections of per capita bingo wagering reported by twelve States (for 1983) to the same population. The estimate of *legal* bingo handle of $3.07 billion is conservative; we are confident that at least this amount was wagered on bingo cards in 1983. The qualification "legal" is important: as the SRC survey noted,[24] in 1974 commercial bingo was almost as widely available in States were it was illegal as in States where this game was specifically authorized. The bingo legalizations that have occurred since 1974 have undoubtedly converted much illegal bingo handle to legal status, making the increase in bingo play somewhat more apparent than real. The tremendous growth of bingo on Indian reservations since 1981, on the other hand, represents for the most part new bingo wagering, some of it at the expense of punchboards, pulltabs, bazaars, raffles, and other charitable gaming.[25]

The retention percentage of 26 percent is a weighted average of retention from bingo reported by twelve States in 1983. This is somewhat lower than the 33 percent commonly assumed to be the retention from commercial bingo; we are reasonably confident that 33 percent retention is too high a figure for U.S. bingo in 1983. In 1983 Nevada's reported bingo win was $2,600,679, or only 5.6 percent of $46,214,380 spent on bingo cards, figures which may puzzle persons familiar with bingo in other States. The explanation is that many Nevada operators offer bingo as a loss leader.

CHARITABLE AND "SOCIAL" GAMING, EXCLUDING BINGO

These games consist of punchboards, pulltabs, raffles, bazaars, "Las Vegas night" casino games, and similar activities. Charitable gaming in general is very lightly regulated. New York, New Jersey, Washington, Michigan, and Massachusetts provide some reporting of handle and revenues from these games, with the regulation and reporting of the Washington State Gambling Commission being exemplary and that of the Commonwealth of Massachusetts good; these jurisdictions aside, reporting formats are inconsistent and highly variable in quality, making estimates of U.S. charitable gaming, excluding bingo, problematic. Five-hundred–odd million dollars in gross wagering at charitable games excluding bingo was tabulated from six large and small States in 1983. For example, for the twelve months ending June 30, 1983, $151.4 million was gambled on punchboards, pulltabs, raffles, and fund raising events in Washington State, with losses totaling $52.7 million, or 34.8 percent of handle.[26] In 1983, $87.1 million was gambled on Massachusetts charity games, raffles, and bazaars.[27] The actual total amount wagered was at least twice the amount we tabulated and may have been three times as large; we are confident that in 1983 at least $1.4 billion was wagered on U.S. charitable games. The retention percentage of 33 percent used in Table A-1 is a weighted average of the gross revenues (losses) as percentages of handle reported from six States.

ILLEGAL GAMBLING

Illegal gambling presents special problems of estimation. The difficulty is neither the games themselves, which have been thoroughly studied,[28] nor any mystery concerning the reasons for their popularity: nearly every newspaper and television station in the country actively stimulates the public appetite for sports betting through massive coverage of sports events complete with betting lines and injury reports, even though there are no legal sports betting opportunities outside the State of Nevada, while numbers is a culturally indigenous game with origins traceable to precolonial European lotteries. The problem is rather a tremendous confusion over the dimensions of these activities—that is, over the volume of illegal wagering. The supposedly "hard" estimates of the amounts of money bet illegally that regularly emanate from law enforcement agency officials are in fact anything but hard and are, moreover, extremely difficult even for interested members of the public to evaluate. At the same time these estimates are among the most important numbers in commercial gambling. From the federal level down to local police departments, law enforcement agency budgets are justified, in part, by the existence of illegal gambling operations. These justifications depend upon the acceptance as facts of two propositions that for persons outside of law enforcement are for all practical purposes impossible to verify that: (1) the volume of illegal wagering is anywhere from $5 billion to $500 billion annually and (2) this illegal business produces billions of dollars of annual profits for organized crime.

The evaluation of these propositions goes to the heart of many of the most intractable issues of American gambling policy. We have already noted that the United States is virtually the only industrialized nation that counts legal winnings as taxable income. The reason other countries do not tax legal payouts is that such taxation stimulates illegal gambling. The conclusion of the 1978 British Royal Commission on Gambling is representative of foreign experience with legal betting tax policies: as regards the taxation of winnings, the commission wrote, "The incidence of illegal betting is in our opinion quite simply a function of the combined rates of duty and levy on betting. It [illegal betting] is not susceptible to effective control by ordinary police methods any more than it was before 1960 [when off-course cash betting was legalized]. . . . The consequences of over-taxing betting are not, as in the case of other duties, merely a loss of revenue and a fall in demand for the taxed commodity. There are serious social evils [i.e., illegal gambling] which would follow from a return to the state of affairs which existed before [essentially tax-free off-course cash betting was legalized in] 1960."[29]

The questions raised by what has been termed the orthodox view of illegal gambling[30]—that it is both enormous and the principal source of revenue for organized crime—do not end with tax policy. Criminalization itself is at issue. If, despite the massive expenditures for the enforcement of antigambling laws that are annually justified by law enforcement estimates of illegal gambling, illegal bookmaking and numbers remain, according to the orthodox view, two of the largest commercial enterprises in the United States, what is the practical effect of gambling prohibitions? The British experience with similar laws is suggestive. In reviewing the operation of the Betting and Gaming Act of 1960, which legalized cash bookmaking (prior to the 1960 Act cash betting had been allowed only at racetracks, and legal off-course betting had been on a credit basis only; the intention was to restrict such betting to, in the commission's phrase, "the wealthier sections of the population"), the Royal Commission found that criminalization had been "hopelessly ineffective. [Illegal] bookmakers satisfied the wish of the ordinary British punter to stake a few shillings on a horse either by operating illegal betting offices or by employing runners to receive illegal cash bets in the street. Instead of suppressing betting among poorer people, the law produced resentment and attempts to corrupt the police, contempt for authority and a bookmaking trade operating outside the law, prey to protection rackets and gang violence. . . . The results [of decriminalizing bookmaking in 1960] were revolutionary. Illegal bookmaking almost completely disappeared. . . . [However] in recent years there has been something of a revival in illegal betting . . . [due to] the introduction of the betting duty . . . [which] gave illegal bookmakers a competitive advantage."[31]

A third and closely related policy question raised by illegal gambling is its potential as a revenue source. How much money is gambled illegally? How profitable is this gambling? Is simple legalization enough to enable either State governments or private businesses to tap these revenues, or must the Internal Revenue Code, as it treats legal winnings, also be amended? What are the practical consequences of State-by-State legalizations, and selective legalizations that allow one form of sports wagering while proscribing closely related forms—for example, the State of New York, which has legalized off-track betting on horse races but continues to prohibit betting on other sports?

None of these questions can receive satisfactory answers while information concerning the nature and dimensions of America's illegal gambling industry remain the exclusive property of impenetrable law enforcement bureaucracies, each with a particular vested interest in maintaining certain public perceptions of bookmaking and illegal numbers, and of illegal gaming and bingo and other games as well, that often appear to bear little relation to the available evidence. The first step towards resolving this confusion is to find as firm a basis as possible for estimating the existing volume of illegal wagering. A review of the history of these troublesome statistics is therefore in order.

The upward limit of the range of current estimates of illegal gambling in the United States is the figure of $450 billion (which includes bets between friends, card games, and other kinds of noncommercial social betting) annually that appears in John Scarne's *Scarne's Complete Guide to Gambling.*[32] This book appears to have been acquired by every public and newspaper library in the United States, and the repetition of Scarne's assertion that "almost 90% or $450 billion of this huge amount [i.e., the $500 billion Scarne estimates is wagered annually] is wagered illegally; only $50 billion legally"[33] in countless editorials and articles and television programs—and its repetition in numerous congressional and State legislative hearings—has established this number in the public consciousness as a kind of received truth.

Estimates by law enforcement agencies, while still involving enormous sums, have generally been much lower. In the late 1950s, Attorney General William P. Rogers put the amount of illegal wagering controlled by organized crime at $10 billion annually. This figure was consistent with a contemporary estimate by J. Edgar Hoover of $11 billion.[34] The famous meeting of organized crime leaders at Apalachin, New York, in November 1957 prompted the Justice Department to make a much higher estimate of the annual volume of illegal betting under organized crime's control: $47 billion, derived in part from Scarne's statement that for every dollar handled by legal operators seven dollars are bet illegally.[35] In August 1961, Sen. John L. McClellan opened hearings before the Senate Permanent Subcommittee on Investigations on the subject of gambling and organized crime with the statement while "the annual revenue from various forms of gambling in the United States . . . cannot be estimated with any degree of accuracy . . . it runs into billions of dollars each year. Moreover . . . the great bulk of these funds are collected illegally.''[36] The subcommittee heard testimony from Scarne to the effect that for every dollar bet legally at racetracks $16.50 was bet illegally off-track. Scarne put the 1960 legal horse-race handle at $3.5 billion and the retention from this amount at approximately $380 million or about 11 percent. Extrapolating from these figures Scarne estimated illegal bookmaking on horse racing at $50 billion and retention, or gross revenues, at $5 billion (10 percent), of which sum ''the bookies hold about $2 billion. Thirty percent of that, $1½ billion, goes to runners and agents, and 15 percent, which is $750 million, goes to corrupt law enforcement agents.''[37] Later in the hearings, Downey Rice, a former FBI agent who had served as associate counsel to the Kefauver committee,[38] characterized Scarne's figure of $50 billion in illegal off-track horse-race betting as ''an educated guess'' with which he did not agree, adding that ''no one has accurate figures'' regarding illegal gambling.[39] The subcommittee concluded its proceedings without reaching a definite answer to the question of the how much money is bet illegally in America.

The next federal evaluation of illegal gambling and organized crime was made by the Commission on Law Enforcement and Administration of Justice established by President Johnson in 1965.[40] The commission made no independent analysis of illegal gambling, citing instead previous ''estimates of the annual intake [gross wagering] . . . vary[ing] from $7 to $50 billion'' and the ''belief'' of ''most enforcement officials . . . that illegal wagering on horse races, lotteries, and sporting events totals at least $20 billion each year.''[41] An unidentified ''analysis of organized criminal betting operations'' indicated to the commission that ''the profit [to organized crime from gambling] is as high as one-third of gross revenue—or $6 to $7 billion each year.'' The reliance the commission placed on these numbers was evidently slight: the paragraph containing them begins with the qualification that ''there is no accurate way of ascertaining organized crime's gross revenue from gambling'' and ends with the disclaimer that ''the Commission cannot judge the accuracy of these figures.''[42]

Following the presidential commission's report two influential books appeared that repeated for a wider readership the estimates of illegal gambling in which the commissioners had reposed so little confidence. Rufus King's *Gambling and Organized Crime*[43] cited a ''general agreement that the total sum spent annually by Americans in all forms of illegal gambling (the yearly ''handle''), runs in the range of $15 to $25 billions. Some reputable estimators double those figures. . . . If the ''take'' [retention] of the gambling promotor amounts to one third of this . . . the income shared by those who control this form of criminal activity would be between $6 billion and $7 billion.''[44] Donald Cressey's *Theft of the Nation,* also published in 1969 and perhaps the most authoritative treatment of organized crime to appear between the Kefauver committee and the spate of books growing out of the 1976 Federal Gambling Commission, repeated the 1967 presidential commission's second-hand estimates (Cressey had been a consultant to the commission) almost verbatim: ''estimates of the amount bet illegally each year range from $7 billion to $50 billion. While it is impossible to determine the calculations on which such estimates are made, there is a consensus among law enforcement officials that illegal betting on horse races, lotteries, and sporting events totals at least $20 billion a year. Cosa Nostra members take about one-third of the gambling gross as their share, so if that gross is in fact $20 billion they acquire some $6 or $7 billion annually.''[45]

By 1970, then, the orthodoxy of gambling and organized crime was firmly established: illegal wagering amounts to anywhere from $7 billion to $50 billion annually; operator retention from this handle is about 33 percent; organized crime (La

Cosa Nostra, the Mafia) derives $6 billion to $7 billion a year from this illegal business, which constitutes its major source of funds. The basis for these estimates and conclusions, which to the public did and still do appear to bear the imprimatur of the United States, was, as far as outsiders can determine, nothing more substantial than the "consensus" and "general agreement" and "belief" among law enforcement officials that these things were so. No independent study of illegal gambling had been made, and no independently gathered data concerning the volume of illegal wagering and the operational characteristics of bookmaking and numbers were available. In 1972—twenty years after the Kefauver committee made "organized crime" household words—the first such data were introduced into illegal gambling estimates in the form of two surveys of legal and illegal wagering by 3,000 New York City adults conducted by Oliver Quayle and Company for the Fund for the City of New York.[45]

For present purposes the most important findings of the fund's report and the Quayle surveys were as follows:

First, illegal gambling was indeed widespread. A quarter of New York City's population, 1.3 million adults, played the numbers, over 40 percent of them daily. A slightly larger number, 1.4 million adults, had bet on one of the major sports—football, basketball, or baseball—in the twelve months prior to the survey. More than 1.6 million adults (of whom about half also bet on sports) bet on horses. Horse-race betting by persons who also bet sports (and therefore were probably, but not necessarily, since the survey included legal sports bets between friends, engaging in illegal gambling) was divided (in dollars) into 34 percent ($117 million) bet at racetracks, 41 percent ($137 million) at OTB, and 25 percent ($84 million) with bookmakers. Since OTB had been in operation for roughly a year at the time of the surveys Quayle sought to determine the effect of legalization on illegal off-track betting. Sixty percent of horse bettors who still patronized bookmakers (who, of course, also offer sports betting) said they bet less frequently with bookmakers than before OTB, leading Quayle to conclude "that OTB . . . has taken a great deal of betting money out of illegal channels" and, further, "that while legalizing sports betting will not do away with bookmaking on sports like football, basketball and baseball, most of the money now bet with bookies on these sports (which is also most of the total money now bet on sports) would flow into a legal operation."[47]

Second, numbers betting totaled $580 million a year, at least 75 percent of which consisted of bets of $2 or less. Sports betting, excluding horses, totaled $688 million, of which $428 million, or 60 percent, was bet illegally with bookmakers. Private, legal bets with friends totaled $225 million or 30 percent, and multiple-choice sports pool cards attracted $35 million, or 5 percent. When added to the $84 million bet illegally on horses these figures produce a gross illegal handle from New York City residents of $1.1 billion in 1971.

Third, five percent of New York City's adult population, or 261,000 persons, were heavy sports bettors (whom Quayle defined as persons betting $500 a year or more). These heavy bettors were only 19 percent of all sports bettors but accounted for 81 percent of all sports betting (and 74 percent of the money bet with bookmakers).

Fourth, in its report, the fund analyzed numbers, bookmaking, and sports cards and produced estimates of the operator retention from gross wagering for each of these illegal businesses. These estimates were: numbers, 42.5 percent; single-event sports wagers with bookmakers, 4.5 percent; horse-race wagers with bookmakers, 17 percent; and sports cards, 60 percent. The application of these percentages to the handle figures derived by Quayle yields the following gross revenue from illegal gambling (losses) by New York City residents: numbers, $247 million; sports betting, $19.3 million; horse-race betting, $14.3 million; and sports cards, $21 million, for total gross revenues (losses) of $301.6 million. The fund, after talking to police officials, settled on a higher estimate of illegal horse-race handle ($150 million to $200 million, as opposed to Quayle's $84 million) and single-event sports betting ($1 billion as opposed to Quayle's $428 million) and used the high end ($600 million) of the "more than half a billion dollars a year" estimate of numbers handle provided by Quayle. Using the fund's higher estimates of illegal bookmaking and numbers these gross revenues (losses) would be: numbers, $255 million; sports betting, $45 million; horse-race betting, $34 million; and sports cards, $21 million, for total gross revenues (losses) of $355 million.

The Quayle surveys and the Fund for the City of New York's report are important for three reasons: first, they were the first large-scale studies of the kind to focus exclusively on gambling behavior; second, they showed that statements putting the operator retention from illegal gambling at one-third of handle are absurd; and third, their findings were used as the basis for an influential subsequent federal estimate of illegal wagering.

There have been several criticisms of Quayle's methodology.[48] Reuter suggests that by using voting records to weight its samples by election districts within assembly districts Quayle imparted an upward bias to their estimates, on the assumption that both voting and sports betting are positively related to income.[49] A more serious consideration is that numbers and sports betting are both vices and illegal. This creates two problems: an assumed reluctance of those responding to admit either to questioners or perhaps to themselves their actual illegal gambling behavior, and, because some persons questioned presumably refused to answer, the impossibility of factoring in the behavior of these nonrespondents. As Reuter points out, Quayle's quota sampling technique provides no meaningful information about nonresponse rates or profiles.[50]

Quayle's estimates of illegal wagering by New York City residents may be compared to a contemporary study of gambling in New York State prepared by the Hudson Institute for the New York State Gambling Commission.[51] From "personal interviews with police officials" and a review of the Quayle surveys the Hudson Institute produced an estimate of numbers handle, which it cautioned "should be considered very rough" for areas outside New York City, of $600 million a year. Relying on police analyses of "wiretapping evidence and seized records which have established a documented total of $926 million" handle by New York City bookmakers, plus "50% for unknown or unrecorded action,"[52] and interviews with police officers in other cities the institute estimated statewide bookmaking handle at $1.2 billion, with an additional $50 million bet on illegal sports pool cards. The institute's estimate for New York State's total illegal handle therefore was: numbers, $600 million; bookmaking, $1.2 billion; and sports cards, $50 million, for a total handle of $1.85 billion. The estimate for operator retention from this handle was: numbers, $300 million (50 percent); bookmaking (including horse-race bets), $120 million (10 percent); and sports cards, $25 million (50 percent), for total gross revenues of $445 million.

An estimate of nationwide illegal gambling in 1973 by Jess Marcum and Henry Rowen should also be mentioned.[53] Using an undisclosed methodology Marcum and Rowen estimated the gross illegal handle of the United States at $22.9 billion, and operator retention (losses) from this amount at $3.52 billion.[54] This study is less important for its estimates of illegal wagering than for the authors' clear demonstration that the 30 percent operator retention assumed by Rufus King and the 1967 president's commission cannot be accurate, and, moreover, had become confused with operator profits, which must, of course, be considerably lower than gross retention.[55]

The next important federal estimates of illegal gambling were compiled by Alfred N. King of the Organized Crime and Racketeering Section of the Justice Department in

November 1973.[56] King's methodology, which has been the subject of considerable discussion, follows.[57] The illegal horse-race *bets* discovered by Justice Department strike forces in New York City in 1971 and 1972 were tabulated. King then took the proportion of illegal to legal *dollars* wagered off-track in New York City reported by Quayle at 37.8 percent[58] and applied this percentage to the total OTB handle for the first six months of 1973 to produce a dollar estimate of total illegal off-track betting for that period. This estimated illegal off-track handle was broken down into weekly figures by averaging to facilitate comparison with weekly average illegal horse-race wagering uncovered by strike forces operating in New York City. From this a "factor of expansion" was developed which was used to "project not only horse bets in New York but all bets throughout the country."[59] To allow for areas in which Justice made no enforcement efforts in 1971 or 1972 King computed a per capita wager, for each such region, and multiplied this figure by each "missed" region's population.

The accuracy of the estimates produced in this manner depends on several assumptions. First, King assumed that enforcement was equal across the country and, moreover, equal as to all varieties of illegal wagering. Second, he assumed that Quayle accurately reported the amount of horse-race betting with bookmakers. Since only persons who bet team sports illegally were asked if they bet horses this may not have been the case. Third, and most important, King's estimates rest on projections from New York City data reflecting horse-race betting *in the only jurisdiction then allowing legal OTB* to national data reflecting all kinds of wagering. Further, as noted, these projections assume constant ratios between crimes and arrests throughout the country. If arrest ratios were higher in New York during the base period than elsewhere the national estimate would be low, and vice versa.[60]

Whatever their reliability, King's estimates were the basis for testimony given by Henry Dogin, deputy attorney general, Criminal Division, Department of Justice, and Edward T. Joyce, deputy chief, Organized Crime and Racketeering Section, Department of Justice, before the Federal Commission on the Review of the National Policy Toward Gambling on May 15, 1974.[61] The Justice Department officials began with an introductory statement of the orthodox view of illegal gambling and organized crime established by the Kefauver committee twenty years earlier: "The President, Congress, and law enforcement officials have concluded that illegal organized gambling is the largest single source of revenue for organized crime. Gambling revenues are used to finance the expansion of organized crime into other illegal activities such as narcotics, hijackings, prostitution, and loansharking. This revenue also provides capital for the acquisition of legitimate businesses. . . . In order to protect its gambling income, organized crime spends millions of dollars to bribe and corrupt criminal justice officials."[62] Dogin and Joyce then proceeded to supply the commission with estimates of illegal gambling based on King's study: "The Organized Crime and Racketeering Section estimated that the profits[63] generated by illegal gambling operations are between $7 billion and $50 billion annually. Gross illegal wagers [presumably handle is meant] probably amounted to between $29 billion and $39 billion in 1973. Wagers placed on sporting events amounted to 64.02 percent; on numbers or policy, 24.9 percent; and on horse racing, 10.9 percent. Organized crime groups controlled 41.9 percent of the gross illegal wagers in 1973, with the resulting profits estimated to have amounted to over $4 billion."[64]

The Justice Department's estimate of illegal handle, $29 billion to $39 billion, is within the meaninglessly wide range of $7 billion to $50 billion published by the 1967 President's Commission. Unlike the commission, however, Justice did not estimate gross revenues (operator retention or losses) on this handle directly. The only part of Dogin's and Joyce's testimony bearing on this point is the statement that organized crime controlled 41.9 percent of the gross illegal wagering and that the "profits"—whether gross revenues or revenues net of operating expenses is meant is unclear—amounted to over $4 billion. Assuming that the $4 billion in profits to organized crime Dogin and Joyce referred to were gross revenues, the percentage organized crime retained from its 41.9 percent of the $29 billion-to-$39 billion total U.S. illegal handle—that is, from a handle of between $12.2 billion and $16.3 billion—was between 24.5 percent (if the organized crime-controlled handle was $16.3 billion) to 32.8 percent (if the organized crime-controlled handle is $12.2 billion). While these percentages are unrealistically high, the alternative assumption that "profits" referred to net revenues after expenses would produce even higher operator retention percentages.

The 1974 Justice Department estimates did not end the debate over the volume of illegal wagering in the United States, which became one of the more controversial issues before the Federal Gambling Commission. In its final report the commission stated that "two years [after Dogin's and Joyce's testimony, Justice] Department officials acknowledged to the Commission that it was impossible for the Department to provide an estimate [of illegal gambling] with any degree of confidence; they could only report accurately on the volume of gambling they had uncovered through actual surveillance and raids. It should be noted that during 1971 and 1972—the period of the Department's most intensive antigambling enforcement—it had acted against illegal operations with a total handle of only $750 million."[65] The commission added that while the FBI had not provided an estimate of illegal handle,[66] "it has released various figures—such as $750 million in payoffs by gambling operations to law enforcement officials—that suggest a total volume of illegal gambling higher than the Commission's adjusted survey estimate."[67] Further, the commission noted that the Bureau of Alcohol, Tobacco, and Firearms "has given estimates [of illegal gambling] as high as $67 billion. However, agency officials told the Commission that this figure was not original but had been extrapolated from estimates made by other agencies."[68]

The Gambling Commission's uncertainty about the volume of illegal wagering had been greatly compounded by the results of a nationwide independent survey of gambling behavior it commissioned from the Survey Research Center of the Institute for Social Research of the University of Michigan.[69] The SRC questioned a national probability sample of 1,736 respondents and a Nevada probability sample of 296 respondents during the summer of 1975 to "determine the extent of gambling activity in the United States, to estimate government revenues that could result from various changes in gambling laws and to examine the social consequences of these changes."[70] The findings concerning illegal gambling were: in 1974, 11 percent of the sample adult population (a projected 15.8 million persons) gambled illegally with bookmakers or on sports cards, numbers, or in illegal card rooms. Of these 15.8 million adults who gambled illegally, 39 percent (a projected 3.9 million) bet at least $50 in 1974 and were classified as "heavy" bettors by the SRC. The aggregate illegal wagering (handle) in 1974 was $5.074 billion, distributed among sports books ($2.341 billion), horse books ($1.368 billion), numbers ($1.064 billion), sports cards ($191 million), and casino games ($110 million). The average annual bet per player was $312, with the average annual expenditure (loss, or operator retention) per player approximately $67, or about $1 billion nationally.[71] The SRC put the standard error of its estimates at "about $10 for the mean annual illegal bet per United States adult. According to sampling theory, this makes the chances six to one against a sample that would underestimate illegal handle by more than $1.4 billion, and forty to one against an underestimate by as much as $2.8 billion, and over six hundred fifty to one against an underestimate as large as $4.2 billion. This makes it certain that actual handle is less than double the sample estimate, even if the sample is badly understating the facts.

In these terms, while our estimate of $5 billion for illegal gambling handle is subject to sampling variation, it is highly unlikely that the 1974 total was more than $8 billion, and it is virtually inconceivable that it should be higher than $10 billion.''[72]

The SRC estimates of illegal gambling were immediately criticized as being too low and remain controversial. An evaluation of these estimates and the methodology used to derive them made for the commission by two Congressional Research Service (CRS) analysts concluded that the survey, as it concerned illegal gambling, was seriously flawed.[73] Specifically, the CRS review pointed out three major weaknesses.

(1) All surveys of illegal gambling rely upon respondents' willingness to admit, and answer candidly questions about, their participation in an illicit activity. Two problems are thus created: First, the identification of persons who engage in illegal gambling is extremely difficult. Illegal handle generated by persons who chose not to admit they gamble illegally cannot accurately be reflected in estimates derived from behavioral surveys. A similar problem exists with estimates (such as the Justice Department's) based on data apprehended by police: there is no good way to project from these data to illegal gambling that is *not* apprehended. For these reasons the CRS concluded that ''no good estimates [of illegal gambling] are currently available.''[74] Second, ''extreme measurement problems'' exist in regard to responses to questions about dollar amounts wagered within a specified period. Gamblers may not remember how much they wagered, or may recall these amounts incorrectly.

(2) The SRC did not conduct adequate tests of the accuracy of responses used to estimate the dollar volume of illegal gambling. In view of the inherent measurement problems, particularly the likelihood that some respondents did not admit to illegal gambling, special studies of the validity of the techniques used to measure both the proportion of illegal gamblers and the amounts wagered were in the CRS analysts' view necessary to determine the accuracy of responses concerning bet sizes and frequencies.

(3) The CRS review agreed with the SRC staff that the apparent close agreement of SRC estimates of legal gambling with published data supports the argument that the SRC estimates of illegal gambling, which were derived in the same way, are similarly accurate. The SRC's comparison of estimated and reported handles appears in Table A-4.[75]

TABLE A-4
TOTAL HANDLE IN THE UNITED STATES, 1974,
AS COMPILED BY THE SURVEY RESEARCH CENTER

Type of Gambling	Handle: Estimate from Sample	Handle: Published Data	Estimates as % of Published Data
Horses at track	$ 7,930,000,000	$ 7,512,000,000	+ 5.2
OTB (N.Y.)	967,000,000	787,000,000	+18.6
Legal casinos	6,076,000,000	6,693,000,000	−10.1
Bingo	1,735,000,000	1,672,000,000	+ 3.6
Lotteries	639,000,000	681,000,000	− 6.6
Total	$17,347,000,000	$17,345,000,000	+ 0.01

SOURCE: *Gambling in America,* Appendix 2, p. 94.

There is however a serious difficulty with this argument. As the CRS analysts noted, the SRC tried to arrive at annual gross wagering by asking a series of questions about betting frequencies and average amounts bet.[76] The data elicited through this questioning were subjected to alternative methods of handle calculation, and the results were compared as an internal check on response accuracy.[77] The SRC study design is a reasonable approach to estimating wagering volumes for forms of gambling characterized by regular, nonrepetitive, and relatively undifferentiated play—games in which most of the handle is bet in roughly similar amounts at daily or weekly intervals. Illegal numbers and the gambling opportunities offered by State lotteries in 1974 (but not the instant games that have since become staples of State lottery menus) are good examples: the bulk of these handles are contributed by players who bet one or two dollars on a daily number or buy a constant number of identical lottery tickets per week in patterns that become individual routines. As with other routine behaviors, such as buying newspapers or groceries, lottery and numbers players are apt to be able to give relatively good accounts of their gambling. Even if some individuals are not able to make accurate responses, or chose not to do so, the remaining "good" responses will still accurately describe the undifferentiated play characteristic of 1974 lottery and numbers gambling.

Unfortunately, neither the SRC's questions nor its evaluation of respondents' answers took sufficient account of a variable characteristic of gambling games with particular importance for general-population surveys of gambling behavior: the relative contributions to handle of small segments of the betting population at forms of gambling offering wide ranges of odds and stakes, low cost (low takeout or operator retention), and real or perceived opportunities for the exercise of skill. Such games create betting markets in which the action of small numbers of players can be very significant in the total gross wagering. Prior to the depression-era legalizations of pari-mutuel betting horse racing was the classic example of such a game. Bets were made through bookmakers operating at racetracks, which by the late nineteenth century were generally dependent on revenue derived from this betting.[78] Like other forms of commercial gambling throughout American history, bookmaking and politics were closely connected. In New York Tammany Hall boss Richard Croker in 1888 banned the recently introduced pari-mutuels, thereby granting a monopoly on horse-race betting to bookmakers, the most important of whom formed the two-hundred-member Metropolitan Turf Association.[79] The "ring" made a betting market in which individual bets of $200,000 to $250,000 (in pre–World War II dollars) were not uncommon while discouraging the $2 bets that are the mainstay of modern pari-mutuel operations. Bets were at fixed odds and relatively low cost, the bookmakers' gross retention being estimated at 8 percent to 9 percent, compared with the 18+ percent retention from pari-mutuel horse-race betting today. The advent of pari-mutuels in April 1940 replaced this high per capita betting with a very much larger number of smaller bettors—including women, who had not been permitted in the bookmakers' ring—whose collective wagering, while at least initially almost certainly less than the unreported booked handles, was sufficient to guarantee the success of the pari-mutuel system. According to *Newsweek,* "The only ones disgusted [at the replacement of bookmakers with pari-mutuel machines in New York] were the plungers, whose heavy bets would just push the odds down. But Mr. and Mrs. Average Citizen found a warm welcome for their $2 gambles, which bookies discouraged as trifling."[80]

The introduction of legal pari-mutuel systems was accompanied by a general criminalization of bookmaking,[81] but despite these measures television and the invention of the point spread gave new life to this form of gambling. Television simultaneously created a national audience for football and basketball to rival that for the traditional "national pastime," baseball, and liberated bookmakers from dependence on syndicated wire services for betting information. Prior to the invention of the point spread bookmakers attempted to equalize betting on sports events by adjusting odds in the manner of horse-race betting, and, while this worked fairly well for baseball, it proved in practice difficult to make a market for football or basketball games by this method. The odds necessary to equalize betting on these games found relatively few takers. The point spread, which appears to have been invented in Minneapolis in the late 1920s,[82] made it possible for bookmakers to offer bets on single football and basketball games at nearly even money, with the bettor risking $11 to win $10 (instead of, for example, $8 to win $1 on a favored football team offered at odds instead of points) if his team ''beats the spread'' of the line quoted when the bet is taken.

Today betting team sports with bookmakers is characteristically repetitive and highly differentiated credit play, in which a small percentage of the clientele contribute a very large percentage of the handle.[83] The Quayle survey defined ''heavy sports bettors'' as ''the 5 percent of the population [of New York City in 1972, or 260,700 adults] who report betting 500 dollars or more in the last year on football, basketball, and baseball combined.'' Although these heavy sports bettors comprised only 19 percent of the 1.4 million New Yorkers who bet one of the three major sports in the twelve months preceding Quayle's survey, they contributd 81 percent of the total sports betting handle (including legal bets between friends) and 74 percent of the bets placed with illegal bookmakers.[84] The SRC survey found that 4 percent of the U.S. adult population (or 5.8 million individuals, using the SRC's 144,129,000 estimate of the resident population) made an illegal sports bet (either with a bookmaker or on a sports card) in 1974; 2.6 percent of the population (or 3.7 million individuals) bet sports with bookmakers, of whom 15.8 percent (or 592,000 individuals) bet $500 or more a year.[85] These heavy sports bettors[86] wagered at least $467 million with bookmakers, or 20 percent of the $2.3 billion the SRC estimated was booked on sports in 1974.[87]

The Quayle and SRC surveys, then, arrived at vastly different estimates of the percentage contribution of ''heavy bettors'' (defined as persons wagering $500 a year on sports with bookmakers a year) to sports book handle. Quayle found that 5 percent of adult New Yorkers or 19 percent of the sports betting population—261,000 persons—bet $500 or more a year with sports books, accounting for 81 percent of all sports betting and 74 percent of sports bookmaking. The SRC survey found that only 4 percent of the adult population of the United States bets sports illegally, only 2.6 percent placed sports bets with bookmakers, and only 0.4 percent—592,000 persons—bet $500 a year or more, accounting for at least 20 percent of the total volume of sports book wagering. Even allowing for the fact that the SRC concluded that the ''Northeast is a hotbed of illegal gambling activity . . . [where] almost one fifth of all adults . . . bet on at least one . . . illegal game in 1974 and where 45 percent of all heavy bettors (wagering more than $200 a year), 50 percent of heavy legal and illegal sports bettors, and 22 percent of heavy illegal sports bettors are located,''[88] it is clear that Quayle found far more heavy sports bettors and found them to be far more significant contributors to sports book handles than did the SRC. Either the Quayle survey found a great many nonexistent heavy illegal sports bettors in New York City or the SRC identified far fewer of these individuals than in fact were present in the U.S. population in 1974.

The available evidence is strongly in favor of the latter alternative. First, the SRC determined that the average annual illegal sports book wager was $623.[89] Nearly everyone with an acquaintance with sports betting would consider this an extremely low figure. Using the SRC's figure of 4.5 percent gross operator retention this $623 in wagering would generate just $28.04 per player annually in operator revenues. At the 1.9 percent Nevada sports books reported as gross retention from sports bets in 1982 operator revenues would be only $11.84 per player annually. The best study of bookmaking to date, Reuter and Rubinstein's *Illegal Gambling in New York*,[90] found the largest bookmaking operation in New York in the middle 1970s to have approximately three hundred customers. If these three hundred customers lost an average of $28 a year this operation would gross only $8,400, an absurdly small amount. The description of bookmakers and their clientele that emerges from Reuter and Rubinstein's definitive study is wholly inconsistent with the SRC's portrait of the average sports book customer. Bookmaking operations are generally small, consisting of wirerooms with no more than three clerks working at any given time and employing perhaps fifty runners, who act as the intermediaries between bettors and the book. Three clerks and fifty runners might service two hundred bettors, each of whose *average* annual gross wagering is $150,000, for a total annual booked handle of $30 million. Assuming operator retention of 4.5 percent, these figures translate into an average annual loss of $6,750 and gross bookmaker revenues (not profit) of $1.35 million. Sports bets range in size from $25 to $5,000, with somewhat higher limits set for special events such as the Superbowl. Small bets are discouraged in the interest of productivity; a large book might require its customers to bet a minimum of $500 per week in increments of at least $50, with the largest book studied setting a minimum bet of $500. Heavy bettors wager amounts that dwarf the figures reported in the Quayle and SRC surveys: Reuter and Rubinstein record that one "Tobias," "a heavy and successful bettor, . . . lost about $200,000 [in] one week."

The nearly inescapable conclusion is that the SRC survey failed to identify a segment of the sports betting population that, while small, contributes a very large percentage of sports book handle, and thereby seriously underestimated the volume of such wagering. The CRS analysts suggest that this may have been the case, pointing out that the "SRC sample was not designed to produce good estimates of the gambling habits of small segments of the population. . . . If there were as many as 500,000 people in the Nation who bet an average of $50,000 annually, the sample used by the SRC has a very small chance of producing good estimates of their gambling activity . . . even if these gamblers were distributed in a way which takes the most favorable advantage of the sample design, there is a very good likelihood that this group would have been missed. . . . If this were the case . . . the true amount of illegal betting might exceed $30 billion a year."[91] Reuter and Rubinstein arrived at similar conclusions: "There is some reason to suspect that [the SRC] estimate for sports betting is an underestimate. The sample did not include any individual with wagering volumes approaching that of the average customer in the bookmaking operations about which we have obtained information in New York. There may be a small population which accounts for a high proportion of total sports betting with bookmakers. If there are 10,000 persons with wagering levels equal to that which we have estimated for the customers of big bookmakers in New York, then the [SRC] figure [of $2.3 billion] would be an underestimate by $1.5 billion or 40% of the total. A sample as small as [the SRC's] 2,000 . . . has only a small probability of including one such person. If he chooses to be a non-respondent, no analysis of non-response, however sophisticated, is going to detect the problem."[92] Simon and Witte likewise consider the SRC estimate of illegal gambling to be low, doubling it to $10 billion as "an upper bound on the total illegal handle."[93]

The Commission on the Review of the National Policy Toward Gambling, which had hoped the SRC survey would end the controversy over the dimensions of illegal gambling in the United States, in the end declined to endorse its estimate of a $5.1 billion illegal handle, citing as reasons its conviction that "the heavy illegal bettor . . . has little incentive to tell the truth" about his wagering, a comparatively low response rate in downtown urban areas, the likelihood that high volume bettors would not know with any degree of precision how much they actually wager, the omission from the SRC totals of money laid off among bookmakers [who were not questioned], and a large number of reports of bettors wagering $100,000 and more annually on sports when the heaviest bettor in the SRC sample admitted to wagering only $30,000.[94] The commission's principal concern was that the SRC's low estimate of illegal wagering would adversely affect law enforcement: "If the survey's estimates of a $5 billion illegal handle are taken at face value, and the Justice Department's estimates of $29 billion–$39 billion are refuted, it might be construed that the incidence of illegal gambling in the United States is only one-sixth to one-eighth of what it is commonly thought to be, and a significant reduction in enforcement activity would follow. Nothing could be further from the Commission's intent.''[95]

Like the 1967 presidential commission before it, the Commission on the Review of the National Policy Toward Gambling concluded its work without producing a definitive answer to the question of how much illegal gambling there is in the United States. Since the commission's final report there have been two further federal estimates of illegal wagering. In 1979 the Department of the Treasury, as part of the Carter administration's offensive against what it termed the ''underground economy,'' published new estimates of illegal gambling in a detailed analysis of untaxed income.[96] The gross handle and revenue estimates appear in Table A-5.

TABLE A-5

GROSS HANDLE AND REVENUES FROM ILLEGAL GAMBLING FOR CALENDAR 1976 AS COMPILED BY THE INTERNAL REVENUE SERVICE IN 1979

Game	Gross Handle (in billions)	Percent Retained (%)	Gross Revenues (in billions)
Numbers	$ 7-9	40	$2.8-3.6
Bookmaking	33-41	15	5-6.2
Other	5.2-6.4	40	2-2.6
Total	$45.2-56.4		$9.8-12.4

SOURCE: U.S. Dept. of the Treasury, Internal Revenue Service, *Estimates of Income Unreported on Individual Income Tax Returns* (1979), pp. 133-37.

The source given for the figure of $7 billion to $9 billion in numbers handle is ''estimate obtained from the FBI,'' which is not further explained. We find this figure to be implausibly high for two reasons. First, the $1.1 billion estimate of illegal numbers produced by the SRC, while subject to the objections that inner-city response rates (where illegal numbers is the dominant form of gambling) were lower than the survey average and are in any case questionable as depending on respondents' admission of illicit activities, should not, given the close agreement of the SRC estimate of otherwise comparable lottery game handles with published data, be off by such a large factor. Second, the expansion of legal State-run numbers games since 1974 cannot under the most pessimistic assumptions have *increased* the market for illegal numbers by any similarly large factor. ''Other'' illegal gambling includes ''dice games, illegal card games, punchboards, coin machines and any other illegal gambling.'' The $5.2 billion to $6.4 billion estimated handle for these illegal games is ''based on 1976 figures from the President's Commission on Law Enforcement Task Force on Organized Crime''; the 40 percent retention from this gambling is from the assumption ''that the return to the bettor is comparable to that for the numbers racket.''

The source for the $33 billion to $41 billion bookmaking handle is again ''estimate obtained from the FBI.'' Reuter criticizes both the FBI's estimate of gross wagering with bookmakers and Internal Revenue's assumption that bookmakers retain 15 percent of handle.[97] This handle estimate does not admit of further analysis in terms of the available data. A figure of 15 percent gross retention from bookmaking is certainly too high. Nevada's legal bookmakers retained a weighted average of 4.9 percent from sports and racing bets in 1982, and this is a more reasonable percentage for gross retention from illegal bookmaking in that year than the 15 percent used by Internal Revenue.

Estimates of Income Unreported on Individual Income Tax Returns turned out to be the last installment of a thirty-five-year attempt to make bureaucratic fantasies of illegal gambling come true through judicious use of the federal imprimatur. The denouement came in 1983, in a wholly remarkable document published by Internal Revenue as *Income Tax Compliance Research: Estimates for 1973–1981.*[98] The approach to the estimation of illicit activities taken by this study is revolutionary: nothing less than an acknowledgment that the evidence for earlier studies, specifically *Estimates of Income Unreported,* was to critics "not impressive . . . [and] consisted essentially of anecdotes or estimates based on indirect methods of questionable validity,"[99] which Internal Revenue now proposed to replace with original research contracted for from a Cambridge, Massachusetts, firm[100] and a promise to "state all of the assumptions [used to estimate illegal activities], together with enough background figures to permit the interested reader to make alternative estimates using the same data, but with different assumptions."[101] "By 1980," it now appeared, "the FBI considered [the estimates of gross illegal wagering of $33 billion to $41 billion that were the basis for the figures in *Estimates of Income Unreported*] to be unreliable." Internal Revenue concluded that while "the overall magnitude of illegal gambling gross revenues continues to be a controversial subject the advocates of the higher estimates . . . have so far failed to produce credible evidence in support of their case."[102]

In the absence of better data the authors of Internal Revenue's *Estimates for 1973–1981* decided to base its new estimates of illegal gambling on the 1974 SRC survey, making due allowance for SRC's probable underestimation of sports betting through failing to capture the wagering of very heavy bettors and subsequent handle growth, and adjusted for both inflation and real growth in illegal wagering since 1974 by analogy with reported changes in wagering on comparable legal games during the period 1973–1979.[103] The results, using the higher and more convincing of the range of estimates provided, appear in Table A-6.[104]

TABLE A-6
ESTIMATES OF ILLEGAL GAMBLING IN 1979
AS COMPILED BY THE INTERNAL REVENUE SERVICE IN 1983

Game	Handle (in billions)	Percent Retained (%)	Revenues (in billions)
Numbers	$ 2.82	49–52	$1.44
Horses	4.61	16.7	0.77
Sports	7.60	4.5	0.35
Sports Cards	0.61	60	0.37
Total Sports/Cards/Horses	$12.8		$1.48
Casinos/Other	0.1	17.3	0.02
Grand Total	$15.7		$2.96

SOURCE: U.S. Dept. of the Treasury, Internal Revenue Service, *Income Tax Compliance Research* (1983), pp. 198–211.

These estimates of illegal handle and revenues are lower, much lower, than the ones usually encountered. They are included here as the latest federal estimates of perhaps the most thoroughly misunderstood activities in America. The reader may choose to rely on these estimates, or on earlier ones, or upon estimates of his own devising as he sees fit. We are persuaded of the independent nature of these latest estimates and regard them as conservative, in the sense that at least this much illegal gambling does in fact occur. They are offered, in the context of this review of the curious history of these statistics, without further comment.

There is every reason to suppose that illegal gambling—like legal gambling—has increased in the five years since 1979. The estimates of gross wagering and gross revenues from illegal gambling that appear in Table A-1 are derived from *Income Tax Compliance Research: Estimates for 1973–1981* through the methodology that follows.

Horse Books/Sports Books/Sports Cards: Increases in illegal horse betting were estimated by substituting 1983 reported legal pari-mutuel horse racing and OTB handles in Internal Revenue's equations in Table G-18 and applying the resulting percentage increase to the 1979 illegal horse handle derived from Internal Revenue's "higher estimates" of unreported income from illegal horse betting. The estimate of 1983 illegal horse handle produced by this methodology is $5.8 billion. Applying a 17 percent operator retention figure to this estimated handle produces estimated gross revenues from illegal horse betting of $986 million in 1983.

Increases in illegal sports book and sports card handles were estimated from the assumption that this illegal wagering increased between 1979 and 1983 by the same percentage as legal sports handle in Nevada between 1979 and 1982. The latter dates were used because the federal excise tax on sports book wagering (which had historically, before its effective elimination in 1983, prevented legal bookmakers from offering price-competitive service compared to their illegal counterparts) was a constant 2 percent during this period. The $7.6 billion illegal sports book and $0.61 billion illegal sports card handles derived from Internal Revenue's "higher estimates" of unreported income from these forms of gambling in Table G-19 are increased by this methodology to $16.8 billion and $1.3 billion in 1983.

Increases in gross revenues from illegal sports books and sports cards since 1979 were arrived at by applying the following operator retention percentages to the estimated 1983 handles for these games: sports books, 4.5 percent, which produces gross revenues of $756 million in 1983; sports cards, 60 percent, which produces gross revenues of $780 million in 1983.

Total illegal sports book and sports card handles are therefore estimated at $18.1 billion in 1983, with gross revenues from these games totaling $1.5 billion. Adding illegal horse handle and revenues to these figures gives total illegal bookmaking and sports card handle of $23.9 billion, with gross revenues totaling $2.5 billion.

Numbers: The $2.82 billion estimated illegal numbers handle derived from Internal Revenue's "higher estimates" of unreported income from illegal numbers in 1979 is increased to $4.89 billion by substituting reported 1983 legal numbers handle of $3 billion in the equations in Table G-17. This methodology may overstate 1983 illegal numbers handle; it might reasonably be argued that legal numbers games have recorded larger handle increases since 1979 than have illegal numbers games. Applying an operator retention percentage of 51 percent to this estimated 1983 illegal numbers handle produces estimated gross revenues from illegal numbers games of $2.49 billion.

Total Illegal Gambling: Adding 1983 estimated handles for books, sports cards, numbers, and miscellaneous other illegal games gives total estimated illegal wagering of $28.9 billion. Total gross revenues from these illegal games are estimated at $5.03 billion. These figures appear in Table A-1.

There is finally the question of exactly what is the value of any of the available estimates of illegal gambling. It will be clear by now that these are not "hard" statistics in any sense of the word. From the Kefauver committee in the early 1950s to Internal

Revenue's estimates in 1979 the production of these numbers was for political or bureaucratic use. Whether the latest estimates released by Internal Revenue presage a more independent and intellectually defensible federal approach to the subject remains to be seen. As Reuter and Rubinstein, the most thorough students of this process, have remarked, estimates of illegal gambling serve principally rhetorical purposes.[105] Their degree of correspondence to reality is relatively unimportant to the government agencies that produce them. Rather, these estimates (as the Commission on the Review of the National Policy Toward Gambling so clearly indicated by its concern that the "low" SRC estimate of sports book handles not lead to reduced enforcement efforts) function as necessary justifications for police and judicial administration policy decisions and resource allocations. These are not trivial considerations. The expenditures for antigambling law enforcement since the days of the Kefauver committee that have been justified by the estimates of illegal gambling here reviewed certainly run into billions of dollars. Wiretapping authority and federal statutes with enormous civil rights implications, of which the RICO (racketeer-influenced and corrupt organizations) provisions (18 U.S.C. 1961-1968) of the Organized Crime Control Act of 1970 have proven to be perhaps the most important example, have similarly been justified by the orthodox argument that illegal gambling is the principal financial support of organized crime.

Regardless of one's personal views—and whether or not one gambles within or outside the law—the issues illegal gambling raises touch us all. The handle and gross revenue numbers for illegal gambling included in Table A-1 are not offered with our endorsement. We do not know the dimensions of illegal gambling in the United States. Neither, we believe, does anyone else. That is knowledge gained. The reader will encounter these estimates again: in newspapers, in televised appeals for his vote on gambling initiatives, as boilerplate for law enforcement budgets, and as justification for laws with implications far beyond illegal gambling. We hope that this short history of an arcane statistic will be useful in the evaluation of some important questions.

NOTES

1. This is because operator revenues are the basis for gambling privilege taxes. Illegal gambling is unfortunately again an exception.

2. Dennis C. Gomes, "Casino Player-Rating Systems: Designing One That Rates," *Gaming Business Magazine,* July 1983, pp. 41–46, reports fifty craps hands and sixty-five blackjack hands per hour, and each hand, particularly at craps, may decide a number of gambles per player. This frequency of gambles far exceeds any other form of commercial gambling. Horse races, for example, occur at twenty- to thirty-minute intervals.

3. Economics Research Section, Nevada State Gaming Control Board (1150 East William Street, Carson City, Nev.), 1983.

4. New Jersey Casino Control Commission, *Monthly Reports of Casino Revenues and Estimated Tax on Gross Revenues* (3131 Princeton Pike, Trenton, N.J.), 1983. The table game win reported in the Casino Control Commission monthly reports varies slightly from the table win reported in the calendar 1983 annual reports filed by each casino with the Casino Control Commission and reflected in Table A-3. The differences are not significant for the purposes of this book.

5. Gomes, "Player-Rating Systems," p. 43.

6. Ibid.

7. Baccarat win-to-drop ratios (hold percentages) are volatile in comparison to other table games because the number of decisions within standard reporting periods is relatively small and may moreover reflect a tremendous range of stakes. As noted in our discussion of gaming, Atlantic City casinos occasionally report monthly losses at baccarat. These losses are apparently produced by the betting of a few very high rollers, persons who purchase and bet $100,000 plaques, whose baccarat play involves a comparatively small number of very large wagers. If for example a high roller makes twenty $100,000 wagers (thereby generating a handle of $2 million), loses seven (or $700,000), and wins thirteen ($1.3 million) *and walks away from the table* his play will have a measurably adverse effect on that baccarat table's monthly hold percentage. In effect, this betting strategy enables the player to beat the edge (between 1.1 percent and 1.2 percent for this game; our high roller, a sophisticated gambler, would probably bet with the banker, where the house advantage is 1.1 percent): he does not make a sufficiently long enough series of wagers for the edge to grind his bankroll away. Of course, he may not win thirteen and lose seven of his twenty bets. He might lose thirteen and win seven, or win all twenty bets, or lose all twenty bets, and so on. As a practical matter Atlantic City baccarat tables beat players over long periods; all casinos report substantial annual baccarat wins.

A second anomaly affecting U.S. baccarat win-to-drop ratios is the fact that in Nevada markers written at baccarat tables are sometimes settled before being dropped, thereby understating baccarat drop at these tables. This practice partially explains the higher reported hold percentages from baccarat in Nevada (21.9 percent) as compared to Atlantic City (13.1 percent) in 1983 (see Table A-3).

8. For a mathematical analysis of *pai gow* as dealt in Nevada casinos, see John M. Gwynn, Jr., "An Optimal Strategy for the Game of Pai Gow," in *Gambling Papers,* ed. William R. Eadington, 13:29–45.

9. Thomas L. Aronson, "Wagering Analysis: Hazel Park Harness, October 1977," unpublished (Washington, D.C.: American Horse Council, 1978).

10. Royal Commission on Gambling, The Lord Rothschild, chairman, *Final Report,* 2 vols. (London: Her Majesty's Stationery Office, 1978), p. 3. British casino win is largely derived from table games (each casino is restricted to a maximum of two slot machines).

11. Lottery gross sales are estimated for calendar 1983 from data supplied by individual lottery administrations and are approximate; actual gross sales for U.S. lotteries in calendar 1983 may have slightly exceeded $5.6 billion.

12. National Association of State Racing Commissioners, *Pari-Mutuel Racing Statistical Summary* (Lexington, Ky.: National Association of State Racing Commissioners, 1983).

13. Horsemen's Benevolent and Protective Association, *Racing Statistics* (Rockville, Md.: Horsemen's Benevolent and Protective Association, 1980); 1980 is the most recent publication of these statistics.

14. The National Association of State Racing Commissioners *Statistical Summary* for 1982 reports New York OTB 1982 handle as $1,711,283,545. This is an error. New York State Racing and Wagering Board, *1982 Annual Report,* gives a figure of $1,521,285,993 for 1982 New York off-track betting handle. This error is corrected in the 1983 NASRC *Statistical Summary.*

15. American Greyhound Track Operators Association, *1983 Summary of State Pari-Mutuel Tax Structures* (North Miami, Fla.: American Greyhound Track Operators Association, 1983).

16. *Gaming Business Magazine,* August 1984, p. 52.

17. Gary Selesner, "California Bell Club—Playing to a Full House," *Gaming Business Magazine,* January 1981, pp. 38–39; Barry Meadow, "The 'Unreported' California Poker Clubs Story," *Gaming Business Magazine,* March 1983, pp. 7–10.

18. Commission on the Review of the National Policy Toward Gambling, *Gambling in America: The Final Report of the Commission on the Review of the National Policy Toward Gambling,* 4 vols. (Washington, D.C.: GPO, 1976), 1:161.

19. *Gaming Business Magazine,* August 1984, p. 52.

20. "Bingo Boom Brings Tribes Profit and Conflict," *New York Times,* March 29, 1983.

21. *Gambling in America,* Appendix 2, pp. 94–96.

22. "Bingo and Break Opens Becoming Big Business," *Public Gaming Magazine,* November 1983, p. 41.

23. *Gambling in America,* Appendix 2, pp. 249–50, 105.

24. Ibid., p. 267.

25. "Bingo Boom," *New York Times,* March 29, 1983.

26. Washington State Gambling Commission, *Statistical Reports for the Quarter Ended June 30, 1983* and *1983 Annual Report.*

27. Commonwealth of Massachusetts, Massachusetts State Lottery Commission, *1983 Annual Report.*

28. Most recently by Peter Reuter, whose *Disorganized Crime: The Economics of the Visible Hand* (Cambridge, Mass.: MIT Press, 1983), includes chapters on numbers and bookmaking that are the clearest and most informed analyses of these businesses available.

29. Royal Commission on Gambling, *Final Report,* pp. 25–26.

30. Peter Reuter and Jonathan Rubinstein, *Illegal Gambling in New York: A Case Study in the Operation, Structure, and Regulation of an Illegal Market* (U.S. Department of Justice, National Institute of Justice, Washington, D.C.: GPO, April 1982), pp. 1–8, provides a history of the development of this ideology, or orthodoxy, of illegal gambling and organized crime.

31. Royal Commission on Gambling, *Final Report,* pp. 24–25. The Royal Commission's conclusions were almost exactly those of New York's Knapp Commission five years earlier (1973): "The criminal laws against gambling should be repealed. To the extent that the legislature deems that some control over gambling is appropriate, such regulation should be by civil rather than criminal process. The police should in any event be relieved from any responsibility for the enforcement of gambling laws or regulations." Knapp Commission, *Report of Commission to Investigate Allegations of Police Corruption and the City's Anti-Corruption Procedures* (New York: George Braziller, 1973), p. 18.

32. John Scarne, *Scarne's Complete Guide to Gambling* (New York: Simon & Schuster, 1961).

33. Ibid., p. 1.

34. Ralph Salerno and John S. Tompkins, *The Crime Confederation* (New York: Doubleday, 1969), pp. 225–35, reprinted in *An Economic Analysis of Crime,* eds. Lawrence J. Kaplan and Dennis Kessler (Springfield, Ill.: Charles C. Thomas, 1976), pp. 46–62, with a useful bibliography.

35. Ibid., p. 49.

36. Permanent Subcommittee on Investigations of the Committee on Government Operations (McClellan Committee), United States Senate, 87th Congress, *Gambling and Organized Crime: Hearings August 22, 23, 24, and 25 and September 7 and 8, 1961,* 3 vols. (Washington, D.C.: GPO, 1961), p. 1.

37. McClellan Committee, *Gambling and Organized Crime,* pp. 83–84.

38. Senate Special Committee to Investigate Organized Crime in Interstate Commerce (Kefauver Committee), *Hearings Before a Special Committee to Investigate Organized Crime in Interstate Commerce,* 19 vols. 81st Congress (Washington, D.C.: GPO, 1950–51). For an evaluation of the Kefauver committee see William Howard Moore, *The Kefauver Committee and the Politics of Crime 1950–1952* (Columbia: University of Missouri Press, 1974).

39. McClellan Committee, *Gambling and Organized Crime,* p. 375.

40. United States President, Executive Order 11236, July 23, 1965. The commission's findings are most conveniently available in a single-volume summary: President's Commission on Law Enforcement and Administration of Justice, *The Challenge of Crime in a Free Society* (Washington, D.C.: GPO, 1967). The chapter dealing with organized crime (pp. 187–210) was published separately in annotated form as *Task Force Report: Organized Crime* (Washington, D.C.: GPO, 1967), with additional source materials.

41. Carl P. Simon and Ann D. Witte, *Beating the System: The Underground Economy* (Boston: Auburn House, 1982), p. 201, state that the commission asked the National Opinion Research Center to estimate the illegal horse-race handle, but rejected the center's estimate of $3.3 billion annually as being too low.

42. *Task Force Report: Organized Crime,* p. 3.

43. Rufus King, *Gambling and Organized Crime* (Washington, D.C.: Public Affairs Press, 1969). See as well King, "Let's Not Deregulate Organized Crime," *Tax Notes,* August 3, 1981, for an argument for retaining federal gambling taxes as restraints on organized crime that endorsed the 1973 Justice Department estimate of $29 billion to $39 billion in illegal wagering annually (for a discussion of this estimate, and the department's admission of its own lack of faith in these numbers, see below) and repeated the "expert consensus" that "the 'take' (profit) from this [$29 billion to $39 billion] would run about one third ($10 billion)." In this article King puts the legal handle in 1979 at $20 billion—a serious underestimate caused by his confusion of casino *win* ($1.5 billion) with the unreported but very much larger casino *handle*—"up from less than half that total a decade earlier," which he uses to calculate the increase in illegal wagering since the 1973 Justice Department estimate on the principle that "it is generally agreed they [illegal operators] draw several times the local patronage: a conservative guess would be a current (1981) illegal handle three times the 1979 legal (i.e., $60 billion), a take [operator retention] of $20 billion, and $4 billion for 'arrangements' [corruption] and protection."

44. King, *Gambling and Organized Crime,* pp. 24–25.

45. Donald R. Cressey, *Theft of the Nation: The Structure and Operations of Organized Crime in America* (New York: Harper & Row, 1969), pp. 74–75.

46. Oliver Quayle & Company, *A Study of the Numbers Game in New York City: Study #1458-A* (New York: Oliver Quayle & Company, 1972), interviewing conducted between February 26 and March 7, 1972, and *A Study of Betting on Sports in New York City: Study #1493* (New York: Oliver Quayle & Company, 1972), interviewing conducted between May 20 and June 7, 1972. Both surveys formed the appendix to *Legal Gambling in New York: A Discussion of Numbers & Sports Betting* (New York: Fund for the City of New York, 1972). The fund, a private foundation created in 1968, sought to evaluate the feasibility and implications of legalizing numbers and sports betting. Its study was undertaken in the context of the recent (1970) legalization of off-track betting and a serious public debate over the adverse effects of criminalized gambling on law enforcement and society in general. These were not new concerns. In 1958 the New York legislature had established a Commission of Investigation whose charges included "keep[ing] the public informed as to the operations of organized crime and problems of

criminal law enforcement in the state'' (S. 2(10), Ch. 989, Laws of 1958). Three years later this commission issued a report that identified the cause of illegal ''professional'' (i.e., commercial) gambling as ''weaknesses in our enforcement system and . . . insufficient deterrents.'' New York State Commission of Investigation, *Syndicated Gambling in New York State* (New York: New York State Commission of Investigation, 1961). Twelve years later the Knapp Commission, investigating gambling-related corruption within the New York City Police Department, came to the opposite conclusion: that ''the criminal laws against gambling should be repealed . . . in any event [the police] should be relieved from any responsibility for the enforcement of gambling laws or regulations.'' *Knapp Commission Report on Police Corruption,* p. 54. In 1971 the legislature required the New York State Off-Track Betting Commission to investigate the social, legal, and fiscal aspects of expanded legalized gambling (Ch. 1014, Laws of 1971), and in February 1972 this commission, reporting as the New York State Commission on Gambling, *Report and Recommendations to Extend Legalized Gambling* (Albany: New York State Gambling Commission, 1961) announced that criminalization had produced nothing beyond futile enforcement efforts, corruption, and the diversion of large amounts of gambling revenue to organized crime. In December 1972 the chairman of the State Assembly Ways and Means Committee released a report (''The Implications of Further Legalization of Gambling in New York State'') reaching essentially similar conclusions. These reports, especially the fund's, persuaded the *New York Times* to overcome its ''reluctance to see the city or state move even deeper into the encouragement of gambling'' and endorse the legalization of numbers on the grounds that this would reduce police corruption and hurt organized crime (editorial, December 13, 1972).

47. Quayle, *Study of Betting on Sports in New York City* (#1493), p. 46. It must be remembered that Quayle's survey was conducted prior to the imposition (in 1974) of the surcharge on OTB payouts.

48. The Quayle surveys and the fund's report are critically evaluated by Simon and Witte in *Beating the System,* pp. 202–24. See as well Reuter, *Disorganized Crime,* pp. 31–32.

49. Reuter, *Disorganized Crime,* p. 32. Quayle found sports betting to be primarily middle-class behavior: *Study of Betting on Sports in New York City* (#1493), pp. 48–49.

50. Reuter, *Disorganized Crime,* p. 32. See as well the discussion in David Melnick and Royce Crocker, ''A Review of Two Studies on Gambling in the United States,'' *Gambling in America,* Appendix 2.

51. Hudson Institute, *Increased Legal Gambling in New York: HI–1736–RR,* 3 vols. (New York: Hudson Institute, 1973).

52. Hudson Institute, *Increased Legal Gambling in New York: HI–1736/2–CC,* p. 6a. The New York City police supplying these figures estimated that perhaps 46 percent of the ''documented total'' was bet by residents of New Jersey and suburban communities or was money ''laid-off'' among the bookmakers themselves. This $1.4 billion police estimate of New York City bookmaking handle includes horse-race bets. New York City bookmaking was, according to the police, highly centralized, with the $926 million in ''documented'' wagering handled by 61 ''principal operators,'' 1,533 runners, and 326 ''others.'' The Hudson Institute apparently decided on the somewhat lower estimate of $1.2 billion for State-wide bookmaking after comparing the New York City police figures to the lower estimates produced by the Quayle surveys. Reuter has criticized the New York City Police Department's estimates of illegal wagering as involving ''an unknown but substantial amount of double counting,'' *Disorganized Crime,* p. 32.

53. Jess Marcum and Henry Rowen, ''How Many Games in Town?—The Pros and Cons of Legalized Gambling,'' *Public Interest* 36 (Summer 1974):25–52. The estimates

of illegal gambling in this article were originally prepared as part of a working paper commissioned by the Twentieth Century Fund and appear in *Easy Money,* Report of the Task Force on Legalized Gambling, sponsored by the Fund for the City of New York and the Twentieth Century Fund, with a Background Paper by David Beale and Clifford Goldman (New York: Twentieth Century Fund, 1974).

54. Marcum and Rowen, ''How Many Games in Town,'' p. 38. The handle and percentages retained by operators for each form of illegal gambling were estimated as follows: sports betting, $12 billion (5.8 percent); horse-race betting, $5.5 billion (18.2 percent); numbers, $2.5 billion (40 percent); casinos, $2 billion (20 percent, as a percentage of *drop* rather than handle); slot machines other than in casinos, $400 million (25 percent); bingo, $300 million (50 percent); and lotteries, $200 million (50 percent).

55. Marcum and Rowen, ''How Many Games in Town,'' pp. 40–41. This study unfortunately repeats a common confusion arising from comparisons of casino gaming and other forms of gambling such as pari-mutuel betting. The authors correctly note that while operator retention from pari-mutuel betting is reported as a percentage of handle, casino win (operator retention) is accounted as a percentage of drop—cash and cash equivalents exchanged for chips or lost directly as the result of cash bets—rather than the (much larger) actual amounts gambled; but then, instead of calculating actual gaming handles, the authors simply equate handle with drop, thereby introducing a noncomparable statistic into their estimates of legal and illegal wagering.

56. Letter from William S. Lynch, chief, Organized Crime and Racketeering Section, Department of Justice, to Dan Melnick, Congressional Research Service, Library of Congress, August 18, 1976, in *Gambling in America,* Appendix 2.

57. This methodology is set forth in the letter from William S. Lynch, ibid., and critically evaluated by Daniel Melnick and Royce Crocker, ''A Review of Two Studies on Gambling in the United States,'' in *Gambling in America,* Appendix 2, pp. 1–15.

58. Quayle, *Study of Betting on Sports in New York City* (#1493), p. 45.

59. Lynch, letter to Melnick, p. 2. According to Melnick and Crocker, this procedure consisted of calculating the difference between the average weekly illegal bets in the first six months of 1973 (as estimated above) and the average weekly illegal horse-race betting uncovered by New York City strike force arrests in 1971 and 1972. This difference was assumed to reflect the proportion of total illegal horse-race betting apprehended by the strike forces. This proportion became the ''factor of expansion'' used ''to calculate the value of all illegal bets on the basis of those bets uncovered by the strike forces nationwide in all kinds of betting.'' Melnick and Crocker, ''Review of Two Studies on Gambling in the United States,'' p. 5. The ''projection for each area is based upon the expansion factor applied to the [illegal] wagers discovered by enforcement *in that area.*''

60. Melnick and Crocker, ''Review of Two Studies on Gambling in the United States,'' p. 14.

61. A summary of testimony by Henry Dogin (deputy attorney general, Criminal Division, Department of Justice) and Edward Joyce (deputy chief, Organized Crime and Racketeering Section, Department of Justice) is given in Appendix 3 to the commission's final report, *Gambling in America,* pp. 15–20.

62. Ibid., p. 15.

63. This is apparently a somewhat garbled reference to the $7 billion-to-$50 billion ''annual intake'' by organized crime from gambling cited by the 1967 presidential *Task Force Report: Organized Crime,* p. 3. What exactly Dogin and Joyce meant is impossible to say: a *handle* of $29 billion to $39 billion obviously cannot generate *profits* of $50 billion.

64. Dogin and Joyce, in *Gambling in America,* Appendix 3, p. 16. The estimates of illegal gambling in New York City were: "Gross illegal wagers . . . amount to over $4.2 billion in 1973. Two-thirds of this total was attributed to wagers placed on sporting events, 22 percent on numbers, and 11.3 percent on horse racing. Organized crime control in these activities was believed to be 50.8 percent of the handle."

65. Ibid., pp. 63–64.

66. On May 10, 1976, Frederick C. Fehl, acting assistant director, Federal Bureau of Investigation, replied to a question (in the course of testifying as to the relationship between gambling and organized crime) concerning the level of illegal gambling to the effect that "the FBI believes that the $50-billion estimate of the volume of illegal gambling quoted by the [1967] President's Commission on Law Enforcement and Administration of Justice was more accurate than the lower $7 billion estimate of the Gambling Commission [the commission made no such estimate; Fehl may have meant the $5.1 billion estimate of the Survey Research Center, for which see below]. There is no one inside or outside organized crime who could provide a viable estimate as to the gross annual national gambling handle. The Bureau has no way it can reliably analyze those estimates." Ibid., p. 500.

67. Ibid., p. 64.

68. Ibid.

69. Maureen Kallick, Daniel Suits, Ted Dielman, and Judith Hybels, Survey Research Center, Institute for Social Research, University of Michigan, "Survey of American Gambling Attitudes and Behavior," in *Gambling in America,* Appendix 2.

70. Ibid., p. i.

71. Ibid., pp. 24–30, 93–98. The operator retention percentages used by the SRC to calculate player expenditures (losses) were sports books, 4.5 percent; horse books, 16.6 percent; numbers, 54 percent; sports cards, 60 percent; and casino games, 15 percent (this last is the percentage win to drop, not handle). These percentages are reasonable.

72. Ibid., pp. 97–98.

73. Melnick and Crocker, "Review of Two Studies on Gambling in the United States," in *Gambling in America,* Appendix 2, pp. 1–15.

74. Ibid., p. 7.

75. This table omits greyhound racing (1974 handle $1.2 billion), *jai alai* (1974 handle $182 million), and card rooms and charitable gaming, for which no reliable 1974 handle statistics are available. The Survey Research Center's total legal handle figure of $17.3 billion in 1974 is thus understated by at least $1.2 billion. This table also includes noncomparable statistics. The "published data" figures for "horses at track," "OTB (N.Y.)," "lotteries," and presumably "bingo" (bingo handle is difficult to obtain; we have been unable to confirm this number) represent gross wagering, or true handle. The "published data" handle for "legal casinos," however, is drop, or the collective bankrolls of casino gamblers. The handle or gross wagering generated from this $6.7 billion drop was a very much larger number.

76. *Gambling in America,* Appendix 2, p. B11.

77. As the CRS review pointed out, these checks did not include external validations of response accuracy. Such tests had been part of the original study design. SRC had, for example, proposed to administer its questionaire to known gamblers to see whether their responses indicated they gambled. Melnick and Crocker, "Review of Two Studies on Gambling in the United States," p. 9.

78. Bookmakers paid racetracks fees ranging from $17.50 to $57.50 per person per day for permission to take bets on racetrack grounds. These fees usually equaled gate receipts—i.e., constituted about half of the tracks' income (Chafetz, *Play the Devil,* p.

378). The criminalization of bookmaking and the more rigorous enforcement of antibookmaking laws that effectively prohibited this form of gambling between 1900 and the start of World War I resulted in the closing of ninety-five racetracks during this period. Mark H. Haller, "Bootleggers and American Gambling 1920–1950," in *Gambling in America,* Appendix 1, pp. 102–43.

79. Chafetz, *Play the Devil,* pp. 266–67.

80. Quoted in Steve Thomas, "The Iron Men," *Thoroughbred Record,* June 17, 1981, pp. 2586–91. This is the best history of New York bookmaking. For a general treatment see David R. Johnson, "A Sinful Business: Origins of Gambling Syndicates in the United States, 1840–1887," in *Police and Society,* ed. David Bayley (Beverly Hills, Calif.: Sage Press, 1977). Haller, "Bootleggers and American Gambling 1920–1950," provides an excellent account of the transition of bookmaking from a quasilegal business prior to the establishment of track-operated pari-mutuels to an illegal off-track horse-race and sports betting enterprise. See as well Reuter and Rubinstein, *Illegal Gambling in New York,* pp. 41–44. Richard Sasuly, *Bookies and Bettors* (New York: Holt, Rinehart and Winston, 1982) is the most recent history of American bookmaking.

81. State antigambling laws were largely rewritten following World War II. Bookmaking is generally prohibited under these modern codes. See Cornell Law School, *The Development of the Law of Gambling: 1776–1976.* Prepared for National Institute of Law Enforcement and Criminal Justice (Washington, D.C.: GPO, 1977), pp. 737–75.

82. For a discussion of point spreads see Neil D. Issacs and Gerald Strine, *Covering the Spread: How to Bet Pro Football* (New York: Random House, 1978). The current use of betting lines and sports information by New York bookmakers is analyzed by Reuter, *Disorganized Crime,* pp. 38–40.

83. The market for professional football betting that is created by this characteristic play is analyzed by Michael E. Canes, "The Market for Pro Football Betting," in *Gambling and Society,* ed. William R. Eadington (Springfield, Ill.: Charles C. Thomas, 1976).

84. Quayle, *Study of Betting on Sports in New York City* (#1493), pp. 2, 7, 31.

85. Kallick, "Survey of American Gambling," in *Gambling in America,* Appendix 2, pp. 11, 29, B9.

86. The SRC variously defined "heavy illegal bettors" as individuals betting at least $50 or more than $200 at year on some form of illegal gambling. Ibid., pp. 2, 27.

87. The SRC did not publish an estimate of gross wagering by heavy sports bettors. Table 1.1-3b ranks bettors by game and dollars wagered. From this table, 6.7 percent of sports book bettors wagered from $500 to $999, or at least 592,000 heavy sports bettors × 6.7 percent = 251,000 individuals × $500 = $126 million + 592,000 heavy sports bettors × 9.1 percent = 341,000 individuals × $1,000 = $341 million, for a minimum gross wager of $467 million. Ibid., pp. 11, 299.

88. Ibid., pp. 10, 25.

89. Ibid., pp. 98, 105.

90. Reuter and Rubinstein, *Illegal Gambling in New York,* pp. 41–79. Much of this material appears in Reuter, *Disorganized Crime,* pp. 14–44.

91. Melnick and Crocker, "A Review of Two Studies on Gambling in the United States," pp. 9–11.

92. Reuter and Rubinstein, *Illegal Gambling in New York,* p. 63.

93. Simon and Witte, *Beating the System,* p. 210.

94. *Gambling in America,* p. 64, and Commission on the Review of the National Policy Toward Gambling, *Second Interim Report* (Washington, D.C.: GPO, 1976), p. 40. The SRC staff defended their estimates of illegal gambling in hearings before the

commission on June 23, 1976, without adding any new material evidence to support them. *Gambling in America,* Appendix 3, pp. 519–24. The SRC survey is reviewed by one of its authors, Maureen Kallick, in Maureen Kallick-Kaufmann, "The Micro and Macro Dimensions of Gambling in the United States," *Journal of Social Issues* 35 (1979):7–35.

95. *Gambling in America,* p. 65.

96. U.S. Department of the Treasury, Internal Revenue Service, *Estimates of Income Unreported on Individual Income Tax Returns,* Publication 1104(9–79) (Washington, D.C.: Internal Revenue Service, 1979), pp. 133–37.

97. Reuter, *Disorganized Crime,* p. 198.

98. U.S. Department of the Treasury, Internal Revenue Service, Office of the Assistant Commissioner (Planning, Finance and Research), Research Division, *Income Tax Compliance Research: Estimates for 1973–1981* (Washington, D.C.: Internal Revenue Service, 1983). The gross wagering (handle) and gross revenue estimates in this document, which are the basis for the illegal gambling handles and gross revenues in Table A–1, are for calendar 1979.

99. Ibid., p. 41.

100. Abt Associates Inc., *Income from Illegal Gambling* (Cambridge, Mass.: Abt Associates, 1982), is the primary research supporting the estimates of illegal gambling.

101. *Income Tax Compliance Research,* p. 1.

102. Ibid., p. 196.

103. The methodology used to derive the estimates of illegal wagering, gross revenues, and unreported income that are contained in *Income Tax Compliance Research* is explained on pp. 195–99. The process of adjusting and updating to 1979 the SRC survey's 1974 statistics was accomplished through a sophisticated game-by-game analysis of the relationships between legal and illegal gambling, and then by applying these relationships to time series of reported legal gambling data for the period 1973–79.

104. Internal Revenue provides handle estimates based on the 1974 SRC survey only. The handle figures in Table A-6 reflect Internal Revenue's 1979 estimates and were derived by applying the retention percentages in this table to the "higher estimates" of 1979 unreported income from Tables G–17, G–18, and G–19. We feel these adjusted, "higher" estimates are more convincing and more accurately describe illegal gambling in the United States in 1979.

Table G–20, which summarizes unreported income from illegal gambling, contains two errors: the 1979 sports betting revenue estimated from survey source alone is given as $0.52 billion. The correct figure, from Table G–19, is $0.32 billion. The total unreported income from all forms of illegal gambling according to the "higher estimates" is incorrectly added as $2.86 billion. The correct total is $2.96 billion.

105. Peter Reuter and Jonathan B. Rubinstein, "Fact, Fancy, and Organized Crime," *Public Interest* 53 (Fall 1978):45–67.

Glossary

Bankroll: The amount of money risked by gamblers, either against casinos (which account bankrolls as drop) or against other gamblers, as in pari-mutuel betting.

Betting: Gambling on events of subjective probability. Horse races, *jai-alai* matches, football games, and other sports are the most important objects of commercial betting, which may be either at fixed or pari-mutuel odds. See Gambling and Gaming.

Bookmaking: One of two commercial systems of gambling on events of subjective probability, the other being pari-mutuel betting. In bookmaking the bettor gambles against the bookmaker, who accepts bets that are contracts to pay winners at fixed odds. The principal objects of American bookmaking are horse racing and team sports. See Pari-mutuel.

Breakage: The odd cents left over after rounding pari-mutuel payouts to the nearest nickel, dime, quarter, half-dollar, or dollar. Breakage, like other pari-mutuel revenue, is distributed according to statutory formulae; it is commonly shared among government, racetracks, and horsemen.

Churn: The recycling, or rewagering, of bankrolls (drop) in games that offer rapid frequencies of gambles. Casino gaming and pari-mutuel betting are the forms of gambling in which churn makes up a significant portion of handle.

Comp: Complimentaries, sometimes including airfare, chartered or wholly private airplanes, room/food/beverage (RFB) privileges, entertainment, and related services provided by casinos to preferred players; hence the vernacular verb "to comp." See Junket.

Drop: The cash and cash-equivalents exchanged for chips in casino gaming. Drop is the players' bankroll; it represents the amount of money players risk against the house.

Edge: The percentage by which the odds in casino games favor the casino. House advantage is a synonymous term.

For games utilizing randomizing devices that obey the law of independent trials the edge can be precisely calculated and is independent of individual player choice or skill. Each bet in a given game has a particular edge, or house advantage: for example, in roulette as offered by Nevada casinos all bets have a house advantage of 5.26 percent except 1-2-3-0-00, which has a house advantage of 7.89 percent. The edge, or advantage, of all bets in a particular game can be weighted by the estimated or empirically determined gross handle on each bet to calculate an average edge, or expected value, for the game. In the case of Nevada roulette this is a simple calculation, since all bets except one have a 5.26 percent edge, making the expected value of roulette for all practical purposes 5.26 percent. In contrast, craps, although utilizing randomizing devices (dice) that obey the law of independent trials, has bets with edges ranging from 1.402 percent to 16.667 percent, making the estimation of an average craps edge, or expected value for this game, a difficult problem requiring extensive empirical observation for its solution.

Games utilizing randomizing devices that do not obey the law of independent trials (of which blackjack and, to a much lesser degree, baccarat are the most important examples) have edges that are in part functions of player choice and skill, and consequently cannot be precisely calculated. Depending on player strategy, single-deck blackjack has an edge, or house advantage, ranging from some negative value (i.e., positive expectation of gain for the player) to about 6 percent. The only reliable way of determining the house advantage for these games is by empirical observation.

Efficient: A concept of economics that is often applied to the analysis of betting markets for both fixed and pari-mutuelly determined odds. In an efficient market all information is so rapidly discounted—reflected in the prices of securities, commodities, horses, or football teams—that no player can obtain a consistent advantage. In other words, in an efficient betting market made by commercial operators who derive revenues from wagers no player can realize long-term gains. In an efficient pari-mutuel horse-race betting market there are no overlays, or favorable betting opportunities created by undervalued horses. Whether U.S. betting markets are in fact efficient is a much-debated question; major pari-mutuel betting markets (i.e., major racetracks that offer high-quality racing) appear to be at least weakly efficient.

Expected Value: In casino gaming, the value to the casino of individual games. As a practical matter, casinos estimate the expected value of specific levels of wagering at particular games in order to make cost-effective evaluations of complimentary room, food, beverage (RFB), travel, and junket policies. See Edge.

Also, the value, or cost, of a particular gamble. See Price.

Fair: A word distinguishing honest from dishonest randomizing devices used to generate gambling events. Honest dice or roulette wheels are fair; loaded dice or warped or rigged roulette wheels are not.

Also, a word distinguishing games of equal and unequal chance, especially lotteries. A lottery in which all receipts are distributed as prizes is fair; a lottery in which some percentage of the receipts is retained by the operator is not. All forms of commercial gambling are, in this usage, unfair.

Fixed Odds: In sports and horse-race betting, the odds paid offered by bookmakers, which bettors accept when placing a bet. Bets at fixed odds are contracts of certain value, as opposed to pari-mutuel odds, which prior to the gambling event (i.e., race or *jai-alai* game) are only approximately known. See Pari-mutuel.

Gambles (noun plural): The risky choices offered by commercial gambling games. Gambles vary greatly from game to game, and are conceptually distinct from some structural characteristics of gambling games such as the availability of credit and from the contextual variables that influence and help to define all forms of gambling.

Gambling: In the most general sense, any activity involving risk, sometimes under conditions of uncertainty. This definition, while accurate as regards American vernacular usage, is too broad to be meaningful. More usefully, gambling is the stake of money or other material consideration on chance, normally as recreation but occasionally, as in the case of professional gambling at games of mixed chance and skill, in the pursuit of financial gain. The element of choice is always present; in games of pure chance, however, choice has no effect on outcomes. Many kinds of risky choice are not gambling. Contests of skill, such as golf or chess, even when played for money, are not gambling: players are betting on their subjective estimates of their skills relative to the skills of their opponents. Games of mixed chance and skill in which the element of skill is predominant when expertly played (of which bridge is an example) similarly fall outside this definition. Gambling is distinguished from investing in that investors purchase equity—for example, common stocks or options to buy some commodity; in contrast, the commodity purchased by gamblers is chance itself. For all practical purposes, however, some forms of speculative investments are gambling: options on essentially nondeliverable stock market index futures, in which the underlying equity represented by the index is theoretical and rarely or never changes hands, is gambling under this definition. In Great Britain, for example, brokers or other persons who wish to speculate on the movement of market indexes may place such transactions through Ladbroke's, a licensed bookmaker, rather than through traders on stock or options exchanges.

Commercial gambling is distinguished from wagering between friends by the fact that all commercial gambling operations are games of unequal chance. A coin toss between two players at even money is a game of equal chance: both people have equal probabilities of gain or loss. Over the long term all commercial gambling ensures financial gains for the operator and corresponding losses for the players collectively. In gaming the house edge or advantage, in the form of the odds at which successful wagers are paid, ensures that over time the casino will extract percentages of the handle, or gross wagering. In betting and State lotteries the operator retains a percentage of the handle before winning wagers are paid: for pari-mutuel betting and State lotteries this percentage retention is statutory; bookmakers extract their percentage through the price, or odds, at which wagers are accepted, or contracted for, and at which winning wagers are paid.

Games of Chance: Games with outcomes governed by statistical probability; lotteries, roulette, craps, slot machines, and big six wheels are examples. Games of chance offer risk but no uncertainty, since the outcomes of all possible series of bets are precisely calculable. Skill is not a factor in determining the outcomes of games of chance. At the odds paid by casinos the players of games of chance have a negative expectation of gain: over the long term they must expect to lose.

Games of Equal and Unequal Chance: Games of equal chance offer all players equal odds or chances of winning. Poker is an example: provided the house has no stake in this game poker favors all players equally, and outcomes depend on the order of cards and the skill with which they are played. Games of unequal chance ensure an advantage to the operator, either through fixed odds paid, as in gaming and bookmaking, or a statutory takeout from gross wagering, as in pari-mutuel betting and State lotteries. All commercial gambling games are by definition games of unequal chance. See Fair.

Games of Mixed Chance and Skill: Games in which both chance and skill, in varying proportions, determine outcomes. Blackjack, baccarat, poker, bridge, and backgammon are examples. In some of these games the element of skill is sufficient to give the expert player a positive expectation of gain: over the long term he can expect to win. Bridge and single-deck blackjack are examples: the former is not used for commercial gambling purposes, and single-deck blackjack has become a rarity in U.S. casinos. The element of skill in determining blackjack outcomes may be reduced in several ways, including dealing from an eight-deck shoe, shuffling after a limited number of hands, or barring skilled players; none of these methods are wholly satisfactory in practice, and expert blackjack players continue to disturb some casino managements. In baccarat, on the other hand, the element of skill does not appear sufficient to give players a positive expectation of gain.

Games of Skill: Games with outcomes wholly determined by skill, of which tic-tac-toe, checkers, and chess are examples. Chance is not a factor in these games. Checkers and chess are games of perfect information, meaning that there is always a best move or series of moves. Games of skill are not used for commercial gambling purposes, for the obvious reason that skilled players would beat the house.

Gaming: Gambling at casino games. Baccarat, bingo, blackjack, craps, roulette, and slot machines are the most important American examples. Bingo, craps, roulette, and slot machines are games of chance, with outcomes that are fixed or *a priori* probabilities. Baccarat and blackjack are games of mixed chance and skill, with outcomes that depend in varying degrees on the elements of choice and player skill.

Handicapping: The estimation of subjective probabilities of the outcomes of horse races, football games, and other events that are objects of commercial betting. See Probability.

Handle: The gross amount wagered at any form of gambling. In pari-mutuel accounting, handle and turnover are synomymous; State lotteries normally account gross wagering as sales. Handle is a partial function of the velocity of dollars through commercial games; it is thus a measure of gambling. See Revenue.

Hold: In casino accounting, win as a percentage of drop; in other words, the percentage of players' bankrolls that casinos win and players lose.

Junket: "Free" travel, rooms, food, beverages, and entertainment at a particular casino/hotel provided to selected players on the assumption their gambling losses will cover these expenses and generate a casino profit. Junket organizers are typically *not* casino employees but agents who are compensated by casinos through sometimes complicated fee arrangements. Modern junket operations originated in Nevada in the early 1960s and today are an important source of preferred players for U.S. casinos. Junkets are prohibited by the British Gaming Act of 1968. See Comp.

Law of Independent Trials: An important distinction concerning the likelihood of outcomes of gambling events. The outcomes of events produced by randomizing devices conform to this law. A simple example is a *fair* coin: the likelihood that the outcome of the next toss of a fair coin will be heads is exactly one out of two, or 50 percent, independent of the outcomes of preceding coin tosses in the series. Fair dice and roulette wheels obey this law. A deck of cards that is not shuffled between deals is an example of a randomizing device that violates the law of independent trials: the likelihood that the next card dealt will be an ace depends on the number of aces that have already appeared and on the total number of undealt cards in the deck.

Line: See Point Spread.

Lottery: A form of gambling in which players purchase chances, in the form of lots or tickets, to share in prizes when the lots are drawn. The traditional elements comprising a lottery are chance, consideration, and prize: if lots are free or prizes are awarded according to skill there is no lottery. Lottery definitions under State laws and constitutions have become controversial through the efforts of State lottery administrations and vendors of lottery games to expand lottery gambling to include video gaming devices and sports betting; see the discussion of State lotteries in Chapter 3.

Odds: The word *odds* means, variously, chance; both the *a priori* and the subjective probabilities of any given outcome of uncertain events, including events used for gambling, such as horseraces or the turn of a roulette wheel; and the return (or odds paid) on successful gambles in relation to the amount staked. State lottery Lotto games, for example, may have fixed odds of winning but pari-mutuelly calculated odds paid, meaning that the probability of winning is determined by the operator while the value of a winning Lotto ticket is a function of the number of winning selections in relation to the total amount bet on the Lotto game. Fixed odds or probabilities of winning are precisely knowable prior to the gambling event—in this case the drawing of winning Lotto numbers. Pari-mutuel odds paid are known only after the gambling event has gone to a decision and the number of winners is revealed. Racetracks and *jai-alai* frontons provide tote boards that display approximate pari-mutuel odds paid for individual pools, such as win, place, and show pools. See Price and Probability.

Overlay: In horse-race betting, a favorable bet created by an undervalued horse. See Efficient.

Pari-mutuel: A form of gambling in which bettors wager among themselves rather than against an operator that originated in Paris in the 1860s as an alternative to off-track betting on horses through bookmakers. In pari-mutuel betting, wagers on a given horse, or betting interest, are pooled, a percentage (takeout) is retained by the operator, and the remaining ("live") money is distributed to the holders of winning pari-mutuel tickets. Pari-mutuel odds paid are a function of the amount of money wagered on the winning betting interest in relation to the total pool on that event; they are thus determined by the bettors themselves (and, of course, by the laws that set takeout percentages) rather than by the operator of the game (as in bookmaking). In France and the United States (Nevada is an exception in that bookmakers are licensed to accept horse-race bets) pari-mutuel betting is the only legal way to conduct horse-race betting; in Great Britain and several of the major Commonwealth nations both pari-mutuel betting and bookmaking are generally allowed.

Payout Interval: With frequency of opportunities to gamble, a variable characteristic of gambling games that governs the rate of gambling activity. At most casino games, for example, payouts are immediate, facilitating rapid, repetitive play; in other forms of gambling, such as bookmaking or lotteries, hours or days may elapse between the gambling event and payouts to winners. Payout intervals must be short in order for recycled winnings to constitute a significant percentage of gross wagering. See Churn.

Payout Ratio and the Probability of Winning: Normally inversely related variables that together provide a continuum of risk/reward values offered by gambling games and that are crucial elements of individual choice among various forms of gambling. Gambling activities that offer only a segment of this continuum—e.g., monthly lotteries, where the single gamble offered is of very low probability of winning and moderately high reward, or ratio of payout to investment—interest a definable and limited segment of the gambling population. Conversely, gambling activities that cover the entire continuum, such as casino gaming, meet a broader range of individual interests and consequently enjoy much wider popular appeal.

Player Participation and Skill: Related but distinct characteristics of gambling activities. Pulling the handle of a slot machine is participation, but it does not involve skill; counting cards at blackjack combines both characteristics into a single activity. Both player participation and the exercise of skill correlate positively with increasing levels of involvement in gambling.

Point Spread: A handicap in the form of points added by odds-makers to the scores of teams in games of predictable outcomes that are the object of betting. Professional football games are the most important example: it is sufficiently easy for expert handicappers to pick the winners of National Football League (NFL) games that without some method of equalizing teams these games would not be suitable objects of large-scale commercial betting. For example, if the New York Jets are given a handicap of 8 points a person betting on the Jets wins only if the Jets beat the opposing team by more than 8 points. Point spreads are betting lines; these lines are made by professional odds-makers and constitute the most important sports information used by bookmakers. The purpose of point spreads is to equalize the amount of money wagered (handle) on each team, or betting interest, not, as is often but erroneously stated, to make the outcome of each game a 50-50 proposition. Lines are formulated from expert opinion and moved upwards or downwards by the number of points needed to equalize the betting of a small number of professional sports bettors; in other words, they are market-determined prices.

Price: The price of gambling is the percentage of the gross amount wagered, or handle, retained by the operator of a commercial gambling business and is equivalent to the losses incurred by gamblers collectively over the long term. The price of commercial gambling is highly variable, ranging from less than 2 percent for some bets at casino table games to more than 50 percent in most State lotteries. Over the long term and (where relevant) provided the player exercises adequate skill, the price an individual pays for gambling will approximate the price of that form of gambling for all gamblers collectively. The outcome of a short series of gambles may, however, bear little relationship to the real price of gambling. For a gambler who makes one bet, loses, and stops, the price of gambling is 100 percent. Conversely, a gambler who makes one bet, wins, and quits, pays no price for gambling and instead realizes an absolute financial gain. Notwithstanding these short-term fluctuations, for gamblers collectively over the long term the price of gambling is calculable for all commercial gambling activities. (Gambling may obviously entail other expenses, such as racetrack admissions, travel costs, and so forth, that are not functions of the gambling activities themselves. While these nongambling but gambling-related expenses are significant considerations, only the cost of gambling itself is meant by price as used in this book.)

The price of gambling must be distinguished from the expected cost, or value, of a particular gamble. The expected value from choosing some alternative is a concept of economics and game theory that may be applied to gambling decisions (and to other risky decisions) with a degree of mathematical precision that may be at variance with real-world gambling decisionmaking. For example, the expected value, in money won or lost, of a specific gamble on an event with outcomes of known probability may be mathematically determined, as long as the odds paid are agreed upon before the event is decided; the risk and the reward of any particular decision—including the decision not to enter the gamble—can be precisely calculated. Such gambles entail risk but no uncertainty; the expected value of all possible decisions is calculable. Examples include the purchase of lottery tickets in drawings where both the number of tickets and the number and value of prizes are known; and craps, roulette, and slot machines.

In contrast, the expected value of a specific gamble under conditions of uncertainty is subjective to the extent that the probabilities of various outcomes are unknown. Poker is an example: both risk, in the form of the draw of cards, and uncertainty, as to the meaning of the actions of other players, are present. A player who keeps careful track of the cards as they appear can know the statistical probability that his opponent holds a pair of aces, but the decision to call or fold involves the subjective estimation of whether in fact he holds them or is simply bluffing. Statistical probability is only part of the information needed to estimate the expected value of gambles under conditions of uncertainty; a poker player who makes all decisions solely on the basis of the statistical probabilities of the distribution of cards without taking bluff into account is an easy victim of players who employ effective bluffing strategies. Pari-mutuel betting and bookmaking on sports may or may not constitute decisionmaking under risk: if all information affecting the outcomes of horse races and football games is immediately discounted and reflected on tote boards, or fully taken into account in betting lines, these gambles are risky decisions, and their expected value may be at least approximately calculated. If, on the other hand, a gambler is in possession of inside information that materially affects the outcome of a horse race or football game the element of risk is reduced or eliminated, and calculations of expected values by other players are valueless. See Risk and Uncertainty.

Odds and price are frequently confused by gamblers and even by the operators of commercial gambling businesses. For example, the statistical probability that 00 will come up in American roulette is 1-in-38 (there being 38 numbers on American roulette wheels); this is often referred to as the odds that 00 will appear. However, a dollar successfully bet on 00 returns $35 (plus the $1 bet), not $38, so that if a player bets $1 on 00 he may expect to lose $2 for every $38 gambled, or 5.26 percent of the amount wagered, the casino's edge for this bet. The price of gambling on 00 at American roulette is thus 5.26 percent of the amount gambled, not the 1-in-38 odds that 00 will be the winning number. Odds and price are related in that commercial gambling at fixed odds, such as casino gaming, must ensure a sufficient return to the operator to cover expenses, tax liabilities, and profit. In pari-mutuel betting odds paid and price may be only indirectly related: the value of winning pari-mutuel tickets (odds paid) is a function of the amount of money bet on the winning horse or betting interest in relation to the total pool, less the takeout (price), or amount removed from the pool before winning tickets are paid.

Probability: In gambling, the likelihood that one among a number of possible outcomes of an event will occur. Two distinct kinds of probabilities describe gambling events: (1) Events produced by randomizing devices that obey the law of independent trials are governed by *a priori,* or statistical, probabilities that may be given precise mathematical expression (for example, the probability that the outcome of the toss of a fair coin will be heads is 1-in-2, or 50-50); (2) The outcomes of horse races, football games, and similar events that are the object of commercial betting have no *a priori* mathematically calculable probability. Odds-makers and bettors handicap, or estimate, the likelihoods of these outcomes by constructing subjective probabilities from a great variety of race and sports information, including past performance, breeding lines, injury reports, weather conditions, and so forth.

Punter: British vernacular for "gambler," usually in the sense of "bettor," meaning a person gambling on events of subjective probability as opposed to casino games governed by *a priori* probability.

Punto banco: One of the family of card games that includes blackjack (twenty-one), baccarat, and chemin-de-fer. The game takes its name from the names of the two players: the bank (banco) and the player (punto).

Rake: A commission deducted from poker and panguingui pots and pai gow winning hands by Nevada casinos, commonly 5 percent.

Randomizing Device: Used to produce series of random events for the purpose of gaming. Roulette wheels, dice, slot machines, and decks of cards are randomizing devices. Horse races, *jai-alai* matches, and greyhound races serve an analogous purpose in pari-mutuel betting; these are not, however, truly randomizing devices. When events of predictable outcome, such as NFL football games, are used for betting purposes outcomes are adjusted through odds or point spreads so that roughly equivalent amounts of money are bet on either team or betting interest.

Retention: In pari-mutuel accounting, the gross amount retained from wagering pools, including taxes, operating expenses, purse distributions, and any other pari-mutuel revenue; synonymous with takeout. For bettors, retention is the price of betting.

Revenue: In commercial gambling generally, the collective losses of gamblers won, or retained, by operators. A portion of this revenue is paid directly to the state as gambling privilege tax. The state also derives direct revenues from commercial gambling in the form of various license fees and admission taxes. In addition to direct revenues the state derives revenue from the income and property taxation of commercial gambling businesses. Revenues—and not handle—are thus measures of the size, or value, of a gambling business, gambling industry, or gambling market. See Handle.

Risk and Uncertainty: Distinct characteristics of gambling decisions that are often confused. Players of all commercial gambling games are at financial risk: games of pure chance, such as roulette, craps, and slot machines, entail risk but no uncertainty, since the outcome of all possible series of wagers at these games is known and may be precisely quantified. Some important gambling games of mixed chance and skill played at equal odds, *games of equal chance* (of which poker is an example), add to risk the quality of uncertainty in the form of bluffing strategies; decisions that fail to evaluate the possibility that other players are bluffing will lose against more expert poker play.

Stakes: Amounts wagered. The range of stakes varies considerably among the different forms of commercial gambling. Lotteries commonly allow stakes of from $1 (or less) to $5, while in pari-mutuel betting the range of stakes is normally from $2 to $100 for a single ticket. Casino games with minimum stakes of $1,000 or more, while not common, are occasionally found. In casino gaming the ratio of minimum to maximum stakes (''table minimums and maximums'') are important determinants of the rate of player loss; high minimum and low maximum stakes increase the rate at which players lose their bankrolls, and, when the demand for gambling exceeds the available number of table games, greatly increase casino productivity, as well, of course, as per capita losses. See the discussion of the debate over table minimums and maximums at Resorts International in Atlantic City in Chapter 3.

Also, in thoroughbred racing, races for which the purse includes money added by the track. Stakes races are graded by the Thoroughbred Owners and Breeders Association as Grade I, II, or III, according to the money added (normally stakes with less than $40,000 added are not considered), the quality of horses competing, handicaps, and the lack of entry restrictions as to State of foaling and so forth, other than sex and age.

Takeout: See Retention.

Tote Board: A large board, usually placed in the infield opposite the grandstand of a racetrack, displaying the current approximate pari-mutuel odds on as many horses, or betting interests, as the board's display capacity can accommodate. The tote board functions in a manner analogous to a stock market ticker-tape, and the information it provides is essential to the efficient working of pari-mutuel betting markets. See Efficient.

Turnover: See Handle.

Win: In casino accounting, gross gaming revenues, or the collective losses of players. The analogous terms in pari-mutuel accounting are retention or takeout.

Bibliography

Abt Associates Inc. *Income from Illegal Gambling*. Cambridge, Mass.: Abt Associates, 1982.

Abt, Vicki, and James F. Smith. "Playing the Game in Mainstream America." In *World of Play*, edited by Frank E. Manning, 50–65. West Point, N.Y.: Leisure Press, 1983.

Adar, Zvi. "Efficiency and Equity of State Lotteries." In *Gambling in America: Final Report of the Commission on the Review of the National Policy Toward Gambling*, Appendix 1, pp. 789–804. Washington, D.C.: GPO, 1976.

Alford, Robert. "Paradigms of Relations Between State and Society." In *Stress & Contradiction in Modern Capitalism*, edited by L. Lindberg, 145–59. Lexington, Mass.: Heath, 1972.

Ali, Mukhtar M. "Probability and Utility Estimates for Racetrack Bettors." *Journal of Political Economy* 85, no. 4 (August 1977): 803–15.

———. "Some Evidence of the Efficiency of a Speculative Market." *Econometrica* 47, no. 2 (March 1979): 387–92.

The Lord Allen of Abbeydale. "Some Reflections on the British Gaming Scene." In *Laventhol & Horwath Second Annual Gaming Conference: The Gaming Industry—1980*, 24–27. Philadelphia: Laventhol & Horwath, 1980.

Ainslie, Tom (Richard Carter). *Ainslie's Complete Guide to Thoroughbred Racing*. New York: Simon and Schuster, 1968.

———. *Ainslie's Encyclopedia of Thoroughbred Handicapping*. New York: William Morrow, 1978.

———. *Ainslie's New Complete Guide to Harness Racing*. New York: Simon and Schuster, 1970.

———. *Theory and Practice of Handicapping*. New York: Trident Press, 1970.

Alsop, Ronald. "Casino Glut in Atlantic City Brings Intense Competition." *Wall Street Journal*, January 14, 1981.

Alvarez, A. "A Reporter at Large: Poker World Series." *The New Yorker*, March 7, 14, 1983.

American Greyhound Track Operators Association. George D. Johnson, Jr., executive director. *1983 Summary of State Pari-Mutuel Tax Structures*. North Miami, Fla.: American Greyhound Track Operators Assoc., 1983.

American Horse Council, Inc. *Standardbred Breeder Incentive Programs*. Washington, D.C.: American Horse Council, 1979, 1982.

———. *Thoroughbred Breeder/Owner Incentive Programs in Pari-Mutuel States.* Washington, D.C.: American Horse Council, 1982.

———. R. Richards Rolapp, president. "Statement in Support of H.R. 4592." U.S. Congress, House, Committee on Ways and Means, Hearings before the Subcommittee on Select Revenue Measures, 97th Cong., 2d sess., March 16, 1982.

———. Thomas L. Aronson, executive secretary, racing committee. "Wagering Analysis: Hazel Park Harness, October 1977." Unpublished, 1978.

Aranson, Peter H., and Roger LeRoy Miller. "Economic Aspects of Public Gaming." *Connecticut Law Review* 12, no. 4 (Summer 1980): 822–53.

Asbury, Herbert. *Sucker's Progress: An Informal History of Gambling in America from the Colonies in Canfield.* New York, Dodd, Mead, 1938.

Ashton, John. *A History of English Lotteries.* London: Leadenhall Press, 1893. Reprint. Detroit, Mich.: Singing Tree Press, 1969.

Ashton, Nancy. "Gamblers: Disturbed or Healthy?" In *Gambling Today,* edited by David Lester, 53–70. Springfield, Ill.: Charles C. Thomas, 1979.

Aspinall, *Aspinall Holdings p.l.c.: Offer for Sale.* Kitcat & Aitken and Raphael, Zorn. Prospectus. November 1, 1983.

Atlantic City Press. "Kean's Pen Stroke Zaps Video Lottery," March 2, 1983.

———. "Palley Pleads Innocent at Brief Arraignment," May 10, 1983.

Aubrey, William E. "Altering the Gambler's Maladaptive Life Goals." *International Journal of the Addictions* 10 (1975): 29–33.

Barclay, Alexander. *The Mirror of Good Manners.* N.p., 1510.

Barnfather, Maurice. "Is Playboy's Luck Running Out?" *Forbes,* May 11, 1981: 58-59.

Becker, Howard S. "Becoming a Marijuana User." *American Journal of Sociology* 59 (November 1953): 235–42.

———. *Outsiders: Studies in the Sociology of Deviance.* Glencoe, Ill.: Free Press, 1963.

Beebe, Lucius. *The Big Spenders.* New York: Doubleday, 1966.

Bell, Raymond C. "Moral Views on Gambling Promulgated by Major American Religious Bodies." In *Gambling in America: Final Report of the Commission on the Review of the National Policy Toward Gambling,* Appendix 1, 161–239. Washington, D.C.: GPO, 1976.

Bender, Eric J. *Tickets to Fortune: The Story of Sweepstakes, Lotteries, and Contests.* New York: Modern Age Books, 1938.

Bendix, Reinhard. *Max Weber: An Intellectual Portrait.* New York: Anchor Books, 1962.

———, and Seymour M. Lipset, eds. *Class, Status and Power.* Glencoe, Ill.: Free Press, 1953.

Berg, Sanford V., and Emery Jay Yelton. "Profits, Payments, and Complementary Products: Additional Ways to Improve Pari-Mutuel Taxation." *National Tax Journal* 29, no. 2 (June 1976): 191–99.

Berger, Peter L., and Hansfried Kellner. *Sociology Reinterpreted: An Essay on Method and Vocation.* Garden City, N.Y.: Doubleday/Anchor, 1981.

Bergler, Edmund, M.D. *The Psychology of Gambling.* New York: Hill and Wang, 1957.

Beyer, Andrew. *Picking Winners.* Boston: Houghton Mifflin, 1975.

Blakey, G. Robert. "State Conducted Lotteries: History, Problems, and Promises." *Journal of Social Issues* 35, no. 3 (Summer 1979): 62–86.

———, and Harold A. Kurland. "The Development of the Federal Law of Gambling." *Cornell Law Review* 63, no. 6 (August 1978): 923–1021.

Blanche, Ernest E. "Gambling Odds Are Gimmicked!" *Annals of the American Academy of Political and Social Science* 269 (May 1950): 77–80.

The Blood-Horse. Editorial, "What's Going on Here," October 15, 1983: 7289.

Blunk, Frank M. "Aqueduct Head Steps up Attack on Jockey Club's 'Dream Track.'" *New York Times,* March 28, 1955.

Boorstin, Daniel. *The Image: A Guide to Pseudo Events in America.* New York: Atheneum, 1961.

Bottomore, T. B. "Marxist Sociology." In *The International Encyclopedia of the Social Sciences,* edited by David L. Sills, 10: 46–53. New York: Free Press, 1968.

Brams, Marvin R., and Harmon Carey. "The Delaware Lotteries: From Failure to Success." Paper presented at the Third Annual Conference on Gambling, University of Nevada, Las Vegas, December 1976.

Brief, Richard P., Samprit Chatterjee, Stephen Figlewski, Jay-Louise Weldon, and Joel Owen. *A Study of the Economic Impact of the Change in the Pari-Mutuel Tax on the Pari-Mutuel Industry in New York State Mandated by Chapter 576 of the Laws of 1978.* Final Report. New York: New York University, Graduate School of Business Administration, College of Business and Public Administration, 1980.

Brinner, Roger E., and Charles T. Clotfelter. "An Economic Appraisal of State Lotteries." *National Tax Journal* 28, no. 4 (December 1975): 395–404.

Business Week. "Atlantic City Gambling Loses its Glow," January 26, 1981: 85–90.

Caillois, Roger. *Man, Play, and Games.* Translated by Meyer Barash. New York: Schocken Books, 1979.

Canes, Michael E. "The Market for Pro Football Betting." In *Gambling and Society: Interdisciplinary Studies on the Subject of Gambling,* edited by William R. Eadington, 108–137. Springfield, Ill.: Charles C. Thomas, 1976.

Carnegie, Andrew. "Wealth." *North American Review,* June 1889. Reprinted in *An American Primer,* edited by Daniel J. Boorstin, 519–30. New York: New American Library, 1968.

Carroll, Robert. "Lotto Winners Take It & Lump It." *New York Daily News,* September 27, 1983.

Chafetz, Henry. *Play the Devil: A History of Gambling in the United States from 1492 to 1955.* New York: Clarkson N. Potter, 1960.

Christiansen, Eugene Martin. "The Gross Annual Wager of the United States (Calendar 1982) Part I: Handle." *Gaming Business Magazine,* April 1984.

———. "The Gross Annual Wager of the United States (Calendar 1982) Part II: Revenues." *Gaming Business Magazine,* May 1984.

———. "The Gross Annual Wager of the United States (1983) Part I: Handle Trends." *Gaming Business Magazine,* June 1984.

———. "The Gross Annual Wager of the United States (1983) Part II: Revenues." *Gaming Business Magazine,* August 1984.

———, and Michael D. Shagan. "The New York Off-Track Betting Law: An Exercise in Selective Decriminalization." *Connecticut Law Review* 12, no. 4 (Summer 1980): 854–69.

Ciccolo, John H. "Taxation of Earnings from Parimutuel Betting." "Optimal On-Track and Off-Track Takeout Rates," with a "Note on Bookmaking." "Taxation of Earnings from Parimutuel Horse Betting." "The Impact of New York City Off-Track Betting Activity on the Revenues of New York State and the Thoroughbred Racing Industry." "The Impact of Increasing Racing Days: Some Preliminary Empirical Results." In *Gambling in America: Final Report of the Commission on the Review of the National Policy Toward Gambling,* Appendix 1, 818–85. Washington, D.C.: GPO, 1976.

Coggins, Russ, ed. *The Gambling Menace.* Nashville, Tenn.: Broadman Press, 1966.

Cohen, Percy S. *Modern Social Theory.* New York: Basic Books, 1968.

Cooke, Alistair. *Alistair Cooke's America.* New York: Alfred A. Knopf, 1977.

Cornell Law School, G. Robert Blakey, supervisor. *The Development of the Law of Gambling: 1776–1976.* National Institute of Law Enforcement and Criminal Justice, Law Enforcement Assistance Administration, United States Department of Justice. Washington, D.C.: GPO, November 1977.

Corney, William J., and William Theodore Cummings. "Information Processing Biases and Gambling Behavior." In *The Gambling Papers: Proceedings of the Fifth National Conference on Gambling and Risk Taking,* edited by William R. Eadington, 13 vols. Vol. 4, *Studies in Gambling Behavior:* 120–30. Reno: Bureau of Business and Economic Research, College of Business Administration, University of Nevada, Reno, 1982.

Cornish, D. B. *Gambling: A Review of the Literature and Its Implications for Policy and Research.* Home Office Research Study no. 42. London: Home Office Research Unit, 1978.

Cotton, Charles. *Games and Gamesters of the Restoration* (*The Compleat Gamester,* 1674, with Theophilus Lucas, *Lives of the Gamesters,* 1714). London: Kennikat Press, 1930.

Council of State Governments. *Gambling: A Source of State Revenue.* Ohio: Council of State Governments, 1973.

Cressey, Donald R. *Theft of the Nation: The Structure and Operations of Organized Crime in America.* New York: Harper & Row, 1969.

Crist, Stephen. "Sangster's Boast Ruffles Bluegrass." *New York Times,* July 23, 1982.

Cuomo, Mario. "Excerpts from Governor Cuomo's Budget Message to the State Legislature." *New York Times,* January 17, 1984.

Custer, Robert L. "Description of Compulsive Gambling." Paper prepared for the American Psychiatric Association Task Force on Nomenclature for inclusion in its *Diagnostic Statistical Manual III.* 1976.

Daily Racing Form. "Cuomo Aide Advocates Privately Run N.Y. OTB," January 11, 1984.

———. "Ky. Bill Would Raise State Racing Taxes," December 3, 1983.

———. *The American Racing Manual: 1982.* Hightstown, N.J.: Daily Racing Form, 1982.

Daley, Arthur. "A Substantial Dream Castle." *New York Times,* September 23, 1955.

DaSilva, E. R., and Roy M. Dorcus. *Science in Betting: The Players and the Horses.* New York: Harper & Brothers, 1961.

Davis, Michael P. "U.S. & Canadian Gaming-at-a-Glance." *Gaming Business Magazine,* July 1983.

Deland, Paul S. "The Facilitation of Gambling." *Annals of the American Academy of Political and Social Science* 269 (May 1950): 21–29.

deSeve, Charles W. "Improved Pari-Mutuel Taxation." *National Tax Journal* 26, no. 4 (December 1973): 591–96.

Devereux, Edward C., Jr. "Gambling and the Social Structure: A Sociological Study of Lotteries and Horseracing in Contemporary America." Ph.D. diss., Harvard University, 1949.

Dielman, Ted E. "Gambling: A Social Problem?" *Journal of Social Issues* 35, no. 3 (1979): 36–42.

Dombrink, John Dennis. "Outlaw Businessmen: Organized Crime and the Legalization of Casino Gambling." Ph.D. diss., University of California, Berkeley, 1981.

Douglas, Mary, and Aaron Wildavsky. *Culture and Risk.* New York: Random House, 1982.

Dowie, Jack. "On the Efficiency and Equity of Betting Markets." Paper presented at the Second Annual Conference on Gambling, Lake Tahoe, Nevada, 1975.

Downes, D. M.; B. P. Davies, M. E. David, and P. Stone. *Gambling, Work and Leisure: A Study Across Three Areas*. London: Routledge & Kegan Paul, 1976.

Downie, Leonard, Jr. "London Court Strips Playboy of Licenses For 2 Casinos." *Washington Post,* October 6, 1981.

Duncan, Carol H. "State and Local Gambling Enforcement: Arrest, Disposition, and Sentencing Statistics." In *Gambling in America: Final Report of the Commission on the Review of the National Policy Toward Gambling,* Appendix 1, 679–744. Washington, D.C.: GPO, 1976.

Durkheim, Emile. *Suicide.* 1897. Reprint. Glencoe, Ill.: Free Press, 1964.

Eadington. William R. "The Economics of Gambling Behavior: A Qualitative Study of Nevada's Gambling Industry." *Research Report Number 11,* Bureau of Business and Economic Research. Reno: College of Business Administration, University of Nevada, Reno, 1973.

———. "The Evolution of Corporate Gambling in Nevada." *Nevada Review of Business and Economics* 6, no. 1 (Spring 1982): 13–22.

———, ed. *Gambling and Society: Interdisciplinary Studies on the Subject of Gambling.* Springfield, Ill.: Charles C. Thomas, 1976.

———, ed. *The Gambling Papers: Proceedings of the Fifth National Conference on Gambling and Risk Taking.* Reno: Bureau of Business and Economic Research, College of Business Administration, University of Nevada, Reno, 1982.

———, and James S. Hattori. "A Legislative History of Gambling in Nevada." *Nevada Review of Business and Economics* 2, no. 1 (Spring 1978): 13–17.

Economics Research Associates. *The Role of Gaming in the Nevada Economy: An Update.* Prepared for the Gaming Industry Association of Nevada and Nevada Resort Association. San Francisco: Economics Research Associates, 1983.

Egan, Leo. "Strong Opposition to 'Dream' Track." *New York Times,* March 26, 1955.

Epstein, Richard A. *The Theory of Gambling and Statistical Logic.* New York: Academic Press, 1967.

Etzioni, Amitai. "Work in the American Future: Reindustrialization or Quality of Life." In *Work in America: The Decade Ahead,* edited by Clark Kerr and Jerome M. Rosow, 27–34. New York: Van Nostrand Reinhold, 1979.

Ewen, C. L'Estrange. *Lotteries and Sweepstakes: An Historical, Legal, and Ethical Survey of Their Introduction, Suppression, and Re-establishment in the British Isles.* London: Heath Cranton, 1932. Reprint. New York: Benjamin Blom, 1972.

Ezell, John Samuel. *Fortune's Merry Wheel: The Lottery in America.* Cambridge, Mass.: Harvard University Press, 1960.

Fabricand, Burton P. *The Science of Winning.* New York: Van Nostrand Reinhold, 1979.

Fact Research, Inc. "Gambling in Perspective." In *Gambling in America: Final Report of the Commission on the Review of the National Policy Toward Gambling,* Appendix 1, 1–101. Washington, D.C.: GPO, 1976.

Feinberg, Alexander. "State Racing Unit Aids Supertrack." *New York Times,* June 22, 1955.

Figlewski, Stephen. "Subjective Information and Market Efficiency in a Betting Market." *Journal of Political Economy* 87, no. 1 (1979): 75–88.

Freund, Julien. *The Sociology of Max Weber.* New York: Vintage Books, 1969.

Friedman, Bill. *Casino Management.* Secaucus, N.J.: Lyle Stuart, 1974.

Friedman, M., and L. J. Savage. "The Utility Analysis of Choices Involving Risk." *Journal of Political Economy* 56, no. 4 (August 1948): 279–304.

Friedman, Robert. *Marxist Social Thought.* New York: Harcourt, Brace and World, 1968.

Fund for the City of New York. Gregory R. Farrell, executive director. *Legal Gambling in New York: A Discussion of Numbers & Sports Betting.* New York: Fund for the City of New York, 1972.

Gamblers Anonymous. Los Angeles: G.A. Publishing, n.d.

Gaming Business Magazine. "Nebraska VLTs: Taking Root or Just a Flash in the Cornfield?," November 1983: 6.

Gardiner, Alexander. *Canfield: The True Story of the Greatest Gambler.* Garden City, N.Y.: Doubleday, Doran, 1930.

Gerth, H. H., and C. Wright Mills, trans. and eds. *From Marx to Weber: Essays in Sociology.* New York: Oxford University Press, 1958.

Goffman, Erving. "Where the Action Is." In *Interaction Ritual: Essays on Face-to-Face Behavior.* New York: Anchor Books, 1967.

Gomes, Dennis C. "Casino Player-Rating Systems: Designing One that Rates." *Gaming Business Magazine,* July 1983: 41–46.

Griffith, R. M. "Odds Adjustments by American Horse-Race Bettors." *American Journal of Psychology* 62, no. 2 (April 1949): 290–94.

Gruen, Arthur. "An Inquiry into the Economics of Race-Track Gambling." *Journal of Political Economy* 84, no. 1 (November 1976): 169–77.

Gwynn, John M. "An Optimal Strategy for the Game of Pai Gow." In *The Gambling Papers: Proceedings of the Fifth National Conference on Gambling and Risk Taking,* edited by William R. Eadington, 13 vols. Vol. 13, *Quantitative Analysis of Gambling: Stock Markets and Other Games,* 28–45. Reno: Bureau of Business and Economic Research, College of Business Administration, University of Nevada, Reno, 1982.

Haller, Mark H. "Bootleggers and American Gambling 1920–1950." In *Gambling in America: Final Report of the Commission on the Review of the National Policy Toward Gambling,* Appendix 1, 102–43. Washington, D.C.: GPO, 1976.

———. "The Changing Structure of American Gambling in the Twentieth Century." *Journal of Social Issues* 35, no. 3 (Summer 1979): 87–114.

Hausch, Donald B., William T. Ziemba, and Mark Rubinstein. "Efficiency of the Market for Racetrack Betting." In *The Gambling Papers: Proceedings of the Fifth National Conference on Gambling and Risk Taking,* edited by William R. Eadington, 13 vols. Vol. 12, *Quantitative Analysis of Gambling: Racing and Sporting Events,* 109–35. Reno: Bureau of Business and Economic Research, College of Business Administration, University of Nevada, Reno, 1982.

Heckerman, David L. "The Economics of Selling." In *The Blood-Horse,* July 18, 1981: 4120–22.

Heneghan, Daniel. "Balley to Buy Former Chairman's Stock." *Atlantic City Press,* January 10, 1984.

———. "British Test for Playboy is Starting." *Atlantic City Press,* September 14, 1981.

———. "Casinos' Lament: December Win Just Not Enough to Pay Bills." *Atlantic City Press,* January 14, 1981.

———. "Codey: Alter View of Casinos." *Atlantic City Press,* January 16, 1981.

———. "Hilton Shelves $250M. A.C. Casino Plans." *Atlantic City Press,* January 17, 1981.

———. "Perlmans Resign from Caesars." *Atlantic City Press,* December 30, 1981.

———. "Perlmans to Refund $7 Million." *Atlantic City Press,* April 1, 1982.

———. "Resorts Agrees to Fine in $4M. Zarin Case." *Atlantic City Press,* September 8, 1982.

Herman, Robert D. "Gambling as Work: A Sociological Study of the Racetrack." In *Gambling*, edited by Robert D. Herman, 87–104. New York: Harper and Row, 1967.

Home Office. *Introduction to the Gaming Act 1968.* London: Her Majesty's Stationery Office, n.d.

Horowitz, Irving Louis, ed. *The New Sociology: Essays in Social Science and Social Theory in Honor of C. Wright Mills.* New York: Oxford University Press, 1964.

Horsemen's Benevolent and Protective Association. R. Anthony Chamblin, executive director. *Racing Statistics.* Annual report. Rockville, Md.: Horsemen's Benevolent and Protective Association, 1960–80.

Hudson Institute. Max Singer, project leader. *Increased Legal Gambling in New York: HI-1736-RR; HI-1736/2CC.* 3 vols. New York: Hudson Institute, 1973.

Huizinga, Johan. *Homo Ludens: A Study of the Play-Element in Culture.* Leyden: 1938. Boston: Beacon Press, 1955.

Ignatin, George. "Taxing Peter to Spite Paul: The Effects of Taxes and Regulation on Sports Gambling." In *The Gambling Papers: Proceedings of the Fifth National Conference on Gambling and Risk Taking*, edited by William R. Eadington, 13 vols. Vol. 9, *Legal, Economic and Humanistic Perspectives on Gambling*, 92–126. Reno: Bureau of Business and Economic Research, College of Business Administration, University of Nevada, Reno, 1982.

Illinois State Lottery. *Third Annual Report.* Springfield: Lottery Division, Dept. of Revenue, State of Illinois, 1977.

Irwin, Will. *Confessions of a Con Man.* New York: B. W. Huebsch, 1909.

Issacs, Neil D., and Gerald Strine. *Covering the Spread: How to Bet Pro Football.* New York: Random House, 1978.

Isaacs, R. "Optimal Horse Race Bets." *American Mathematical Monthly*, May 1953: 310–15.

Janson, Donald. "Jersey Casinos Expect First Monthly Deficits since Their Openings." *New York Times*, January 14, 1981.

———. "Revenues Soaring at Jersey Casinos." *New York Times*, November 20, 1983.

Jennings, Rienzi Wilson. *Taxation of Thoroughbred Racing.* Lexington, Ky.: University of Kentucky, 1949.

Jockey Club. Letter from John W. Hanes, Christopher T. Chenery, and Harry F. Guggenheim to Ashley Trimble Cole, chairman of the New York State Racing Commission, September 20, 1954. Reprinted in New York State Racing Commission, *Annual Report for 1954*, 18–20.

Johnson, David R. "A Sinful Business: Origins of Gambling Syndicates in the United States, 1840–1887." In *Police and Society*, edited by David Bayley, 17–47. Beverly Hills, Ca.: Sage, 1977.

Joyce, Kathleen M. "Public Opinion and the Politics of Gambling." *Journal of Social Issues* 35, no. 3 (Summer 1979): 144–65.

Kallick, Maureen, Daniel Suits, Ted Dielman, and Judith Hybels, Survey Research Center, Institute for Social Research, University of Michigan. "Survey of American Gambling Attitudes and Behavior." In *Gambling in America: Final Report of the Commission on the Review of the National Policy Toward Gambling*, Appendix 2, 1–454. Washington, D.C.: GPO, 1976.

Kallick-Kaufmann, Maureen. "The Micro and Macro Dimensions of Gambling in the United States." *Journal of Social Issues* 35, no. 3 (1979): 7–35.

Kaplan, Lawrence J., and James M. Maher. "Economics of the Numbers Game." *American Journal of Economics and Sociology* 29, no. 4 (October 1970): 391–408.

Kaplan, Lawrence J., and Dennis Kessler, eds. *An Economic Analysis of Crime: Selected Readings.* Springfield, Ill.: Charles C. Thomas, 1976.

Kellogg, John L. "The Federal Tax Treatment of Winnings, Losses, and Expenses of the Sports and Casino Bettor." In *The Gambling Papers: Proceedings of the Fifth National Conference on Gambling and Risk Taking,* edited by William R. Eadington, 13 vols. Vol. 5, *Studies in the Business of Gambling (1):* 1–25. Reno: Bureau of Business and Economic Research, College of Business Administration, University of Nevada, Reno, 1982.

Kennedy, Robert F. "The Baleful Influence of Gambling." In *Gambling,* edited by Robert D. Herman, 169–77. New York: Harper & Row, 1967.

Kerr, Clark. "Introduction: Industrialism with a Human Face." In *Work in America: The Decade Ahead,* edited by Clark Kerr and Jerome M. Rosow. New York: Van Nostrand Reinhold, 1979.

Killingsworth Associates. "Trends in Pari-Mutuel Taxation of Thoroughbred Racing in the United States and Canada." Lexington, Mass.: Killingsworth Assoc., 1983.

Killingsworth, Liddy & Co., Inc. "The Impacts of Reducing the Takeout." Arlington, Mass.: Killingsworth, Liddy & Co., 1980.

———. "The Nature of Wagering Markets and the Implications for Pari-Mutuel Regulation and Taxation." Arlington, Mass.: Killingsworth, Liddy & Co., 1981.

King, Rufus. *Gambling and Organized Crime.* Washington, D.C.: Public Affairs Press, 1969.

———. "Let's Not Deregulate Organized Crime." *Tax Notes* (August 3, 1981): 259–62.

Kinloch, Graham C. *Ideology and Contemporary Sociological Theory.* New York: Prentice Hall, 1981.

Kinsey, Robert R. "The Role of Lotteries in Public Finance." *National Tax Journal* 16, no. 1 (March 1963): 11–19.

Klein, Heywood, and Ronald Alsop. "Playboy Loses 2 London Casino Licenses, Clouding Plan for Atlantic City Operation." *Wall Street Journal,* October 6, 1981.

Klein, Howard J., and Gary Selesner. "Results of the First Gallup Organization Study of Public Attitudes Toward Legalized Gambling." *Gaming Business Magazine,* July 1983.

———, Gary Selesner, and Michael P. Davis. "Gaming Industry Report, 1982: A Revolution at the Starting Gate." *Gaming Business Magazine,* February 1983, 5–56.

Knapp Commission. *Report of Commission to Investigate Allegations of Police Corruption and the City's Anti-Corruption Procedures.* New York: George Braziller, 1973.

Knapp, Terry J. "A Functional Analysis of Gambling Behavior." In *Gambling and Society: Interdisciplinary Studies on the Subject of Gambling,* edited by William R. Eadington, 276–94. Springfield, Ill.: Charles C. Thomas, 1976.

Kogan, Nathan, and Michael A. Wallach. "Risk Taking as a Function of the Situation, the Person and the Group." In *New Directions in Psychology III,* edited by George Mandler, Paul Mussen, Nathan Kogan, and Michael A. Wallach, 110–278. New York: Holt, Rinehart and Winston, 1967.

Koza, John. "Who Is Playing What: A Demographic Study." *Public Gaming Magazine,* April 1984: 36–72.

Kornblum, Alan. *The Moral Hazards.* Lexington, Mass.: D. C. Heath, 1976.

Kretz, James M., and Carol H. Duncan. "Police Attitudes Toward Gambling Enforcement." In *Gambling in America: Final Report of the Commission on the Review of the National Policy Toward Gambling,* Appendix 1, 565–73. Washington, D.C.: GPO, 1976.

Kusyszyn, Igor. "'Compulsive' Gambling: The Problem of Definition." *International Journal of the Addictions* 13 (1978): 1095–1101.

———. "The Gambling Addict Versus the Gambling Professional: A Difference in Character?" *International Journal of the Addictions* 7, no. 2 (1972): 387–93.

Ladouceur, Robert, and Marie Mayrand. "Evaluation of the 'Illusion of Control'." In *The Gambling Papers: Proceedings of the Fifth National Conference on Gambling and Risk Taking,* edited by William R. Eadington, 13 vols. Vol. 4, *Studies in Gambling Behavior:* 61–78. Reno: Bureau of Business and Economic Research, College of Business Administration, University of Nevada, Reno, 1982.

Lasch, Christopher. *The Culture of Narcissism: American Life in an Age of Diminishing Expectations.* New York: Warner Books, 1979.

Lawrence, Robert G. "All About Purses." Annual article in *The Thoroughbred Record,* edited by Timothy T. Capps, April 29, 1981: 1915–22; May 12, 1982: 2509–18; June 8, 1983: 2806–18. Lexington, Ky.: Thoroughbred Publishers, 1981–83.

Lesieur, Henry. *The Chase: Career of the Compulsive Gambler.* Garden City, N.Y.: Doubleday/Anchor Press, 1977.

Lindner, Robert M. "The Psychodynamics of Gambling." *Annals of the American Academy of Political and Social Science* 269 (May 1950): 93–107.

Livingston, Jay. "Compulsive Gambling: A Culture of Losers." *Psychology Today* 7 (March 1974): 51–55.

Looney, Douglas S. "A Big Loss for a Gambling Quarterback." *Sports Illustrated,* May 30, 1983: 30–31.

Lownes, Victor. *The Day the Bunny Died.* Seacacus, N.J.: Lyle Stuart, 1982.

MacDonald, Dwight. "A Theory of Mass Culture." In *Mass Culture: The Popular Arts in America,* edited by Bernard Rosenberg and David Manning White, 59–73. New York: Free Press, 1959.

Mahon, Gigi. *The Company That Bought the Boardwalk: A Reporter's Story of How Resorts International Came to Atlantic City.* New York: Random House, 1980.

Mangione, Thomas W., and Floyd J. Fowler, Jr. "Enforcing the Gambling Laws." *Journal of Social Issues* 35, no. 3 (1979): 115–28.

———, Floyd J. Fowler, Jr., Frederick E. Pratter, and Cynthia L. Martin. "Citizen Views of Gambling Enforcement." In *Gambling in America: Final Report of the Commission on the Review of the National Policy Toward Gambling,* Appendix 1, 240–300. Washington, D.C.: GPO, 1976.

Manis, Jerome, and Bernard Meltzer, eds. *Symbolic Interaction: A Reader in Social Psychology.* Boston: Allyn & Bacon, 1972.

Marcum, Jess, and Henry Rowen. "How Many Games in Town?—The Pros and Cons of Legalized Gambling." *The Public Interest* 36 (Summer 1974): 25–52.

Martindale, Don. *The Nature and Types of Sociological Theory.* Boston: Houghton Mifflin, 1960.

Martinez, Tomás. *The Gambling Scene: Why People Gamble.* Springfield, Ill.: Charles C. Thomas, 1983.

Massachusetts, Commonwealth of. Massachusetts State Lottery Commission. *1982 Annual Report.* Braintree, Mass.: Massachusetts State Lottery Commission, 1982.

Mattiace, Peter. "Casinos Lobbying for Less State Controls." *Bergen County* (N.J.) *Record,* January 16, 1981.

Matza, David. *Delinquency and Drift.* New York: Wiley, 1964.

McDonald, John. "Off-Track Betting on Horseracing: The Effect of a New Player in an Old Cooperative Game." In *The Game of Business.* Garden City, N.Y.: Doubleday & Co., 1975. Anchor Books, 1977: 246–65.

Mead, George Herbert. *Mind, Self and Society.* Chicago: University of Chicago Press, 1934.

Mead, Margaret. *And Keep Your Powder Dry.* New York: William Morrow, 1942.

Meadow, Barry. "The 'Unreported' California Poker Clubs Story." *Gaming Business Magazine,* March 1983, 7–10.

Melnick, Daniel, and Royce Crocker. "A Review of Two Studies on Gambling in the United States." In *Gambling in America: Final Report of the Commission on the Review of the National Policy Toward Gambling,* Appendix 2. Washington, D.C.: GPO, 1976.

Menke, Frank G. *Down the Stretch: The Story of Colonel Matt J. Winn.* New York: Smith & Durrell, 1944.

Merton, Robert K. *Social Theory and Social Structure.* Glencoe, Ill.: Free Press, 1957.

Miers, David. "The Mismanagement of Casino Gaming." *British Journal of Criminology* 21, no. 1 (January 1981): 79–86.

Mills, C. Wright. *The Sociological Imagination.* London: Oxford University Press, 1959.

Minsky, Terri. "Playboy Enters British Court Today on License Renewal." *Wall Street Journal,* September 14, 1981.

Monopolies and Mergers Commission, Secretary of State for Trade and Industry. *Pleasurama PLC and Trident Television PLC and Grand Metropolitan PLC: A report on the proposed merger of Pleasurama PLC and Trident Television PLC and on the merger situation between Grand Metropolitan PLC and Trident Television PLC.* London: Her Majesty's Stationery Office, 1983.

Moore, William Howard. *The Kefauver Committee and the Politics of Crime 1950–1952.* Columbia, Mo.: University of Missouri Press, 1974.

Morgan, W. Douglas, and Jon David Vasché. "Horseracing Demand, Parimutuel Taxation and State Revenue Potential." *National Tax Journal* 32, no. 2 (June 1979): 185–94.

Morris, John. *An Exposure of the Arts and Miseries of Gambling.* Cincinnati, Ohio: 1843.

Murtagh, Judge John M. "Gambling and Police Corruption." *Atlantic Monthly* 206 (November 1960): 49–53.

Musante, Michael J. *Pai Gow.* Las Vegas: MJM Enterprises, 1981.

National Association of State Racing Commissioners. *Pari-Mutuel Racing Statistical Summaries.* Lexington, Ky.: National Association of State Racing Commissioners, 1950–83.

Nevada. State Gaming Control Board. *Direct Levies on Gaming in Nevada, an Analysis of the Rates and Structure by All Levels of Government, for the Fiscal Years Ended June 30, 1976–1983.* Carson City: State Gaming Control Board.

———. *Nevada Gaming Abstracts: 1973–1983.* Carson City: State Gaming Control Board.

———. *Quarterly Reports for the Years 1973–1983.* Carson City: State Gaming Control Board.

———. "Summary of Statewide Drop, Fill, and Win, Calendar 1982." Carson City: State Gaming Control Board, 1982.

———. Audit Division, Dennis C. Gomes, chief. *Investigation of the Background of Alvin Ira Malnick and His Financial Relationship with Caesars World and/or Its Stockholders and Executives,* March 5, 1976. Reprinted in *Rouge et Noir News* 12, no. 3 (September 30, 1980): 3–40.

New Jersey. *Annual reports* filed by operating casino/hotels with the Casino Control Commission of the State of New Jersey. Trenton: New Jersey Casino Control Commission, 1980–83.

New Jersey. New Jersey Casino Control Commission. *Annual Reports: 1979–1983*. Trenton: New Jersey Casino Control Commission.

———. *In the Matter of the Casino License Application of Boardwalk Regency Corporation: Casino License Application Proceeding*. "Statement of Issues." John J. Degnan, Attorney General of New Jersey, Attorney for State of New Jersey, Dept. of Law and Public Safety, and Robert P. Martinez, director, Div. of Gaming Enforcement. Trenton: New Jersey Casino Control Commission, January 1980.

———. *Monthly Reports of Casino Revenues and Estimated Tax on Gross Revenues: June 1978–December 1983*. Trenton: New Jersey Casino Control Commission.

———. "The New Jersey Casino Industry's Net Income: 1978 through 1982." Trenton: New Jersey Casino Control Commission, April 5, 1983.

New Jersey. New Jersey Election Law Enforcement Commission. "Special Report of Contributions and Expenditures Re Public Question #1, 1976 N.J. General Election—Authorizing Casino Gambling in Atlantic City." Trenton: New Jersey Election Law Enforcement Commission, 1977.

New Jersey. New Jersey State Commission of Investigation. Arthur S. Lane, chairman. *Recommendations on Casino Credit Controls*. Trenton: New Jersey State Commission of Investigation, 1983.

New Jersey. New Jersey State Lottery. *Annual Reports: 1972–1983*. Trenton: New Jersey State Lottery.

New Jersey Sports and Exposition Authority. *1982 Annual Report*. East Rutherford, N.J.: New Jersey Sports and Exposition Authority, 1982.

———. *1983 Annual Report*. East Rutherford, N.J.: New Jersey Sports and Exposition Authority, 1983.

New Jersey. State of New Jersey Dept. of Law and Public Safety, Div. of Law. Irwin I. Kimmelman, Attorney General. "Formal Opinion No. 5—1982" (concerning the legality of video lottery devices). Trenton: State of New Jersey Department of Law and Public Safety, June 22, 1982.

New Jersey. State of New Jersey Dept. of Law and Public Safety, Div. of Gaming Enforcement. Robert P. Martinez, director. *Statement of Exceptions and Investigative Report Re the Casino License Application of Resorts International Hotel, Inc.* Trenton: Division of Gaming Enforcement, December 4, 1978.

———. *Report to the Casino Control Commission with Reference to the Casino License Application of Boardwalk Regency Corporation*. Trenton: Division of Gaming Enforcement, January 22, 1980.

Newman, Otto. *Gambling: Hazard and Reward*. London: Athlone Press, 1977.

Newsday (Long Island, N.Y.). "Harrah's Cites N.J. Rules in Delaying Plan for Casino," January 20, 1981.

———. "N.J. Dec. Casino Revenue off 19.3%," January 14, 1981.

New York Daily News. "City to Get Video Poker," August 19, 1981.

———. "Hilton delays work on N.J. casino," January 16, 1981.

New York Post. "Atlantic City's red ink chasing casino builders," January 20, 1981.

New York. City of New York. *Mayor's Citizens' Committee on Off-Track Betting: Plan for Legal Off-Track Betting in the City of New York*. New York City: 1963, 1964.

New York City Off-Track Betting Corporation, *1982 Annual Report*. New York: New York City Off-Track Betting Corporation, 1982.

———. *1983 Annual Report*. New York: New York City Off-Track Betting Corporation, 1983.

New York. Commission to Study and Investigate the Thoroughbred Industry in New York State. Robert J. Morgado, chairman. *Report.* Albany: Executive Chamber, March 31, 1977.

New York. Court of Appeals. *People ex rel. Lichtenstein* v. *Langan* 196 N.Y., 260 (1909).

New York. New York State Commission of Investigation. David Brown, chairman. *Review of the Financial Condition of the New York Racing Association.* Albany: New York State Commission of Investigation, 1976.

———. Warren E. Downing, executive assistant. *Syndicated Gambling in New York State.* New York: New York State Commission of Investigation, February 1961.

New York. New York State Commission on Gambling. Kent H. Brown, chairman; Wallace M. Wyncoop, executive director. *Report and Recommendations to Extend Legalized Gambling.* Compiled by commissioner Joseph J. Weiser. Albany: New York State Gambling Commission, February 1, 1973.

New York. New York State Dept. of Audit and Control. *Audit Report* (#NY-St-35-64). Albany: State Dept. of Audit and Control, March 9, 1964.

New York. New York State Joint Legislative Task Force to Study and Evaluate the Pari-mutuel Racing and Breeding Industry in New York State. Jon J. McCloskey, executive director. *A Discussion Paper on the New York Racing Association.* Albany: March 1, 1980.

———. *First Interim Report.* Albany: July 1, 1978.

New York. New York State Racing Commission. Ashley Trimble Cole, chairman. *Annual Report for 1954.* New York: New York State Racing Commission, 1954.

New York. Office of the Comptroller of the State of New York. *Audit Report* (#NY-St-14-72). Albany: Office of the Comptroller, December 31, 1971.

———. *Audit Report* (#NY-AUTH-2-78; #NY-AUTH-1-79). Albany: Office of the Comptroller, January 18, 1978; December 26, 1979.

New York. State Assembly Ways and Means Committee. "The Implications of Further Legalization of Gambling in New York State." New York: Assembly Committee on Ways and Means, December 1972.

New York. State Dept. of Taxation and Finance. *Annual Statistical Review of Pari-Mutuel Tax Operations for the Racing Season of 1982.* Albany: Dept. of Taxation and Finance, 1983.

New York. State of New York Department of Law. Robert Abrams, Attorney General. Opinion concerning the legality of video lottery devices, in a letter to John D. Quinn, director, New York State Lottery, dated September 8, 1981. Albany: State of New York Department of Law, 1981.

New York. State of New York Executive Chamber. Hugh L. Carey, governor. *Executive Budget for the Fiscal Year April 1, 1982, to March 31, 1983.* Albany: 1983.

New York. New York State Lottery. "Rules and Regulations," Rev. 2/10/83. Albany: New York State Lottery, 1983.

———. *Annual Report.* Albany: New York State Lottery, 1976–83.

New York. New York State Racing and Wagering Board. *Annual Report.* New York: New York State Racing and Wagering Board, 1973–83.

New York Times. "Aqueduct Calls Meeting on Plans," February 10, 1955.

———. "Bingo Boom Brings Tribes Profit and Conflict," March 29, 1983.

———. "Cole Backs Plan for Super-Track," February 16, 1955.

———. Editorial, "Gambling Odds," December 13, 1972.

———. Editorial, "The Betting Addiction," December 28, 1983.

———. "Gambling Foots the Bill for Massachusetts Arts," July 17, 1983.

———. "Hearing Ordered on Racing Plants," March 18, 1955.
———. "Jockey Club Gives Approval to Plan," September 23, 1954.
———. "Lottery's 'Fat One' Showers Cash on Spain," December 23, 1983.
———. "New State Gaming Plan Runs into Legal Tangle," August 20, 1981.
———. "Playboy in London Loses Casino Fight," October 6, 1981.
———. "Purchase of Four Local Race Tracks: Nonprofit Group Discloses Offer," July 8, 1954.
———. "Racing Group Petitions for Right to Obtain State's Four Tracks: Commission Asked to Approve Purchase Price of $32,616,750 and to Grant 25-Year Betting Privileges," September 17, 1955.
———. "Track Plan Wins Banking Support," February 2, 1955.
Nisbet, Robert. *Prejudices: A Philosophical Dictionary.* Cambridge, Mass.: Harvard University Press, 1983.
———. *The Quest for Community.* New York: Oxford University Press, 1953.
———. *The Twilight of Authority.* New York: Oxford University Press, 1975.
Novick, David. *An Economic Study of Harness Horse Racing.* Santa Monica, Ca.: David Novick Assoc., 1962.
———. "Economic Outlook of the Racing Industry." *The Blood-Horse,* July 22, 1974, 2760–66.
———. *Economics of the Pari-Mutuel Business.* Santa Monica, Ca.: David Novick Assoc., 1963.
———. "Economics of the Thoroughbred Industry." *The Blood-Horse,* (annually) July 1965–79.
O'Connor, James. *The Fiscal Crisis of the State.* New York: St. Martin's Press, 1973.
Offe, Claus. "Political Authority and Class Structures: An Analysis of Late Capitalist Societies." *International Journal of Sociology* 2 (1972): 73–108.
Oreskes, Michael. "Cuomo Studies Restructuring of State OTB." *New York Times,* January 25, 1984.
Orwell, George. *1984.* 1949. Reprint. New York: New American Library, 1961, 1981.
Pankoff, Lyn D. "Market Efficiency and Football Betting." *The Journal of Business* 41, no. 2 (April 1968): 203–14.
Parsons, Talcott, and Edward Shils, eds. *Toward a General Theory of Action.* New York: Harper, 1951.
Pawel, Miriam. "NY Racing Assn. Asks to Run OTB, Vows Higher Take." *Newsday,* January 24, 1984.
Peagam, Norman, and Frederick Kempe. "Playboy to Sell British Casinos for $31.4 Million." *Wall Street Journal,* November 4, 1981.
Pescatrice, Donn R. "The Inelastic Demand for Wagering." *Journal of Applied Economics* 12, no. 1 (March 1980): 1–10.
———. "An Interstate Off-Track Betting System." *National Tax Journal* 32, no. 2 (June 1979): 209–13.
Peterson, Virgil W. "Obstacles to Enforcement of Gambling Laws." *Annals of the American Academy of Political and Social Science* 269 (May 1950): 9–20.
Philadelphia Daily News. "Tracks: Too Many Purses," October 25, 1983.
Philadelphia Inquirer. "Brandywine to Give Way to Mall," October 29, 1983.
———. "Six Numbers Add Up to $4.2 Million," December 18, 1982.
Pollack, Andrew. "Electronics Invades Gambling." *New York Times,* January 21, 1984.
Potter, David M. *People of Plenty: Economic Abundance and the American Character.* Chicago: University of Chicago Press, 1954.

Pratter, Frederick, and Floyd J. Fowler, Jr. "Police Perceptions about Gambling Enforcement." In *Gambling in America: Final Report of the Commission on the Review of the National Policy Toward Gambling*, Appendix 1, 461–93. Washington, D.C.: GPO, 1976.

Public Gaming Magazine. "Bingo and Break Opens Becoming Big Business," November 1983: 39–48.

———. "Washington State Keeps Demographic Tabs on Instant Lottery Winners," February 1982.

Public Gaming Newsletter: A Private Report to Government and Industry on Public Gaming. Rockville, Md.: Public Gaming Research Institute (twice monthly), 1973–83.

Pugh-Roberts Associates, Inc. *The Future of Thoroughbred Racing in the United States*. Cambridge, Mass.: Pugh-Roberts Assoc., 1975.

Puzo, Mario. *The Godfather*. New York: Putnam, 1969.

Oliver Quayle and Co. *A Study of the Numbers Game in New York City: Study #1458-A*. New York: Oliver Quayle & Co., 1972.

———. *A Study of Betting on Sports in New York City: Study #1493*. New York: Oliver Quayle & Co., 1972.

Quinn, John Philip. *Fools of Fortune*. Chicago: G. Howe, 1890.

Reuter, Peter. *Disorganized Crime: The Economics of the Visible Hand*. Cambridge, Mass.: MIT Press, 1983.

———. "Enforceability of Gambling Laws." In *Gambling in America: Final Report of the Commission on the Review of the National Policy Toward Gambling*, Appendix 1, pp. 551–64. Washington, D.C.: GPO, 1976.

———, and Jonathan B. Rubinstein. "Fact, Fancy, and Organized Crime." *The Public Interest* 53 (Fall 1978): 45–67.

———. *Illegal Gambling in New York: A Case Study in the Operation, Structure, and Regulation of an Illegal Market*. Washington, D.C.: GPO, 1982.

Riesman, David. *Abundance for What? and Other Essays*. Garden City, N.Y.: Doubleday, 1964.

———. *The Lonely Crowd*. New Haven, Conn.: Yale University Press, 1961.

Ritchie, James E. "The Changing Role of Government in Gaming." In *Laventhol & Horwath First Annual Gaming Conference: The Gaming Industry–1979* (New York City, October 1979), 6. Philadelphia: Laventhol & Horwath, 1979.

Roach, James. "Jockey Club Gives State Track Plan." *New York Times*, September 21, 1954.

———. "Officials Named by Jockey Club To Activate 'Super-Track' Plan." *New York Times*, June 3, 1955.

Rose, Nelson. "The Legalization and Control of Casino Gambling." *Fordham Urban Law Journal* 8, no. 2 (1979–80): 245–300.

Rosett, R. N. "Gambling and Rationality." *Journal of Political Economy* 73, no. 6 (December 1965): 595–607.

Rouge et Noir News. "Alice in Wonderland: New Jersey Version—Book II," 13, no. 6 (June 30, 1981): 1–4.

———. "The Atlantic City Scam," 13, no. 1 (January 28, 1981): 1–4.

Rouge et Noir Resort Management Report. "The 1981 Prospects for N.J. Casino Gaming Industry," 4, no. 1 (January 29, 1981): 3–6.

Royal Commission on Betting, Lotteries, and Gaming 1949–1951. Henry Urmston Willink, chairman. *Report*. London: Her Majesty's Stationery Office, 1951. Reprint. 1956.

Royal Commission on Gambling. The Lord Rothschild, chairman. *Final Report.* 2 vols. London: Her Majesty's Stationery Office, 1978.

Rubinstein, Jonathan B. "Gambling Enforcement and Police Corruption." In *Gambling in America: Final Report of the Commission on the Review of the National Policy Toward Gambling,* Appendix 1, 600–632. Washington, D.C.: GPO, 1976.

Salerno, Ralph, and John S. Tompkins. *The Crime Confederation.* New York: Doubleday, 1969.

Salmans, Sandra. "British Casinos Sale by Playboy." *New York Times,* November 4, 1981.

Samuels, Howard J. "The Off-Track Betting Experiment in New York." *Howard Law Journal* 17, no. 4 (1973): 731–57.

Sasuly, Richard. *Bookies and Bettors.* New York: Holt, Rinehart and Winston, 1982.

Scarne, John. *Scarne's Complete Guide to Gambling.* New York: Simon & Schuster, 1961.

Scientific Games, Inc. *Washington State Lottery: Preliminary Analysis of Lottery Players.* Version I. Norcross, Ga.: Scientific Games, 1983.

Selesner, Gary. "California Bell Club—Playing to a Full House." *Gaming Business Magazine,* January 1981, 38–39.

———. "U.K.'s Ladbroke: Betting on and Betting in the U.S.," *Gaming Business Magazine,* June 1982, pp. 4–49.

Shearer, Lloyd. "The Gamble Playboy Lost." *Parade,* December 13, 1981.

Simon, Carl P., and Ann D. Witte. *Beating the System: The Underground Economy.* Boston: Auburn House, 1982.

Simpson, George. *Emile Durkheim.* New York: Thomas Y. Crowell, 1963.

Skolnick, Jerome H. *House of Cards: Legalization and Control of Casino Gambling.* Boston: Little, Brown, 1978.

———. "The Social Risks of Casino Gambling." *Psychology Today,* July 1979: 22–27.

Slater, Philip E. *The Pursuit of Loneliness: American Culture at the Breaking Point.* Boston: Beacon Press, 1970.

Smith, Vernon L. "Economic Theory of Wager Markets." *Western Economic Journal* 9, no. 3 (September 1971): 242–55.

Snyder, Wayne W. "Horse Racing: Testing the Efficient Markets Model." *Journal of Finance* 33 (September 1978): 1109–18.

Spiro, Michael H. "On the Tax Incidence of the Pennsylvania Lottery." *National Tax Journal* 27, no. 1 (March 1974): 57–61.

Sprowls, R. Clay. "On the Terms of the New York State Lottery." *National Tax Journal* 23, no. 1 (March 1970): 74–82.

Starkey, Lycurgus Monroe, Jr. *The Christian Church and Gambling.* Washington, D.C.: General Board of Christian Social Concerns of the Methodist Church, n.d.

———. "Christians and the Gambling Mania." In *Gambling,* edited by Robert D. Herman, 225–33. New York: Harper and Row, 1967.

———. *Money, Mania, and Morals: The Churches and Gambling.* New York: Abingdon Press, 1964.

Stead, W. T. *Satan's Invisible World Displayed.* New York: World Publishing, 1972.

Sternlieb, George, and James W. Hughes. *The Atlantic City Gamble: A Twentieth Century Fund Report.* Cambridge, Mass.: Harvard University Press, 1983.

Stocker, Frederick D. "State Sponsored Gambling as a Source of Public Revenue." *National Tax Journal* 25, no. 3 (September 1972): 437–41.

Straus, Anselm. *George Herbert Mead on Social Psychology.* Chicago: University of Chicago Press, 1964.

Suits, Daniel B. "Gambling Taxes: Regressivity and Revenue Potential." *National Tax Journal* 30, no. 1 (January 1977): 19–35.

Sullivan, George. *By Chance a Winner: The History of Lotteries.* New York: Dodd, Mead, 1972.

Thomas, Steve. "The Iron Men." *The Thoroughbred Record* 213, no. 24 (June 17, 1981): 2586–91.

Thompson, William N. "Casino Drives in Colo., Ark. Likely to Die." *Gaming & Wagering Business* (formerly *Gaming Business Magazine*), October 1984: 43–46.

Timberlake, James H. *Prohibition and the Progressive Movement, 1900–1920.* Cambridge, Mass.: Harvard University Press, 1963.

Tocqueville, Alexis de. *Democracy in America.* New York: Random House, 1954.

Tsukahara, Theodore Jr., and Harold J. Brumm, Jr. "Economic Rationality, Psychology and Decision-Making Under Uncertainty." In *Gambling and Society: Interdisciplinary Studies on the Subject of Gambling,* edited by William R. Eadington, 92–107. Springfield, Ill.: Charles C. Thomas, 1976.

Twentieth Century Fund. *Easy Money.* Report of the Task Force on Legalized Gambling Sponsored by the Fund for the City of New York and the Twentieth Century Fund, with a Background Paper by David Beale and Clifford Goldman. New York: Twentieth Century Fund, 1974.

United States. Commission on the Review of the National Policy Toward Gambling, Charles H. Morin, chairman, James E. Ritchie, executive director. *Gambling in America: Final Report of the Commission on the Review of the National Policy Toward Gambling.* 4 vols. Washington, D.C.: GPO, 1976.

United States Congress. Senate. Senate Special Committee to Investigate Organized Crime in Interstate Commerce (Kefauver Committee). *Hearings Before a Special Committee to Investigate Organized Crime in Interstate Commerce.* 81st Congress, 2nd Session, pursuant to S. Res. 202, and 82nd Congress, 1st Session, pursuant to S. Res. 60 and 129. 19 vols. Washington, D.C.: GPO, 1950–51.

———. *Third Interim Report.* 82nd Congress, 1st Session, S. Rep. 307. Washington, D.C.: GPO, 1951.

———. *Final Report.* 82nd Congress, 1st Session, S. Rep. 725. Washington, D.C.: GPO, 1951. Republished as *The Kefauver Committee Report on Organized Crime.* New York: Didier, n.d., and *Report of the Special Senate Committee to Investigate Organized Crime in Interstate Commerce.* New York: Arco, 1951.

United States Congress. Senate. Permanent Subcommittee on Investigations of the Committee on Government Operations (McClellan Committee). *Gambling and Organized Crime: Hearings: August 22, 23, 24, and 25, and September 7 and 8, 1961.* 87th Congress, 1st sess., pursuant to S. Res. 69. 3 vols. Washington, D.C.: GPO, 1961.

———. *Gambling and Organized Crime: Report.* 87th Congress, 2nd Session, S. Rep. 1310. Washington, D.C.: GPO, 1962.

United States. Department of Justice, Henry Dogin, deputy attorney general, Criminal Division, and Edward T. Joyce, deputy chief, Organized Crime and Racketeering Section. Testimony before the Commission on the Review of the National Policy Toward Gambling, May 15, 1974. In *Gambling in America: Final Report of the Commission on the Review of the National Policy Toward Gambling,* Appendix 3, 15–20. Washington, D.C.: GPO, 1976.

———. William S. Lynch, chief, Organized Crime and Racketeering Section. Letter to Dan Melnick, Congressional Research Service, Library of Congress, August 18, 1976. In *Gambling in America: Final Report of the Commission on the Review of the National Policy Toward Gambling,* Appendix 2. Washington, D.C.: GPO, 1976.

United States. Department of the Treasury, John E. Chapoton, Assistant Secretary for Tax Policy. Statement before the Subcommittee on Select Revenue Measures, House Committee on Ways and Means, United States Congress, March 16, 1982.
———. Letter to Senator Paul Laxalt, May 21, 1982.
United States. Department of the Treasury, Internal Revenue Service. *Estimates of Income Unreported on Individual Income Tax Returns.* Publication 1104(9-79). Washington, D.C.: Internal Revenue Service, 1979.
———. Office of the Assistant Commissioner (Planning, Finance and Research) Research Division. *Income Tax Compliance Research: Estimates for 1973–1981.* Washington, D.C.: Internal Revenue Service, July 1983.
United States. District Court for the District of Delaware. Stapleton, District Judge. Opinion, Civil Action No. 76-273, concerning the Delaware State Lottery Sports Lottery. Wilmington: United States District Court for the District of Delaware, August 11, 1977.
United States. Federal Bureau of Investigation, Frederick C. Fehl, acting assistant director. Testimony before the Commission on the Review of the National Policy Toward Gambling, May 10, 1976. In *Gambling in America: Final Report of the Commission on the Review of the National Policy Toward Gambling,* Appendix 3, 498–502. Washington, D.C.: GPO, 1976.
United States President. Executive Order 11236, July 23, 1965.
———. President's Commission on Law Enforcement and Administration of Justice. Nicholas deB. Katzenbach, chairman; James Vorenberg, executive director. *The Challenge of Crime in a Free Society.* Washington, D.C.: GPO, 1967.
———. President's Commission on Law Enforcement and Administration of Justice. Nicholas deB. Katzenbach, chairman; James Vorenberg, executive director. *Task Force Report: Organized Crime.* Washington, D.C.: GPO, 1967.
Uston, Ken. *Million Dollar Blackjack.* Hollywood, Ca.: Scientific Research Services, 1981.
———, and Roger Rapoport. *The Big Player.* New York: Holt, Rinehart and Winston, 1977.
Vatz, Richard E., and Lee S. Weinberg. Quoted by Andrew Beyer, in "Psychiatrists Ill-Advised On Gambling," *Washington Post,* July 3, 1983.
Vermont. State of Vermont Office of the Attorney General. John J. Easton, Jr., attorney general. Opinion No. 83-9, concerning the legality of video lottery devices. Montpelier: State of Vermont Office of the Attorney General, September 13, 1982.
Vermont. Vermont Lottery Commission. *Annual Report 1978.* Montpelier: Vermont Lottery Commission, January 2, 1979.
Wagner, Walter. *To Gamble, Or Not to Gamble.* New York: World Publishing, 1972.
Wall Street Journal. Editorial, "A Bad Bet," December 28, 1983.
———. "Indian Bingo Has Big List of Reasons Stock is Risky as It Plans Initial Offering," July 1, 1983.
———. "In North Dakota, a Blackjack Game is an Act of Charity," January 14, 1982.
———. "Trident Holders Back Purchase of Playboy's Casinos in the U.K.," January 6, 1982.
———. "Resorts International Laying off up to 400 at Atlantic City," January 12, 1981.
———. "Using Loophole in Treasury Rule, Casinos Said to Help Launder Illegal-Drug Money," March 17, 1983.
Wallace, Ruth, and Alison Wolf. *Contemporary Sociological Theory.* New York: Prentice Hall, 1980.
Warshaw, Robert Irving. *Bet-A-Million Gates: The Story of a Plunger.* New York: Greenberg, 1932.

Washington State. Washington State Gambling Commission. Keith Kisor, executive director. *Statistical Reports for the Quarter Ended June 30, 1983*. Olympia: Washington State Gambling Commission, 1983.

———. *Report to the Governor and Legislature: 1981*. Olympia: Washington State Gambling Commission, 1981.

Weaver, Warren, Jr. "Flat-Track Bill Passes and Goes to Governor Harriman." *New York Times,* April 3, 1955.

———. "Harriman Backs Super Race Track." *New York Times,* March 1, 1955.

———. "Jockey Club Urges Harriman to Join Move to Rebuild Tracks." *New York Times,* February 1, 1955.

Weber, Max. *The Protestant Ethic and the Spirit of Capitalism.* New York: Scribner, 1930.

———. *Theory of Social and Economic Organization.* 1925. Translated by A. M. Henderson and Talcott Parsons. New York: Free Press, 1957.

Weinstein, David, and Lillian Deitch. *The Impact of Legalized Gambling: The Socioeconomic Consequences of Lotteries and Off-Track Betting.* New York: Praeger, 1974.

Weiss, Harry Bischoff, and Grace M. Weiss. *The Early Lotteries of New Jersey.* Trenton, N.J.: Past Times Press, 1966.

Westby, David L., and Allen Sack. "The Rationalization and Commercialization of College Football in the Late Nineteenth Century." *Journal of Higher Education* 47, no. 6 (November/December 1976), 625–48.

Whyte, William. *The Organization Man.* New York: Simon & Schuster, 1956.

Williams, Francis Emmett. *Lotteries, Laws, and Morals.* New York: Vantage Press, 1958.

Wilson, Allan N. *The Casino Gambler's Guide.* New York: Harper & Row, 1970.

Winthrop, John. "A Modell of Christian Charity." In *An American Primer,* edited by Daniel J. Boorstin, 28–41. New York: New American Library, 1968.

Wynn, Stephen A. "Expansion of Legalized Gaming and Factors that Will Influence It." In *Laventhol & Horwath Second Annual Gaming Conference: The Gaming Industry—1980* (New York City, October 1, 1980), 36–39. Philadelphia: Laventhol and Horwath, 1980.

Yankelovich, Daniel. "Work, Values, and the New Breed." In *Work in America: The Decade Ahead,* edited by Clark Kerr and Jerome M. Rosow, 3–26. New York: Van Nostrand Reinhold, 1979.

Zola, Irving Kenneth. "Observations on Gambling in a Lower Class Setting." In *Gambling,* edited by Robert D. Herman, 19–31. New York: Harper & Row, 1967.

Index